Merry Christmas!

Love,
Maggie

A Touchstone Book
Published by Simon & Schuster
New York London Toronto Sydney

DAVID BIANCULLI

DANGEROUSLY FUNNY

THE UNCENSORED STORY OF THE SMOTHERS BROTHERS COMEDY HOUR

 Touchstone
A Division of Simon & Schuster, Inc.
1230 Avenue of the Americas
New York, NY 10020

First Touchstone hardcover edition December 2009

TOUCHSTONE and colophon are registered trademarks of
Simon & Schuster, Inc.

For information about special discounts for bulk purchases,
please contact Simon & Schuster Special Sales at
1-866-506-1949 or business@simonandschuster.com.

The Simon & Schuster Speakers Bureau can bring authors to your live event.
For more information or to book an event contact the Simon & Schuster
Speakers Bureau at 866-248-3049 or visit our website at
www.simonspeakers.com.

Designed by William Ruoto

Manufactured in the United States of America

10   9   8   7   6   5   4   3   2   1

Library of Congress Cataloging-in-Publication Data
Bianculli, David.
    Dangerously funny / by David Bianculli.
        p.   cm.
    Includes bibliographical references and index.
    1. Smothers Brothers comedy hour.   2. Smothers Brothers.   I. Title.
    PN1992.77.S63B33   2010
    791.45'72—dc22   2009036843

ISBN 978-1-4391-0116-2
ISBN 978-1-4391-0953-3 (ebook)

Permissions on page 383.

To Tom and Dick Smothers,

for their trust, their cooperation,
and especially their patience

Contents

Introduction

Six months after the tragic events of 9/11, at the US Comedy Arts Festival in Aspen, Colorado, five defiantly outspoken performers were saluted for their often costly efforts to exercise their First Amendment rights as comedians. One was Bill Maher, who lost his ABC late-night talk show *Politically Incorrect* after remarking of the Al-Qaeda terrorist hijackers who commandeered passenger airliners and steered them into the World Trade Center and the Pentagon, "Staying in the airplane when it hits the building—say what you want about it, it's not cowardly." Another was stand-up comic and civil rights advocate Dick Gregory, who not only challenged segregation by becoming the first black comic to headline in all-white nightclubs, but also demonstrated alongside Martin Luther King Jr. and Medgar Evers in history-making confrontations in Montgomery and Selma. Still another was George Carlin, whose infamous "Seven Words You Can Never Say on Television" and "Filthy Words" comedy album routines sparked a free-speech battle that went all the way to the Supreme Court. And rounding out this handful of brave, bold humorists were Tom and Dick Smothers.

Significantly, the Smothers Brothers received their Freedom of Speech Award from comic David Steinberg, whose controversial mock sermons on *The Smothers Brothers Comedy Hour* played a key part in having that variety show yanked and the brothers fired, despite three successful seasons on CBS from 1967 to 1969 and an announced renewal for a fourth.

"The most innovative variety show on television shut down because of political pressure," Steinberg told the audience in Aspen that night. "But the Smothers Brothers got their revenge. Never giving up, they sued CBS—and they won. And they forever became prominent symbols in the fight for free speech."

Accepting the award, Tom Smothers joked, "Of course, many of you recognize the fact that we are not the *original* Smothers Brothers. I'm sure they would have loved to have been here to receive this award. But the original Smothers Brothers passed away in 1969."

As jokes go, that one cuts very close to the bone.

On the surface, it's patently ridiculous. The Smothers Brothers are, of course, the same siblings who began performing as folk satirists in 1959, and whose half-century career has outlasted almost all comic teams on stage, screen, and television. Tom, who plays guitar and unleashes elaborate fibs and heated emotional outbursts, and Dick, who plays bass and acts as the grounded and weary straight man, have a history as a comedy team that covers more years than the Marx Brothers, Stan Laurel and Oliver Hardy, Bud Abbott and Lou Costello, Dean Martin and Jerry Lewis, Dan Rowan and Dick Martin, and even George Burns and Gracie Allen.

In another way, though, Tom was being painfully honest. Part of the Smothers Brothers *did* die when CBS wrested their show away from them. Oh, they were vindicated in court, proving that they had not violated any terms of their agreement in providing shows for the network. And over the years, they starred in several subsequent TV showcases, including a brilliant run of reunion specials and series in the 1980s for CBS, the very network that had shunned them two decades before. In addition, they never failed to find steady work in nightclubs.

However, by becoming unexpected martyrs to the cause of free speech, the Smothers Brothers lost their most influential national TV platform just when that freedom mattered the most. Like Elvis Presley when he was shipped off to the army, or Muhammad Ali when he was stripped of his heavyweight title for refusing to fight in Vietnam, the Smothers Brothers were nonconformist iconoclasts, pop-culture heroes yanked from the national spotlight in their prime. Muhammad Ali became the champ again, and Elvis returned to record many more number-one hits, but Tom and Dick Smothers never again enjoyed the influence or mass popularity of *The Smothers Brothers Comedy Hour*. In terms of introducing and encouraging new talent, pushing the boundaries of network television, and reflecting the youth movement and embracing its antiwar stance and anti-administration politics, the show was, quite literally, their finest *Hour*.

What, exactly, made the Smothers Brothers so important a guiding force in the 1960s? Mostly, they were in the right place at the right time, reacting to the '60s as events unfurled around them. They were the first members of their generation with a prime-time pulpit, and they used it. Each season, the average age of their writing staff got younger, and the satiric edge of the material being televised—or censored—got sharper. Yet in an era when most families still watched television together, in the same room on the same TV set, the greatest and most impressive achievement of *The Smothers Brothers Comedy Hour* was that it spoke to and attracted young viewers without alienating older ones. With its humor, guest list, and high caliber of entertainment, it bridged the generation gap at a time when that gap was becoming a Grand Canyon–like chasm.

The *Comedy Hour* introduced fresh talent—from in-house future stars Pat Paulsen and Mason Williams to such emerging rock groups as Buffalo Springfield, Jefferson Airplane, and the Who—

while making room for veteran stars from movies, TV, even vaudeville. On one show, Kate Smith shared billing with Simon and Garfunkel. Another show featured Mel Torme, Don Knotts, and Ravi Shankar. Musicians came on not to perform their old or current hits, but to unveil new ones—a bold departure from established practice. The Beatles even provided the brothers with a US exclusive—the videotaped premiere of "Hey Jude"—and in the middle of the Smothers Brothers' battles with the CBS censors, George Harrison showed up in 1968 as a surprise guest to offer moral support. "Whether you can say it or not," Harrison urged them on the air, "keep *trying* to say it." And they did. First, individual words and phrases that CBS found objectionable were cut from skits after rehearsals or edited out of the final master tape. Then entire segments were cut because of their political, social, or anti-establishment messages.

For every battle the Smothers Brothers won, CBS sought and got revenge. When *The Smothers Brothers Comedy Hour* wanted to open its third season by having Harry Belafonte singing "Don't Stop the Carnival" against a backdrop reel of violent outbursts filmed in and around that summer's Democratic National Convention, CBS not only cut the number completely, but added insult to injury by replacing it with a five-minute campaign ad from Republican presidential nominee Richard M. Nixon.

Politics, and politicians, play a big part in the story of *The Smothers Brothers Comedy Hour*. Even though the show poked fun at President Johnson and criticized his Vietnam War policies, LBJ's daughters were fervent fans. Yet more than once the chief executive of the United States called CBS Chairman William S. Paley to exert pressure on the Smothers Brothers. *The Smothers Brothers Comedy Hour* even ran its own candidate for president, Pat Paulsen, whose tongue-in-cheek campaign was a brilliant deconstruction of the 1968 presidential race. Paulsen had become popular delivering fake editorials on the show, such as the one in support of network censorship ("The Bill of Rights says nothing about Freedom of Hearing," he told viewers, adding, "This, of course, takes a lot of the fun out of Freedom of Speech"). Paulsen moved effortlessly onto the actual campaign trail, where real candidates such as Robert F. Kennedy got and played with the joke, and the show hired a former California gubernatorial campaign manager to offer behind-the-scenes advice.

With regime changes both at the White House and at the CBS New York headquarters known as Black Rock, the Smothers Brothers' days were numbered. Once Nixon ascended to the presidency, Tom Smothers insists he was targeted in a way that both predated and prefigured Nixon's enemies list and the sneaky tactics of the "Plumbers." Nixon pushed for greater governmental control of broadcast media at the same time well-placed Nixon allies, from new CBS programming chief Robert D. Wood to *TV Guide* publisher Walter Annenberg, adopted hard-line stances against the sort of envelope-pushing content the Smothers Brothers were trying to present in prime time. Both sides got increasingly, exponentially petulant and combative. Tom Smothers fought too fervently for every word and idea, and slipped obscenities into scripts just to tweak the censors, who promptly removed them. Eventually, Tom lost his own sense of humor while railing against the network suits. CBS executives, on their part, grew impatient and resentful at having to defend or discuss the Smothers Brothers everywhere they went, and began to both change the rules and enforce them ruthlessly.

Undeniably, CBS wanted Tom and Dick Smothers off the air because of the ideas they were espousing on their show, but eventually removed them by claiming that the brothers had violated the terms of their contract by not delivering a copy of that week's show in time. It was like the feds busting Al Capone: the crime for which he was convicted was a mere technicality, but it got Capone off the streets. In the case of CBS and the Smothers Brothers, they got them off the air. Fired, not canceled, as Tom Smothers invariably corrected people in an effort to set the record straight.

A few years later, in the case of *Tom Smothers et al. v. Columbia Broadcasting System, Inc.,* the US District Court in California ruled that CBS, not the Smothers Brothers, was the party in violation of its contract. But by then, the duo's prime-time platform had long been torpedoed and their influence stolen from them. The attitude they reflected would continue to flourish on *Rowan & Martin's Laugh-In,* but only briefly. In late-night TV, it would find its closest approximation, within a decade, on *Saturday Night Live,* which as recently as the 2008 presidential race proved itself a vital, arguably invaluable, popculture component in analyzing and advancing what was, and wasn't, funny about national politics and politicians. But in prime time, where the Smothers Brothers once dared to offer the same sort of probing and timely humor, the concept of relevance in entertainment shows would become an endangered species, if not completely extinct.

During its three-year reign, however, *The Smothers Brothers Comedy Hour* was about as topical, influential, and important as a TV show could get. Tom Smothers, for the last half of the '60s, was like a mod Zelig or a hippie Forrest Gump, appearing almost everywhere the times they were a-changin'. In 1967, Tom was present, and an occasional onstage presenter, at the Monterey International Pop Festival, scouting such breakthrough acts as the Who, Jefferson Airplane, and Ravi Shankar. In 1968, Tom was an early champion of the Broadway show *Hair,* and instrumental in bringing the show to the West Coast. In 1969, Tom could be found at the bedside of John Lennon and Yoko Ono, playing guitar and singing with Lennon as a group of friends recorded the classic anthem "Give Peace a Chance."

Yes, there was sex, and there were drugs, and everything else associated with the '60s, from freedom and peace to foolishness and paranoia. Both the Smothers Brothers and CBS, in the end, agree that they overreacted at the time—but remembering how polarized and sensitive society was then goes a long way toward explaining how pitched those battles got, and why.

This book is not, however, some quaint remembrance of a show with a moral stand that has no bearing to modern times. Think of the Smothers Brothers as a pop-culture *Grapes of Wrath*. When Michael Moore takes his time in the spotlight during a live Oscar telecast to scold President George W. Bush for sending America to war without due cause, the Smothers Brothers, in spirit, are there. When the Dixie Chicks make an anti-Bush comment onstage and suffer a backlash from conservatives before reemerging triumphantly with a new hit and a slew of Grammy Awards, the Smothers Brothers are there. When Bill Maher resurfaces on HBO's *Real Time with Bill Maher,* or when Jon Stewart skewers politicians and the media on Comedy Central's *The Daily Show with Jon Stewart,* the Smothers Brothers are there. When Stephen Colbert attempts a comedic run for the presidency, the Smothers Brothers are there. It's worth pointing out, though, that contemporary outspoken comedians and programs reside today on cable. When CBS fired Tom and Dick Smothers, there *were* no cable networks. They had not been invented. And nearly forty years after the network pulled *The Smothers Brothers Comedy Hour* from prime time, there's still no true modern-day equivalent on broadcast network television—no series that speaks truth to power, pushes boundaries, and champions new art and artists in quite the way Tom and Dick Smothers did.

"I run into people," Tom Smothers told the crowd at the Free Speech Tribute in Aspen, "who say, 'Don't you wish you guys had a television show right now? You could say anything you want!'

"That's an illusion, isn't it?" he asked. "The language is there. You can say any language you want . . . you can talk about violence, graphic sex. But I'm not hearing anything being particularly *said*. And if we had a show today, I don't think we could say anything more than we did back then."

The closer you look at *The Smothers Brothers Comedy Hour*—season by season, show by show—the more you understand the generational, artistic, and moral duels being fought in the '60s, and how quickly small confrontations mushroomed into all-out war on several fronts. Year to year, the shows said it all: Tom and Dick Smothers looked different, acted differently, and protested more brazenly and passionately. What they managed to say and do was important, and what they were prevented from saying and doing was no less meaningful.

The Birth of the Smothers Brothers
(and the Smothers Sister)

T he catchphrase that ended up defining the Smothers
Brothers—Tom's angry exclamation to Dick "Mom always
liked you best!"—didn't surface until many years into the
duo's stage, recording, and TV act. Until then, their act consisted of
funny parodies of folk songs and the brothers' sparkling verbal byplay: Dick trying to extol the virtues and describe the histories of
various tunes, while Tom digressed, meandered, misbehaved, interrupted, and acted, basically, like an impish little brother—though, in
real life, he was the elder of the two. This went on for several years
and many record albums, until, onstage and on TV, Tom ad-libbed
the complaint that launched their career to a new level, and made
sibling rivalry, as much as musical revelry, the cornerstone of the
Smothers Brothers.

Their eighth LP, released in August 1965, got its title from Tom's
angry opening line: *Mom Always Liked You Best!* The rest of the
routine—no music, just a long, comic argument, expanding upon
scattered remarks (and that catchphrase) first heard on their November 1964 *Tour de Farce* album—was a litany of perceived slights from
their childhood.

"My mom and my brother would get together and say, 'We don't like you!' " Tom complains to the audience. And: "More than any-thing in the whole world, I wanted to have a dog of my own. I asked my mom. I said, 'Mom, I want to have a dog like my brother, Dickie Smothers. You remember me, I'm Tommy Smothers. And I never got to have a dog!' "

Dick defends himself: "Now hold it a minute. Before we go any further, you know you had your own pet already."

"A crummy chicken," Tom grumbles.

The real story of the Smothers brothers' childhood was quite differ-ent. Their mother didn't favor one boy over the other, and, as chil-dren, they played together often and nicely. Things weren't always that funny growing up, either. Their father died when they were very young, a POW fatality in the last months of World War II. Dick was ejected accidentally from a moving car, suffering injuries that made him deaf in one ear. Their mother, after the death of her hus-band, struggled through bouts of alcoholism and several tenuous marriages and relationships, often leading to her children being farmed out, separately or together, to live with relatives. Those children included not only Tom and Dick, but a sibling who may be a surprise even to fervent Smothers brothers fans: younger sister Sherry. And it's Sherry, after all these years, who reveals another sur-prising fact about the Smothers family history: there really *was* a pet chicken.

First genealogy, then poultry.

Thomas Bolyn Smothers Jr., father of Tom, Dick, and Sherry, was born in Winston-Salem, North Carolina, in 1908. He graduated from West Point in the class of 1929, becoming a career soldier and eventually earning the rank of major. (His West Point yearbook de-scribed him as answering to the nickname of "Smo," being a good baseball player and a knowledgeable sports fan, and being determined and independent, "although he has never startled anyone with his academic record.") He married Ruth Remick in 1935, and was stationed on Governors Island in New York, where his two boys were born, making them instant "army brats." Thomas Bolyn Smothers III was born February 2, 1937, Richard Remick Smothers followed on November 20, 1939—and shortly thereafter, the entire family made a dramatic relocation, when Major Smothers was reassigned to an army base in the Philippines.

They weren't together long. Little more than a year later, rumblings of danger in the Pacific led, as a precaution, to the slow but steady evacuation of many military families. Major Smothers's wife Ruth, now pregnant with their third child, was sent back to the States with her two boys. They resettled in Altadena, California, just north of Pasadena, finding solace with Ruth's relatives. (There's a picture of young Dick, taken stateside on December 7, 1941, the day the Japanese attacked Pearl Harbor and drew the United States into World War II.) Tom and Dick never saw their father again. Their sister, Sherry, born September 18, 1941, in Pasadena, never saw him at all. But he did send Ruth a giddy, congratulatory radiogram six days after their daughter's birth, signing off with his old West Point nickname: "BLESS YOU YOU RASCAL STOP YOU CAN CALL YOUR SHOTS AM TICKLED PINK OVER SHARON'S ARRIVAL BE CAREFUL LOVE SMO."

Back in the Philippines, on Corregidor, their father was among the American troops fighting the Japanese on the Bataan Peninsula on West Luzon Island. In April 1942, the lengthy isolation and lack of supplies and reinforcements for American and Filipino troops led to unbearable levels of malnutrition, and 75,000 soldiers surrendered at once. The Japanese, unprepared to deal locally with so many prisoners, set them on a brutally sadistic forced sixty-five-mile march to a prison camp in San Fernando. Along the way, guards killed and tortured prisoners indiscriminately, buried others alive, and withheld food and water to intensify the agony of the rest. So many prisoners of war perished on that merciless journey that it became known as the Bataan Death March. Major Smothers survived that march and survived more years as a prisoner of war. He was imprisoned, under horridly inhumane conditions, aboard three different Japanese POW ships. According to information provided to Tom, his father died when the last of those ships, en route to Korea, was bombed mistakenly by Allied pilots. He was a victim of friendly fire. The date was April 26, 1945—less than five months before the Japanese government surrendered to end World War II.

His young namesake, Thomas Bolyn Smothers III, was four when he last saw his father and eight when his father died. Dick has no vivid memories of living in the Philippines, but Tom does. "I remember it raining, and my father taking me out and running in the rain," he recalls. In addition to the flash rainstorms, he remembers the loud sounds of mosquitoes ("terrifying"), and mosquito nets, and the fact that the legs of their beds were placed in pans of water "so certain things wouldn't crawl up." He also remembers that the maid taking care of them would use bacon grease to smooth out Dick's hair—a fate Tom escaped. "About two hours later, in that heat," Tom remembers, laughing, "the smell was just awful."

Back in the States, in Altadena, young Tom remembers being "eight or nine" when informed, in the most general terms, of his father's fate. "My mother brought me in, sat me down, and said, 'Your daddy was caught in the war and died.' I remember she turned to me and said, 'Now you're the man of the house.' Tough, for a nine-year-old. She was crying. I was crying, too."

Then there was the accident. Dick was three, Tom was five, and mother Ruth was driving them somewhere in the family car, a dazzling 1932 Packard (picture a getaway car Bonnie and Clyde might use). There were no seat belts then: for safety's sake, young Dick was placed in the front seat, within easy reach ("Mama's right arm, when she wasn't shifting, was on you," he recalls). Except, on this particular trip, Dick kept whining about how he wanted to sit in back with his brother—and after one too many whines of "I wanna be with Tommy!" Mom relented, and Dick climbed in back.

Unfortunately, this particular 1932 Packard model came equipped with what were called "suicide doors"—doors that opened toward the rear of the vehicle, and thus were perfectly (or imperfectly) designed to catch the wind if opened while the car was in motion. The Packard was going about thirty miles an hour—and for a moment or two, after he reached for the shiny handle and opened the rear door, so was Dick.

"All of a sudden," Tom says, "we're feeling air coming in the car. I look around, and Dickie's not there."

"I landed on my head and fractured my skull," Dick says, picking up the story. "That's why I'm deaf in one ear." All because he wanted to sit with his brother.

A few years later, Dick remembers a different man of the house: Orville Hood, whom his mother married in the mid-1940s, but whose stature in the household, like the fate of Major Smothers, was somewhat unclear to the younger Smothers brother. "He adopted us," Dick recalls of Orville, "but I was always worried what was going to happen to Orville when Daddy came home. You know: 'If Daddy comes home, Orville can't be here!' So I didn't quite get it . . . but I knew that wasn't going to go over well."

Things didn't go over that well anyway. For the Smothers brothers, and their Smothers sister, childhood and adolescence unfolded in an environment that could charitably be described as unstable. Their mother, in Tom's words, "had drinking problems," which made the entire situation "kind of high maintenance." Throughout their childhood, Ruth was in and out of rehab and state hospitals, leaving her children with others as she tried, with little success, to conquer her alcoholism. After Hood left, while Tom and Dick still were in high school, Ruth met her next husband while the two of them were attending Alcoholics Anonymous. Neither sobriety nor the marriage lasted very long. "She went back to drinking, then he went back, then he deserted her," recounts Sherry. "The drinking, between the both of them, destroyed him." A brief fourth marriage followed— "to someone we really never knew," Sherry says—after which Ruth took back her original married name of Smothers. Sherry, too, got the Smothers name back, while still in junior high. Tom and Dick had never changed theirs to anything else, making it one of the few things in their childhood to remain constant.

"Tommy was quite a filter," Dick says, recalling how, when Dick was in first or second grade, Tom would tell him that their mother had fainted—when, Dick finally understood years later, "she was passed out drunk." It was about that time when Ruth placed the boys in military school, where they lived instead of at home. Dick lasted one year, Tom two. And Tom remembers, more than once, enduring corporal punishment in front of his classmates for such infractions as not making his bed properly. "You'd get swats," he recalls, and it's not much of a stretch to imagine Tom Smothers's problems with authority stemming from this fatherless, regimented period. "I remember thinking, 'You won't break my spirit!' "

"Your boy is very, very stubborn," one officer at the school informed Ruth, referring to young Tom, then in third grade. "He could either turn out to be a great man, or maybe a criminal, but I don't know."

During their childhood, together or separately, Tom, Dick, and Sherry were shipped out, at different times and in various configurations, not only to a succession of schools, but to assorted nearby relatives and friends. Dick went to live for a while with his aunt and uncle—Dick Remick (Ruth's brother) and his wife, Winifred—in

Sunland, halfway between Altadena and San Fernando. When young Dick returned, Sherry lived with them next, even accompanying them when they moved to Chico, north of Sacramento, so Uncle Dick could attend college. Tom lived with them too, at one point, but he and brother Dick spent more time under the guardianship of Ruth's parents, Ed and Bertha Remick, in Tujunga, just south of Sunland. One year, while attending Verdugo Hills High School in Tujunga, Tom and Dick were sheltered at a nearby home for asthmatic children—even though neither of them had asthma.

Despite the upheaval, there were times of normal childhood antics and activities. For a while, Tom, Dick, and Sherry—now *there's* a marquee name—were living together in Altadena in adjacent attic rooms, the boys sharing one, Sherry alone in the other. At age nine, Tom organized a neighborhood charity benefit in someone's backyard, showcasing all the local kids. Tom, already interested in gymnastics, did lots of acrobatics and an animal act, showing off tricks he'd taught his dog, Toby. Yes, it was his dog, not Dick's, though there were plenty of other family pets–many of whom, like Tom's mythical pet chicken Frank from the *Mom Always Liked You Best!* LP, sounded slightly surreal. For starters, Toby turned out to be a girl dog. The family had other dogs at Altadena, and the entire block shared a "neighborhood tortoise that made the rounds"—slowly, no doubt. And it was when visiting Grandpa Remick that Tom and Dick got the seminal inspiration for Frank.

"Our grandparents had a chicken coop," Sherry says, "and they had a blond chicken that they named Brownie." This particular chicken was so loved and pampered, it was shown the highest form of flattery and favoritism: "They never ate Brownie."

Also in Altadena, Sherry remembers Tom getting in trouble with stepfather Orville for sneaking out the bathroom window to go to the neighbor's house and watch TV—the first television set on the block. "Tom was always in mischief," Sherry says, but he also was protective of his younger siblings.

"Tom has always been the responsible one," Sherry says. "He's always been the one that felt he had to take care of the whole family. So he was in a different place, so to speak." Dick, who was head cheerleader in high school while Tom competed in gymnastics, remembers a similar protectiveness from his brother. "My perception," Dick recalls, "is that he took care of me."

When Sherry was a freshman in high school, and living with Uncle Dick and Aunt Wini, Tom would drive north just to pick her up and take her on outings. "He would drag me out to the beach when he was in high school—a senior!—with his friends, and I would sit and watch all the girls go gaga. He was very popular. They both were."

Sherry also recalls Dick teasing her ruthlessly. "It was just normal brother-and-sister stuff," she said, laughing. "Dickie was brutal at times—he said some pretty damned funny stuff to me in the teenage years. I would ask him, 'What's sex appeal?'" she recalls, "and he would answer, 'Don't worry, you don't have any.'"

Even when younger, the children did everything they could together: played together, fought together, got in trouble together. There were big vacant lots filled with lemon trees where Tom and Dick grew up, and they would steal lemons, set up a stand, and sell lemonade—then make more of a profit by selling somewhere else. "We'd sell it in front of our uncle's coffee shop, and then he'd give us a dollar to go in front of the drugstore and sell it there instead," Dick remembers with a laugh. He also recalls getting in trouble with Tom for cutting down some royal palm trees ("Tommy was engineering"), and being forced to dig up the stumps, or try to, as punishment. "They got in a world of trouble for that one," Sherry says, laughing.

But through it all, despite it all, or because of it all, there was, and remains, a strong familial bond. "Tom had a thought that siblings who had to grow up with a dysfunctional life sometimes have a stronger bond," Sherry says. "And we have a pretty good bond. They are the two most special people in my life—and they are very, very, very good to me." Dick now lives fifteen minutes away from Sherry in Florida, while Tom's family and winery are in Northern California, at an idyllic place called Remick Ridge, named after his mother and grandfather.

"I always thought they were amazingly devoted to her," Ken Fritz, the brothers' onetime manager and production partner (with Ken Kragen), says of Tom and Dick's relationship with their mother. "They were very concerned and protective of her, because she was fragile." Fritz also saw a tight bond between the two brothers— "They were a unit, those two guys"—even though Tom, describing his own relationship with Dick, remembers it more as normal fraternal friction, "salt and pepper all the time." Except, that is, for the real spice—the music.

2

The Smothers Brothers—
All Three of Them—Take the Stage

A love of music is what eventually changed the Smothers brothers into the Smothers Brothers. And it started early, with family sing-alongs in the family's death-trap automobile. "When we were going back and forth to Grandma's house in the old Packard," Tom told me on National Public Radio's *Fresh Air with Terry Gross* in 1997, "we always sang songs. We'd sing 'Down in the Valley,' 'Home on the Range'—all these songs, we'd be singing." ("Down in the Valley," tellingly, wound up as one of the songs on their first album, the only one they sing and play completely straight, without jokes or interruption.)

When Tom was nine years old, he began asking—pestering, really—for a guitar. And he got one, from a surprising source. Brother Dick later got a guitar—a beautiful blond-back Martin four-string that was stored under his bed, neglected and unused. So when the time came, Dick's guitar was used as partial payment for Tom's first quality guitar, an even more beautiful golden Gibson. "My mother, who supposedly liked me best," says Dick, with the deadpan delivery of a true straight man, "had me sell my guitar for a down payment on Tommy's."

Tom credits Burl Ives, a folksinger who popularized traditional folk tunes in the '40s, as his first influence on guitar, just as he credits '50s TV star George Gobel, a few years later, as his first comedic influence. (It's no coincidence, but it is sweet to note, that both Ives and Gobel eventually were featured as special guest stars on *The Smothers Brothers Comedy Hour.*) And while Tom was learning to play guitar, and to act silly, Dick was learning to sing and act—and learning, in the process, he had a voice others considered quite special.

Both brothers, though, came out of their shells rather slowly. Dick remembers his first performance in front of a group at a church Christmas pageant when he was five or six—forgetting every word he was supposed to deliver, but *never* forgetting how awful that felt.

Tom, in grade school, was drawn to both guitar and piano but had difficulty reading sheet music. Years later, he learned that his problems were caused by the same thing that made academics so challenging in school: he has dyslexia, a condition that made both notes and letters scramble out of order as he tried to read them on the page. He could learn music by ear, though, and the guitar by feel and repetition, so he pursued music, like gymnastics, with a passion.

Tom started his first band in 1948, when he was in fifth grade. It was a trio—"clarinet, piano, and me," he recalls—and Dick was not a member. They were formed to play one song, the then-runaway hit "Now Is the Hour" (recorded by both Gracie Fields and Bing Crosby that year). But in high school, there were other groups, everything from pickup barbershop quartets to bands thrown together for school assemblies. One group, the Casual Quartet, featured Tom, Dick, and two other classmates. Another, with Tom, Dick, and one other member, was called the Trite Trio. Dick sang but didn't play; he didn't yet have his signature upright bass. And while Tom played guitar and sang, he also started to joke around a bit.

"I'd introduce us, and I knew I was funny," Tom says. "I understood I was funny, but I didn't learn the craft of it until much later in my life." He recalls watching classmates freeze up and scramble desperately for words while trying to bluff their way through oral book reports. He just played variations on that comic theme—even when playing the class clown himself. If he showed up late to class, instead of sliding quietly into the back of the room, Tom would go to the front of the class and address the teacher in a deadpan, rambling speech: "My apologies. I'm late. To all the kids for whom I disrupted class, I apologize to you students for my lateness. To you, my teacher, I apologize also, and promise it's never going to happen again." Recounting this story, Tom laughs. "By this time, she's grabbed me by the ear and dragged me down to the principal's office, and I'm going, 'What did I *do*?' "

In performances, Tom realized almost instinctively that awkwardness, long silences, even disconnected and incomplete thoughts were his friends, and became part of his arsenal. He knew as a youngster, somehow, what comedian Andy Kaufman would explore two decades later—that attitude could matter as much as jokes, and vulnerability and discomfort, if presented correctly, could be their own rich rewards. "I always kept saying, 'I hope something comes to me,' " Tom says of those first comic attempts at thinking on his feet. "But," he adds, "I found out that something *would* always come to me, if the tension got higher."

It was as a teenager, seeing the wry, meek, and constantly digressing standup comic George Gobel on *The Ed Sullivan Show,* that cemented for Tom the idea of his fumbling onstage persona. "He was talking about losing a bowling ball, and I said, 'Oh, wow, that's funny!' He didn't tell a single joke, but I was laughing. And I thought, Well, I'd like to do *that*! . . . He didn't do jokes, he did attitude." So, as emcee at school functions or as spokesman for his own musical group, Tom would play with deadpan delivery, long silences, and goofy asides.

The most crucial influence at that point in the development of the Smothers Brothers, though, was Ted Misenheimer, a band teacher and choir director at the Redondo Beach High School. At that point, all three Smothers siblings had reunited and were living together. Tom transferred to the high school as a senior, Dick already was there as a sophomore, and Misenheimer ended up drafting them both into a very small and specialized vocal program—the madrigal choir. Not only did it give both brothers a taste for music from other lands and times, but it gave them an appreciation of their vocal abilities, alone and especially together.

Tom was selected first, singing bass, and Dick, who had been singing bass in choir since sixth grade, offered to sing tenor, because that was the only vocal part that needed to be filled. So they started singing together, paying more attention to harmonies and dividing their vocal parts differently and with more subtlety.

"I'm not a true tenor," Dick says. "Two more notes, and I could have been a David Gates, an Art Garfunkel, or one of those guys. I was faking it." Dick's "faking it," though, was good enough to impress "Mr. M," with whom Dick stayed in contact until the teacher's recent death. ("He always prayed for me," Dick says fondly. "I was on his list. And he was *so* proud of the Smothers Brothers.") Dick's "faking it" also was good enough for him to win awards for his vocal ability—and get the attention, and respect, of his big brother.

"Dick was the best tenor in the South Bay area of Redondo Beach where we went to finish up high school," Tom says. That measure of respect was what turned Dick from annoying little brother into convenient singing partner. It made Tom reach down two entire school grades to include his brother in the quartet, and the trio, and eventually their first paying gigs.

"When we were in high school," Tom says, "the only reason we started singing was because he was the best tenor. He was really good." Because of that connection, Tom says, "I got to know my brother really well. Without that, we'd have been kind of strangers." Dick, too, credits the madrigal choir with giving the brothers both a bond and a direction: "It was one of the reasons we got into this business." Otherwise, Dick's career plan was to become a teacher, like his Uncle Dick, or a school principal. Tom had inclinations and interests of his own, including architecture, but music spoke to him most. "I don't know what drove Tommy," Dick says. "He always had this thing of wanting to do things musically. He would practice for hours with a harmonica and a guitar."

Tom graduated from high school in 1955. His high school yearbook photo shows a dapper, smiling young man in a jacket and bow tie, with short, well-groomed hair. Dick's smaller sophomore photo, by contrast, displays longer and more disheveled hair, glasses, and a more serious expression. Tom moved north to attend San Jose State, and Dick eventually graduated high school and started attending junior college at Fullerton, south of Los Angeles. This is when they could have gone their separate ways: Dick still had plans to pursue a career in education, while Tom, studying advertising at San Jose State, began performing solo, running the synchronized card-stunt halftime show at college football games and experiencing, for the first time, the thrill of drawing laughs from large crowds.

Instead of branching out solo, however, Tom kept making room for and working with his little brother, eventually persuading him to transfer and join him at San Jose State. The two would continue to perform in various small-group permutations, getting their first "paid" gig at a college beer hall. The pay was beer and pretzels, but it was a start.

Next stop: the Kerosene Club, a tiny college hangout at San Jose where college kids sprawled on couches, drank too much beer, and yelled at the amateur acts who dared to perform in front of them. Tom and Dick would perform there, but not well.

As a duo, the Smothers brothers—not yet the Smothers Brothers—were bombing. "Tom wasn't that comedically developed," Dick recalls, "and I was not developed as a straight man." Their musical repertoire was thin, and so were their prospects—so much so, Dick recalls, that at the end of one particularly forgettable set in front of a typically boisterous drunken crowd, Tom made an announcement to the audience. "Anybody who wants to join us," he said, "who has got some songs and knows what they're doing, talk to us afterward."

This very open audition process resulted in a young man walking up, with his leg in a cast from a skiing accident, to offer his services. His name was Bobby Blackmore. He had a nice smile and a pleasant voice, knew a lot of songs, and played a tenor guitar, like Nick Reynolds of the Kingston Trio. That was more than enough for Tom and Dick, because the Kingston Trio, at that point in 1958, was an inspiration in more ways than one.

The Weavers, a folk group that included activist banjo player Pete Seeger, had scored a big hit with a recording of Huddie Ledbetter's "Goodnight Irene" in 1949, but popular music was changing drastically in the late 1950s, splintering off into several different directions. Elvis Presley exploded onto the scene in 1956, electrifying the charts with five number-one hits that year alone (including three monsters in a row: "Don't Be Cruel," "Hound Dog," and "Love Me Tender"). Also in 1956, Harry Belafonte released his best-selling *Calypso* album, turning "Banana Boat (Day-O)" into a Top 10 hit. (A dozen years later, Belafonte would take part in one of the most notorious censored segments of *The Smothers Brothers Comedy Hour.*)

In 1957, Pat Boone, Perry Como, and Andy Williams ruled the charts, but so did Presley, Buddy Holly and the Crickets ("That'll Be the Day"), Jimmie Rodgers ("Honeycomb"), Johnny Mathis ("Chances Are"), and the Everly Brothers ("Wake Up Little Susie"). And in 1958, the year Tom and Dick Smothers were trying to find their way and a new lead singer, many number-one hits were either nascent rock 'n' roll (Danny and the Juniors' "At the Hop," the Silhouettes' "Get a Job," the Coasters' "Yakety Yak") or funny novelty tunes (David Seville's "Witch Doctor" and "The Chipmunk Song," Sheb Wooley's "Purple People Eater").

But one group bucked all the trends—and in so doing, started its own. The Kingston Trio, picking up where the Weavers had left off, sang folk songs in tight harmonies and told stories about the songs' origins as part of their act. The clean-cut young men had started singing together at a fraternity luau and quickly developed a strong local following in Palo Alto, California, less than twenty miles north of where Tom and Dick were studying at San Jose. In the summer of 1957, the Kingston Trio got a one-week booking at San Francisco's the Purple Onion, which extended to the end of the year. In 1958, they recorded their first album for Capitol Records, and one song lifted from the album, "Tom Dooley," became a number-one hit in November. It was the song that, in essence, launched the modern folk movement and the careers of just about everyone who played an acoustic guitar and got a record contract in the early 1960s.

But to the Smothers brothers, the Kingston Trio offered more than just a general direction. "Tom Dooley," with its spoken introduction about the song's meaning and history, provided a template Tom and Dick would use to shape and perfect their stage act. More specifically, the path from Northern California college gigs to auditioning at the Purple Onion would be one the Smothers brothers would follow as well. Which is why Bobby Blackmore's knowledge of folk music, and his snazzy Martin tenor guitar, made him instantly attractive to Tom and Dick.

"He knew a lot of Harry Belafonte tunes," Dick says of Blackmore, "so we said, 'Wow, this is great!' Our repertoire increased by about 300 or 400 percent—and that's when we went up to the Purple Onion."

They went up after a detective in the audience offered to be their first manager and arrange an audition in San Francisco. So in January

1959, this detective-manager crammed Tom, Dick, and Bobby into his car and drove north. It was a case of perfect timing: the Kingston Trio, after becoming headliners at the Purple Onion, had released "Tom Dooley" as a single and sold three million copies. The group was now at a rival North Beach club in San Francisco, the even hotter hungry i, and the managers of the Purple Onion were willing to try almost any act that might reach that same level of success.

"They had auditions the first Tuesday of every month, or something like that," Tom recalls. Phyllis Diller was headlining at the Onion then, and, without the Kingston Trio, other acts ranged from lounge singers to flamenco dancers. "We auditioned, and someone was talking out in the audience, and I said, 'Shut up!' And people thought that was very funny—and it was. So all of a sudden they hired us. We couldn't believe it."

Barry Drew, the manager of the Purple Onion, really liked the act: Tom played guitar and offered rambling introductions, Bobby played tenor guitar and banjo and sang, and Dick sang. But Drew had some suggestions. At the audition, Drew said that Dick should play an instrument, because he was just standing there. Tom suggested an upright bass, and Drew thought that would be fine. Drew also suggested they should call themselves the Smothers Brothers, even though one of them was neither a Smothers nor a brother. When that suggestion was considered unacceptable, Drew came up with an alternative means of billing: the act at the Purple Onion, he suggested, would open under the irreverent name of Smothers Brothers and Gawd.

That, too, was agreed upon, but there was one more snag. The next opening at the Onion, they were told, was in two or three months. But no sooner had Tom and Dick returned to San Jose and school than the Purple Onion called back. A singer was sick, and so was the flamenco act, so could they start next week? They could, and they did.

Dick couldn't afford to buy an upright bass on his own, so Drew cosigned for it—at three hundred dollars, paid over eighteen months. Tom gave Dick some cram lessons in how to play ("Tommy plays the guitar," Dick explains, "and the bass is just the bottom four strings of the guitar, so all you do is just outline some chords for folk, and most of them were real simple"). They practiced furiously that week, trying to perfect a handful of songs, but perfection didn't come easily. Dick was a quick study, but Tom was both impatient and imperfect. "We'd practice on a song while driving from San Jose to San Francisco," Tom says. "Bobby would be driving, Dick would be in the backseat, and I would be in the front seat with a guitar, working on harmonies. Then the first time we'd get onstage, I'd forget the chords, I'd forget the words. At first, it was just scary. So we always said the first thing to do was to get onstage. Get onstage. Because that's where you're going to learn all your skills, primarily."

The Smothers Brothers and Gawd opened at the Purple Onion in February 1959, signed to a two-week contract with options to extend in additional two-week increments. The set was compact— three songs, fifteen minutes, three times nightly—and so was the venue. The Purple Onion held about one hundred fifty people, and the stage was some eight feet square, backed by a brick wall. It was like a dingy comedy club, before there were comedy clubs.

Onstage, Dick played the bass, nervously, and didn't talk. Bobby talked occasionally, but only to introduce certain songs, and his introductions were no more complicated than, "And here's a song Belafonte sang." It was Tom who did almost all the talking—and at first, even Tom wasn't sure at all about what he was saying.

"I would make up an introduction about each song—I'd just make it up," Tom recalls. "And I'd make it up different every night. Every single night. We'd sing the same three songs, it's all I knew. Every night. Three shows a night. And every single show would be a different introduction, because I truly believed that people knew when you were repeating yourself.

"A song could be sung again and again, because I've heard songs again and again. That was legitimate. But when people were talking, I always assumed it was the first thing that would come out of their mouths. About a week into it, Dickie said to me, 'Those ad libs are starting to get pretty thin.' I was reaching for straws."

"Why don't you repeat one of those things?" Dick asked.

"Oh, no man," Tom replied. "They'll know. The audience will know." But after a few weeks of the audience laughing at Tom straining onstage to think of something to say, Tom took his brother's advice and repeated an ad lib from a previous show—and it got big laughs. He tried it the next show, repeating the same line. Again, big laughs.

"What a discovery! Isn't that amazing!" Tom remembers thinking. "They don't know!" From that point on, Tom wasn't ashamed to repeat lines, and the laughs between songs began to increase.

Tom and Dick conspired to sneak in their sister Sherry to see some of their early Purple Onion shows. "I was always sitting there beaming, of course, and laughing my head off," she said. She was only seventeen, and the club was restricted to patrons age twenty-one and older, but carrying Tom's guitar case as an "assistant" was good enough to get her through the door. And she wasn't the only Smothers underage at the Purple Onion: Dick was only nineteen when they started. There and elsewhere for the next two years, Tom would slip his own ID to his brother whenever there was a problem. Offstage, and onstage, Tom shouldered a lot of the responsibility.

"We were a trio the first professional year," Dick says, "and two of us didn't have to talk. Tommy did all the talking, and Bobby and I sort of pretended we were tuning. There was a comfort—I've always had a comfort . . . of knowing the songs and music, and that's all I had to do."

The Purple Onion appearance was so successful, the club kept extending their contract, eventually covering sixteen straight weeks and signing them for an additional sixteen weeks after a summer booking at the Wagon Wheel at Lake Tahoe, Nevada. Meanwhile, the trio made its first local TV appearance, on San Francisco's *Bright and Early Show*, in March, and, like the Kingston Trio, picked up lucrative high school graduation shows during the summer. ("We'd go off and make $150 in one night," Dick says, "which was a fortune for us!" The Kingston Trio commanded ten times that amount, but for the Smothers Brothers and Gawd, it was a windfall.) An advance story in The *San Mateo Times* for March 12, 1959, boasts that the Smothers Brothers would be featured at the Burlingame "Polynesian Grad Night." There is no mention of Gawd.

Nor was the name of Gawd taken, in vain or in any other manner, in a July 31 story in the *Reno Evening Gazette,* which ran a story on Tom, Dick, and Bobby, and an accompanying photo, identifying them only as the Smothers Brothers. "The young Smothers Brothers," said the Nevada paper, "have a unique three-part harmony and unamplified guitar and banjo format that is going over strongly."

As the months wore on, Bobby's billing as one of "the Smothers Brothers" may have worn thin. And while the Purple Onion was happy to have them back, and the Nevada booking may have been seen as a first step in the general direction of Las Vegas, the end of 1959 showed relatively little promise. In October the Smothers Brothers—as they had come to be billed officially—were one of nine acts booked in Oakland in a one-night variety show celebration of a new building complex housing the Church of Jesus Christ of Latter-day Saints. In hindsight, the Smothers Brothers were the biggest act on the bill. Back then, all nine might be said to be equally unknown.

The frustrations of group friction and the threat of career stagnation came to a head when Bobby Blackmore married a professional ice skater and decided to return with her to her native Australia. He quit the group, and Tom and Dick, not even knowing if they would continue, didn't try to talk him out of it.

"He could not tolerate Dick and me," Tom says. "It was kind of hard to be a third party. It was Tom and Dick Smothers, and this one guy. Neither one of us really were fond of him," Tom adds, laughing. "At first, we liked him a lot, and then . . ."

But in the end, all was forgiven. When the Smothers Brothers got their CBS variety show, they invited Bobby Blackmore to join them for a one-shot reunion. He accepted, and the TV audience got to see the three of them performing together in 1967.

Yet back at the end of 1959, there was no guarantee the Smothers Brothers as a two-man band would survive even to see 1960. Dick had gotten married, too, to Linda Miller, and was about to resume his plan of finishing college to become an elementary school teacher.

"I was going to go back to school," Dick recalls. "We were very, very close to breaking up the act at that time. It could have gone either way." The new lease on life came courtesy of another folk trio: the Limeliters, a new act that had performed in San Francisco at the hungry i while the Smothers Brothers were at the Purple Onion. This is how intimate, interconnected, and friendly the folk music world was at that time: One of the founding members of the Limeliters, Lou Gottlieb, had been an arranger for the Kingston Trio. The other two, Glenn Yarbrough and Alex Hassilev, had performed as a duo in Aspen the previous winter and invested their earnings in a small folk club they christened the Limelite. (The group was named after the club, not the other way around.) At the end of 1959, after Bobby Blackmore's departure and Dick's marriage, Yarbrough offered Tom and Dick Smothers a deal. Go to Aspen and work at the Limelite for eight weeks, guaranteed, as a duo—for only $200 a week salary, but free room and board.

The offer was meager, but so were the balances in Tom's and

Dick's bank accounts, and this paycheck would be split two ways, not three. Dick remembers having only twenty dollars in his checking account when Yarbrough made the offer, but because he had a checking account in California, he was given a newfangled thing, good only in that state at the time, called a VISA credit card.

"It got us as close to the state line as we could get," Dick says, "and then we stopped and played a couple of quarters or nickels in a slot machine in Elko, Nevada, and won a little mini-jackpot, and that got the gas that got us all the way to Aspen. By the skin of our teeth, by the hair on our chinny-chin-chin, we got there. And we had no idea if it was going to be a struggle [as a duet], like it was in the Kerosene Club a year earlier. We didn't really know. We didn't sense the movement, how much more professional we were."

Almost instantly, when they took the stage in Aspen in the winter of 1960, they would find out.

Tom and Dick Shoot for Paar

I n the middle of February 1960, three events occurred that would
become significant historical markers in the history of comedy.
One was in Aspen, Colorado, where Tom and Dick Smothers
stepped onstage for the first time as a professional duo. Seven years
later, to the very month, they would have their own weekly variety
series on CBS. But their act, as it became known, began that evening.
Another February 1960 milestone was in Chicago, Illinois, where an
equally unknown talent, a young accountant named Bob Newhart,
would make his first-ever appearance before a live audience, purely
to record a debut album that would become the first comedy LP ever
to reach number one on the charts. (More on that later.) Finally, the
third event was in New York, where Jack Paar, host of NBC's popular *Tonight* show, would run afoul of his own network's censors, walk
off the air, and quit his high-profile talk show in protest of their interference.

Paar, who had succeeded Steve Allen as host of NBC's pioneering late-night national talk show (then called *Tonight!*), dominated
late-night TV from 1957 to 1962. Actually, "dominated" is too mild
a description. Except for late-night movies and other local programs,
Jack Paar *was* late-night TV. No other national network program
competed in the time slot until 1964, two years into Johnny Carson's

amazing thirty-year reign on *The Tonight Show*, when ABC tried to counter-program the genial, funny Carson with the acerbic, scowling host of *The Les Crane Show*. But Paar, for five years, held the late-night championship belt without ever being contested. He had power and clout, and enjoyed an intelligent, savvy audience—partly because of the late hour, partly because of his genuine interest in his guests, but also because of his quick wit, his emotional honesty, and unpredictability and occasional volatility. In his time, for his time, Jack Paar was as big as Johnny Carson—who, in *his* time, was bigger than David Letterman and Jay Leno put together and then some.

But in 1960, censors ended up driving Paar off TV, at least temporarily. The *Tonight* show, also known as *The Jack Paar Show,* was broadcast live for its first two seasons, then, with the advent of new technology, taped at 8:00 p.m. ET for delayed broadcast. That allowed for greater flexibility in booking guests, but also allowed time for NBC's censors to tamper with the show, which they did on February 10, 1960, when Paar told, or attempted to tell, his now-infamous "water closet" joke.

The joke itself has largely been forgotten, but shouldn't be. By today's standards, it is so innocuous, so absurdly inoffensive, that it illustrates perfectly the restrictive and puritanical nature of the networks of its day. Essentially, here was the joke, which Paar relayed in his opening monologue: A woman visiting Switzerland was looking to rent a room, and, after visiting an inn, wrote a follow-up note wondering "if there was a W.C. around." W.C. was an abbreviation for water closet, or toilet, but the recipients of the note were unfamiliar with the term and presumed the initials stood for the nearby Wayside Chapel. Their descriptive reply, to NBC's censors, was completely unacceptable.

"I take great pleasure in informing you that the W.C. is situated nine miles from the house you occupy," the note began. It added helpfully, "You will no doubt be glad to hear that a good number of people bring their lunch and make a day of it, while others, who can afford to, go by car and arrive just in time." After more such mild misunderstandings, the letter concludes: "I shall be delighted to reserve the best seat for you if you wish, where you will be seen by all . . ."

Paar taped the monologue and the show, went home, and learned only when he watched the show on TV that his three-minute joke had been cut and the time filled by news bulletins. The morning papers ran headlines about Paar's "obscene" joke, which, in this case, was obscene but not heard. Paar went to work and asked the network to allow him to show the excised three minutes on that night's program. NBC refused, and Paar taped his program as usual—except, on that February 11 show, he stunned the studio audience, cohost Hugh Downs, and the NBC censors and executives by tearfully announcing he was leaving the *Tonight* show: "There must be a better way of making a living than this, a way of entertaining people without being constantly involved in some sort of controversy." Paar walked off, leaving a stunned Downs to finish the show and an equally stunned NBC little choice, given the controversy already brewing, but to broadcast it a few hours later.

There's a great postscript to that controversy. A month later, after a parade of guest hosts had filled the late-night slot, Paar returned to a standing ovation and began his monologue with the impish phrase, "As I was saying before I was interrupted . . ." He then smiled and said, "When I walked off, I said there must be a better way of making a living. Well, I've looked, and there isn't." Paar got his show back and kept it long enough to showcase the Smothers Brothers, who would appear thirteen times during Paar's final year as host of *Tonight*.

In that same February of 1960, Tom and Dick took the stage at the Limelite and performed for the first time as a duo. They stood the way they would stand onstage for the next fifty years—Tom at Dick's right, a configuration designed so that Tom would be at Dick's good ear, rather than his deaf one. The brothers weren't sure how their voices would go over without a lead singer, how the audience would relate to them, or even how they would relate to each other. The transformation, according to them both, was like a bolt of lightning. By shedding their third member and almost stumbling on to the idea that Dick could play the role of straight man and interact with Tom conversationally as well as musically, the real Smothers Brothers were born, virtually overnight.

"Once we got onstage," Dick says, "within the first couple lines—boom! It was just there. There was just something about the naturalness of being two."

"We didn't think we could do it," Tom admits. "Bobby Blackmore, he always sang lead, and we sang harmony, and so we had to learn these different songs and we didn't think we had strong enough voices to carry them. Pretty soon, we're singing solos and doing comedy. It was amazing!"

Part of the Smothers Brothers' rapid growth in Aspen was due to the deep talent pool there, and the folk music tradition of swapping and sharing songs. Tom and Dick loved learning obscure traditional numbers they could fold into their act—and that fed their repertoire. Meanwhile, the earnestness with which most of the other folkies performed ("a lot of songs about hanging," is how Tom jokingly summarizes them, taking an obvious swipe at "Tom Dooley") was something the brothers had an easy time ridiculing—and that fed their comedy. "Anybody that sang, they took it so seriously," Tom says.

The close-knit folk community in Aspen included teenaged Judy Collins, who had grown up in nearby Denver and who opened for Tom and Dick on their first night. (Eight years later she would score her first Top 10 hit with "Both Sides Now.") Also hanging around, during those salad days of harmony and harmoniousness, were Walt Conley, a black folksinger who also played and hosted folk events in nearby Denver; Bob Gibson, who would slide in and out of town with his twelve-string guitar; and Mason Williams, an unknown guitarist and composer who was tipped to the Smothers Brothers' standing-room-only Aspen shows by a friend. "You've never seen anything like them," Mason was told—and he hadn't. Before too many years, Tom and Mason would become best friends. Hanging around together after shows, late into the night, all these musicians traded songs and guitar chords like baseball cards—learning a new song, or unfamiliar standard, by offering one of their own. Two future Smothers Brothers staples, "Tzena, Tzena, Tzena" and "John Henry," were acquired during these musical swaps.

While their audiences and their repertoire were increasing exponentially, the Smothers Brothers still were a long way from the big time. With more songs from which to choose and different avenues of comedy to explore, Tom and Dick found it tough to agree which songs to play during a given set. On occasion, those quarrels would escalate from the philosophical to the physical, with boys being boys, and brothers being brothers. Future Smothers Brothers manager Ken Kragen, who at the time was representing the Limeliters, remembers a snowy day in Aspen when a long line of people was waiting to get into the club where Tom and Dick were about to play. "Tom and Dick walked up there, arguing over something," Kragen says, "and they got in a fight. They were now wrestling in the snow, right next to the line of people who were waiting to go in and see them at the club."

Some of that combativeness would play out onstage, as Dick would begin to talk more, slowly assuming the role of the straight man. It wasn't a rapid evolution: "I just slowly edged my way in—Tommy was always the rock," Dick says. Yet even in the earliest days of the duo, with Tom providing most of the song introductions, their fraternal familiarity allowed the brothers to improvise easily and playfully, and to expand their routine whenever a new line got a big laugh—which was often.

"We'd learn a song, and then things would happen," Dick says. "It would take its own direction. It was like a boat with no rudder." Tom agrees, remembering the Aspen days as the time he and Dick discovered not only lots of new music, but also their own identity as a stage act. They had come to Aspen singing Kingston Trio songs and Harry Belafonte calypso numbers—the stuff they'd sung when backing Blackmore—but quickly sailed into uncharted territory. "That's where the definitive part of the Smothers Brothers was founded," Tom says. He added, "The comedy just took over. And I kind of got waylaid musically, because the comedy became our central focus."

The next job to come, after the Limelite gig ended, was in Denver, through a connection made with Walt Conley. Sam Sugarman, the owner of a low-rent sports bar on Colfax Avenue's rough-and-tumble eastern stretch, had decided to bet on the growing folk music scene and redesign his place as a folk club. He renamed it the Satire, and very quickly offered Conley the chance to run the place and perform there—especially if he could book that hot new group from Aspen, the Smothers Brothers. He could, and did—and they all crashed in Conley's apartment above the club, along with other familiar and less familiar faces from the folk scene.

"My wife and I scrubbed the apartment," Dick says, remembering their way of paying their room and board. In the club, his wife waited tables, and though Tom and Dick were paid the same $200 weekly sum they had gotten in Aspen, overhead was cheap. ("We ate on fifteen bucks a week," Dick says.) The Smothers Brothers soon turned the Satire into one of Denver's most popular night spots.

"Folk music back then, in the early '60s, was like the comedy stores were in the '80s and '90s," Tom says. "Anybody could get up." But there were solid opening acts, and headliners, along with others who tried to earn their way onto the roster. In Denver in the summer of 1960, Walt Conley was the opening act, the Smothers Brothers were the headliners, and one of the wannabe performers who had just come to town, having hitchhiked from Minneapolis, was Bob Dylan. Conley's recollection is that Dylan not only played at the Satire, with Tom Smothers privately making fun of his vocal style from the back of the room, but crashed at Conley's apartment for three weeks, when both Tom and Dick were living there also. Both brothers have only sketchy memories of Dylan from that time, though, and Conley may be mistaken. Other accounts have Dylan staying elsewhere in Denver that summer. But Dylan, at the time, would have been nineteen years old, a totally unknown and scruffy out-of-towner, so may have flown beneath the radar of the Smothers Brothers for the most part.

"We only ran into him once or twice," Tom says, when asked about Dylan and that summer in Denver. "He was always somewhere we'd just been." In January 1961, their paths would cross again—both Bob Dylan and the Smothers Brothers would hit New York City for the first time that same month—but in the meantime, and for a while, Tom and Dick would enjoy greater success.

"We got hot so fast after that," Tom says of the time spent in Colorado. He and Dick packed up and returned to San Francisco, where the Purple Onion was delighted to rehire and showcase them. Before the year was out, an acetate of their nightclub act was recorded there as a sample, with an eye toward recording their debut comedy album.

This was a particularly smart and well-timed move. In February, as the Smothers Brothers were rebooting themselves in Aspen, a thirty-year-old Chicago accountant named Bob Newhart had taken the stage at the Tidelands Club in Houston, Texas, to record his comedy routine in front of a live audience. Until then, the only people to see his "act" were coworkers and friends, who laughed heartily as New-hart conducted imagined one-way conversations—a driving instruc-tor talking to a bad woman driver ("How fast were you going when Mr. Adams jumped from the car?"), a press agent advising Abe Lin-coln just before Gettysburg ("You changed four-score and seven to 87? . . . Abe, that's meant to be a grabber"). Newhart had recorded his routines for the fun of it, and a tape eventually made its way to a Chicago disc jockey, who forwarded it to a record executive from Warner Bros. The label offered Newhart a contract and agreed to pay to have his next nightclub appearance recorded for the album. The only thing was, Newhart had no nightclub appearance booked, and never had. So they found a club with an open date, two weeks later in Houston, and Newhart stepped out as a professional stand-up comic for the first time. If he was nervous, he sure didn't sound it.

The resultant album, *The Button-Down Mind of Bob Newhart,* was released in May 1960 and quickly became the first comedy album to hit number one on the charts. The second comedy album to attain that rank was Newhart's follow-up effort, *The Button-Down Mind Strikes Back!,* released later that same year, in September 1960. That album was recorded, in part, at San Francisco's hungry i nightclub, where Newhart was appearing at the same time the Smothers Broth-ers were across the street, making their triumphant return appear-ance at the Purple Onion. Newhart saw their show, and the brothers saw his. "We were all just struggling stand-up guys," Newhart says.

Even so, by selling enough comedy albums to top the charts in 1960, Bob Newhart had blazed a trail the Smothers Brothers could follow, just as the Kingston Trio had revitalized folk music two years earlier. Tom and Dick offered the best of both worlds—folk music and comedy—and were poised perfectly to tap both markets by land-ing a record deal. That also was the opinion of Irv Marcus, West Coast regional manager for Mercury Records. (Eventually, Marcus would become one of the Smothers Brothers' several managers.) He arranged for an acetate recording of the act at the Purple Onion and sent it around. It was played for Mercury recording director David Carroll, who was asked whether he wanted to record the duo himself, which he agreed to do. Carroll became not only their record producer and A&R man, but, as future Smothers manager Ken Fritz put it, "David Carroll was really the father figure for them."

The first Smothers Brothers album was called *The Songs and Comedy of the Smothers Brothers! at the Purple Onion*—but that title's a little dishonest. The Smothers Brothers recorded there, but those performances weren't used on the album, only the introduction that opens the album. "The shows were good," Dick explains. "I think they just blew it on the recording end. But we were committed—plus, we owed them for giving us our first break, so we just said, 'Live, at the Purple Onion!' " Dick says the performance heard on the album eventually was recorded, as a Plan B substitute, at the Tideland Club in Houston. It wouldn't be released until May 1961, but by then, thanks to their first trip to New York, and in particular to Jack Paar, Tom and Dick would be certifiable showbiz stars.

The Smothers Brothers arrived in New York in January 1961, in the middle of the coldest, most brutal winter in twenty-eight years. They were booked at the Blue Angel, an uptown club, as the opening act for Pat Harrington Jr., who had achieved fame as Guido Panzini, the ersatz Italian golf pro appearing from time to time on Paar's *Tonight* show. On the program, he never broke character, but his nightclub act was more freewheeling and presented under his real name. (In the '70s, Harrington would find another level of fame as Schneider the handyman on the CBS sitcom *One Day at a Time*.) The Harrington connection turned out to be priceless for Tom and Dick, because he eventually lobbied, successfully, for Paar's talent booker to take a look at them. But first, the Smothers Brothers—who at this point had no record album to promote, no national TV exposure to point to, and no East Coast performance experience—had to prove themselves to the legendarily tough New York audience. Success didn't come immediately. It took about a week.

"New York is pretty damned big," Tom wrote in a letter to sister Sherry postmarked January 16, 1961. In the letter, Tom goes on to boast about the "name entertainers" who showed up to catch the Smothers Brothers in action their first week in Manhattan—not only supportive fellow fledgling comic Bob Newhart, but Anne Bancroft, Jack E. Leonard, composer Richard Rodgers, Shelley Berman, and "perky Peggy King," a singer who had been a regular on *The George Gobel Show* and promised to bring Gobel—Tom's original comic inspiration—the following week. "So far, no definite TV shows," he wrote, citing Jack Paar and Perry Como as "tentative," but sounding upbeat nonetheless: "First time in New York, you can't get everything!"

But they did. Harrington came through for them, and a representative from the *Tonight* show made it to the Blue Angel. He liked what he saw and told Tom and Dick to bring their instruments and show up at Rockefeller Center to audition for the producer. They hailed a cab and went to the *Tonight* offices, where they performed "The Fox," a new routine they'd fleshed out onstage in New York. It starts with a silly introduction from Tom, shifts to a song sung by Dick, which is interrupted by Tom, who does some very loud quacking to ruin a folk song about a fox hunting ducks and geese. As Tom quacks, the song screeches to a halt and the brothers have a heated argument, with Tom being outrageously, delightfully immature. "We'll call you," the producer said, and that was that. Almost.

Shortly before the Smothers Brothers were scheduled to leave the Blue Angel and head back west, Paar's young talent coordinator called back. A booking had fallen through, so if the duo could make an 8:00 p.m. taping, they could be on the show. They showed up early for camera blocking and rehearsal, and the stage manager, asking them to just talk through their act, seemed singularly unimpressed. Tom remembers the stage manager explaining some very discouraging hand signals—one that meant "speed it up," another that meant "stop and get off."

"I thought we were going to get to talk to Mr. Paar," Tom said, hoping for one of those coveted postperformance moves from the stage to where Jack Paar would be sitting.

"Ah, well, I don't think so," the stage manager said.

The talent coordinator, seeing things were going badly, slipped Tom and Dick back to meet Paar before the show. Paar was polite but initially standoffish. "Hi, boys," he said. "You're folksingers, right? I like folksingers. I just hate hillbillies." Then he stared at them warily and asked, "What's the difference between hillbilly and folk music?"

"Well," Tom replied nervously, like a kid caught unprepared for a pop quiz, "hillbillies sing higher." Paar roared with laughter, asked the brothers a little bit about themselves, and the stage was set. By meeting Paar backstage, and tickling his fancy, the Smothers Brothers had passed the most important audition of all.

Dick wasn't sure, at first, whether Paar really was on their side. "The show starts," Dick recalls, "and he starts to introduce us. He says, 'I've got to tell you, this next act, I've never seen before.' He totally divorced himself from us! Then he says, 'And I never heard of them before. They've got a funny name—Smothers Brothers—it's not made up. But their dad, their dad was an army man, he was killed in the war. And they're folksingers. I don't like folksingers generally. I like Burl Ives. But . . . come on out, boys! Come on out!' "

"What kind of an intro is *that*?" Dick remembers thinking. But then Paar asked Tom the same question he had thrown at Tom previously and privately, now knowing that Tom had a home-run answer. "What's the difference between hillbilly singing and folk music?" he asked Tom, as if for the first time. "I guess hillbillies sing higher," Tom replied, just as he had before.

"And the way he said it," Dick says, "because he looked so frightened, the audience fell on the floor!" Then they performed "The Fox," with all Tom's loud quacking, infantile bickering, and Dick's straight-faced singing ("I could hardly squeak out the words, I was so nervous," Dick says)—and they killed. The host immediately invited them over to the panel and anointed them as stars with an assessment that was pure Paar: "I don't know what you guys have," he told Tom and Dick at the end of their debut *Tonight* show appearance on January 28, 1961, "but no one's gonna steal it."

"His setup was so perfect," Dick says appreciatively of Paar's showmanship. "Letting them see us for a second, dismissing us, and setting up Tommy's line so they saw his character a little bit before we got into the music—it was huge." Tom uses the same word, *huge*, to describe that late-night show's impact. "At that time, if you succeeded on that," Tom says, "you were immediately a star. It was that important." Their "huge success" on Paar's program, Tom says, was obvious within twenty-four hours. "The next day, going to work, we couldn't walk in the streets," he says. "We couldn't go anywhere without people saying, 'Hey! Smothers Brothers! You guys! I saw you last night!' " Paar would retire from the *Tonight* show a year later, but before he did, the Smothers Brothers would appear as guests thirteen times.

The Smothers Brothers, on the Record

"T hings are looking up for us," Tom wrote Sherry on February 11, 1961. "We should be making a lot of loot pretty soon. Keep your fingers crossed. When things start to pop, I'll get you all the clothes and stuff a young college girl . . . could want . . . Our record on Mercury will be released . . . I don't know when, and don't care—it's really bad anyway."

That assessment was a bit premature. Record producer David Carroll wasn't any happier than Tom about their Purple Onion recordings, so alternate arrangements were made to record Tom and Dick at the Tidelands. In May 1961, Mercury Records released *The Songs and Comedy of the Smothers Brothers! at the Purple Onion*—only nine songs, but enough to keep the Smothers Brothers on the album charts for a full year.

"That *Purple Onion* album might be our best album," Dick says, "because it's just . . . the essence of early Smothers Brothers. And that material, we really, really knew. That's a major difference, which I never stated before. The *Purple Onion* album was *everything* we knew. Our whole career. Which, at that time," he adds, laughing, "was a year and a half."

It's a significant distinction. Routines on all subsequent albums, both Tom and Dick explain, were pieced together in editing, culling the best ad libs from two or three days' worth of shows, and building them subsequently into a cohesive whole. Once the records were released, those grafted-together routines became after-the-fact blueprints, the comedy frameworks upon which the Smothers Brothers would expand their act.

Their debut album, though, was different. "The first album, you could have just set the microphone stand and kept it on," Dick says. And Tom says that the first album didn't just capture the essence of their act at that time, but captured it all. "They cleaned us out!" Tom says. "This was the totality of what we had!"

To be honest, they didn't have much. Dick had yet to step fully into his role as the straight man and still relied on Tom to do all the song introductions. Of the nine songs on the LP, two were totally no-nonsense, no-comedy vocal performances, of "Down in the Valley" and "I Never Will Marry." "I'm still really surprised when we hear an old record, or we hear an old performance on television, how well our voices blended," Dick says, adding, "I never thought of ourselves as really singers. It was just the singing to get to the jokes."

Those jokes, in those innocent times, are what popped off the vinyl the most. Tom's stage persona, at this point, was solidified as the impish, misbehaving "younger" brother, and he often tiptoed as closely as he could to what was acceptable as "good taste" humor. Only one year after Jack Paar was censored for trying to tell a joke about a bathroom, Tom slipped in some good ones. Talking about the sailors of "Dance, Boatman, Dance," Tom said they would go into town and "pick up their oars." Singing "Pretoria," he added the line, "You sleep with me, I'll sleep with you." "Jezebel" was good for lots of slightly risqué jokes about prostitution. And conversely, before massacring "Tom Dooley," Tom promises to perform it in "its original virgin."

While the Smothers Brothers' act would evolve very quickly over the next few albums, the release of this first LP placed them as relative pioneers in both the comedy and folk recording fields. For the Smothers Brothers to establish their own beachhead so early—especially so early in their young careers—was impressive on its own, and even more so in context. The 1961 release of *The Songs and Comedy of the Smothers Brothers! at the Purple Onion* may have been three years behind the Kingston Trio's first album, and one year behind Bob Newhart's, but it was released a year before the debut albums by Bob Dylan and Peter, Paul and Mary, and two years before the first albums by Bill Cosby and the Beatles.

With the album out, and in the wake of several appearances with Paar, the Smothers Brothers had no problem landing solid bookings at nightclubs and universities across the country. Their return visit to New York, and the Blue Angel, earned a rave review in the *New York Times* in May 1961, the same month their album came out. Robert Shelton wrote: "The appeal of the Smothers Brothers totals more than one Tom Smothers plus one Dick Smothers. It is a result of a good deal of musical acumen and a fresh type of stinging satire, directed at a field wide open for it—folk music." Shelton nailed the dynamic of the brothers and described it nicely. "Tom's foolery," he wrote, "reflects the speech pattern of a frightened tenth-grader giving a memorized talk at a Kiwanis meeting," which brother Dick's "cherubic look suggests that he may have just won a Boy Scout merit badge for bass-playing." Together, Shelton wrote, the Smothers Brothers "use a merciless variety of musical and comedy devices to smother the folk-song craze in wit."

Jack Paar had given Tom and Dick their first national TV exposure just four months earlier, and here they were, being celebrated in the *Times*. Their next big national TV exposure, coincidentally enough, came courtesy of Paar's predecessor at the *Tonight* show, Steve Allen, a pioneering TV comedian who loved to discover and work with new talent, had switched networks and was starting a prime-time variety series that fall on ABC. "Whenever I started a new series, I was always looking for new faces," Allen said. "So I had seen these two new faces at that point, and they joined our group . . . I thought they were just terrific."

The Smothers Brothers became regulars on that series, appearing on most of its installments before it was canceled quickly at the end of the year. Yet in the last half of 1961, the show exposed young Tom and Dick to loads of talented young regulars and guest stars. Pat Harrington Jr., who had gotten the brothers in to see Paar, was a regular on ABC's *The Steve Allen Show,* as were Tim Conway and Don Knotts, and guests included Bill Dana, Louis Nye, Buck Henry, Carl Reiner, and Jim Nabors. The writer-producers on the show included Stan Burns and Mike Marmer, both of whom ended up writing for *The Smothers Brothers Comedy Hour.* Dick says, "Steve Allen was real important in keeping the momentum going for the Smothers Brothers . . . We did thirteen of those shows, and that sort of generated some interest, so Mercury said, 'How about a second album?' But in the meantime, we hadn't been working on new material."

Club dates intensified, and Tom and Dick couldn't write new material fast enough. That was true in a literal sense. Their contract with Mercury Records committed them to two albums per year, yet fulfilling that obligation proved nearly impossible. From the start, Mercury sent acetates of upcoming albums by new folk artists, just in case Tom and Dick might find something worth covering or lampooning hidden in its grooves. So did rival record companies, which was one sign of how quickly the Smothers Brothers had achieved some degree of respectability. Tom remembers Columbia Records sending over for consideration an advance acetate of what would be the first album by Bob Dylan, released in March 1962. Dylan hadn't made that strong a first impression on Tom when their paths crossed in Colorado in 1960, and his initial recordings didn't make a strong second impression, either. Decades later, Tom imitates Dylan's nasal whine and unique phrasing and, though Tom says he's a big Dylan fan now, admits of that first acetate exposure, "I couldn't hear the melody. Dickie and I always were captivated by melody . . . The words were kind of incidental. I was hearing those songs and saying, 'I don't hear anything here.' "

With such slow progress, the duo's second LP, *The Two Sides of the Smothers Brothers*, didn't appear until sixteen months after the first—and was padded out by Carroll's face-saving, time-saving idea of dividing the album in half. One side, of comedy, was recorded live at the Crystal Palace in St. Louis. The other side, a series of "straight" studio recordings with orchestra, included no-jokes renditions of such songs as "Stella's Got a New Dress" and "The Four Winds and the Seven Seas." "We didn't have enough [comedy material] for the album," Tom recalls, "so we had to do straight songs."

Regardless, the album was no throwaway. It included a few routines that would become Smothers Brothers classics and which sparkled even in these nascent versions. In "Cabbage," Tom interrupted the singing of "Boil That Cabbage Down" to tell his version of the building of the transcontinental railroad, where workers risked life and limb to build bridges "across deep cravisses [Tom's intentionally incorrect pronunciation], with vicious pumas in the cravisses." Dick kept correcting Tom on his historical inaccuracies, lengthening the routine into a six-minute home run, and in so doing demonstrating how much their comedy had grown since the last album. "I Don't Care" was a quick laugh at the expense of the refrain of "Jimmy Crack Corn," in which Tom would keep repeating "I don't care," even (especially) after Dick told him that wasn't the way the song went. "I don't care."

Most significant of all was the album's leadoff number, a story song called "Chocolate." It's familiar Smothers Brothers: Tom stretching to complete thoughts and answer questions, Dick patiently but firmly poking holes in Tom's silly stories. "I fell in a vat of chocolate,"

Tom starts the song, and Dick stops the singing to press for details. The capper comes when Tom sings, "I yelled 'Fire!' when I fell into the chocolate," Dick asks why, and Tom sings and shouts, "I yelled fire because no one would save me if I yelled 'CHOCOLATE!' " " 'Chocolate,' " Dick says admiringly, "had a great punch line."

The next years were a whirlwind. On their albums, TV appearances, and in concert, the Smothers Brothers were totally apolitical, even though politics in 1962 and beyond was getting increasingly volatile and polarizing, as the Cuban Missile Crisis pushed President John F. Kennedy to the brink of nuclear war over the issue of secret Soviet missiles established in Cuba. Thirteen months later, JFK would be assassinated, and Vice President Lyndon Baines Johnson would ascend to the presidency. Despite the Reverend Martin Luther King Jr.'s hopeful and peace-seeking "I Have a Dream" speech during the march on Washington, the year 1963 would be marred by violence, with national television carrying more of it to viewers who were aghast, or should have been, by what they were witnessing. Police attack dogs and fire hoses were turned on civil rights demonstrators in Birmingham, Alabama. Civil rights leader Medgar Evers was killed by a sniper in Jackson, Mississippi. Four young girls were killed when a black Birmingham church was bombed.

Also in 1963, folk and protest music continued to grow, despite some forces trying to control what was being said and sung. ABC premiered *Hootenanny,* a folk-song performance series, that year but refused to allow blacklisted singer Pete Seeger and others to appear on it. Several performers, including Dylan, refused to appear on the show in protest of its perpetuation of the blacklist. The Smothers Brothers did appear on *Hootenanny,* in a concert taped at New Jersey's Rutgers University.

Hootenanny wasn't the only showbiz outlet resisting change and dissent. In May 1963, Dylan was at a dress rehearsal for *The Ed Sullivan Show* when he was told one song he planned to sing, "Talkin' John Birch Paranoid Blues," was unacceptable to Sullivan and CBS. Instead of substituting another number, Dylan walked off and never appeared on Sullivan's hit show. Two weeks later, Dylan's second LP, *The Freewheelin' Bob Dylan*, hit record stores—but this time, CBS-owned Columbia Records had demanded the removal and replacement of the "John Birch" number. (The delightfully clever and funny song finally surfaced before the end of the decade on one of the first bootleg albums ever made.)

In 1964, Dylan's next album title said it all: *The Times They Are A-Changin'*. It was the year he became the folk prophet for a generation, even as the Beatles appeared on *The Ed Sullivan Show* and sparked their own musical revolution. The Beatles had six number-one hits that year.

LBJ signed the Civil Rights Act into law and was elected president. And at the University of California at Berkeley, after students were denied permission to set up tables on campus dispensing information in support of civil rights activities, they banded together into what they called the Free Speech Movement, ultimately taking over the administration building and staging a nonviolent protest they called a "sit-in." (One of their organizers also coined the phrase later adopted by, and associated with, Yippie leader Jerry Rubin: "Don't trust anyone over thirty.") The music was getting a little louder, the hair was getting a little longer, and the divide between generations was getting a little deeper. As the counterculture raised its voice, so did defenders of the status quo. It was the same fight the Smothers Brothers ultimately would undertake later at CBS—and, amazingly, with some of the same people.

To protest the actions of the Berkeley protesters, the general manager of a CBS-owned Los Angeles TV station KNXT used his own airwaves, in December 1964, to deliver an on-air editorial. This was a brand-new phenomenon in local TV, but several station executives in California took to it quickly and eagerly.

"The pandemonium and chaos created by a group of witless agitators at the University of California campus in Berkeley," this particular editorial began, "is making a mockery of one of the world's greatest educational institutions. KNXT believes it should be dealt with quickly and severely to set an example for all time for those who agitate for the sake of agitation." Those harsh, unyielding words were written and delivered by Robert D. Wood, who, in addition to being the station's general manager, also was vice president of CBS Television Stations. Four years later, as CBS Network president, he would fire Tom and Dick Smothers.

So where were Tom and Dick Smothers? For the most part, focused on their careers and families, not politics. In January 1963, Tom had married Stephanie Shorr, whom he called Stephi. Their son, Thomas Bolyn Smothers IV, was born in May 1965. By that time, Dick and Linda already had two children, Susan and Dick Jr. Whenever possible, when Tom and Dick were on the road, the families accompanied them on tour. Success brought a lot of touring— not only big venues in New York and Las Vegas, but scores of college towns, tapping a market opened by, yes, the Kingston Trio. Tom and Dick both had dropped out shy of completing college and weren't supporting any political causes yet, but they enjoyed a large and enthusiastic student following. That kept them busy, as did their exhaustive recording schedule.

In the two-year stretch of 1963 to 1964, they released four albums: *The Smothers Brothers Think Ethnic!* (February 1963), *Curb Your Tongue, Knave!* (November 1963), *It Must Have Been Something I Said!* (April 1964), and *Tour de Farce: American History and Other Unrelated Subjects* (November 1964). The albums contain scant evidence of political commitment or awareness, but each is a portrait, trapped in amber (vinyl, actually), of the brothers' impressive and swift development.

On *The Smothers Brothers Think Ethnic!*, their third album, Dick does more of the intros and has much more of a presence. This LP includes their first recorded version of "The Fox," the song they did on their star-making Jack Paar appearance, and also includes such other now-iconic routines as "Venezuelan Rain Dance" (a misleading buildup to a performance of "Hava Nagila"); "The Saga of John Henry" ("When John Henry was a little baby, sitting on his daddy's knee," Tom sings, "his daddy picked him up, threw him on the floor, and said, 'This baby's done wet on me!'"); and their version of the Oscar Brand song "My Old Man," in which the brothers sing about emulating their father's professions.

"My old man's a sailor," they sing. "What do you think about that?" They describe his uniform and habits, and at verse's end add, "And someday, if I can, I'm gonna be a sailor the same as my old man." For the second verse, Dick sings solo, substituting "anthropologist" for "sailor," and running through the same litany: "He wears an anthropologist's collar, he wears an anthropologist's hat . . ." For the final verse, Dick takes on a tongue twister—a daringly high-risk one: "My old man's a cotton-pickin', finger-lickin' chicken plucker," Dick sings. "What do you think about that?" Tom snickers and replies, "You better not make a mistake." From this album on, Tom and Dick were fully formed as the Smothers Brothers. They had their rhythm and their roles, and each successive album added at least one new great routine to their comic arsenal.

On *Curb Your Tongue, Knave!*, the new triumph was "I Talk to the Trees," the second song they chose to lampoon from *Paint Your Wagon. It Must Have Been Something I Said* includes the first song on a Smothers album that has a message other than just comedy. "Crabs Walk Sideways," released a few months before the Civil Rights Act was passed, was the story of an interracial romance. "Herman was a lobster," Tom explains in his intro, "and Sally was a crab." The lyrics tell of a tale of parental intolerance and prejudice: "Crabs walk sideways and lobsters walk straight / and we won't let you take her for your mate."

Tour de Farce: American History and Other Unrelated Subjects arrived near the end of 1964. "Siblings," its spoken-word opener, commits to vinyl for the first time the sibling-rivalry battle that would become their trademark. ("Dickie Smothers had a dog," Tom complains to the audience, "and I used to sit around in the backyard and draw in the dirt." Then, turning to Dick, Tom says, "Mom got you a dog, and I didn't get a dog. I had a chicken.") "Siblings" also contains Tom's first album utterance of one trademark phrase—the screamed, childish retort "Oh, yeah??" Another track, "American History II-A," contains another: "Mom always liked you best," Tom complains to Dick. The audience laughter let them know they were onto something special.

Tour de Farce also is notable because Mason Williams accompanies them, uncredited, on backing guitar, and provides two short songs, "Life and the Song of Life" and "Time and the Song of Time," that were more cerebral, subtle, and odd than most of the duo's output. The first (which would resurface as "Life Song" on 1968's *The Mason Williams Phonograph Record,* sung by the composer) is a twenty-second song consisting of Tom and Dick singing three quick questions: "Isn't life beautiful? Isn't life gay? Isn't life the perfect thing to pass the time away?" It was a new flavor for the Smothers Brothers, and Tom welcomed it—and Mason—immediately. When Tom and Dick began planning *The Smothers Brothers Comedy Hour,* Mason Williams became the chief coconspirator.

Each LP stretched and defined the brothers a little more, but the albums continued to capture the start of the process, not the more polished end result. On deadline to produce an album, they'd record some shows, edit their ad libs together into a routine, release the album, then spend months honing that routine onstage—until the next album deadline approached, and the process repeated itself.

"All the best of our comedy material was never recorded!" Dick complains. "It was lost! Everybody says, 'That's a great album!'—and I say, 'Oh, God, if you'd only known how good we had the routine down before they made us do another one.' "

The albums, though, had fans, lots of them—and it's surprising, more than four decades after their release, how many of those songs can be sung verbatim by those fans. Ken Burns, the documentary filmmaker behind such brilliant PBS programs as *The Civil War, Jazz, Baseball*, and *The War*, got wide-eyed as a child when he talked to me about "My Old Man," his favorite Smothers Brothers song from that period. "They were ratifying my father's existence, and therefore, by extension, mine," Burns says of the Smothers Brothers, recalling his dad's profession, "by singing, 'My old man's an anthropologist—what do you think about that?' " And Burns, the usually so-serious historian, bursts into song himself, running correctly through all the lyrics about "an anthropologist's raincoat" and "an anthropologist's hat" and such—and beaming widely when he gets to the capper, singing, "And someday, if I can, I'm gonna be an anthropologist, the same as my old man."

When I interviewed him for this book, Bill Maher also raved about the Smothers Brothers and, unprompted, sang a song that was a particular favorite. "I had their albums," he said. "Before their TV show, I was a fan. I have three of their albums still. And whenever I get together with Tommy, I always crack him up by singing 'Mediocre Fred.' " It's the song, from *Tour de Farce*, about a guy who seems totally boring, until the unexpected final verse—which Maher sang with impressive accuracy and unchecked enthusiasm: "When the full moon rose, he'd climb over the moat / And find some people sleeping / And he'd bite their throats / Mediocre, dull Fred." Maher laughed loudly. "I mean, come *on*!" he said appreciatively.

Churning out two albums a year, the Smothers Brothers began to amass money for the first time and cultivate private interests. "Dick was flying airplanes," David Carroll, their record producer and father figure, recalled. With both Dick and Tom married, Carroll believed that the brothers never applied themselves to develop any new material unless absolutely forced to by record contract commitments. "They've been lazy ever since they started, and they still are today," Carroll said in 1998, sounding more resigned than disapproving. "As they gained fame, if you want to call it that, they were still busy doing other things."

At this point in their career the Smothers Brothers considered television an ancillary activity—like the record albums—a way to promote their key activity, live touring. Coffeehouses had warmed to the Smothers Brothers, and so had some Vegas lounges and hotels, but Tom and Dick also were accepting bookings at local college and high school auditoriums—anything that promised a young crowd and a shot at a larger gate than the usual 125-seat club.

On Halloween 1964—the night Tom Smothers says he became politically aware—they were playing a high school auditorium in Elkhart, Indiana. Dick's mother-in-law had died of cancer, so Tom and Dick had printed special souvenir programs that were sold at all their concerts by local volunteers, with the proceeds donated to the American Cancer Society. Promoters routinely waived any percentage from these sales and that agreement was in place that night, according to Ken Fritz. But this show was sparsely attended, and the promoter confronted Fritz and the brothers afterward, demanding a percentage from the program sales. The demand was refused, Tom threatened to take the guy to court if he persisted, and everyone began to pack up.

"And the next thing I know," Fritz says, "the Indiana police show up with those big Smokey the Bear hats, and the promoter points at me and says, 'That's the guy who owes me the money.' "

One cop told Fritz he'd have to come to the station for questioning. As Fritz was led out by the police, Tom followed and told them, "Any place Ken Fritz is going, I'm going, too." The police started to put Fritz in a squad car, and Tom attempted to follow. "Don't try it," one cop warned him. "I'm going to get in the car with him," Tom insisted. "Don't try it," the cop repeated, more forcefully. But Tom did.

"The cops grab Tommy," Fritz recalls, "and hit him on the back of the head with a big flashlight. And there's blood everywhere. And now this fight starts between the troopers and Tom and me, and Dickie's yelling, 'Don't hit my brother!' . . . And in the middle of the fight, we were holding our own, I thought, quite well. And then the next thing I know, I woke up, and my face was up against the hubcap of the police car." Fritz had been knocked out by a blackjack-type weapon ("We're lucky we weren't killed"). After he came to, he and the Smothers brothers were arrested and carted away.

"We end up being handcuffed," Fritz says. "Tommy goes to the hospital, comes back with stitches in his head, and the two of us got pretty well roughed up." At the station house, Tom, Dick, and Fritz are charged with resisting arrest, interfering with an arrest, and disorderly conduct. "We got the crap knocked out of us in that place!" Fritz says.

Tom calls that his "first personal experience of social injustice" and the thing that opened his eyes to the idea that when protesters and demonstrators complained about police brutality, perhaps they weren't exaggerating. Prior to that night, Tom admits, he "didn't buy it" but "all of a sudden, I had nine stitches in my head from the back of those eight-battery flashlights. . . . And that's when I began to say 'Wow . . . this is the reality that happened to *me*. And I'm a *Smothers brother*!"

Immediately after their arrest, the Smothers Brothers were back to business. Their *Tour de Farce* LP was released the next day, and the same month brought a guest appearance on *Burke's Law*, the ABC series produced by Aaron Spelling, in which Tom and Dick played tycoons in the episode called "Who Killed the Richest Man in the World?" The same Four Star Television company was looking to showcase the Smothers Brothers in a sitcom of their own, and their appearance here, without their instruments or music, was an on-air test run. It went well enough for Spelling to give the go-ahead for what eventually would become *The Smothers Brothers Show*.

Spelling soon would become a major TV mogul—thanks to *The Mod Squad*, *Charlie's Angels*, *The Love Boat*, and *Fantasy Island*. On the surface, the Smothers Brothers, their management team, and Spelling all were aiming to ride the next big pop-culture wave, which appeared to be the fantasy situation comedy. In 1963, *My Favorite Martian* had become an instant hit; in it Ray Walston playing an alien with amazing powers who lived with, and complicated the life of, the only person who knew of his real powers and identity. In 1964, *Bewitched* had become an instant hit; Elizabeth Montgomery played a witch with amazing powers who lived with, and complicated the life of, her mortal husband, the only person who knew of her real powers and identity. So in 1965, Spelling and Richard Newton, cocreators of *The Smothers Brothers Show*, cast Tom as an apprentice angel, returning after being lost at sea to live with, and complicate the life of, his brother Dick, a formerly freewheeling bachelor who is the only one who knows of his late brother's real powers and identity.

The Smothers Brothers Show seemed designed almost perversely to identify the strengths of Tom and Dick, and then willfully ignore them. The plots, which had angel Tom fulfilling weekly missions from an unseen and unheard angel supervisor named Ralph, kept Tom and Dick apart most of the show—even though they were best when playing together. The show took away their instruments, their singing, and their freedom to ad lib, which is where their humor grew most naturally. It took away their audience, filming the series out of sequence, like a movie. What's worse, the scripts assigned most of the scenes and dialogue to Tom, even though Dick was a much quicker study. Tom, in fact, had problems memorizing lines and even reading cue cards. Every bad decision that could be made was made. Tom and Dick felt, when episodes were being filmed, that the show wasn't working and didn't feel right—but it was the brothers' first TV series, and no one would listen to them.

"The attitude at those times," explains Ken Kragen, one of their managers at the time, "was that the performer didn't have any clout or leverage. You came in, you acted, you read the script that was written, and you went home. They were allowed no input into the show whatsoever."

Even at the start of Spelling's career as a producer, he was attracted to high-concept ideas and willing to go with the latest trends. After two seasons, in 1965 he changed ABC's *Burke's Law*, a light-hearted police drama, into *Amos Burke—Secret Agent*, to capitalize on the new James Bond craze. Spelling also launched a *Burke's Law* spinoff, *Honey West*, built around Anne Francis as a sexy private eye with loads of electronic gadgets and her own pet ocelot. All of a sudden, he had three shows vying for his attention—and *The Smothers Brothers Show*, his first sitcom, was the most far afield.

Tom and Steffi's child, Thomas Bolyn Smothers IV, was born in May 1965, just as the sitcom was gearing up for production. Staying in one town and doing a TV series was supposed to be a respite from the grueling schedule of one-night concert appearances, but didn't work out that way. By July, when production shut down temporarily so Tom and Dick could honor a previously scheduled month-long gig at the Flamingo Hotel in Las Vegas, things had gotten untenable. Compared to the demands of filming *The Smothers Brothers Show*, the grueling Vegas performance schedule was a vacation for Tom.

"The show was extremely hard on Tom," Dick says, "because he had all the words—*all* the words—and they didn't know it was hard for Tommy to learn all the words. So it was extremely hard on him, compared to me."

"Dick was being snubbed," Tom says, referring to the sitcom writing staff. "They weren't writing for him. They were writing for me. I was stuck with thousands of words . . . it was sixteen-hour days, every day." Something had to give—and what gave was producer Phil Sharp. After five episodes he was replaced, at Tom's urging, by producer-director Fred De Cordova. It was his work with TV's comedy pioneers—such as Jack Benny, George Burns, even George Gobel—that carried the most weight with Tom and gave him the most hope.

De Cordova's approach was to multiply, divide, and conquer. He hired dozens of writers to come up with concepts and scripts. The sitcom's instrumental theme song was replaced by one sung by the Smothers brothers, explaining the premise: "My brother Tom was lost at sea without his water wings," Dick sings, "and now he is an angel, and he tries to do amazing things." Tom and Dick opened and closed each show by addressing the audience directly, an old Benny and Burns breaking-the-fourth-wall trick, taking the opportunity to loosen up, reflecting their less regimented nightclub act.

Tom and Dick were able to hire a few friends as extras: Pat Paulsen got a few bucks by running out of a building in one scene, and Tom and Dick's sister Sherry also clocked some work.

After *The Smothers Brothers Show* had died an ignominious death after one season, Dick told a reporter, "Tom got nothing out of the series but an ulcer."

The Smothers Brothers Show was not without its fans: One of them was Bill Maher, who "loved" what he called "the angel show," and credits Tom with giving him the comedy bug: "I couldn't have been older than seven years old," Maher recalls, "and I imitated Tommy in his stuttering manner from the 'angel show' at our Christmas party. I think it's the first time I remember getting laughs—literally."

For Tom and Dick, *The Smothers Brothers Show* was a frustrating, forgettable experience. They had no reason to suspect it at the time— but when the final episode of *The Smothers Brothers Show* was rerun in September 1966, that opportunity was just around the corner.

5

"High Noon on the Ponderosa"

It wasn't innovation or inspiration that led CBS to unveil *The Smothers Brothers Comedy Hour* in the winter of 1967. It was desperation.

It was *Bonanza*.

At that point in the mid–1960s, *Bonanza* dominated television, and its time slot, the same way *All in the Family* did in the 1970s, *The Cosby Show* did in the 1980s, and *Seinfeld* and *ER* did in the 1990s. Audience levels for *Bonanza* were as vast as the Ponderosa, with the series claiming half of all viewers watching TV at that hour each Sunday, then the pivotal, most-viewed night of the week.

As David Steinberg, whose controversial sermonettes would play an unintended part in the premature demise of *The Smothers Brothers Comedy Hour*, explained, "*Bonanza* was the number-one hit on NBC. It was the biggest show in the country . . . It's hard to imagine what it was like when there were only three networks. *Bonanza* was the Goliath."

Bonanza had broken out of a very crowded field. The series, starring Lorne Greene as rancher patriarch Pa Cartwright and Pernell Roberts, Dan Blocker, and Michael Landon as grown sons Adam, Hoss, and Little Joe, premiered in 1959, the year the three networks had combined to schedule an astounding total of thirty prime-time

Westerns. *Bonanza* had one secret weapon at the start: it was the first network Western to be broadcast in color, and NBC's parent corporation, RCA, which manufactured TV sets, initially scheduled *Bonanza* on Saturday nights to give appliance dealers something colorful and exciting to showcase on all their window and store display TV sets, when couples were out walking, shopping, and perhaps in the market for their first color television.

When *Bonanza* premiered, the three most popular shows on television were Westerns. *Gunsmoke*, which had begun the "adult Western" trend with its CBS debut four years earlier, was at the top, followed by NBC's *Wagon Train* and another CBS Western, *Have Gun—Will Travel*. Despite a glut of other Westerns, and the disadvantage of being shown on TV's least-viewed night, *Bonanza* climbed into the Top 20, at which point NBC relocated it to 9:00 p.m. ET Sundays—and the tumbleweed juggernaut began rolling over everything in its path.

In its first season on Sunday, *Bonanza* rose to the number-two slot, nestled comfortably between *Wagon Train* and *Gunsmoke*. Its first victim was *The Real McCoys,* a former Top 10 comedy for ABC that CBS had acquired and thrown into the fray opposite the Cartwrights. *The Real McCoys* plummeted instantly and was canceled. In rapid succession, so did a doomed parade of other CBS offerings, new and old. *The Judy Garland Show,* despite such guests as Barbra Streisand, Tony Bennett, Mel Torme, Ethel Merman, and Peggy Lee, lasted six months. *The Twilight Zone*, Rod Serling's venerable fantasy anthology that had premiered the same season as *Bonanza* in 1959, was moved against it, and died four months later. *Perry Mason,* the father of all courtroom dramas, had enjoyed a popular eight-year run until CBS pitted it against *Bonanza*. A year later, *Perry Mason* was dismissed, with no hope for appeal. CBS finally thought it had come up with the solution in *The Garry Moore Show*, a variety series that had ranked as high as number 12 (for the 1961–62 season) before the host called it quits and took a self-imposed hiatus from network television. From 1958 to 1964, Moore's show, which introduced Carol Burnett as a supporting player, had been a reliable, lucrative success until Moore, weary of the grind, pulled the plug on his own show. When Moore was persuaded to revive his beloved series in the fall of 1966, scheduled opposite *Bonanza,* how could it fail?

Hugely, that's how. Despite all those years of residual goodwill, Moore was no match for the Ponderosa clan. Before long, even with the Top 10 *The Ed Sullivan Show* as its CBS lead-in, *The Garry Moore Show* was the lowest-rated show on television, while NBC's *Bonanza* was well on its way to being crowned TV's most popular series for the third year in a row. CBS didn't want any more *Moore,* but didn't have any one-hour dramas in the pipeline ready to go as a midseason replacement.

Fred Silverman, the TV programming innovator who eventually would run the entertainment divisions of ABC and NBC, was at CBS in the mid-'60s, the newly installed twentysomething vice president of Daytime Programming. The head of programming for CBS at that time, Mike Dann, encouraged Silverman to sit in on all the programming meetings, even for prime time, so Silverman can recall the failures and the frustrations of those times quite clearly.

"I was privy to the succession of turkeys that they scheduled in the nine o'clock Sunday time period," Silverman said. "They did everything in the world to try to compete with *Bonanza* . . . They had Judy Garland in there, and *The Real McCoys,* and dopey situation comedies like *My Living Doll,* with Julie Newmar." (She played a shapely female robot, owned by Robert Cummings. The show lasted one season, and Cummings didn't even bother to stick around for the last few episodes.)

"They had a show called *Made in America,*" Silverman continued, "where they had people come on and tell their success stories— how they made a million dollars or more." That one lasted a month.

"You know, they did just the worst array of shows that you could ever imagine."

Mike Dann, head of programming for CBS then, didn't dispute that characterization. "*Bonanza* was killing me on a big night," Dann recalled, adding, "I just called up the [William] Morris office and said, 'I need a show—a variety show—because I'm just in terrible trouble on Sunday night.' And they said, 'How about the Smothers Brothers?' I just said to them, 'Can you get them ready?' "

His thinking, he explained, was that a variety show could be created from scratch in a few months, while any other genre would take too much valuable time to get up to speed. "Months later," Dann said of the new Smothers series, "they were doing just great, and everybody was saying it took a lot of courage for me to do it. It didn't take any courage! They were the only show I could get ready!"

Actually, it was a bit more complicated than that.

Once *The Smothers Brothers Show* was canceled, the brothers were happy to resume their nightclub touring schedule and accept TV guest spots on other shows. The sitcom's final telecast was in September 1966—the same month *The Garry Moore Show* returned to CBS and began its rapid downward spiral against *Bonanza*.

Most of 1966 was a tumultuous year, and not a terribly successful one, for the Smothers Brothers. Their sitcom presented its last original episode in April, yet—as was common practice at the time—stayed on the air in reruns until September, when CBS launched its new fall shows. That meant an additional five months when the duo's least impressive work was shown weekly on nationwide TV.

Meanwhile, the team's only record album that year, released in February, was a studio LP called *The Smothers Brothers Play It Straight*. It was a labor of love, not a contractual throwaway, and was recorded over a period of months—evenings and weekends—while *The Smothers Brothers Show* was in production. The performances and arrangements were tasteful, and the song selections innovative. The Beatles' "Yesterday" was covered only five months after its release, making the Smothers Brothers among the first to recognize it as an instant standard. Also on the album was Dick singing solo on "The First Time (Ever I Saw Your Face)," six full years before it became a number-one hit for Roberta Flack. But except for a pair of novelty numbers, *Play It Straight* had the brothers doing just that. They weren't trying to be funny on their album, and weren't very successful at being funny on their sitcom.

As their sitcom duties wound down, the Smothers Brothers returned to the road and made a few TV guest appearances in 1966 that would prove very serendipitous very shortly. They appeared on a few episodes of NBC's *The Andy Williams Show,* on a CBS summer replacement variety series called *The John Gary Show,* and reunited with Jack Benny on his first special for NBC, *The Jack Benny Hour.* The personal lives and relationships of the Smothers Brothers, though, hadn't weathered their own sitcom experience very well. The bonds between Tom and Dick, after their first professional failure, were more frayed and fragile than usual, and things at home weren't necessarily better. By September, Tom and Stephi officially separated.

Professionally, neither CBS nor the William Morris Agency, which represented the Smothers Brothers, had given up on them. Variety was almost as popular a TV genre then as the Western: CBS had major hits in *The Red Skelton Show, The Jackie Gleason Show,* and *The Ed Sullivan Show,* while NBC scored big with *The Dean Martin Show* and the Bob Hope specials, and ABC succeeded with the boldly bland *The Lawrence Welk Show.* But while those shows and stars were popular, they weren't getting any younger, and one powerful Hollywood player took notice.

Abe Lastfogel, who headed the William Morris talent agency

from the 1930s until the end of the 1960s, went to CBS chairman William S. Paley and handed him a list of the stars headlining his various variety shows. Attached to Lastfogel's list, according to Ken Kragen, who has represented the Smothers Brothers at various points in their career, were the ages of those stars. Sullivan was in his sixties. Skelton and Gleason were in their fifties. Even among the competition, maturity ruled: Hope and Welk were past sixty, and Martin, the baby of the bunch, was closing in on fifty. The Morris agency also took out a trade ad reinforcing the message that the Smothers Brothers was a "young" act.

Kragen recalled that Lastfogel insisted to Paley, " 'You need something young. You need to have some young people here. You should put the Smothers on with a show.' And he kept pumping for that."

To Kragen's surprise, Paley—who had just turned sixty-five himself, yet remained in power in defiance of his own company's retirement policy—agreed, and the brothers were offered a variety show. It was scheduled to begin in the fall of 1967, but when Moore's series tanked so quickly, Dann accelerated the order and asked if the brothers would like to start their show six months early—in the Sunday time slot opposite *Bonanza*.

"We were all skittish about it," Kragen recalled. Tom Smothers, though, saw the death slot as a golden opportunity, Kragen recalled. "Tommy said: 'Hey, if we succeed, it will be big. It will be a big deal. And if we fail, no one will blame us. So let's go. I want to go now.' "

Part of Tom's eagerness was that he saw the opportunity to demand—and get—something he wanted desperately after feeling so powerless on their *Smothers Brothers Show* sitcom: creative control. And because CBS was so desperate, the prospects for any new series lasting more than a few months opposite *Bonanza* were slim. The Smothers Brothers had such a clean-cut, nonthreatening image, the network thought it was risking little and truly had nothing to lose.

"I said, 'We won't do it unless we have control of the thing,' " Tom recalled. "And I was not thinking politics, I was not thinking social commentary. I was thinking creative control in the most classic sense of the word. I wanted to work with writers I could work with."

To this day, there's no consensus about the specifics of the agreement. Dann said he granted the brothers creative leeway but not absolute freedom, while other CBS executives balked at the thought of anyone putting such a promise in writing. Perry Lafferty, the West Coast entertainment executive for CBS, insisted, "They didn't have creative control. Nobody in the history of television, to my knowledge, in the entertainment genre had creative control on a series, except Danny Kaye. I have never heard of another person that had creative control . . . The censors still prevailed."

Fred Silverman concurred. "I don't think it was in a contract . . . I seriously doubt that CBS would make a contract like that. I'm sure that one of the senior executives probably said to them, 'Well, don't worry about it. I mean, you'll have your way.' But I can't imagine that they would put that in writing."

"I just know," insisted Tom Smothers, "that William Morris said, 'CBS goes with all your conditions' . . . I remember talking with Perry Lafferty and Michael Dann. I said, 'I've got creative control.' There was never a fully executed contract for the whole show," Tom explained. "There was an intent paper signed, and somehow the show got started and we're working . . ."

Indisputably, Tom had the right to hire and fire. He set out to assemble a team of producers, writers, and performers who would help, rather than hinder, the creation of the sort of show he had in mind. It was a show that would draw on the entire history of TV variety while at the same time making TV history of its own.

From the very beginning, *The Smothers Brothers Comedy Hour* was designed to have one foot in the past, one foot in the present—and, before too long, at least one eye on stirring up a little trouble. At first, though, Tom and Dick Smothers were intent mostly on entertaining as large an audience as possible—and CBS, at that point in the increasingly tumultuous '60s, was expecting, and rooting for, the same thing. As CBS executive Lafferty said about TV shows, and viewers, in those polarizing, volatile times: "We weren't looking for shows that rocked the boat. The boat was already being rocked. We were trying to quiet them down."

6

Revolution in a Shoe Box

The tumult of 1966 was almost unavoidable, no matter where you turned.

Musically, the year began with Simon and Garfunkel's first number-one hit, "The Sounds of Silence." Other chart-toppers that year reflected the cultural awakenings and clashes percolating to the surface. The Beatles topped the charts with "We Can Work It Out" and "Paperback Writer," but also stopped touring and got embroiled in the furor over John Lennon's offhand remark to a journalist that the Beatles were "more popular than Jesus." Soul music was well represented by the number-one hits of 1966 [the Supremes' "You Can't Hurry Love" and "You Keep Me Hangin' On," the Four Tops' "Reach Out (I'll Be There)," Percy Sledge's "When a Man Loves a Woman"], but so were plenty of other genres, from the soft folk-rock of the Mamas and the Papas ("Monday, Monday") and the Association ("Cherish") to harder-edged groups both imported (the Rolling Stones with "Paint It Black") and domestic (the Young Rascals with "Good Lovin' "). Yet it also was a year when the novelty song "Winchester Cathedral," with Rudy Vallee–type crooning by the New Vaudeville Band, could top the charts as well, along with Staff Sergeant Barry Sadler's unapologetically, defiantly hawkish ode to the military, "The Ballad of the Green Berets." Young fans could vault the Monkees, a created-for-TV band launched that September in its own NBC sitcom, to number one with "Last Train to Clarksville" and "I'm a Believer" before the year was out, yet the Beach Boys, clobbered by the British Invasion and the attempt to emulate it, could bounce back with the revolutionary "Good Vibrations." It was a year when Frank Sinatra could top the charts with "Strangers in the Night," only a few months after his daughter, Nancy Sinatra, had done the same thing with "These Boots Are Made for Walkin'." And while Bob Dylan didn't have a number-one hit that year, his LP *Blonde on Blonde* had a stunning lasting impact. That same year, Dylan vanished from public view after a near-fatal motorcycle accident, taboo-busting comedian Lenny Bruce died from an overdose, *Star Trek* premiered on TV, California declared LSD illegal, and the US Supreme Court established arrested suspects' rights with its *Miranda v. Arizona* decision ("You have the right to remain silent . . .").

Near the end of that year, on November 17, 1966, CBS presented the Smothers Brothers with an initial deal memo for what would become *The Smothers Brothers Comedy Hour*. A month later, their representatives got a formal contract—never finalized, but duly honored—agreeing to a series launch in February 1967, a renewal option by April 1, and the promise of a second-season summer replacement series production deal should the new show survive that long. Basically, Tom and Dick were given two months to create a one-hour prime-time network TV show from scratch. They drew from experiences and acquaintances old and new, by settling on what they wanted to do, and, by elimination, what they were determined *not* to do. With creative control, or at least the belief they *had* creative control, they set out with a vengeance. And their secret weapons, during this intense and innovative planning stage, included Mason Williams and a shoe box.

Mason Williams had been in and out of the brothers' lives for several years, having first met and befriended them during their first performances as a duo in Colorado in 1960. Mason, who had grown up in Oklahoma City, was a promising young folksinger and musician with markedly eclectic tastes and a very broad knowledge of different musical genres. ("I worked in a record store in Oklahoma City," he says, "and decided that I would listen to every record in the store. It was a major education, one album at a time. I got a taste of everything that's out there.") His own career in music, however, was detoured by an early marriage and two years of active duty with the navy. Mason was stationed on Coronado Island, southwest of San Diego, from 1961 to 1963, playing on evenings and weekends at clubs, bars, and PTA meetings. By the time his enlistment was over, so was his marriage, and Mason returned to Oklahoma City to find work but eventually found better work back in California, with a Los Angeles music publisher who offered him $200 a month to come out and write songs. He arrived in January 1964, using LA as a home base while taking any job within driving distance—which for Mason, who loved to drive, meant as far east as Hunstville, Alabama. In California, he lived with Ed Ruscha, a childhood friend who, like Mason, had moved west from Oklahoma City. Ruscha was an artist whose way of thinking, about art and life, definitely influenced Mason a great deal.

One of Mason's hometown venues that year was the West Hollywood club the Troubadour, which later would serve as a career launching pad for Elton John, James Taylor, and others. It helped launch Mason's career, too, because of a recommendation by a Smothers. Not Tom or Dick, but sister Sherry, who was working there. When her brothers asked her if she'd seen anyone impressive performing there, she mentioned Mason Williams.

"Tom called me up," Mason recalls, "and I went up to his house on Doheny Drive, brought my demos, and we spent an afternoon together." Within a week, Mason was backing the brothers onstage and playing on their *Tour de Farce* album. Mason went on the road with Tom and Dick, joining their loose national tour with opening act Esther and Abi Ofarim, backing up that Israeli duo on guitar, but providing discreet backup as accompanist for Tom and Dick as well. "I sat behind them onstage every night," Mason says. "One of the things they liked about me was that I didn't get in the way—I knew how to be there musically, but not to overplay." And as Mason learned their music, he also studied their comedy. "Every night, they'd be working on pieces in the dressing room," he says, "and I'd be sitting there and hear them discuss what was wrong with it, and how to fix it, 'Don't jump on my line,' 'Speak slower.' They were very knowledgeable about a lot of that stuff."

By the time the *Mom Always Liked You Best!* album was released in 1965 (recorded, in part, at the Troubadour), five of the songs performed by Tom and Dick were compositions by Mason Williams: "The Three Song," "We Love Us," "Long Time Blues," "The Tattoo Song," and "The Last Great Waltz." He helped producer David Carroll edit the comedy albums, coproduced (with Carroll and Ken Fritz) and was musical director for *The Smothers Brothers Play It Straight,* which included three of Mason's songs: "Wanderlove," "The Write of Songs," and "They Are Gone." Then, when the sitcom was canceled and Tom and Stephi separated, Tom suggested that he and Mason share a place on Kings Road. Mason got a job writing for NBC's *The Roger Miller Show* variety series, and one day in November, Tom came home and told his new roommate, "Hey, CBS just gave us an offer to be on TV at nine o'clock on Sunday night, opposite *Bonanza.*"

Tom and Dick approached the new show with a passion that was missing from their sitcom effort—and with harsh lessons learned from that show, lessons which would inform their next one.

"Tommy had been so upset over the way the 'angel' show went," Mason recalls. "He said, 'I'll never do a show again where the audience isn't part of the mix, because I want real reactions from people.' " Tom also was adamant, from the start, that the show they present to the studio audience shouldn't be much longer, in terms of time, than the one shown on the air. If the wait between sketches or segments became prolonged, Tom thought, the studio audience would get restless, "and you're ruining the mechanism we go by, which is the audience's reaction."

What Tom had in mind, from the very beginning, was a show that would be paced almost like his beloved live variety shows from TV's Golden Age—the early Jack Benny specials, the George Burns "vaudeo" sitcom. Both of those shows were broadcast from the same CBS stage on which Tom and Dick would tape *The Smothers Brothers Comedy Hour*, one of many TV traditions of which the brothers not only were aware but were actively embracing.

Dick says, "We wanted traditional stuff. We wanted dancers for production numbers. We wanted a real good singing group . . . And we wanted musical acts and we wanted skits. And," he adds with a smile, "the Smothers Brothers." There was a genuine appreciation of the performers and programs that had preceded them, and a burning desire, especially from Tom, to find, introduce, and support the next generation of talent. With that in mind, the mandate was clear, and so was the blueprint: *The Smothers Brothers Comedy Hour* would plant one foot in the past and one in the future, straddling time and the growing generation gap by bringing old and new entertainment and entertainers into the same prime-time tent.

From *The John Gary Show*, where Tom and Dick had liked the material they'd been given as guest stars, they hired writer-producers Saul Ilson and Ernest Chambers to produce *The Smothers Brothers Comedy Hour*. They previously had written for Danny Kaye, whose CBS Television City offices Tom and Dick were about to inherit. Kaye's producer had been Perry Lafferty, now the West Coast CBS programming executive for CBS, so Ilson and Chambers had the network's confidence from the start ("They knew the rules," Lafferty said, "and how things are supposed to go"). They also had enough experience to mount a variety show quickly, especially from those same CBS studios—and if Tom and Dick had handpicked Ilson and Chambers, the clashes with producers that troubled the Smotherses' sitcom were less likely to recur. Stan Harris, director of *The John Gary Show*, was also brought aboard, and, in time, so was Gary's in-house vocal group, the Jimmy Joyce Singers.

Before the end of November, less than two weeks after getting the initial CBS offer, news of the show broke in the press. New York *Daily News* TV columnist Kay Gardella pegged the launch date of a new Smothers Brothers series as February 8, and noted in her lead paragraph that the creators of the upcoming variety hour "want to erase the impression once and for all that the boys are returning in their same old situation comedy." Writers Saul Ilson and Ernest Chambers were quoted as calling it "a very different game" and "hip and contemporary," and said they were "scouting for a strong stable of writers."

They got them, quickly. No sooner had the Smothers Brothers guest-starred on *The Jack Benny Hour* special on NBC than they had Saul Ilson and Ernest Chambers hire two of Benny's veteran writers, Hal Goldman and Al Gordon, to join their staff. Then came Mike Marmer, whose writing credits included shows by two true TV comedy pioneers, Steve Allen and Ernie Kovacs. Stan Burns, another Steve Allen writer whose credits also included two rather distinctive sitcom genre spoofs, *F Troop* and *Get Smart,* signed on, as well as Allan Blye, a young Canadian writer whom Tom drafted personally after seeing a show he'd written in Canada. When NBC canceled *The Roger Miller Show* in January 1967, a month before *Comedy Hour* was to premiere, Tom took advantage of Mason's sudden availability and brought him aboard as the last official member of the inaugural writing staff. Because they were by far the youngest, Blye and Mason ended up working together.

"There was Hal Goldman and Al Gordon, who were older fellows," Blye explains, "and Mike Marmer and Stan Burns, who were middle-aged guys, and Mason Williams and myself, who were like the young puppies. We were in our twenties."

"Saul and Ernie . . . didn't want to hire me," Mason says, "but Tommy said, 'No, I insist.' So I came to the show and didn't have an office. I sat in the same office with Allan. He had a desk. I didn't. I was just sitting on the other side of the desk."

With three generations of writers generating material, it's no wonder *The Smothers Brothers Comedy Hour* managed to seem reassuringly old-fashioned and playfully fresh at the same time. Parts of the show came straight from Broadway, and from memories of vaudeville—but other portions deconstructed, and gently ridiculed, those very traditions in much the same way the brothers had lampooned folk music. Guests were treated with respect and allowed to showcase their strengths and favorite performance pieces, but they also were encouraged to go out on a limb, participate in comedy sketches, try something new, and even poke fun at their own images a bit. The previous TV series that most directly inspired *The Smothers Brothers Comedy Hour*, and spring from the same family tree, begin with the Jack Benny and George Burns shows on CBS. The lineage includes NBC's brilliant satirical variety showcase *Your Show of Shows* (a prime-time *Saturday Night Live* precursor starring Sid Caesar, Imogene Coca, and Carl Reiner), the technically innovative comedy of Ernie Kovacs, and the butcher-the-sacred-cows approach of NBC's *That Was the Week That Was*, an Americanized version of a British series that used music and comedy to remark on current events. David Frost, Buck Henry, and future *M*A*S*H* star Alan Alda were players on NBC's *TW3*, as was singer Nancy Ames, who got to sing such wittily vitriolic Tom Lehrer compositions as "The Vatican Rag" and "Pollution." "I didn't find that show unfunny, I've got to tell you," Dick says of *TW3*. "And when we talked about our [variety] show, in front, we said we wanted to be socially relevant."

"When they were trying to come up with a [musical] theme for the show," Mason says, "they put the word out that anyone could submit an idea for it." Nancy Ames was appearing at the Sands Hotel in Las Vegas, and Mason was there with her, as both accompanist and, at the time, boyfriend. "She was rehearsing her act. I was playing in the key of C, and then I played an E chord, which was a mistake, and slid it up to an F chord. Gosh, I thought, that's an attractive mistake. Then I said, 'Since the Smothers Brothers' whole career is based on mistakes, maybe we should create a song that's just full of mistakes—or the same mistake, repeated over and over.' " Mason laughs and adds, "Same as their career."

Tom's only guiding hint to Mason was that he wanted the theme to be "a new take on vaudeville," so Mason and Nancy Ames consciously crafted a sort of soft-shoe melody, complete with Smothers-like musical errors. "We wrote that in November of 1966, and made a demo right there in Las Vegas."

Mason sent it to Tom, who presented it to the producers and CBS, who said, "No, no. You've got to use something like 'Thanks for the Memories.' It's got to be something they recognize." Tom, who thought it was a "terrific" song, insisted: "It doesn't matter. They'll recognize it after they hear it a couple of times!" Other people wanted their songs used, so it was, in Tom's words, "a little bit of a fight"—but in the short time allotted before the series launch, no other viable alternatives came forth. Almost by default, the Mason Williams–Nancy Ames composition, orchestrated by the show's newly hired musical director Nelson Riddle (famous for recording with Frank Sinatra and others), became the series', and the brothers', theme song. "It became their signature theme," Mason says, "even to this day."

At the same time, and especially after being released from his writing duties at *The Roger Miller Show*, Mason was generating other ideas for Tom and Dick's new TV show. Some thoughts and suggestions were new, while others were recycled from personal notations made years before.

"Mason had a phenomenal creative period when he was in the service," Ken Kragen says. "He was in the military, and very bored, and he sat around, played his guitar, and wrote in his journals. He had enormous journals: they were like these big, old-fashioned accounting journals, real big. The kind that look like Scrooge sitting at his desk . . .

"And he carried them around with him, these huge journals, and he wrote every idea that came into his head—spontaneous, fragments, anything. And in that period of a couple of years, most of the great things that Mason did, material and stuff that was later used, came out of those bits and pieces and fragments of thoughts."

In December 1966, Mason's journal included not only the latest hires for *The Smothers Brothers Comedy Hour* ("Nelson Riddle picked for Musical Director of the show," he wrote, "also the Anita Kerr Singers"), but an astoundingly ambitious and wide-ranging wish list under the heading of "Guest ideas." The initial roster of proposed guest stars included Spencer Tracy and Katharine Hepburn (together), Butterfly McQueen (Prissy, the excitable maid from *Gone with the Wind*), Shirley Temple Black (before she reemerged as a political figure), and Bette Davis. On the same page, under "More guest ideas," Mason listed such names as composer-conductor Leonard Bernstein, Beatles producer George Martin, not-yet-reclusive actor Marlon Brando, and—as an early hint that *The Comedy Hour* was interested from the start in reflecting a political perspective—Mario Savio.

Savio was one of the key members of the Berkeley Free Speech Movement, the December 1964 student protests against which future CBS executive Robert W. Wood had editorialized passionately while general manager of a California CBS TV station. A student protester as a guest star on a variety show? Clearly, this was no ordinary program.

"I remember Tommy and I watching television, and there was some sort of independent thing Mort Sahl had on at that time," Mason says. (Sahl, a topical comedian and satirist who had started at San Francisco's hungry i, at that point was cohost of *Both Sides Now*, a nationally syndicated talk program seen locally on KTTV. Sahl offered comic rants and espoused political philosophies; he was countered by station anchor George Putnam, widely credited as the model for vapid Ted Baxter on *The Mary Tyler Moore Show*.) Mason continues, "Tommy would say, 'Man, this is so much more interesting than what's on the networks.'"

Tom certainly was right in his assessment of a lack of topicality on the network level. When *The Smothers Brothers Comedy Hour* arrived at midseason in 1967, the other new entries replacing fall flops included *Mr. Terrific* (nerd as temporary superhero), *Captain Nice* (nerd as temporary superhero), and *The Invaders* (loner insists aliens have landed on and infiltrated our planet). On TV, escapism was almost everywhere you looked—all the Smothers Brothers had to do to build a reputation for topical comic commentary was to say anything at all.

While Mason was writing for a rival prime-time variety series already, he was more than happy to help his roommate plan his new show. They placed a shoe box in the foyer of their apartment, in which they threw scraps of paper noting ideas, guest suggestions—anything that might lead to a spark, a sketch, a booking, a new direction. "When it came time for the show," Mason says, "we dug the damned thing out, and there were two to three pages of solid ideas, of things we wanted to explore. It could be a guest's name—don't forget so-and-so—or just a single idea."

As the show was being formulated quickly, ideas were coming from all directions. By coincidence, Danny Kaye was vacating his offices just as Tom and Dick were staffing up, so they inherited a great workspace at Television City: rooftop offices to go along with the fabled soundstages used by Benny and Burns. "We had fifteen or twenty offices in one area, up on the top floor of CBS," Ken Kragen says. "For us, it was pretty good. The writers' cubicles were tiny, but we had a decent setup up there. And it was so convenient, because the rehearsal halls were just around the corner, and the tape stages were downstairs."

"We went through a door and we walked across the roof," Dick recalls, "and it was . . . hot mopped in gravel on either side of a wooden path. It sort of made some turns, and you go into this office, and there was a whole suite of offices there. And it was just exciting, putting everything together. All these young, good-looking, and healthy-looking people starting off on an adventure." Dick continues, smiling, "The exciting thing was for Tommy and me to seek out our executive assistants, who turned out to be very beautiful young ladies who were highly qualified." Tom's marriage had been in trouble before the series began; Dick's would be over before the series ended.

Dick also recalls fondly that the offices and dressing rooms were outfitted with closed-circuit TV, so you could monitor internal CBS feeds and in-building rehearsals from the various stages, even for other shows. Weeks before *Comedy Hour* premiered, he remembers watching the internal CBS feed of what is now known as Super Bowl I—and also recalls watching, with interest, Red Skelton's rehearsals for *The Red Skelton Show*. Skelton intentionally put in all sorts of off-color jokes just to perplex the network's head of program practices, William Tankersley. Tankersley would, in time, be the network's point man in most of its censorship battles with the Smothers Brothers. But Skelton, they soon realized, was just misbehaving during rehearsal for the fun of it. "He'd put on the dirtiest shows you've ever seen!" Dick says. "And during the live [evening] show, Red had a thing of laughing at his own jokes. He was laughing at all the dirty jokes they didn't say!"

With offices in place and writers divided into teams, the format for the series came together very quickly. It had to. Some building blocks were obvious, and at first effortless: Tom and Dick would open and close each show, and provide one lengthy performance piece from their rock-solid stage act. Guest stars would be introduced by one or both brothers, and either perform solo or appear in a sketch, then return for a themed finale featuring the entire company. Musical groups might provide an additional song or two, and so might Dick, with or without his brother. The show's company of singers and dancers would be incorporated into the action when possible—and always would appear in the opening credits, as a dancing band carrying signs identifying the week's guest stars, with a big bass drum emblazoned with the show's title.

"I don't know who thought of that!" Dick says appreciatively. "What a great opening that was!" The "who" was brother Tom, who had insisted that the show hire eight singers, a dozen dancers, and a huge band—then devised the opening credits sequence as a way to use them all. The orchestra, under Nelson Riddle's direction, would play the theme offscreen, while the dancers would march, dance, and pretend to play, and the singers, also offscreen, would sing their tuneful, wordless accompaniment. "We decided it would be nice to have real dancers involved in the opening, so they got to participate," Mason remembers. "Tommy said, 'I really want to load this show up with talent.' This was one of the things that they could do every week, so they were there, at least." And it wasn't just the dancers whose presence and paychecks were justified, in part, by appearing in the opening credits. The same trick was used to help secure a regular spot, and salary, for one of Tom and Dick's friends, who carried the bass drum in those early shows and hid behind a giant fake mustache. The friend's name: Pat Paulsen.

Booking for the show—an unknown entity, in the kamikaze slot, hosted by relative youngsters—was difficult at first, but thanks to various showbiz connections, not impossible. Jack Benny was such a fan of the young comedy team that he agreed to come aboard, especially when asked by his own former writers, Al Gordon and Hal Goldman, who promised to write his *Comedy Hour* spots. CBS persuaded Ed Sullivan, whose long-running variety show served as the Smothers Brothers' lead-in, to appear at the top of the first show to introduce Tom and Dick to viewers, a potent endorsement. And Tom, on a recent *Tonight Show* appearance hosted by Johnny Carson, had so delighted fellow guest Bette Davis that, when she was approached to appear on *Comedy Hour,* she agreed to make a rare prime-time TV appearance—but *not* on the first show.

"On the first show," Mason says, "you couldn't get anybody to be the star. Finally, Jim Nabors stepped forward—he was a big star at that time." His Marine Corps sitcom, *Gomer Pyle, U.S.M.C.,* had finished the previous TV season second only to *Bonanza,* making it CBS's most popular program, and Nabors its most popular personality. The network, by delivering both Sullivan and Nabors, certainly was giving the Smothers Brothers its best shot. Also signed for the opening show, eventually, was Jill St. John, a red-headed starlet who, in 1966, had been a featured guest star in the premiere of ABC's pop hit series *Batman,* and a supporting player in the glitzy, trashy movie *The Oscar.* The cast was set. The set was built. The script was written, rewritten, and rehearsed. On January 22, 1967, on Stage 33 at CBS

Television Studio, it was performed, twice, before an audience, and taped and edited for broadcast.

"The first show came off beautifully," Mason wrote in a journal entry for January 25. "Virtually everything worked. It was good." Within two weeks, Mason would learn whether his opinion was shared by the American viewing public—if anyone bothered to tune in to watch.

And So It Begins:
The Smothers Brothers Comedy Hour

At 9:00 p.m. ET on February 5, 1967, *The Smothers Brothers Comedy Hour* premiered to an unsuspecting but not inattentive nation. The premiere had about as much advance hype as a midseason replacement could hope to get. *TV Guide* had given the *Comedy Hour* premiere a coveted half-page "Close-Up" feature. Ed Sullivan not only featured the Smothers Brothers on his live variety show the Sunday before, but on the night of the premiere, promoted *Comedy Hour* at the end of *The Ed Sullivan Show,* then stayed around to introduce the boys, and their show, from his own New York stage. The bit, like another bit of cross-talk later in the show, was taped but loose enough to look and feel live.

"Well, hello again, ladies and gentlemen," Sullivan begins. "Now I'd like to help kick off the premiere of an exciting new comedy show which you're all going to enjoy for a long, long time, starring Tom and Dick Smothers. Now, first of all, they really are brothers," Sullivan says, launching into a family-album slide show to which he provides commentary. "They were typical American kids, average in every way . . ."

The earliest photos show Tom and Dick as young children—a collection of baby pictures, snapshots of them as young boys (in and out of their childhood military academy uniforms), and a backyard photo of them with their mother and Grandma Remick, the latter identified by Sullivan as "the Smothers Brothers' mother's mother." No mention is made of Tom and Dick's father, or his fate in World War II, nor are there any mentions, or photos, of Tom and Dick's sister Sherry. The narrative jumps quickly to and past the high school years (showing Tom on the gymnastics team and Dick in a track uniform), vaulting directly to their showbiz beginnings. "They started out as a trio," Sullivan says, offering a biographical fact few viewers knew to be the truth—and making it a punch line of sorts by showing a photo of the brothers flanking Red Skelton. "Unfortunately, they felt the one in the middle had no talent," Sullivan continues, "so they decided to go it alone." If Bobby Blackmore, the actual original third member of the Smothers Brothers, were watching the premiere, it's doubtful he found that particular joke amusing.

In short order, Sullivan throws the show to Hollywood and the brothers, dressed smartly in matching red blazers, white shirts, and black ties. They open their portion of the show by launching into "I Wish I Wuz in Peoria," from their very first album—just a snippet, enough to have Tom make an intentional mistake so they can stop the music and talk about being nervous on their new show. "Welcome to *The Smothers Comedy Brothers Hour!*" Tom says, which leads into the literal parade of credits, with an unrecognizable—and, at that point, unrecognized—Pat Paulsen holding the bass drum. "I was merely asked to play the drummer in the band in the beginning," Pat explained. "Tommy wanted to keep me around there, and that way I'd get paid scale and could stay in town."

After the opening credits and commercials, the brothers return, stepping on the illuminated Tiffany-style mini-stage that became their visual trademark. (The Tiffany theme didn't yet extend to the background set, though. Mason described the first show's background set this way: "It looks like somebody shot their car seat, skinned it, and made a set out of it.") Tom and Dick, guitar and bass at the ready, thank Ed Sullivan for the introduction and mention the guest stars: Jim Nabors, Jill St. John, and some surprise cameos by unbilled "walk-ons." Then they do their first full set piece: "Venezuelan Rain Dance," which, as on their *Think Ethnic!* album, runs more than six minutes. It establishes not only the comedy dynamic of excitable Tom and grounded Dick, but also their impressive musical ability (when they launch into "Hava Nagila," it becomes not just a punch line, but a rousing performance).

After the commercial break, Tom introduces Jill St. John, who sings "L.O.V.E." while flanked with dancers and decked out in what looks like a floor-length, kimono-sleeved slick yellow raincoat. But when she opens her coat with arms outstretched, she looks more like a pop-art butterfly: the inner lining is bright paisley, and she's wearing a bright red beaded pantsuit. "The dress cost twelve hundred dollars, which was a lot of money in those days," Mason recalls. "Everyone backstage was just stunned by the fact they were willing to spend twelve hundred dollars on one dress for one number." Tom and Dick chat with Jill St. John afterward, then disperse so that Dick can introduce the next sketch, in which Tom and Jill St. John play Romeo and Juliet. Tom gets big laughs for his broken bogus Shakespearean dialogue, and the sketch establishes what would become a popular recurring element of *The Smothers Brothers Comedy Hour*: "Any time you had a female guest, they were probably going to do a famous love story," says Mason. "That turned out to be very hip. It provided a platform for you to invite these female stars on."

Next comes Nabors, in his improbably rich and deep singing voice, belting "The Impossible Dream" from *Man of La Mancha* (which had opened on Broadway fifteen months earlier). Afterward, Dick asks Nabors about the song's meaning, playing straight man as he listens to Nabors's Gomerish description of "Don Coyote" as a "Spanish Walter Brennan."

Sullivan returns, in another coast-to-coast conversation, to start the second half of the show. Then Tom introduces the Anita Kerr Singers, bandleader Nelson Riddle and his orchestra, and brother Dick, all of whom perform "What the World Needs Now." Dick rejoins Tom, whose after-song chat is interrupted by the show's first walk-on: "Come on out, you old son of a gun!" The person who enters greets Tom warmly, shakes hands with a befuddled Dick, and leaves, with the audience laughing because they have no idea who the guy is. "Tommy, who was that?" Dick asks, a bit irritated. "Artie Bowser," Tom explains. "One heck of a guy. Down at the Cocoanut Grove there, parking cars." In reality, Artie marks the show's first speaking appearance by Pat Paulsen, who gets laughs just from his deadpan, hangdog expressions and quiet demeanor.

"Pat has that television face where he just has a lot going on without a lot of activity," Mason says. "That's how Tom would bring people on the show. He was always giving people little shots to see how they would do."

Another unrecognizable person enters next, prompting Dick to yell at his brother and tell him to stop it with the walk-ons by unfamiliar "friends." Dick leaves angrily, and Tom looks offstage. "Sorry," he says, "my brother says we can't use you." The rejected guest says, "Well, it's all right" then comes into the audience's view. It's popular entertainer and TV star Danny Thomas, who shakes hands with Tom and leaves.

Nothing at all in that first *Comedy Hour* was topical, much less controversial . . . but it wasn't always intended that way. Five days before the premiere episode was taped, CBS sent out a descriptive press release that, among other things, promised something new. "The brothers," it said, "also introduce a unique feature in television comedy, an editorial. The premiere editorial deals with the war on poverty." A correction was sent out before the premiere, deleting any mention of the editorial. Tom, who was to deliver it, didn't approve of his own performance. The first *Comedy Hour* editorial eventually appeared in the fourth show—presented by the show's first home-grown rising star, Pat Paulsen.

The second show was taped before ratings for the first were released, so everyone was flying blind, unaware of whether their program had attracted an audience at all. At this early point, CBS wielded its influence to showcase network stars and Columbia recording artists on the new Smothers series. Sometimes this corporate synergy was a plus: both Pete Seeger and Simon and Garfunkel recorded for the company's record label, and Eddie Albert of *Green Acres,* a vaudevillian at heart, was a welcome guest. Unfortunately, for the second *Comedy Hour* show, Albert came as a package deal with his sitcom costar Eva Gabor, who was awful. She rejected a sketch written especially for her, in which she was to play Marie Antoinette to Tom's Robespierre, and demanded it be replaced with a skit based on a *Green Acres* scene she and Albert already had played on their sitcom, about his teaching her to drive. Albert, solo, explained and sang "Guantanamera," the first of several times that song would be performed on the series. But other than that, the week's special guests didn't add much. "I don't like parts of the second show," Mason wrote in his journal.

Even in a show that would be one of their weaker first-season efforts, this hour had several notable elements. The background, behind which the brothers performed, had been redesigned by scenic designer Romain Johnston. (He and director Stan Harris based the curtain and the lit stage's Tiffany motif, according to Harris, on the Tiffany-designed Palacio de Bellas Artes mosaic curtain in Mexico City.) Pat Paulsen was featured again, this time pretending to be a celebrity audience member, an Australian tennis pro (this allowed Pat to demonstrate his slow-motion tennis bit from his nightclub act).

Also pointed out, in the audience, was Tom and Dick's mother, Ruth, who was asked by her sons to stand. "How come you liked my brother best?" Tom asks her, and she just smiles. Later in the show, Tom and Dick, perhaps in her honor, do their famous "Mom Always Liked You Best" routine, including the bits about the wagon and the "crummy chicken."

There were, on this otherwise forgettable show, two tiny signs of rebellion. One was the booking, at Tom's insistence, of an unfamiliar rock group singing an unfamiliar song: the Turtles, lip-synching to "Happy Together." The song is harmless, but the timing is crucial. The show was taped on February 3, and "Happy Together," the group's first single, didn't hit *Billboard*'s Top 100 until February 11, the night before the program was televised. It reached number one, proving and *The Smothers Brothers Comedy Hour* could help make new hits, even by new acts. And there was one other gauntlet thrown in that show, as part of their introduction to old vaudeville standards.

"We're going to present some pungent social comment on the pressing issues of the day," Tom promises, adding, "We're going to delve into the controversial issues and the material that faces our society today."

Dick interrupts him and says, "Tommy, we're not going to do anything of the sort."

"We are going to make social comment," Tom insists, "and we are going to talk about what's going on in the world today."

Dick launches into a series of songs, each of which Tom describes as being either outdated or, at its core, controversial. Finally, he objects to the all-Irish lineup in the song "McNamara's Band," and Dick relents. The two of them update the lyrics as "McNamara's Integrated Band"—playing for comedy even as Tom fulfills his promise to be topical. Not bad, but the next show was much, much better.

Writers Hal Goldman and Al Gordon got their old boss Jack Benny to appear, bringing buddy George Burns with him—and those writers had the brilliant idea of bringing out Burns and Benny dressed as Dick and Tom, red blazers and all, and adopting their respective personalities. "And now," announcer Roger Carroll boomed a few minutes into the show, "two of the brightest, freshest faces in show business today," and Burns and Benny come out in silhouette, carrying the brothers' instruments. The lights come up, the studio audience applauds and laughs, and the two showbiz veterans launch into their act—which, in this case, is the Smotherses' act. "Mom always liked you best!" Benny shouts, and even hits Burns in the arm the same playful way Tom hits Dick. They "do" Tom and Dick beautifully, which reveals how much of Benny's masterful timing is in Tom's halting character, and how much straight-man mastery Dick has developed as well. Benny and Burns symbolically pass the baton to the Smothers Brothers and endorse them as the new generation.

During the rest of the show, the veteran performers joke about working for these youngsters ("Us working for these kids," Burns complains to Benny, "is like General Eisenhower working for Gomer Pyle"), then team with them for a closing number designed to help the tenured comedians appeal to teenagers. Benny plays an electric violin, Burns claims to play an electric cigar ("I plug it in, smoke it, and it turns me on," he explains, getting the show's first drug joke past the censors), and the four of them sing the big "modern" closing number—"Winchester Cathedral," a two-month-old novelty hit that echoes the sound of ancient vaudeville.

On the basis of these early shows, the press paid attention to the ratings and gave the Smothers Brothers their due. "Have the bravos of the Ponderosa finally met a couple of tough hombres they can't outdraw?" asked the *New York Times* on February 14. After two showings, *Comedy Hour* was doing phenomenally well—beating *Bonanza* its second week, though finishing behind ABC's movie night—

and, according to the *Times*, doing especially well in the thirty biggest cities monitored by A. C. Nielsen, "where the comedians outdrew the cowboys . . . and got a 36 share of the available audience to *Bonanza*'s 26." The article quoted an unnamed CBS source, who sounds an awful lot like executive Mike Dann, as saying, "The attitude here is, 'My gosh, we may be stuck with a hit!' " Before too long, many within CBS would feel that way, but without any sense of gleeful irony.

Testing the CBS Censors—
the First Encounters

Getting Jack Benny and George Burns to guest star was a tri-umph in and of itself. Having them do new material, espe-cially material presenting them in a new way to a new audience, was a bonus, a winning strategy the show would replicate immediately. And as the ratings trickled in, showing that *The Smoth-ers Brothers Comedy Hour* was sustaining a strong, reliable second-place finish in the former "kamikaze slot," a sense of euphoria and ambi-tion set in. The show, clearly, was attracting and holding a large, and largely new, audience—not merely drawing viewers from NBC and ABC, but also luring people who didn't watch much television.

The next batch of shows played to that new audience, and to the show's strengths. Veteran stars brought back to goof around with the Smothers Brothers included movie star Bette Davis, entertainer Jimmy Durante, and *Garry Moore Show* sidekick Carol Burnett. Meanwhile, for the young audiences, rock acts booked included Paul Revere and the Raiders, a return appearance by the Turtles, and, most impressively, Buffalo Springfield.

Most veterans of the *Comedy Hour* interviewed for this book share the perspective that the show didn't delve into politics for the first dozen or so programs, but a closer look at show number four disproves that recollection. The guests were Bette Davis, Bob Crane from the hit CBS sitcom *Hogan's Heroes,* and Buffalo Springfield—and for a variety show, the political content was substantial.

Tom and Dick open the show with a discussion of a theory about a correlation between clothes and politics. "You can tell who's running the country," Tom insists, "by how much clothes people wear." Ordinary people, who can't afford too many layers of clothing, Tom explains, are "the less-ons." "So," Dick asks, "who's running the country?" "The more-ons," Tom replies. Later in the show, Dick jokes with Bob Crane about his sitcom, set in a Nazi POW concentration camp, and tells him, "I didn't know war was so much fun." It might have been a pointed barb, since Dick and Tom's father died as a POW, but Crane points the barb elsewhere: "The peace," he replies, "hasn't been too many laughs, either." Then the two of them launch into "Pollution," the Tom Lehrer song written for, and first heard on, *That Was the Week That Was* ("The city streets are really quite a thrill / If the hoods don't get you, the monoxide will").

Bette Davis, playing Marie Antoinette in the sketch foolishly rejected by Eva Gabor, does a delightful job sending up her own serious movie star image—and, in character, even makes some "let them eat cake" pronouncements poking gentle fun at LBJ's Great Society social programs. But the most daring political commentary of all comes during the featured musical act, when Stephen Stills led Neil Young and the rest of Buffalo Springfield in a rendition of his new song, "For What It's Worth," recorded just two months earlier. Stills wrote the song as a reaction to the Sunset Strip riots, when Los Angeles police imposed a curfew on young people attending nightclubs, and a mass demonstration—with mass arrests—resulted. The song, which wasn't even in the Top 40 when the program was taped, was an important, potentially incendiary pop-culture counterpunch. Tom softened the blows by twice interrupting Buffalo Springfield's performance, and playing against the lyrics for comedy. When Stills sang "There's a man with a gun over there / telling me I've got to beware," the camera cuts to Tom, dressed in Western garb like an outlaw. After the line about "a thousand people in the street / singing songs and carrying signs," Dick is shown holding a sign saying, as in the lyric, "Hooray for our side." Stills smiles approvingly both times, the studio audience laughs and applauds—but the message gets out. And for what it's worth, "For What It's Worth" soars up the charts in the weeks afterward and eventually becomes a generational anthem.

It was an important booking, as was special guest star Bette Davis, whose skit with Tom gave the producers another key piece of their variety-hour puzzle. "She set the stage for all these other sort of older big stars, like Greer Garson and Lana Turner," Mason says. "They knew they were going to be treated well and come off well. You'll have fun, and the public will see you again in a new light." Tom looks at his performances opposite Davis and cringes, upset that he put so much energy into the booking and planning and other elements of the show that when it came time to act in front of the audience, he found himself reading cue cards instead of connecting fully with his costar. But the Oscar-winning actress clearly enjoyed herself ("She was great in comedy, and on the stage—she loved it," said director Stan Harris), and the result, on camera, only made Tom seem even more scattered, befuddled, and funny.

Tom might have been even more overworked, at that point, had he not vetoed the suggestion that he star in a segment planned for but dropped from the opening show: an on-air editorial. Instead, he suggested it be given to Pat Paulsen, who at that point had appeared on the show only twice (outside of the opening credits, that is), in those walk-on bits as a car-park attendant and tennis pro. As vice president of "the Smothers Brothers Corporation," Pat's dour expressions and barely audible monotone were perfectly suited to lampoon local station editorialists, who had begun appearing on TV only a few years before.

The subject of the first editorial was "Safety in Automobiles." It was a timely and touchy subject—Ralph Nader's *Unsafe at Any Speed*, the book that launched a new era of auto-safety awareness, had come out only two years before—yet Paulsen's editorial had no controversial punch whatsover. It was delivered almost totally in doublespeak, a combination of Norm Crosby–like malaprops and incoherent mumbling. But Paulsen's dry, droll delivery got big laughs, and a post office box address superimposed at the end, offering copies of the speech to anyone sending a self-addressed, stamped envelope, drew an unexpectedly large response.

"The first one," Mason explained, "is making fun of the concept of editorials. But later on, they became a vehicle for comments on social issues . . . First, it was about form; then it got to be about content."

The writers had rented an actual post office box to supply an authentic address, but forgot about it until the Beverly Hills post office phoned the *Comedy Hour* production company to come get their mail. "The postmaster called and said, 'We've got a lot of stuff here,' " Ken Fritz recalls. Fritz promised to send someone to pick it up, and the postmaster warned him that it wouldn't be that easy. Eventually several vans had to be dispatched to gather the more than fifteen thousand letters that arrived each week. Many decades before the internet, the response was an early example of true TV interactivity.

The next show—featuring Carl Reiner from *Your Show of Shows,* Barbara Eden from NBC's *I Dream of Jeannie,* and Paul Revere and the Raiders—wasn't that impressive. The program was interesting only for its lengthy finale, which used Paul Revere and the Raiders as an excuse for a Revolutionary War USO skit employing the entire company: Reiner as an eighteenth-century Bob Hope, Eden as a "Miss Louisiana Purchase" beauty queen, and the rock band and the Smothers Brothers as so many musical Yankee Doodles. More noteworthy is what wasn't shown—the first example of a sketch being rejected almost outright by the CBS censors. It was called "Sex and the Single Student" and was intended as a comic look at the new sexual frankness and freedom. The sketch that aired contained nothing clever, much less daring or shocking.

"That was a piece that the censors just absolutely gutted," Mason remembers. "This was one of the first examples of running into a subject they wouldn't let you expound on at all. I remember Tommy and I sat at his house, and went over it, and tried to make something out of it. They just wouldn't let us."

That first bout of censorship didn't register strongly, nor did some concerns in the next show, which featured Carol Burnett as special guest star, and included sketches in which Carol and Tom play two people who meet under various circumstances, including at KKK rallies and nudist colonies. "I do remember Carol coming and saying, 'Let's push the envelope,'" Mason says. Carol Burnett was highly regarded at CBS, so much so that they gave her and Tom enough leeway to appear as nudists, hidden behind well-placed shrubbery. What's left of the sketch is greeted as audacious and naughty by the studio audience, but for the second week in a row, the original scripts had been blue-penciled heavily by the network.

Burnett, at this point, already knew she would be hosting her own CBS variety show in the fall, broadcast from an adjoining studio at Television City. Neither she nor the brothers, though, were aware of how close she had come to getting the variety show slot given to them instead. In 1962, when she left *The Garry Moore Show*, Burnett was given what she calls "a very unusual contract" by CBS. It was a ten-year deal, requiring two guest spots and one special a year, and including one additional provision: within the first five years of the contract, all Burnett had to do was call up CBS and say she wanted to do a one-hour variety series, and the network would commit instantly to thirty shows, pay or play. "We were five years into that contract, and I really needed the money," Burnett says. "It was the week before the five years would be up, and I had just moved to California with my husband, Joe Hamilton. We said, 'Maybe we should make that call.'" They did. In the last week of December 1966, Carol called CBS executive Mike Dann and said, "I really want to push that button and do that variety show." She placed that call a mere two weeks after CBS signed the Smothers Brothers for midseason. Had she phoned a little earlier, she, rather than Tom and Dick, most likely would have been selected as the replacement for her old boss, Garry Moore. Instead, Dann tried at first to talk her into accepting the starring role in an already written sitcom pilot called *Here's Agnes*. Burnett balked and held CBS to the terms of her contract. They agreed to give her a variety show beginning that fall. *The Carol Burnett Show* ran for eleven years. "I'm so glad," she says, "I didn't do *Here's Agnes*."

On her *Comedy Hour* guest spot, Carol joked with Tom, sang with Dick, and sang and clowned with them both, demonstrating without doubt she was ready to step up to a new level. On the same show, so did Pat Paulsen, delivering his second editorial, this one on "Keeping Our Cities Clean." While loaded with nonsense phrases, this one also contained, for the first time, some quotable one-liners. "Litter is something we are all against," Pat said. "Oh, it's all right, in its place . . ." And he scrunched up his face and waited for the audience to catch up to the joke. Once again, he was a hit.

At this point, Tom was close to being overwhelmed by the dual responsibilities of performing and production. A divorce action filed by Stephi was postponed because Tom, according to court papers, was "too busy to think." Early clashes with CBS censors were irritating, but Tom was unaware of how pitched the battles were about to get or even how widespread they were for others at the network. Yet there was a perfect example, occurring at that exact time, of CBS fighting to keep from its airwaves what it considered controversial material.

The case in point was *Mark Twain Tonight!*, the one-man Broadway show written and performed by actor Hal Holbrook, based on the books, letters, and speeches of Mark Twain. Mike Dann had seen and loved Holbrook's stage show, and, to his credit, wanted to present it in prime time on CBS. With David Susskind as producer, the program was scheduled and promoted to be televised as a ninety-minute special on Monday, March 6, 1967. Holbrook, who reshaped the show and substituted material constantly, agreed to a one-week preparation schedule: rehearsals Monday through Wednesday, camera blocking Thursday and Friday, filming on Saturday and Sunday, and televising the final cut on Monday. All went well into Wednesday, when Susskind showed up and said CBS objected to certain material Holbrook was performing. One objection was to the anti-war tone of some of Twain's remarks. The other objection was to the repeated usage, in passages from *The Adventures of Huckleberry Finn*, of the word *nigger*. Though the word is used, in context, either to expose racism as ugly or to dramatize Huck's eventual rejection of bigotry, its use by Twain is a hot-button issue even today. In 1967, with civil rights an inflamed battle, it couldn't have been hotter.

"In some places in the South, racism was really out of control," Holbrook says now, "and we were watching it all over the television screen. And the other thing was this war we'd gotten ourselves tangled up in, and we were beginning to realize, at that point, that we got our foot in a bear trap." Holbrook had chosen those passages precisely because of the Vietnam War and the racial divide, and what he saw as Twain's applicable, universal truths about war and equality. When he got news of the network's objections, his reaction was simple but unyielding: Tell CBS, he told Susskind, that we can stop rehearsals and not have a show—or that the show will go on as planned, with absolutely no cuts.

"They were trapped, really," Holbrook says, "and of course I knew that. I knew they were committed, and trapped, so it wasn't like I was cavalier. I just knew I had a tremendous amount of influence there, and if I was able to stand my ground, that probably I'd win . . . And I did. He came back in a couple hours and said, 'Okay, Hal. They've agreed to it.' And we went and did it." The result: one of the best television programs of the 1960s—and a kindred spirit, with *The Smothers Brothers Comedy Hour*, of making serious points through humor.

"You can make statements, political statements, with what we generally call humor," Holbrook says. "But humor is often interpreted as something soft. Well, it isn't always soft at all. And if you can use a sense of humor, you can use the 'ignition' function of comedy—using something funny to explode an idea that is serious and political."

In the first *Comedy Hour* taped after *Mark Twain Tonight!* was televised, the Smothers Brothers did just that. They presented the third, and easily most controversial, Pat Paulsen editorial: "Should the Use of Firearms Be Restricted?"

It starts with doublespeak, then shifts to speak: "If you're old enough to get arrested, you're old enough to carry a gun." And: "A gun is a necessity. Who knows, if you're walking down the street, you'll spot a moose." And, while brandishing a pistol: "Stand up and be counted. Let's preserve our freedom to kill." Then, as the announcer begins to recite the post office box number to send requests for copies of the editorial, Pat's gun goes off and kills the announcer in midsentence. Maybe it doesn't sound like much, but on TV in 1967, there was nothing quite like it.

Yet by leavening its viewpoints with humor and entertainment, *Comedy Hour* was adding to its national audience. That same seventh *Comedy Hour* show featured a lavish, ultra-mod fashion show, music, and comedy with beautiful actress Inger Stevens (who played Queen

Isabella to Tom's Christopher Columbus), and, as special guest star, Jimmy Durante. The highlight of the show, and one of the most intimate moments from the entire series, showcased Durante, sitting on the side of the stage bathed in a single follow spot, singing "Young at Heart," with a lovely arrangement by Nelson Riddle. A little music, a little fashion, and a little "ignition" comedy—it was a formula that worked well, and, on a week when *Bonanza* was preempted by a special telecast of *Annie Get Your Gun*, gave *The Smothers Brothers Comedy Hour* its first first-place win in its Sunday time slot. An estimated 14.2 million TV households—more than one in four homes equipped with television—tuned to *Comedy Hour* that night.

Neither CBS nor the Smothers Brothers had any way of knowing it, but that was the largest audience the series would ever attract.

From Hit Status to Elaine May Not

I n March 1967, CBS and the Smothers Brothers didn't know what
hit them—but were about to learn they *were* a hit. Lightning had
struck instantly, but confirmation traveled slowly. Back then, national ratings from the A. C. Nielsen Company were delivered every
two weeks, not overnight, and television critics for magazines and
daily newspapers were similarly unhurried. In that era, TV shows
were not previewed for critics (not yet, though the Smothers eventually had a hand in changing that). Programs were reviewed after the
fact and often not until several representative episodes had been sam-
pled. Only the trades could be counted on to react quickly, though
not often excitedly. The premiere of *The Smothers Brothers Comedy
Hour*, according to *Variety*, was "neither here nor there nor hip nor
square."

In fact, those first *Comedy Hour* shows were produced on such an
advance schedule—nine days between the taping and the telecast—
and the ratings released so tardily, there were no expectations, and
there was very little feedback from the network or the press. Even
after Nielsen released its second bimonthly report of *Comedy Hour*
ratings, with the stunning news that the second episode of *Comedy
Hour* had beaten the unstoppable *Bonanza*, neither the brothers nor
the network knew quite what to think.

"There certainly were celebratory phone calls, and everybody was kind of walking on air," Fred Silverman, then running daytime for CBS, recalled. "But at first there was some caution. Everybody thought, 'Maybe it was a fluke, it was sampling'—there were any number of things. 'We better wait for a second rating.' The second rating came in," Silverman continued, referring to the ratings book that showed *Comedy Hour* beating *Bonanza* one week, "and we said, 'We better wait for a third rating.' By the third rating, we were ecstatic. We didn't lose any viewers. Everybody knew we had a hit."

The third ratings book for the Smothers show estimated its two-week audience at more than 12 million TV households—not quite as large as the 14.5 million for NBC's *Bonanza*, but many millions more than even the most optimistic projections. Already, a pattern had emerged: *The Smothers Brothers Comedy Hour* reliably outperformed ABC's Sunday night movie offering. This was at a time, a decade before the introduction of home video, when movies on TV were one of the medium's most popular genres and considered special events unto themselves.

As the unexpected news about the ratings made the rounds, the cast and crew of *Comedy Hour* were producing and taping the seventh show—the one with Jimmy Durante, Inger Stevens, and the second appearance by the Turtles. Just after that, the sixth show, with Carol Burnett, was broadcast by CBS. That's when everyone started to take notice and to believe that this midseason replacement out of nowhere was achieving the unthinkable.

The *Washington Post* acknowledged the phenomenon, crowning *The Smothers Brothers Comedy Hour* "the hit of the second season," but the reporter for the newspaper didn't even pretend to understand it. "Over the last three audience measurement reports from the A. C. Nielsen Co.," Lawrence Laurent wrote, "the program has succeeded in doing what had been considered impossible. It knocked *Bonanza* out of first place. In the most recent report," he added, "*Bonanza* was down to fifteenth place and the *Brothers Smothers* was in twenty-third place. The question now becomes 'Why?'"

Laurent couldn't begin to explain it. He didn't much like the show ("More than anything, it resembled an amateur hour that was produced on a big budget"), or care for the brothers themselves ("the act was generally considered to be one of limited appeal") but conceded that its success couldn't be attributed to the notion that viewers were happy to sit still for any old variety series that followed the popular *Ed Sullivan Show*. Were that the case, *Garry Moore* would not have crashed in the same time slot. The truth of the matter was plain to see, if you looked at it from the other side of the generation gap. *The Smothers Brothers Comedy Hour* wasn't any old variety series. It was a *new* variety series, one that managed to appeal to a different, younger demographic while hanging on to the more traditional *Sullivan Show* audience.

Stan Harris, director of *Comedy Hour* that first season, recalled, "Everyone was saying, 'How can this be?' . . . We were bringing in an audience that was not watching television. That's what happened." Silverman, with a chuckle, explained, "It was kind of funny, because there was this bright, shiny, young-appeal show sitting in between *Ed Sullivan* and *Candid Camera* and *What's My Line*. So it was like a hiccup in the middle of the schedule."

While the *Washington Post* reported the show's success begrudgingly, *Variety* revisited the series on the heels of the hour featuring Carol Burnett. Proclaiming that *The Smothers Brothers Comedy Hour* "continues in a top level in its highly competitive Sunday slot," *Variety* jumped aboard the *Comedy Hour* bandwagon. "The presentations are geared to laughs for the younger and perhaps more adventurous members of the family," the reviewer noted perceptively.

Riding the waves of both ratings and critical success, the Smothers Brothers returned to the studio to tape their eighth show. The guests were Tony Randall, singer Jack Jones, and a trio of shapely female puppets designed by Sid and Marty Krofft. It was a fairly innocuous show, filled with old-fashioned production numbers (Randall embodying, and singing, "Lucky Lindy" while dancing on the wing of a biplane) and vaudeville bits (Dick's verbal byplay with the Krofft puppets was a weak echo of Ed Sullivan's conversations with the cute Italian mouse puppet Topo Gigio). The edginess, what little there was of it, was slipped into the Lucky Lindy sketch, with "Lucky Lindy Smothers" (Tom) making several jokes about the appeal of airplane glue. One of the show's obvious highlights was Pat Paulsen, finally given the spotlight to re-create some of the bits from his own stage act as a folksinger. He offered drolly rambling, seemingly endless introductions to songs he never played, got applause for singing single lines of lyrics from his own songs ("I was standing in the street when a very ugly man came up and tied his horse to me"), and even more applause for starting, then stopping, a song from the hit Off-Broadway musical *The Fantasticks* ("Try to remember," Paulsen sang, then pretended to forget the chords and lyrics that came next). Paulsen, in short, was a hit.

That week's Smothers Brothers closing skit, written by Mason Williams and Allan Blye, utilized all the guest stars. It featured Jones as a singing minstrel, telling the tale of a princess (one of the Krofft puppets) in love with a prince (Tom), who gets turned into a frog by a wicked wizard (Randall). Dick got big laughs by flying in from the rafters as the Good Fairy, who ended up changing the wizard into another frog and running off with the princess himself. Costume designer Sal Anthony was the real star here, getting hearty laughs from the studio audience for the cartoonish outfits worn by the prince, fairy, and frogs—but Tom chose this odd, make-believe battlefield to have his first real run-in with the CBS censors.

As frogs, Tom and Tony Randall were to punctuate their dialogue with the croaky sound of "ribbet, ribbet." Tom wanted to slip in an occasional "frigget, frigget," which CBS refused to allow. At the afternoon and evening tapings of the show, Tom made the substitutions anyway. CBS reacted by taking the audio of Tom saying "ribbet" from somewhere else on the tape and editing it into the sound track. When the program was broadcast on Easter night, all the TV audience heard was "ribbet," but if you watched Tom's mouth closely, you could see that he was saying something else entirely.

Director Stan Harris recalled, "CBS said, 'You cannot do that. You've got to say ribbet. Ribbet ribbet, but not frigget, frigget.' It's so stupid! And all these things are so stupid, when you think about it."

"Oh, there was a great deal of carrying on about the 'ribbet,'" moaned former CBS executive Perry Lafferty. During subsequent battles over program content, Lafferty often sided with the brothers, but with this first offense, he agreed with the censors. "You can't say, 'Frigget, frigget, frigget, frigget!' There's worse than that today on cable, but not then . . . [on broadcast TV]," he said. "That's colloquial for 'fuck it!'"

Mason Williams, coauthor of the offending sketch, defends Tom's taping-day defiance as the instinctive reaction of a comic performer. "Tommy was willing to be funny onstage to get the [studio] audience to react," Williams said. "So he was going to say 'frigget' if it got a big laugh. It wasn't just the idea of spitting in the censor's eye. It was like, 'This is a funnier line; it's going to get a bigger response.' But that's the first really blatant example of the network actually overdubbing, changing the content."

On this point, at least, the Smothers Brothers got the last laugh. Midway through the second season, they mounted an operatic *Mutiny on the Bounty* spoof and took full advantage of the name of their style of warship—one that happened to be a very handy homophone (a word that sounds the same as another, but is spelled differently and has a different meaning). That way, Dick Smothers explained with a deep chuckle, Tom and anyone else in the sketch ". . . could say 'frigate' all he wanted!'"

Because of the still-standard delay between tape day and telecast night, Tom's eighth-show "frigget" mini-mutiny was followed, two days later, by the Sunday telecast of the previously taped seventh show—the one in which Jimmy Durante stopped the show with "Young at Heart," Pat Paulsen delivered an editorial on gun legislation, and the Turtles returned to sing "Happy Together" for the second time in five weeks. NBC's *Bonanza* was preempted that night for a TV version of a Lincoln Center musical production of *Annie Get Your Gun*, starring Ethel Merman and Jerry Orbach. When the two-week ratings came in, there was no more denying the appeal, and power, of *The Smothers Brothers Comedy Hour*.

The first week, A. C. Nielsen credited the Carol Burnett episode of *Comedy Hour* with reaching 12.8 million TV households, not far behind the 14.6 million for *Bonanza* and ahead of the 10.5 million for ABC's telecast of the movie *The Haunting*. The second week in that latest ratings period, *Comedy Hour* took advantage of the absence of *Bonanza* to win the time period for the first time. The *Comedy Hour* with Jimmy Durante drew 14.2 million TV households, its biggest audience yet, compared to 13 million for ABC's *Move Over, Darling* movie and 11 million for *Annie Get Your Gun*. For the two-week period—and these were the numbers that screamed success in the CBS corridors—NBC's long-dominant *Bonanza*, with one show, averaged 14.6 million TV households, and was ranked number 4. *The Smothers Brothers Comedy Hour*, with two shows, averaged 13.5 million, and was ranked number 8. It was the first time *Comedy Hour* had ended a ratings period ranked in the Top 10, and this was only seven weeks into a twenty-episode midseason run.

It's hardly coincidental that once those ratings came in—and *Comedy Hour* hit the Top 10 and came within striking distance of *Bonanza*—CBS decided, on March 23, 1967, to exercise its option and renew *The Smothers Brothers Comedy Hour* for the coming 1967–68 season.

The very next day, the Smothers Brothers taped their ninth show. Despite the Top 10 status and the freshly inked contract renewal, they ran into their first serious, infuriating battle with CBS. The network censored a sketch in its entirety and refused to let it air. Ironically, it was a sketch about censors.

One immediate benefit of *Comedy Hour*'s rapid success was a power shift in the booking of guests. Instead of accepting, gratefully and a little desperately, almost any acts sent their way, the show's staff became pickier. The original concept of bridging the generations was continued, but *The Smothers Brothers Comedy Hour*, like *Saturday Night Live* in the following decade, quickly became *the* place to be seen. At this time in TV history, networks and sponsors routinely exercised influence to book guests, but the *Comedy Hour* staff began to balk.

"When the show got hot," Mason Williams said, "the ad agencies wanted to load this show up with their talent. So we kept going to Tommy and saying, "Man, don't. We don't want to service these types of acts over and over and over. Ask us who *we'd* like to write for a little more, and who would *you* like to write for—and that's when people like Pete Seeger came into the scene."

Actually, Pete Seeger would not arrive until the start of the second season, but discussions began about having him on and shattering the seventeen-year prime-time TV blacklist against him. Tom and Dick indulged themselves in the second half of their debut hit season by hiring as guest stars some of the people who had supported the Smothers Brothers with TV guest spots earlier in their career, such as Steve Allen and the lesser-known variety-show host John Gary, a fleetingly popular singer. The Smothers Brothers even invited Bobby Blackmore, who had worked with Tom and Dick back when they all performed as a trio, to reunite briefly for one show. And musically, they continued to support not only new groups, but new music from those groups.

"The first battle we won," Mason Williams explained, "was playing different music. When we went to them [CBS] and said, 'We want to present new music,' they said, 'Oh, no, no. Television is not about new music. Television is Broadway, or hits, or Americana. We don't want things on the TV that aren't familiar, or that people don't already like.'

"We said, 'No, we have these new music acts—the Turtles, the Doors, you name them—they're the cutting edge of the youth and the music. We want them to play what they're excited about, not what they're tired of.' And we actually proved our point. What happened was, we began to be a place where the record industry gladly would have their acts perform, because we *broke* records. It was the first time [TV] variety had done that." That claim denies the impact of Ed Sullivan, among others—but *Comedy Hour* definitely had a "new" feel in its approach to music on TV.

The ninth installment of *The Smothers Brothers Comedy Hour* was a power play of sorts, with Tom both indulging his whims and exercising his, and the show's, clout. Among the musical guests that week were the Blues Magoos, a rock quintet from the Bronx that vanished from the scene after one Top 10 hit, "(We Ain't Got) Nothin' Yet." And the group didn't even play that hit on the *Comedy Hour*. They opted for another, newer song—described by Tom, in his introduction, as "their far-out brand of psychedelic music." Images on the camera were oversaturated intentionally, in an effort to make the band look even more "mod." In retrospect, they look almost impossibly young and pretentious. The show's other musical guest that night was Israeli singer Esther Ofarim, the Smothers Brothers's former opening act, given her second *Comedy Hour* showcase in nine shows. Unlike the Blues Magoos, however, Ofarim was worth the prime time. Previously, she introduced what would now be called "world music" into the show and had enjoyed a global hit with her recording of Mason Williams's "Cinderella Rockefella," also featuring her husband, Abi Ofarim. This time her vocal trio performance with Tom and Dick, "The Three Song," was a delicate rendition of an intricate number written by Mason Williams, who was getting the chance to work more of his compositions into the show. ("This was a song that came to me in a dream," he said of "Three Song," adding, "It was so powerful, I got up and wrote it down.") In the same show, Ofarim's solo performance of "Motherless Child" was gorgeous.

Yet the star of that ninth show, by far, was Elaine May. With her former improv partner Mike Nichols, May had made the type of free-form, audacious comedy albums that Tom Smothers listened to before he and Dick began making their own. Their humor, and their topics, were modern, playful, and often impish. As a recording act and stand-up duo. Nichols and May had broken up in 1961, the same year the Smothers Brothers released its introductory *Live at the Purple Onion* LP. Since then, May had appeared on TV only rarely and chosen her guest spots carefully. Like former partner Nichols, she appeared as a guest star on NBC's American version of *That Was the Week That Was* and reunited with Nichols for a joint appearance on *The Jack Paar Program* in 1965. Getting Elaine May as a guest star, in and of itself, was a coup. Having her willing to not only perform in but also help polish and help write a three-part sketch about Hollywood movie censors was a golden gift. Until, that is, CBS snatched it away.

This *Comedy Hour* was scheduled to be televised on April 9, 1967, the night before ABC's telecast of that year's Academy Awards. A segment in which Dick and Tom introduced vintage movie clips, falsely introducing them as being from the year's nominated films, was one tie-in to the Oscars ceremony. In another, Tom played a nominee practicing his acceptance speech so obsessively that he was blind to his wife's increasingly absurd efforts to gain his attention. By the end of the skit, his wife, played by May, had an earring dangling from her nose, a lit cigarette inside her ear, an unlit cigar in her mouth, and her husband's bowler hat on her head. It may not sound very funny, and it wasn't.

In structure, the controversial three-part sketch was vintage Nichols and May, with Tom Smothers inheriting the Nichols role. In the first part, Tom Smothers and Elaine May played censors, taking notes on a film they were watching. TV viewers saw Tom and Elaine staring straight ahead and the movie projector flickering over their heads, but saw no movie images themselves. "I want the word 'breast' taken out of the dinner scene," she complained, suggesting substitutions: arm first, then wrist. "My heart beats wildly in my wrist whenever you're near" becomes the accepted change. In the second part, the duo again play censors, but different characters. This time they're conservative, married censors—and not married to each other, either, though what they see onscreen causes their glasses to fog and compels Tom to grab Elaine's knee in a fit of passion and exclaim, "My heart beats wildly in my wrist whenever you're near!" In the final part, they play two fashionably dressed young people, watching the movie in a theater and being dumbfounded, rather than shocked, by the inanity of the film's dialogue, especially the "heart beats wildly in my wrist" line.

The first draft of the sketch, suggested by May and expanded upon by the Smothers staff, was less subtle, and was toned down by May. As she explained at the time, "The original script I received was full of innuendos and was about censoring movies that are obviously dirty, with titles like 'Black Whips and Red Lips' and 'Wild Strawberries and Sour Cream over Naked Flesh.' I thought I was toning it down."

Not enough, though, for CBS, which objected to all three

sketches, even in their revised script form. Specifically, there were issues with the "heart beats wildly in my breast" line that was the basis of all three connected sketches, and with the second sketch, which showed two censors worked up into a frenzy by the material they were watching. The network wanted those changes made, but Tom held firm, arguing that May was a comic writer of stature and that it would be insulting to edit material she had helped craft especially for the show. Invoking his supposed right of creative control, Tom demanded that the trio of "Clean Movies" sketches be rehearsed and taped without any editorial changes. They were. But once they were taped, the battle only escalated.

Tom recalls going into an office with CBS executives Mike Dann, Perry Lafferty, and Tom Dawson to view the skits, with the agreement that if the material as performed was funny, it could stay in the show. One Tom, the one in the sketches, thought it was funny. The other Tom, then the CBS Network president, did not. Tom Smothers refused to approve isolated edits or changes. As he explained in a deposition for his eventual court case against CBS: "I never said it was all or nothing. There was no alternative. I felt it was all. I didn't think it would be nothing."

In the end, it was Dawson's call—and he chose nothing, demanding that all three sketches, adding up to eleven full minutes of air time, be cut from the show.

"If it was cut," explained Perry Lafferty, Dann's West Coast assistant at CBS, "that became a management decision. Censors would never have the authority. So it had to be taken up to the president of the network . . . the program head and the president had to say 'cut it.' The censors would never do that alone."

Nor, had it gotten back to the head CBS censor in New York, would the sketch even have raised an objection. That's one of the major revelations about this pivotal confrontation in the history of CBS and the Smothers Brothers: had the standoff been considered serious enough to involve standards and practices boss William L. Tankerlsey, who was not consulted on the appropriateness of the "censor" sketch, he now says he would have approved it.

"When the Elaine May thing came up, I hadn't heard of it," Tankersley told me in 2008. "Our president at the time, Tom Dawson, was out there, and he got wind of that, and he turned it down. I didn't see it. To be perfectly honest with you, I would have accepted it. It was a funny scene . . . It's hilarious! And I would have said, 'Look, fellas. You're not going to make fun of the censors, but that's a funny scene. As a onetime thing, you've got it.' " Instead, Dawson got his way, wielding his power in a way that would turn Tom Smothers from loyal employee to agitating adversary. "No president ever interfered before," Tankersley said of Dawson's unilateral decision. "He was defending a department as best he could, but it wasn't wise, in my opinion."

Mason Williams, recalling the timidity of network television at that time, said, "You couldn't say the word 'pregnant,' you couldn't say 'God.' " The Smothers Brothers never expected May's skit to be that sensitive or received so negatively. Ken Kragen, one of their managers at the time, found himself trying to act as a buffer between Tom and the network and having a difficult time making total sense of either side. As for Tom's insistence that he had creative control, Kragen tried to explain the distinction to his client this way: "Creative control, yes. Ability to do anything you wanted, no." At the same time, Kragen found it absurd that real censors objected to fake censors saying, "You can't say 'breasts' on television," on television.

"It was dramatic because it was asinine," Kragen said. "God, on British television at that point, you could say anything. When the Smothers Brothers' show was ultimately syndicated to England right in that same time period, because it was the hottest show in America or one of the hottest, the British looked at it and went, 'What's the

controversy about? . . . This isn't controversial at all.' They were saying 'fuck' on English television in those days. It didn't translate."

Mason Williams agreed. "We were not very much aware of the
censors when we first started," he said. "They'd keep a low profile.
I'm convinced that one of the things CBS didn't like about the [Elaine
May] show was that we pointed out that there *were* censors and gave
them a persona. In other words, we basically said, these are the guys
that own the saloon and wear a black hat. It's not really true," he
added with a chuckle and a shrug. "It was two guys."

To Tom, though, the censors suddenly were the men behind the
curtain, and he was just as upset that his contractually promised creative control didn't hold up in practice as he was that objections had
been raised in the first place.

"That was probably the first time I really was angry," he admitted. "I kept saying, 'I've got creative control!' They said, 'Well, Program Practices. We have our rules.' I said, 'Where are the rules?
Show me the rules so I can adjust to these rules.' And the rules were
'No vulgarity,' that kind of thing. But that was the extent of it. So
there *were* no rules."

Director Stan Harris saw Tom boil over when CBS wouldn't
back down. "Tommy, like [he did] later on, threatened to leave the
show," Harris said. "I don't know how they calmed him down, but
he was furious. I must say," Harris added, "that not many other people were that adamant. We were incensed, but I would never say, 'I'm
going to quit the show.'"

Tom did threaten to quit but capitulated and worked with the
show's producers to replace the objectionable material in time for
broadcast. There was plenty of time, because *The Smothers Brothers
Comedy Hour* was being preempted April 2 for a rebroadcast of the
previous year's *Death of a Salesman* special—a brilliant version of the
Arthur Miller classic, starring Lee J. Cobb as Willy Loman. That

preemption would come in handy for another reason as well, but neither CBS nor the Smothers Brothers were aware of that yet.

Meanwhile, there was a censored show to doctor. Some of the missing eleven minutes were filled by an extra Esther Ofarim number already in the can, and the rest by a lengthy question-and-answer session from the fourth show. Tom and Dick took questions from the audience at both the afternoon (dress) and evening (air) tapings that day. One set of Q&A exchanges, from the evening taping, was broadcast in that fourth program. The other, from the afternoon dress rehearsal, was recorded but shelved, then unearthed to replace the scuttled Elaine May sketches. Look closely and you'll see Tom and Dick wearing outfits and standing in front of scenery that appear nowhere else in the ninth show, but do match those from episode four. Yet it worked, because Tom and Dick were so casually entertaining: like the Beatles at press conferences, they were quick on their feet and could come up with a witty rejoinder to almost any query. (Man in audience: "Does it pay to act ignorant?" Tom: "Very well." Woman in audience: "Could you say hello to my son, who's thirteen today?" Tom: "You don't look like you're old enough to have a son thirteen years old. Twenty-two, twenty-three . . . but thirteen?" Audience member: "Which of you is the kid brother?" Tom and Dick, pointing to each other: "He is.") "When they would do these question-and-answer pieces," Mason Williams recalled, "sometimes they would be ten or twelve minutes long, because you could just edit them down to whatever size you wanted."

Tom could claim one piece of satisfaction from the otherwise gutted Elaine May show, however. The Smothers Brothers' opening number that week was "Cabbage," a song from their second album. It was a song about workmen toiling to build the transcontinental railroad, and Tom, painting a slightly different word picture than he did on their 1962 album, described the railway workers as "inching their way across the vast bosom of America." When the audience laughed, Tom smiled mischievously and said, "Thought I'd throw a little sex in the show." So while there was no "breast" in that week's show, at least there was a "bosom."

And though CBS won that battle, the network did not emerge unscathed. One week after the censored *Comedy Hour* appeared on CBS, one of the censored skits written by Elaine May appeared for all to see—reprinted in full in the *New York Times*.

Bylined "by Elaine May," the sketch was prefaced with the following italicized explanation: *"This is the first part of a three-part sketch that Miss May wrote for 'The Smothers Brothers.' It was ruled out for 'bad taste.' "* Then came the full sketch—slightly different, in parts, from the one recorded for the show, since both Elaine and Tom improvised certain lines, but certainly close enough to make the point and to include the word *breast*.

Tom insists he didn't leak the script but was delighted that it was printed by the *Times,* and admitted it was a trick he learned to employ from then on. ("Oh, yeah," Tom said, referring to subsequent squabbles with CBS and how he'd amass public support. "I'd pick up the phone and call someone at one of the papers. I wouldn't even know him.") *The Smothers Brothers Comedy Hour* had discovered an important ally.

"You could read it," Dick Smothers said about the reprinted sketch, "and say, 'There's nothing offensive about that' . . . It's so stupid anybody would even *care* about censoring that!"

"The newspaper was not lined up with TV the way it is today," Mason Williams explained. "We started realizing that we could play one against the other. We could go to the press and address our grievances, in a format that was news . . . We started realizing that we could use the press as leverage against the censors."

Also in the *New York Times*, Tom was quoted then as accusing CBS of "a real infringement of our creative rights," and, describing the meeting in which Dawson, Dann, and Lafferty accused Tom and

Dick of "bad taste" for the censorship sketch, both named and slammed the network executives. "It left me with a great amount of disrespect for them as far as *their* taste is concerned, and you can quote me on that." The paper quoted him on that. More than a decade before the existence of *People* magazine or *Entertainment Tonight*, it was a rare on-the-record look at backstage bickering regarding a hit TV show.

"I think the network got Tom's attention by doing that," Mason Williams said. "Because it was after that ninth show that more and more of this [controversial material] began to creep into the script and into the show." If CBS hadn't drawn a line in the sand over the Elaine May sketches, Williams concluded, *The Smothers Brothers Comedy Hour* "probably would have continued in a more traditional vein." Telling Tom no, in Williams's opinion, "was a big mistake."

Becoming More Creative, and More Substantive

As Tom and Dick engaged in their first serious fight with CBS, the entertainment industry itself was embroiled in an even larger battle of its own. On March 29, 1967, the American Federation of Television and Radio Artists (AFTRA) authorized the first strike in its history. It was a fight over staff announcer contracts and first-time newsmen salary levels—a very limited segment of the AFTRA membership—but the guild, eighteen thousand members strong, supported the work stoppage, and virtually all TV production ground to an instant halt. Johnny Carson refused to host *The Tonight Show* during the strike, and when NBC began rerunning episodes without his approval, he quit in protest entirely, though he returned three weeks later with a much fatter contract. Respected CBS News anchor Walter Cronkite refused to cross the picket line, and so did NBC's David Brinkley, though Chet Huntley, his on-air partner on *The Huntley-Brinkley Report,* carried on without him. The strike lasted only thirteen days and was stopped just in time, virtually to the minute, to facilitate the live broadcast of that year's Academy Awards telecast on April 10.

The night before the Oscars, CBS broadcast the absurdly censored Elaine May edition of *The Smothers Brothers Comedy Hour,* the last installment taped before the AFTRA strike stopped production. When the strike ended, the only way CBS could get a fresh *Comedy Hour* onto the air the following Sunday was to speed up the production schedule considerably. Instead of a leisurely nine days between taping and telecast, there was a two-day turnaround: tapings on Fridays, broadcasts on Sundays. And since there was no scheduled preemption until the series went on summer hiatus, the Smothers Brothers would maintain that same frenzied pace, working almost without a net, for the rest of the 1966–67 TV season. If, as they say, the show must go on, they'd have to. And the *Comedy Hour* gang loved it. Pushing up the deadline not only made the comedy more topical but also gave CBS less time to mess with it.

"If there was one moment when we had our chance, when the opening was there to drive through," Ken Fritz says, "that was it." He added, "It was like you had a direct megaphone from Television City to everybody in the country."

The brothers pounced on the opportunity immediately. In the opening moments of the first show after the strike, Dick talked of being glad to be back, while Tom claimed he enjoyed the strike, didn't forgive that easily, and spun around his guitar to show a placard on the back saying, ON STRIKE and UNFAIR! The brothers agreed to disagree, and Dick segued to the opening credits by saying "Good night, David," to Tom, who replied, "Good night, Chet." Those were the nightly signoffs by *The Huntley-Brinkley Report* coanchors— and the Smothers Brothers, by taking opposite sides of the AFTRA strike issue, were reminding viewers that Huntley and Brinkley had done the same.

The following week's show began with another ripped-from-the-headlines topic and a subversive political subtext. On the morning of April 21, 1967, the day episode eleven of *Comedy Hour* was taped, a right-wing military junta took control of the government of Greece. At virtually the last minute, Tom and Dick substituted an opening welcome that would be seen by American viewers two days later, one in which Tom wants to be the first to recognize this new Greek government, while Dick, ever the calming influence, explains that's not up to Tom to do. But Tom persists, saying he likes the way, in Greece, they "threw up the government." Dick corrects him, saying he meant threw *out* or threw *over,* but Tom stands firm: "They got sick of the government, and just *blecch!,* threw it up!"

That would have been an innocuous bit of topical humor, but Tom didn't stop there. "Even right here in this country," he shouts defiantly to Dick and the studio audience, "if there's something we don't like, we have the right, as members of this country, to stand right up and throw the government right out! March right over, and throw them right out!"

"Wait a minute, Tommy," Dick says sternly. "You *love* this country."

"I know I love this country," Tom replies. "I'm not too sure about the *government!*"

"That is *not* how he feels!" Dick says, turning directly to the audience. "Tommy does *not* advocate throwing over the government." Then, turning back to his brother, Dick says, "You don't, do you?"

"I don't advocate throwing over the government," Tom admits sheepishly. Then, with a smile, he adds, "I was just saying that to keep them on their toes."

What an amazing sentiment for a prime-time variety series to present, even in jest, given the tensions of the times. And the brothers' brazenness didn't stop there. The next show, Dick all but dares Tom to be controversial again, asking him to name the most surprising thing that had happened in the world that week. This was a week in which, among other things, heavyweight champion Muhammad Ali had been stripped of his title because of his opposition to the Vietnam War—but Tom goes the lighter route, citing instead Elvis

Presley's marriage to Priscilla Beaulieu. "That knocked me out," Tom says with a goofy grin. "Six days, he's been married now. Six days—that's a Hollywood record!" Despite that toothless opening, though, the Smothers Brothers conclude with a bold antiwar bite.

After Dick notes that the following Sunday will be Mother's Day, Tom addresses the TV audience sincerely and says, "There's a very special Mother's Day card that has been put out this year. It's not for you to send, it's for your mother to send. It's a mother's prayer for peace, and it's beautifully written. The ladies who worked it up are hoping that a million mothers will send this card to their congressmen and senators." Dick adds, "And this will also show the president that the people of this country will support every effort he makes in his quest for world peace."

Tom then displays the front of the card, with its childish scrawl and crayon-drawn flower, and reads the cover message written and designed (originally for an art show) by Lorraine Schneider. The message is now famous and sounds harmless, but back then it was brand-new and politically divisive. The message: "War is not healthy for children and other living things." (Tom misreads the message slightly, on-air proof of his struggle with dyslexia.) Tom also reads the inside of the card, which is even more direct: "For my Mother's Day gift this year," it reads, "I don't want candy or flowers. I want an end to killing. We who have given life must be dedicated to preserving it. Please talk peace." Tom and Dick offer their address at Television City, telling viewers to write if they're interested in ordering cards, and that their mail will be forwarded to the proper place. (That place was Another Mother for Peace, a new activist movement spearheaded by TV writer-producer Barbara Avedon, then a scriptwriter on such shows as *Bewitched* and later the creator of the feminist flashpoint *Cagney & Lacey*.) CBS was incensed—"We do not permit political positions," executive Mike Dann scolded them after the show was taped, referring to his network's entertainment shows—and the entire closing was cut by the network before the show aired.

On those same shows, other barriers were being tested. The first poststrike show ended with a finale called "Doors," where doors of various shapes and sizes were opened to reveal Tom, Dick, and the rest of the company dispensing rapid-fire one-liners. This was in April 1967—five months before NBC presented the first pilot special for *Rowan & Martin's Laugh-In*, whose "comedy wall" was built on the same premise. On another *Comedy Hour*, Nancy Wilson was a prominently featured guest and sang a playful duet with Tom at a time when the mere appearance of black entertainers on TV still could, and in this case did, generate hate mail. Yet another show ended with a comic sketch called "Phantom of the Discotheque," in which Dick played a long-haired deejay named Larry Stanley Dillinger (" . . . affectionately known as old LSD," a line that was targeted by censors), and guest star Dom DeLuise plays a trigger-happy cop who shoots Tom's Phantom in the back and only *then* says, "Stop, or I'll shoot!"

"That was one of the first digs at law enforcement," Mason Williams says. "It was subtle; you might not even notice it. But there were discussions [of police brutality] at the time, so that some people would get that. It passed through [the censors] without remark. They didn't get it. They just thought it was a benign joke, but other people read stuff into it."

Pat Paulsen delivered two more editorials during this stretch, one on the "War on Poverty" ("You can't just give poor people money—poor people will just go out and buy clothes and pay rent") and another on "Should Our Divorce Laws Be Changed?" ("Why can't a man go into court and calmly say, under oath, 'I hate her guts'? Or a woman say, 'I hate *his* guts'? Or, in the case of a bigamist, 'I hate *their* guts'?") Pat also dressed up as Smokey the Bear, making fun of a popular public service announcement by asking, "What is the number-one cause of forest fires?"—and answering, to the studio audience's delight, "Trees." It was during this first poststrike run of shows that Pat began being billed in the opening credits. Pat Paulsen had officially arrived.

Tom's eye for talent, and desire to push boundaries, continued with musical guest stars as well. Jefferson Airplane, a new San Francisco rock group, taped its first *Comedy Hour* appearance *before* its first single, "Somebody to Love," entered the Top 40. On that May 7 show, most viewers were seeing and hearing lead singer Grace Slick and the rest of the Airplane members for the first time—and, most likely, seeing the light-show elements behind them for the first time as well. As Slick sang "Somebody to Love," Tom simultaneously showcased Glenn McKay, the artist who developed the concept of dropping colored oils and waters into trays and projecting the images onto the background as what he called psychedelic light shows. Unlike Buffalo Springfield, whose tone was softened by inserted comedy bits, Jefferson Airplane was presented at full strength, and the week that performance was televised, the group sold thousands of records and earned its first hit.

"That was produced live," Mason recalls of McKay's visuals. "He was performing at the same time they were." Ken Kragen adds, "Nowadays it would seem a little tame, but it was revolutionary at the time. It was really something fresh and new that nobody else was doing." Grace Slick caught on to the brothers' hidden counterculture sensibility right away: "They looked like just nice, next-door guys—and they weren't. They were really tilted."

How tilted—and how gifted—became apparent in the next hour, the fourteenth and best show of the first season. The guest roster was typically eclectic: It included Simon and Garfunkel (seven months before the duo's music would be used throughout the hit movie *The Graduate*) and actress Janet Leigh (seven years after she had starred in Alfred Hitchcock's *Psycho*). The hour included sharp jabs at censorship and the CIA, and ended with an intentionally unsettling commentary on the unequally approved limits of sex and violence on television. But from start to finish, while ambitiously trying to say so much in a mass-medium network variety show, the hour succeeded at being very funny, entertaining, musical, as well as bold.

On this Mother's Day show, Tom and Dick pay homage to mothers by having Janet Leigh play an atypically sexy representation of a sweet old mom, and by, for the second time in the series, recognizing their own mother in the audience. Simon and Garfunkel sang two songs—their latest single, "59th Street Bridge Song (Feelin' Groovy)," on which Tom and Dick join in at the end, and "Cloudy," which is shot in the style of a music video long before that term had even been coined. "Cloudy" was an album track from *Parsley, Sage, Rosemary and Thyme*, Simon and Garfunkel's latest LP, and was another example of the Smothers Brothers encouraging their musical guests to do what they wanted. "Paul was very shy at the time," Tom says. "I was a big fan of his. I always thought that he was pretty deep." Mason adds, "We were so enamored, Tommy and I, of the Simon and Garfunkel album that had these songs on it . . . This was a big thrill for us."

In short segments, Tom and Dick take aim at both CBS and the government. For the former, Tom and Dick make their first defiant stand against, and on-air mention of, the network censors. Brandishing the Elaine May script of the sketch that had been banned from broadcast a few shows before, Dick says, "The censors, for various reasons of their own, they just didn't let us show it." Tom adds, "The sketch was about censors," drawing a laugh from the studio audience. Then Dick says, "They decided we could show it to you after all," and Tom holds up the script itself. "Page three," he says. "This page was especially well written." Then Tom says, looking directly into the camera, "Elaine, we *told* you we'd get this sketch on!" They were letting the national audience know they'd been stifled—perhaps the first time an entertainer had done that on TV since Jack Paar walked off the *Tonight* show in protest of the censored water closet joke.

Another segment, taking aim at the Central Intelligence Agency, features young comic Jim Connell, playing a nervous, meek CIA agent interviewed by Dick about his top-secret clandestine activities. "This is the first time I know of any show bringing on a CIA agent," Dick announces proudly. When Dick asks how many communists the CIA has uncovered, the agent replies, "Not counting our own men? Four thousand men and women, and a dog." Dick asks, "How can a dog be a communist?" And the agent replies, "I don't know. We tortured him, and he wouldn't talk." At the end of the interview, the agent says he's about to parachute into an international trouble spot. "Asia?" Dick guesses. "Berkeley," the agent replies. Tricky stuff, for 1967. So was the show's good-bye segment, when Tom and Dick addressed the audience and turned very serious. "Today is Mother's Day 1967," Dick says. "And it is really not a very happy occasion for thousands of mothers in our country, and throughout the world. Because their sons are not with them on this day, but instead are at war." "So won't you please join us tonight," Tom adds, "in the sincere hope and plea to all the world leaders that next year will be a happy and much more peaceful one."

In addition to all that, in this one exceptional hour, were two terrific set pieces. The first featured Janet Leigh and Tom in an enactment of "The Last Great Waltz," the Mason Williams composition recorded by Tom and Dick two years earlier. The song tells of a waltzing master who is so good that no one dares dance with him—until he meets a woman with a peculiar physical attribute . . . a third leg. The rest of the sketch has jokes that are both physical (Leigh appearing to dance on a tripod of high-heeled legs) and musical (with Janet Leigh counting 1,2,3 and Tom counting 1,2, moving their feet accordingly, the song pays off with a new double meaning provided by Mason as the closing lyric: "Though we are different, we took a chance / and found true love in an offbeat romance").

Comedy Hour writer Allan Blye says, "It was brilliant musically *and* lyrically. The concept of a great waltzer with three legs, who meets a great waltzer who has two legs, and they do it in five-four time—it was brilliant. And on television, it was absolutely right."

Guest star Janet Leigh also figured in the show's ambitious finale, "Billy the Kid's Birthday Party." At thirteen minutes, it was the longest TV sketch the Smothers Brother would ever present, and it made room for everybody. Leigh plays Belle Starr, the sexy saloon keeper. Pat Paulsen plays Doc Holliday, Dick plays Frank James, and featured players Jim Connell and Hamilton Camp play Bat Masterson and Jesse James, respectively. All are done up in Western garb, as are the skit's balladeer narrators, Paul Simon and Art Garfunkel. They sing special lyrics, written by Mason, to the tune of the traditional folk song "John Hardy Was a Desperate Little Man," the 1928 Carter Family recording of which was part of Harry Smith's seminal *Anthology of American Folk Music,* which Paul Simon, like Bob Dylan and anyone else deeply into folk music in the 1960s, revered almost as a musical bible. "This was something these guys could get into easily," Mason says of Simon and Garfunkel. "Simon wouldn't do something silly or too stupid. But he liked the fact that we were trying to make a philosophical point."

Tom plays Billy the Kid, who is a reluctant guest at his own surprise party. Eventually, when presented with a birthday cake, he refuses to make a wish, then wishes he were dead. Obligingly, all the Western outlaws draw their six-shooters, and Billy is about to die—until Frank stops everyone and says, "Maybe killing's not the answer. Maybe *love* is the answer." Billy accepts the suggestion and grabs Belle, ready for passion, but she stops him. "You can't do that in front of millions of people," she tells him. Doc Holliday objects, too. "You can't do that on television—make love," he tells Billy. "That's disgusting." Bat Masterson agrees: "You can kill on TV, but you can't make love." Billy looks confused: "That don't seem right. That seems weird." "We're just wasting time," Belle says. "Love just ain't acceptable." They all take aim at Billy, say "Happy birthday, kid," and fire. He slumps to the ground, clutches his chest, and starts gasping. Belle leans over him and whispers, "Hey, kid, I thought this was supposed to be a *comedy* show." "Well," Billy says, "you can't be funny *all* of the time." And he dies. Simon and Garfunkel, to the tune of "John Hardy," sing the closing moral: "No, you can't be funny all of the time. Sometimes there's things to say / And the least expected time and place / Can give impact to what you say . . . Like Billy the Kid's death day."

Anyone who still considered *The Smothers Brothers Comedy Hour* "the least expected time and place" to encounter "things to say," after this ambitious hour, simply wasn't paying attention.

11

Homegrown Talent: Pat Paulsen, Leigh French, Mason Williams

Most people close to Tom Smothers agree that one of his biggest passions, and greatest gifts, is discovering and nurturing new talent. The final shows of the first season are a perfect illustration of this. Pat Paulsen developed from an unknown walk-on to a beloved star delivering comic editorials and giving the writers one guaranteed spot where issues could be addressed head-on. Leigh French, a member of the Committee comedy troupe, is introduced as a "member of the audience" during a question-and-answer session and charms them so completely that she returns the following season as a regular. And Mason Williams, after serving as one of the show's writers all season and having many of his songs performed by others, steps into the spotlight himself for the first year's final show. A year later, his recording of "Classical Gas" would give him a number-two *Billboard* hit. By season two of *Comedy Hour*, all three of these Tom Smothers discoveries were stars, sharing top billing whenever they appeared on the program.

"I was always looking for new people," Tom says. "I absolutely fell in love with talent." He claims Pat Paulsen as his first real discovery, and Leigh French and Mason Williams as other early ones. "If I thought they were good, I was arrogant enough to assume that everybody would understand and agree with my taste. That *this* is funny, that *that* is a good singer—and to have that platform to present it was just great . . . I was so excited to be able to present a new song or someone they hadn't heard before."

Tom's instincts as a discoverer and nurturer of new talent were excellent. Appearances on *The Smothers Brothers Comedy Hour* helped propel the careers of so many talents—including Glen Campbell, George Carlin, John Hartford, David Steinberg, and the Who—it's tempting to imagine what might have been, had the show remained on the air a few more years, with Tom unearthing and showcasing talent into 1970 and beyond. It's not that much of a stretch to envision Tom Smothers, not Lorne Michaels of *Saturday Night Live*, as the tenured tastemaker, in both comedy and music, for a new generation of TV viewers.

But in May 1967, still turning shows around on a two-day deadline, Tom was less concerned with building an empire than with getting to the finish line. After the "Billy the Kid" show, there were seven hours left to produce, including one that would be put on ice until the following New Year's Eve. Luckily, Tom had friends on whom he could call for help, including Steve Allen, who had given the Smothers Brothers their first jobs as part of a comic ensemble, and singer John Gary, from whose summer variety show Tom recruited a lot of backstage and onstage talent. Even more luckily, the ratings, and thus the viewers, were with him, giving Tom more muscle to follow his own instincts.

NBC's *Bonanza* had begun a cycle of summer reruns at that point, but that hardy Western, like crime procedurals in a more modern TV era, proved almost as popular the second time around. Even so, of the five remaining *Comedy Hour* shows rated by Nielsen that season, two of them beat *Bonanza* outright and won their Sunday time slot. (In its last two-week rating period for the season, *Comedy Hour* was ranked ninth, *Bonanza* fifth.) And while the network's practice of promoting its own stars was still in evidence, with Martin Landau and Barbara Bain from *Mission: Impossible* guest starring on one show and Jim Backus from *Gilligan's Island* on another, other bookings were less conventional. Sonny and Cher showed up, providing ample evidence of the chemistry they would provide when given their own CBS variety show four years later. Former child star Margaret O'Brien made her first TV variety show appearance in a decade, and the Association and Jefferson Airplane made return visits, performing new songs before they entered the Top 40: "Windy" and "White Rabbit" respectively—the latter, once again, backed by fiercely psychedelic images, as Grace Slick sang, "Remember what the dormouse said: Feed your head." One week after its *Comedy Hour* unveiling, "White Rabbit" was a Top 10 hit, and "Windy" went all the way to number one.

During this period, while the Smothers Brothers didn't get into any headline-making trouble, they still continued to get in a jab or two, and a jam or two, almost every week. The weekly "cold open," the brief intro where Tom and Dick would talk briefly before the opening credits, remained a way to play off recent headlines and events. In one, Tom notes the problems America is having with certain of its allies, and also notes the US military budget of $50 billion annually—concluding that, with that price tag, "We don't need more allies. We need more enemies." In another, Tom notes that high school and college students are about to graduate, and Dick says simply, "Things are a little messed up right now." Tom offers a message to the graduating class of 1967: "Soon you'll be leaving those hallowed halls and those walls of ivy, and those segregated schools, and go face the world, with its tenseness, turmoil, and tumult. But be not afraid. Throw your chest out and keep your backbone straight. Keep your head up high, keep your eyes on the sky. Throw your chin out," Tom says, "and you'll walk right into a truck." The punch line is goofy, but the premise, which got out to the national audience, was dead serious. And the week after the Emmy Awards, Tom uses the opening moments of his show to thank the academy for awarding *Comedy Hour* an Emmy, until Dick corrects him, pointing out that *The Andy Williams Show* won in their category instead. "I must have been more stoned that night than I thought." At a pivotal point in the culture when "stoned" meant drunk to one generation and high to another, that one slipped through.

Other segments, though, caused more problems. A sketch called "One Man's Country," billed as "a political soap opera of the sixties," starred Jim Backus as an LBJ caricature called Father Barbecue, sporting a "Hail to the Chef" barbecue apron. (It was an allusion, explains original *Comedy Hour* writer-producer Ernest Chambers, to the vintage *One Man's Family* radio serial, which centered on a stockbroker named Henry Barbour, known as Father Barbour, and family.) Margaret O'Brien played his Southern-accented daughter, and Tom played his potential son-in-law, who had punctured an eardrum to avoid the draft. CBS executive Frank Stanton, a close friend of President Johnson, wasn't happy about the sketch—but neither was Tom. It was a last-second replacement for a sketch that hadn't quite developed to anyone's satisfaction. "It was an emergency fix," Mason says. "Of all the pieces the show did, this is the one Tommy hated the most or thought was the most artless."

The same show closed with two segments whose objections by program practices, in retrospect, seem absurdly silly. In their closing good-byes, Tom and Dick were permitted to announce they were profiled in the current issues of a national magazine but forbidden from identifying the publication. "We can't tell you which one," Tom says wickedly, "but go down to your newsstand and take a *Look*." Just before that, a sketch features Tom and Dick, in red jerseys and white vaudeville-era skimmers, singing "The Banana Pickers Song," after a comic preface in which they rave about bananas and their uses. "We peel them and we puff them as fast as we can," Tom jokes.

Indicative of how humorless the overall climate was in 1967, that sketch elicited an immediate response from the Banana Council of Southern California, who fired off a letter to the show. "We must point out," insisted one paragraph of the three-page letter, "that various governmental studies and our own studies have been unable to find any of the effects or qualities attributed to the banana by the young people who smoke the dried lining of the fruit. We feel that we must ask that a public retraction on a subsiquent [sic] program be made." And, yes, CBS made the brothers provide that retraction, on the very next show. "Last week we had a song about bananas," Tom said during a Q&A segment, "and we had some repercussions from the banana industry, and we want to apologize . . ." Dick added, "We demeaned the banana, and we didn't really mean to." Tom, though, got the last laugh, literally, by holding a different fruit and saying, just before popping it into his mouth, "We have a tangerine now—and does anybody in the audience have a match?"

Nothing allowed the program to delve more overtly into the drug culture, though, than Leigh French. A fresh member of the San Francisco improvisational comedy troupe the Committee, she caught the eye of writer-producer Ernest Chambers, and of Tom, who immediately set about concocting ways of working her flower-child aura and comedy into the show. The first attempt, a slam-dunk success, introduced her the same way Tom had worked Pat Paulsen into one of the program's first shows, by hiding her in the audience and calling upon her for what appeared to be a spontaneous conversation. And, for the most part, it was.

Initially, the writers had concocted a skit featuring Leigh French, based on the Berkeley radical character she performed in the Committee. But when she met with the writing and production staff, she politely refused the concept. She and Tom chatted about the changing times—peace, drugs, music, freedom, alternative lifestyles—and it became clear to everyone in the room that she was very funny, with an improviser's quick wit. More important, in those earliest days of flower power, Leigh French clearly was the real deal. She had split her time between San Francisco, performing with the Committee and attending all the various be-ins, and living in a teepee in New Mexico. She was a beautiful young woman, with straight brown hair tied in long pigtails adorned with daisies. Listening to the topics and byplay between Tom and Leigh, one of the staffers said, "Let's write that!" And again, Leigh politely demurred. "I said, 'Let's *don't* write that.' Let's just rap.'" (Rap, younger readers might be relieved to know, at that time meant "to talk.")

So they did. On that June 1967 show, Tom begins the spot by standing onstage alone, leading the audience in a sweet but serious sing-along version of "If I Had a Ship" (a Kingston Trio song from 1965, written, notably, by Mason Williams). Still singing and strumming, Tom descends the stairs of the stage, walks along the front row of the audience, and notices a young woman in the second row, daisies in her hair, wearing a bright yellow dress. She isn't singing along—she's playing along, twanging a Jew's harp held between her lips. Tom asks her to stand, and they begin talking. It's a wonderful bit, and there's the sense that the audience never suspects it's watching something staged. Tom, for one of the few times on *Comedy Hour*, plays the straight man, feeding questions to Leigh and reacting to her laid-back comments with surprise, delight, and confusion. Except for a handful of talking points to rely upon as an outline and an agreed-upon name for her character, Tom and Leigh improvised the entire six-and-a-half-minute conversation. "It was absolutely not written," she says, calling the dialogue "very spontaneous and very real between the two of us."

When Tom singles her out, Leigh explains that she's hitchhiked to Los Angeles from the Haight-Ashbury district of San Francisco, and that she's in the *Comedy Hour* audience because "somebody laid a ticket on me to come here, and, y'know, anything that's free, y'know, is a groove." She adds, "TV is so weird, anyway, y'know. You never expect anything far-out to happen in a TV studio." But she compliments Tom on his sing-along, with its message of love and happiness. "I just started to blossom," she tells Tom. "I'm glad I could be part of that blossoming," Tom says, shooting a nervous, naughty look at the audience. "You really were, man. You really turned me on." Tom, after a pause Jack Benny would have admired, asks, "What do you mean, exactly, by 'turning you on'?" "Turn on," she explains, "is, like, if you press a certain button and you get kind of like a high-frequency response in your soul, sort of." And so it goes: Leigh tossing out the latest hippie slang, and Tom acting as a combination reporter-interpreter for Middle America. "You're really groovy, man," she tells him. "You're really too much. Wow. I love you." When he asks if she watches the show, she calls it one of the few "far-out" things on television. She mentions the bright colors and the fantasy sketches, and the psychedelic background behind the Jefferson Airplane, and says how much she enjoys watching his show on her TV—but with the sound off, and the vertical hold adjusted so the picture is rolling out of control, and while simultaneously playing music by the Beatles or the Mothers of Invention. "This is really the highest show I've ever been on," she says, "and I've never used television before." Asked for her favorite hippie slogan, she offers, with a sly smile, "Keep America green, folks—and grow oregano." The audience laughs deeply, and Tom, sensing the crowd's approval, takes the opportunity to shift gears and offer a more serious sentiment.

"We laugh a lot," Tom says, "but I would like to say to this young lady, and to a lot of young people around, I admire you and the thing that's happening, very much. Because it's all gentle, it's peace, and it's love, what they're trying to present." With gratitude, she presents him with a gift, making him an honorary flower child by handing him a small pouch filled with something that helps flowers grow. "Love?" Tom asks. "No," she says. "It's something that's really stronger than love: fertilizer." The segment ends with Tom asking her name. "Goldie," she says. "And what's your last name?" he asks. "Keefe," she replies. As she returns to her seat, the other audience members applaud her warmly.

Leigh French was twenty-one years old—nine years younger than Tom—when she made her first *Comedy Hour* appearance, and she was an immediate hit. The timing of her introduction was impeccable: the Beatles' *Sgt. Pepper's Lonely Hearts Club Band* had been released less than two weeks earlier, with the group's unprecedented sonic surrealism, colorful costumes, and flagrantly long hair and facial hair kicking off what came to be known as the Summer of Love. Leigh French and *The Smothers Brothers Comedy Hour* were right there from the start, reporting from the front, as comic correspondents poised on the edgy edge of the generation gap.

"In the original [outline]," Mason Williams explains, "We said, 'Let's give her the name Mary Jane Roach.' We did that on purpose, because we knew the censors would spot that, and we knew they'd come back to us right away and say, 'No, you can't say that'—because 'mary jane' is a joint, and, of course, a roach is a smoked joint. So we'd say, 'Okay, we'll just pick a different name . . . Acapulco gold was around at that time, and keefe was another name for marijuana as well. So we had already started to lay things into the script that we knew were going to come out. We put the most obvious things in the script, and had more subtle replacements already in mind." Tom reassured producer Ernie Chambers that the only drug references were the obvious "tea" and "high" jokes; and Chambers, in turn, reassured the network censors. "About a month later," Chambers recalls, "my wife and I were walking along the Sunset Strip, and we walked into a head shop and there was a big poster on the wall, and it said, 'A puff of keefe makes a man strong as a thousand camels.' I did not," Chambers adds, "share that information with Program Practices."

When she returned the following season as the slightly renamed Goldie O'Keefe, she was able to get away with even more drug-culture double entendre—partly because the censors still were a generation behind the times, and partly because Leigh was so fresh-faced and innocent-looking. "She was so beautiful," Mason recalls, watching a video of her first appearance. "She looks almost like an Indian maiden." "She was so stunning," Tom agrees. "Beautiful. It was really hard to work with her." He admits that at that point in his life, with his marriage dissolving, he was attracted to Leigh, and was by no means alone. "I mean, *everybody* was trying to get to her," he says, laughing. "With her pigtails, her beautiful eyes, that face—oh, yeah." He laughs even harder, remembering that no matter how much she bewitched the cast and crew, no one, according to Tom, got even close. She would, however, get noticed by the critics, and get rave notices, in season two when she began doing her "Share a Little Tea with Goldie" spots.

Meanwhile, season one was winding down, the show itself was generating national press, and so was its first breakout star, Pat Paulsen. Just as Leigh French was making her *Comedy Hour* TV debut, *Newsweek* was crediting Pat Paulsen with "some of the freshest comedy of the season," citing everything from his mock editorials to his Smokey the Bear. Simultaneously, *TV Guide* published a five-page cover story on the Smothers Brothers, billed as "the stars of the hottest new show on TV." Assessing what their *Comedy Hour* had accomplished against

NBC's *Bonanza* since February, *TV Guide* noted approvingly, "If the Brothers haven't won so far, neither have they lost. And against all that *Bonanza* beef, just holding one's own verges on the miraculous." The article also featured a rare interview with the boys' mother, at that time on her third marriage and known as Mrs. Ruth Berk. Asked if she really liked Dick best, the mother of three laughed and replied, "You love all your children. But that Tommy was the biggest bunch of trouble."

The day after taping the penultimate show of the first season, Tom and Mason took a road trip to Northern California and the Monterey International Pop Music Festival, held June 16 to 18. Attracting an estimated two hundred thousand fans, it was the first counterculture music festival of its kind, paving the way for Woodstock two summers later. For Tom and Mason, it was a new-talent-recruitment field trip.

Back at Television City, Tom still had two more TV shows to complete before taking a summer break. One was what was called a "banked" show—a program taped in June, yet held in reserve until December, when it would air as a New Year's Eve show (without forcing the cast or crew to work over the holidays). Because it wouldn't be seen for six months, it had to be entirely devoid of any topical references or material. It was a casual affair, featuring Eddie Albert, the Irish Rovers, and two old friends from the very early days of the Smothers Brothers. One was Judy Collins, who opened for them in Colorado when they made their 1960 debut as a duo. She appeared on *Comedy Hour* a full year before reaching the pop charts with her version of Joni Mitchell's "Both Sides Now." On this show, Collins beautifully covers "I Think It's Going to Rain Today," a song by a writer who had yet to record an album of his own, Randy Newman.

The other performer from the brothers' past was an even older acquaintance: Bobby Blackmore, who played with Tom and Dick in

1959, when the Smothers Brothers were starting out as a trio. Tom and Dick introduce him to the audience, explain their early history, and perform "Tzena, Tzena, Tzena," from the first Smothers Brothers LP. Blackmore, who played banjo and sang in the original act, plays tambourine and sings, adding a deeper voice to the mix, but not much else. The whole thing looks uncomfortable and strained, as if Pete Best had been asked by the Beatles to reunite for a one-shot appearance.

Tom accepts the Pete Best simile without hesitation. "Yeah, it was like that," he says. "It felt like that. We were not quite in sync."

The other, the final show of season one, was shown during a Nielsen ratings "dark week," when no ratings were tabulated, so there was no pressure to compete strongly against the other networks. And not only were there no ratings, there was no money. "We were over budget," says Stan Harris, who, after being one of several directors fired by Tom, returned for part of the second. "We didn't have any money left."

So the twentieth and final show of season one was conceived as a family affair, presenting not only highlights from previous shows (such as Bette Davis as Marie Antoinette) and a few pretaped and banked guest appearances (including Jefferson Airplane performing "White Rabbit"), but also a talent show featuring the program's resident company and backstage staff. The Jimmy Joyce Singers sing "The Bells of Rhymney," complete with hand-rung bells. The Louis DaPron Dancers got to strut their stuff—and, in the most unusual feature of the hour, so did writing partners Allan Blye and Mason Williams, in the world premiere performance of Mason's "*(Whistle) Hear!*" a song that eventually resurfaced on his *Mason Williams Ear Show* LP.

"It was really a wonderful moment for me," Blye says—and Mason, after taking this first on-camera step, soon would launch a successful recording career.

The *Comedy Hour* company, by this point, was exhausted. The second half of the season's shows had been produced under an unforgiving schedule. Tom had clashed more frequently, and angrily, with director Harris, and with writer-producers Chambers and Ilson and network executives. "To put a show on the air," Tom said at the end of the first-season finale, "it takes one hundred twenty-five people working against each other"—and there seemed to be some ring of truth to that punch line. "It's been a long, hard season," Dick said to Tom as they closed out that final first-season show, "and we're all looking forward to a little rest."

"The end of each season, going into summer," Mason says, "it's always like a shipwreck. And you're spit up on the beach, kind of wondering what happened."

What happened was this: *The Smothers Brothers Comedy Hour* had premiered at midseason as a desperation "Hail Mary" pass by CBS and ended the season, six months later, as a surprise hit.

Season Two:
Breaking the Blacklist of Pete Seeger

idway through the first season of *The Smothers Brothers Comedy Hour,* when ratings and a spirit of celebration were unexpectedly high, CBS executive Mike Dann flew to Los Angeles and visited the set to demonstrate his gratitude.

"You guys have done a great job," he said to Smothers associates Ken Kragen and Ken Fritz, referring to everyone working on the series. "What do you need, what do you want, what can the network do for you?"

Without hesitation, Fritz replied, "Give us Pete Seeger."

And with that, CBS and the Smothers Brothers embarked on one of the most memorable battles in their stormy three-year association—and emerged, finally, with a truly great moment in television history.

The Smothers Brothers had requested Seeger as a guest before, early on, but been turned down. The reason he topped their list was obvious. Not only was Seeger one of the most prominent and inspiring examples of an outspoken, liberal, and defiantly principled mass-market entertainer, but he was indirectly responsible for the Smothers Brothers having a career in the first place.

Seeger was a founding member of the Weavers, the folk quartet that almost singlehandedly jump-started the modern folk movement in the 1940s and 1950s. The group's first single was a two-sided smash, featuring a remake of Huddie Ledbetter's Depression-era "Goodnight Irene" and a translated version of the Israeli folk song "Tzena, Tzena, Tzena." The single topped the charts in the summer of 1950, paving the way for a string of folk hits—and an even longer string of very popular imitators and successors, including the Kingston Trio and Peter, Paul and Mary.

In that same summer of 1950, the book *Red Channels* was published. Subtitled *The Report of Communist Influence in Radio and Television*, it identified individuals and organizations it claimed had affiliations with, or sympathy for, the Communist Party. This publication (by *Counterattack* magazine, "the newsletter of facts to combat Communism," started by three former FBI agents) fed the communist witch hunts and gave ammunition to Republican senator Joseph McCarthy from Wisconsin, who rode his anticommunist crusade to temporary but formidable heights by relying on *Red Channels* and other uncorroborated sources. In the 1950s, if your name was in *Red Channels,* you stood a good chance of being effectively blacklisted from appearing on radio or TV—and Pete Seeger was listed, on page 130, as a "Folk Singer" with such allegedly subversive associations as singing at rallies for Yugoslav relief and May Day 1950.

Some of those accused in *Red Channels* were big enough, or fortunate enough, to escape relatively unscathed: Arthur Miller, Leonard Bernstein, Lee J. Cobb, Burl Ives. For others, it meant the end of a career, and, in at least one case, the end of a life. Philip Loeb, costar of the CBS sitcom *The Goldbergs*, was named in *Red Channels.* Despite his protestations of innocence, CBS and the show's sponsor, General Foods, dropped both him and the series. It reappeared, on NBC, a year later but without Loeb. In 1955, still a victim of the blacklist, Loeb killed himself.

Coincidentally, it was in 1955 that Seeger was called before the House Un-American Activities Committee to defend himself. By that time, the Weavers had disbanded (they staged a comeback concert later that year), but Seeger refused to be a cooperative witness. He also refused to take the Fifth Amendment, as many before him had done, and instead argued that while he was ready and eager to discuss his life and his music, other avenues of inquiry were none of the committee's business.

"I decline to discuss, under compulsion," he testified, "where I have sung, and who has sung my songs, and who else has sung with me, and the people I have known. I love my country very dearly, and I greatly resent this implication that some of the places that I have sung and some of the people that I have known, and some of my opinions—whether they are religious or philosophical, or I might be a vegetarian—make me any less of an American." Six years later, for refusing to answer questions posed by the HUAC, Seeger was convicted on ten counts of contempt of Congress and sentenced to a year in prison. A federal court of appeals unanimously reversed the decision in 1962, without Seeger's having to serve any time. Meanwhile, since being named in *Red Channels* in 1950, Seeger had not appeared on national television—and that unofficial but very effective blacklist didn't end with his successful court appeal.

From 1950 until 1967, Seeger's appearances on TV were few, fleeting, and sometimes downright sneaky. "I'd given up the idea of trying to do network TV," Seeger told me. "I would get on little local shows occasionally. I used to call it cultural guerrilla tactics. I'd be doing a concert at a college somewhere, and I'd drop down to the local TV station and say, 'I'm giving a concert tonight—could I mention it on your program?' They'd say, 'Oh, yeah, I remember the

Weavers and "Goodnight Irene"—what are you doing these days?' And I'd say, 'Well, I go from college to college singing,' and give a plug for it, and I'd be on my way before anybody could call up to object, 'Why did you let that commie bastard on there?' I was a moving target."

In the 1960s, despite the ongoing blacklist, Seeger found his way onto the fringes of network TV, appearing on a pair of unsponsored Sunday morning programs. One was the religious series *Lamp Unto My Feet,* and the other was the arts anthology *Camera Three.* Both series, coincidentally, were televised by CBS. And both of Seeger's appearances, by a somewhat staggering coincidence, were approved by William Tankersley, the CBS vice president for program practices who would be the network's head censor for all three years of *The Smothers Brothers Comedy Hour.*

"I'm the one that gave the okay for Sunday morning," Tankersley said of Seeger's unsponsored TV appearances. "We'd been trying to help him to restore his standing." Dann also took credit, though Tankersley disputed that.

In any event, when Seeger's name came up again as a possible guest on *The Smothers Brothers Comedy Hour*—now that the show was an unqualified hit and the brothers at this point had yet to cause much trouble with the network—the suggestion was met more receptively. Exactly why, and by whom, is harder to decipher.

Perry Lafferty, West Coast programming head for CBS, wrote in his unpublished memoir, *We Can Put the Laughs in Later,* that the breaking of the Seeger blacklist was political in more ways than one. It began, Lafferty said, when President Lyndon Johnson phoned from the White House to complain about a skit lampooning him. LBJ was calling the network, at his daughters' behest, to ask CBS to be more reasonable. The call, according to Lafferty, was placed from LBJ directly to CBS founder William S. Paley (even though Paley's second in command, Frank Stanton, was Johnson's close personal friend).

Paley called Mike Dann, who ran CBS entertainment in New York, who called Lafferty, and soon thereafter, Lafferty and *Comedy Hour* producers Saul Ilson and Ernie Chambers were summoned to New York by Paley, who asked them to please take it easier on LBJ, and asked, in return, "Is there anything I can do to help you keep the brothers in line?" Ilson, according to Lafferty, said yes: approve Seeger. Paley made the call to Dann, and that was that.

At least in that version. According to three separate interviews—with executive Dann and Smothers managers Kragen and Fritz—the offer to do something as a reward for high ratings came from Dann, and the instant Seeger request came from Fritz. Tankersley says Tom asked him directly, and he approved it, so long as Seeger didn't sing a controversial song. And according to Mason Williams, the request for the booking was at his instigation, once the show was proven popular. "Tommy had said to me, 'We can have anybody on the show we want, so who are your heroes?' And I said, right off the bat, 'One of my heroes is Pete Seeger.' " Any or all of those versions could be true, with each piece of the puzzle leading to, and interlocking with, another.

And clearly, Seeger was a hero to the Smothers Brothers as well. Their entire act, utilizing and joking around with folk music, owes everything to the stage persona and eclectic, ethnic repertoire of the Weavers. When Tom and Dick recorded their first album in 1961, one of the numbers they sang—and hilariously deconstructed and destroyed, while still playing and singing it wonderfully—was "Tzena, Tzena, Tzena," made famous eleven years before by the Weavers. "I wanted Seeger in because he's a famous folksinger," Tom said. "Like the Weavers and all those people, he's a legend to me."

The most persuasive account comes from writer-producer Saul Ilson, who corroborates Lafferty's account of meeting with Paley while adding some telling details. According to Ilson, President Johnson did indeed call Paley directly after the barbecue sketch—

phoning him at home at three o'clock in the morning—and, in Paley's words, "took my head off." Johnson was offended, and wanted the Smothers Brothers to lay off. "Look," Paley said to Ilson, "I don't appreciate being woken up by the president. Could you guys just lay off for a while?" When Ilson and Chambers agreed to try, the chairman of CBS offered a favor in return—and the producers immediately asked to book Seeger, whose prime-time TV appearances had been vetoed by the West Coast. "Go ahead and book him," Paley said just as quickly, Ilson recalls, and that was that.

In any case, the brothers were given the green light for Seeger, and the show instantly booked him as the second season's special opening guest. "We decided to put him on the season's first program," Chambers told the *New York Times* proudly in August 1967, "because it is the most significant thing we'll do all year." And when word got out, the letters poured in—tens of thousands of them, in advance of the program even being aired. "I am shocked you are considering putting on an anti-American nonentity such as Pete Seeger on the Smothers Brothers' show—and on the premiere, yet!" wrote one angry correspondent. "This is just a short thank-you note," wrote a more encouraging one, "for your courage in bringing to our screens a man who deserves to be heard and seen." Reaction was polarized, but, at that point, so was the entire country.

During the summer of 1967, the Summer of Love, every week seemed to present another seismic shift in pop culture or current events. It started on June 1, with the release of the Beatles' *Sgt. Peppers Lonely Hearts Club Band* and never let up. The Smothers Brothers were still taping the last of season one's shows in June when the Six-Day War erupted between Israel and Egypt, when *To Sir with Love* premiered in theaters, and when Scott McKenzie's anthem "San Francisco (Be Sure to Wear Flowers in Your Hair)" hit the Top 40, luring flower children and other free thinkers—including Tom Smothers and Mason Williams—to the Monterey Pop Festival.

The rest of the summer was no less lively. Number-one hits, in order, included Aretha Franklin's "Respect," the Association's "Windy," the Doors' "Light My Fire," and the Beatles' "All You Need Is Love"—an unbelievably diverse sampling of styles and messages. Movie screens were lit up by the violent slow-motion ballet of bullets in the climax of *Bonnie and Clyde* and by Sidney Poitier's defiant demand for racial equality in the Deep South detective drama *In the Heat of the Night* ("They call me *Mister* Tibbs!"). Race riots swept across Detroit, and LBJ announced plans to send 45,000 more troops to Vietnam. Along came Pete Seeger.

"Oh, that was a tremendous opportunity," Seeger said. "I thought very carefully of what I would do." He decided to open with "Wimoweh," an audience sing-along from his days with the Weavers (based on the same Zulu folk tune from Africa, "Mbube," that inspired the Tokens' 1961 pop hit "The Lion Sleeps Tonight"). He'd close with his own "Where Have All the Flowers Gone?" followed by a sing-along to "Guantanamera" and a portion of Woody Guthrie's "This Land Is Your Land," two songs with potent but understated messages. And in between, he'd present the title song from his brand-new album, a new composition called "Waist Deep in the Big Muddy." That was the plan, anyway.

Meanwhile, the Smothers Brothers, having secured enough of a triumph by booking Seeger, approached the rest of their second-season opener with a very nonthreatening attitude. Janet Leigh, who had performed so charmingly as a guest the previous season, was asked back, and Bobbie Gentry, whose "Ode to Billie Joe" was the country's number-one record, was invited on to sing that song and another number—and, as a bonus, to serve as an obvious bridge between Seeger's folk purism and the new genre known as folk rock. Pat Paulsen would do another editorial, but on a relatively benign topic, "Should Gambling Be Legalized?" When you have Pete Seeger as a guest, you don't need to make waves. You're already presenting a tsunami.

According to Lafferty, Seeger arrived in time for camera blocking the day before the show was taped. Among those sitting in the audience bleachers that day, in addition to Lafferty, were producer Ilson and one of the West Coast censors, Charles Pettijohn. When Seeger performed "Big Muddy," Pettijohn turned ashen, and Lafferty held his chest, turned to Ilson, and asked, "Which side is a cardiac arrest?"

The song had been inspired, Seeger explained, by a news photo of American troops in Vietnam slogging through some deep river in the Mekong Delta. Seeger saw the song as a powerful allegory: each verse, soldiers trying to ford a river would get deeper and deeper into a quagmire, eventually getting up to their necks as their commanding officer orders them forward. Midway through the song, the captain drowns, a victim of his own stubborn stupidity, and the sergeant takes charge and orders his men to turn back. Seeger set the song in World War II, but—just as the 1970 movie and later TV series *M*A*S*H* were set during the Korean War but echoed Vietnam-era antiwar sentiment—both its meaning and its target were clear. "It didn't mention Johnson by name," Seeger said, "and it didn't have to."

The sixth and final stanza was the one that made CBS brass the most apopleptic. "Every time I read the papers," Seeger sang, "that old feeling comes on—we're waist deep in the Big Muddy, and the big fool says to push on." Seeger was singing this five weeks after Johnson had committed more troops to Vietnam, and CBS found it unacceptable. Meetings were held that night, and the morning of taping, in which Dann and others suggested compromises, such as having Seeger drop the final verse. Seeger refused, and Tom backed him up. "That stanza is the whole point of the song," he insisted. "He's got to sing the whole song." At dress rehearsal, and again at the evening show (both of which, as always, were taped), Seeger performed "Big Muddy" intact.

Between the September 1 taping and the September 10 season premiere telecast, however, CBS put its corporate foot down and brought its corporate scissors out. "Big Muddy" was sliced from the broadcast, ruled unacceptable by network standards. This ruling was despite the fact that Seeger's *Waist Deep in the Big Muddy* LP had been released the previous month without incident—by Columbia Records, a division of the CBS empire. Record albums, though, could be bought by the faithful and ignored by the rest. Television was out there for everyone to see, and angering people, especially people in power when individual station licenses could be challenged and revoked by the Federal Communications Commission, was not in a network's interest.

That outlook certainly explains the 1967 fall season in which *The Smothers Brothers Comedy Hour* found itself. While Tom and Dick were breaking the blacklist of Pete Seeger, other popular shows that fall included such escapist fare as *The Flying Nun, The Beverly Hillbillies,* and *Gentle Ben*. It's no wonder the Smothers Brothers attracted such attention, and such scrutiny—and no wonder, when they open the Seeger show talking about returning for the new TV season, Tom says to Dick, "I think it's a privilege and a shame to be part of it."

Even the edited show broadcast that night by CBS was nothing of which to be ashamed. Except for one drug joke keyed to the new TV season ("I hope every week you'll keep turning on with us," Tom told viewers impishly), the brothers were on their best behavior. They did their classic "I Talk to the Trees" bit lampooning the *Paint Your Wagon* standard, and Dick sang the title song from his new solo album, *Saturday Night at the World* (a song written, and subsequently recorded on his own album, by Mason Williams). Bobbie Gentry sang two songs, looking every bit as sultry as the "Mississippi hippie" described by *TV Guide*. Tom and Janet Leigh did a not-too-naughty comedy sketch about an unzipped zipper, and Paulsen, editorializing on the issue of legalized gambling, said, "In looking into this issue, we will find many pros . . . and cons." All very entertaining. All very safe.

Then, to open the second half of the show, we join Pete Seeger, already in progress, leading the audience in a boisterous "Wimoweh" sing-along. The studio audience is not only singing, but laughing, enjoying Seeger's sound effects and general exuberance. By the time Dick says, "Ladies and gentlemen, meet Pete Seeger," he's already triumphed. He's already back, and the studio audience clearly loves him.

After "Wimoweh," Seeger starts strumming his guitar as Tom asks him to set up the next number. The tune Seeger is strumming is the opening of "Waist Deep in the Big Muddy," and it's obvious both of them know, at this point, they're walking around a musical land mine. Tom is urging Seeger to explain the song and its meaning, but Seeger quickly demurs. "I tell too many stories," Seeger says, explaining to Tom he'd rather let the song stand by itself and let people reach their own conclusions.

Suddenly, there's a jolting cut to a clip of the audience applauding. When the camera returns to Seeger, he's suddenly holding a banjo, not a guitar. "He was about to play 'Waist Deep' . . . so you can *see* that cut," Mason Williams notes. What's missing is unfortunate—but what remains is a highlight, of 1967 or any other year.

Accompanying himself on banjo, Seeger hushes the studio with "Where Have All the Flowers Gone?" and earns chilling, appreciative applause for the answer to the lyrical question, "Where have all the young men gone?" The answer: "They're all in uniform—when will we ever learn?" He goes back to guitar for "Guantanamera," and to the banjo for "This Land Is Your Land," fading out after the first few verses. According to both Seeger and Tom, though, that was always the intention. Only "Big Muddy" was missing—and the rest of Seeger's act that survived the censors, drawing from both the dress and air tapings, was beautiful: a masterful performance and a remark-able comeback by a uniquely principled and talented entertainer.

"Pete's unusual," Mason Williams said appreciatively after watching a tape of Seeger's performance. "He really shows you! You could be a great singer, you could be a great instrumentalist, and you could be a great songwriter. But you could never be Pete Seeger un-less you embraced humanity the way he does."

More than one out of every five TV households tuned to CBS that night to see Pete Seeger, but he and Tom were no less focused on what they *couldn't* see. As with the Elaine May sketch from season one, the issue of censorship was taken to the press, which reported it eagerly. "It's important for people to realize," Seeger told *Newsweek*, "that what they see on television is screened—not only for good taste, but for ideas."

13

The Who Explodes

T wo full summers before the generation-defining performances and mass gathering at Woodstock, Northern California played host to a weekend celebration of music that paved the way and made lots of memorable music and history of its own. The Monterey International Pop Festival was held June 16 to 18, 1967, smack in the middle of the Summer of Love. The Beatle's *Sgt. Peppers Lonely Hearts Club Band* blared from the loudspeakers between acts, but the acts onstage were no slouches, either.

Some acts at Monterey—Buffalo Springfield, Jefferson Airplane, the Association, Simon and Garfunkel—already had appeared on *The Smothers Brothers Comedy Hour* during its first season. Others, such as Indian sitar master Ravi Shankar and the Byrds, would appear subsequently. That wasn't a surprise, because as part of his summer vacation, Tom Smothers attended Monterey as both an occasional onstage host and, as always, an unofficial talent scout, always on the lookout for new acts, new energy, new ideas. Monterey had plenty of them, including the major American showcase launches of Janis Joplin (as riveting lead singer of Big Brother and the Holding Company), Jimi Hendrix (titular star of the Jimi Hendrix Experience, astounding the audience with his guitar prowess and star power two years before doing the same at Woodstock), and Shankar, as well as a reputation-making set by Otis Redding, a soul singer who would leave Monterey as a newly embraced crossover star.

Tom Smothers was onstage and at the microphone to introduce Otis Redding to the Monterey audience that weekend, and also, on one of Big Brother and the Holding Company's two performances, to introduce Janis Joplin. But when I asked Tom about introducing those now-legendary singers, his answer was as unexpected as it was amusing.

"No kidding," he said, his voice getting louder and higher with excitement. "I *did*?"

Yes, he did. And Tom also did, that weekend, what he insists he's done only two other times in fifty years as an entertainer. He went onstage stoned. (The other times, for the record: in the mid-'60s with Roger McGuinn at an appearance at Indiana University's Little 500, the bicycle race dramatized in the movie *Breaking Away;* and in the 1970s with brother Dick, appearing in, and bored by, a regional stage production of *Stop the World—I Want to Get Off.* All three times, he noted, went badly.) Tom's justification for smoking dope at Monterey, he explained, was that the audience clearly was stoned, so he should get on their wavelength. He succeeded at that, if nothing else.

But there *was* something else—something that led to one of the most famous moments in the entire history of *The Smothers Brothers Comedy Hour.* Another act vying for instant notoriety that weekend at Monterey was the Who, which at that point in 1967 had yet to break out big in the States. The group's first concert performance in America had been only a few months before, and its only appearances on American TV had been filmed performances from Britain, imported by ABC's *Shindig.* The Who, before Monterey, was a relative minor player and late arrival, in the British Invasion. But after Monterey—after Pete Townshend's slashing guitar work, John Entwistle's thumping bass, Keith Moon's manic drumming, and

Roger Daltrey's defiant, stuttering vocal on "My Generation"—the Who had arrived. At the end of their set, they destroyed their instruments, an unprecedented act of anarchy that made their reputation at the same time.

Tom booked them immediately for the second season of *Comedy Hour,* scheduling them for the third show. But once the show was taped, on September 15, 1967, Tom was so excited by the results that he rushed it to air two days later, pulling such a late substitution that *TV Guide* still had that night's show listed as featuring George Burns and Herman's Hermits.

Instead, the second show of season two featured Bette Davis (making a return appearance), Mickey Rooney (his first), and the Who. The lineup was a perfect example of the show's express intent to bridge the generation gap and mix old and new elements of show business.

For the old, there was Rooney, born to a vaudeville family and first achieving major stardom opposite Judy Garland when both were teens. There was Davis, who in this return appearance played Queen Elizabeth I in a skit opposite Tom's Earl of Essex. It was a role with which she was quite familiar, having played the same queen in *The Private Lives of Elizabeth and Essex* in 1939, and again in *The Virgin Queen* in 1955. Now here she was, again, in 1967, in full royal regalia, relishing the chance to joke around with Tom and poke fun at her own image. She also plays Rooney's loyal wife in a *Death of a Salesman* spoof, trying to cheer up her despondent spouse by pointing out, "You've got a beautiful home, and an attractive wife who doesn't mess around." In the timid TV atmosphere of the 1960s, that line was so naughty and unexpected, the studio audience laughs and applauds with glee.

The audience also laughs, appreciatively and almost conspiratorially, during the cold open between Tom and Dick, in which Dick chastises his brother for stretching the truth. "I'm sure the country can accept a whole lie," Tom shoots back, taking a political slant without mentioning politics at all. "We do it all the time." But when Tom introduced the Who, no one—not even Tom—was prepared for what happened next.

"Several months ago, I was at Monterey," Tom began. "It was there we saw this new group called the Who." The quartet began by lip-synching to a recording of, and pretending to play, their latest release, "I Can See for Miles"—so new that it wouldn't hit the Top 40 for another five weeks. It's shot in a very groovy, *Austin Powers* style (this is, after all, the original article), and drummer Moon is so unconcerned with maintaining the illusion of playing that he knocks over his cymbal partway through and just laughs.

Then, between songs, Tom enters to introduce the band members and engage in some friendly banter. But where he's usually the representative of the younger generation, these mod rockers are even younger—seven to nine years younger—and brimming with attitude. Suddenly, Tom is thrust into the authority-figure role, and the members of the Who are the ones ready and eager to misbehave.

"You must be Roger," Tom says, turning to the lead singer.

"I must be," Roger replies, deadpan.

"Well, are you?"

"Yeah."

"And where are you from?"

"Oz," Daltrey replies, with a wicked smile.

Turning to Keith Moon, Tom asks, "The guy who plays sloppy drums—what's *your* name?"

"My friends call me Keith," Moon says. "You can call me John."

Finally, Tom introduces the group's next number, identifying it as "My Generation" and promising, "This is excitement."

It certainly was. This was no lip-synch pretend performance. This was a hard-driving, in-your-face musical gauntlet ("Hope I die before I get old"), being performed live to tape, with a surprise ending designed as a very real, very loud surprise indeed. In addition to destroying their instruments, as they had at Monterey, the Who planned to climax this rendition of "My Generation" by firing off an explosive charge hidden inside Moon's bass drum. That was the plan. The reality was a bit . . . bigger.

At the afternoon dress rehearsal, Daltrey recalls, the special-effects cannon was loaded with a charge and set off, but without impressive results. (Daltrey, very descriptively, recalls it as sounding "a bit like a wet baby's fart.") So the order was given to double the charge, but that wasn't enough for Keith Moon, known for his impulsive recklessness.

"I didn't know," Daltrey says now, "that Moon had the pyrotechnic guy from the studio in his dressing room with a bottle of brandy, and a few hundred dollars in his pocket, and was gearing him up to overcharge this thing. We didn't know anything, until it went off. And when it went off, my God!"

Townshend had stabbed his amplifier with his guitar, smashed his guitar on the ground, and was standing in front of Moon's drum set, throwing his guitar in the air, when the cannon with the over-packed explosive charges went off. Moon was blown backward a bit, and Townshend was blown forward, with enough ferocity that his hearing was damaged permanently and his hair was singed.

"I was in my dressing room, but I heard it," Paulsen said. "I could have been *home* and heard it."

Daltrey says, accurately, "If you watch, Pete's patting his hair, trying to put his hair out. His hair was *alight*! That's why he's banging his hair." Daltrey also remembers seeing something that *isn't* available on video, because it was off camera, on the side of the stage: Bette Davis, in full Queen Elizabeth regalia, and Mickey Rooney, watching the Who perform. When the cannon went off, Daltrey says, he looked offstage at the veteran movie stars and saw something he'll never forget.

"Bette Davis was on the floor," Daltrey recalls, "and Mickey Rooney was jumping up and down shouting for more! She passed out . . . She fainted!"

And the performance wasn't quite over yet. Townshend, amid all the smoke and confusion after the explosion, charged Tom, unstrapped his acoustic guitar, and smashed and kicked it to bits—after which Tom said timidly to Dick, "I'd like to borrow your bass for a minute."

Tom looks so rattled that it almost seems Townshend grabbed and destroyed his guitar out of anger, but Tom confirms it was a cheap prop guitar and a planned bit. He was surprised that Townshend had the presence of mind to go through with the sight gag—"and the reason I looked horrified," Tom explains, "was because I was looking for people with shrapnel in the head after that explosion."

"The whole place was in an uproar," Daltrey says. "It was a wonder someone wasn't killed . . . It was very close to the knuckle."

Dick Smothers agrees. "It was by the grace of God nobody got hurt," he says. After the chaos, it was his job to segue to the *Death of a Salesman* sketch, which he describes as "one of America's great modern tragedies." Then, pointing back to the stage where the smoke from the Who is still wafting, Dick gets a huge laugh by ad-libbing, "You just saw another one." ("I was so sorry for those guitars," Dick recalls thinking as he witnessed the Who's explosive campaign of intentional destruction. "I can't stand to see things ruined, and I'm thinking of the poor people that save for their guitars—and these guys break them up every time!")

What the audience had seen, though, was TV history in the making. *The Smothers Brothers Comedy Hour* was putting everyone on notice: It wasn't afraid to make a little noise.

The Generation Gap Widens, Even on TV

I n the fall of 1967, everything seemed to be changing, shifting, or ripping apart. Opposition to the Vietnam War was stepping up, with major antiwar demonstrations in Washington, DC, New York, and elsewhere. In Oakland, folksinger Joan Baez was arrested, with 123 other protesters, for blocking the entrace to the Armed Forces Induction Center. The antiwar rock musical *Hair* opened Off-Broadway, launching New York's Public Theater and a string of hit singles, covered by other artists. (Both Baez and *Hair* eventually would be featured on *The Smothers Brothers Comedy Hour*.) Two immensely influential movies featuring nonconformist antiheroes, *Cool Hand Luke* and *The Graduate*, packed theaters. The Beatles pushed the psychedelic envelope with *Magical Mystery Tour*, while the reclusive Bob Dylan resurfaced, with another ahead-of-his-time tonal shift, with his countrified *John Wesley Harding*. And *Rolling Stone* magazine published its first issue that fall, featuring John Lennon on the cover, and a free roach clip as an added incentive for a subscription.

Having successfully shepherded blacklisted folksinger Pete Seeger back to prime-time television and showcased the Who in all its explosive rebelliousness, *The Smothers Brothers Comedy Hour* would appear to have started season two off on a very strong foot. Not only was it a Top 20 show for the network, and virtually the only series on television that spoke to a new generation of viewers and actually tried to say something, but it was back to a more leisurely production pace, allowing the writers and producers to plan ahead and spend more time on postproduction. Yet each of those assets had a downside and, in addition, there were other factors, outside and inside the Smothers Brothers camp, that made season two a more contentious experience from the start.

The flip sides to the various *Comedy Hour* triumphs were these: the more the program was sought out, supported, and taken seriously by the counterculture, the more it began to alienate the more conservative status quo. In the first season, the only installments of *The Smothers Brothers Comedy Hour* failing to reach at least a 30 share in the Nielsen ratings (in other words, reaching at least 30 percent of the homes watching television at that hour) were programs pitted against the Emmy and Tony awards shows. But after Seeger and the Who, audience levels began dipping a bit. And while *Comedy Hour* still carried the residual clout of being a Top 20 show the previous season, ranked sixteenth, that carried less weight at CBS because of its crushing prime-time dominance at the time. ABC had only two Top 20 shows that season, *Bewitched* and *The Lawrence Welk Show.* NBC, other than top-ranked *Bonanza,* had four. The rest—thirteen out of twenty—belonged to CBS. So while the Smothers Brothers' show was a welcome, remarkable success, especially in its time slot, it wasn't the network's favorite son. Even in the variety genre, *The Red Skelton Show, The Jackie Gleason Show,* and *The Ed Sullivan Show* all drew more viewers in the 1966–67 season. And the new season, in the fall of 1967, brought new variety-show competitors to the table: another CBS entry, *The Carol Burnett Show,* as well as the September showing of a special test pilot for a proposed new NBC series called *Rowan & Martin's Laugh-In.* That latter special, with all its quick-cut comedy and rapid-fire nonsense, was such a hit that NBC launched *Laugh-In* as a midseason entry, just as CBS had the season before with the

Smothers Brothers. Before long, Tom and Dick were outflanked by popular newcomers on both sides: *The Carol Burnett Show* presented old-fashioned, apolitical sketch comedy in the old *Your Show of Shows* mold, while *Laugh-In* took the anything-goes blackout approach of Ernie Kovacs and applied it to everything from slapstick and one-liners to graffiti and Tiny Tim.

Those were the pressures from without, but the *Comedy Hour* production also had plenty of pressures from within. These pressures, from staff disagreements and censorial restrictions to political pressure and sibling rivalry, all percolated and festered in season one, but intensified significantly in season two. And the return to a looser production schedule, while allowing more time for each show to be crafted, also meant more time for each show to be meddled with, and picked apart, by the increasingly vigilant and sensitive program practices representatives. Before too long, the push and pull between the writers and the censors became a time-sapping, counterproductive game. By examining the on-air programs with behind-the-scenes memos and early-draft scripts, you can measure the fight to say something on *The Smothers Brothers Comedy Hour* not only by what was broadcast, but by what wasn't.

During season one, most of Tom's fights were creative ones, having to do with the show itself. He fought to have his own TV monitors, like the ones CBS West Coast executives such as Perry Lafferty had, so he could keep an eye on rehearsals while away from the set. He fought angrily, and constantly, with director Stan Harris and others, trying to get them to realize his vision of the pace and shape of various comedy sketches. Tom always asked for, but could never get, super-quick edits for the show's comedy blackouts—it wasn't until *Laugh-In* premiered, Mason Williams recalled, that Tom pointed to the TV screen and complained that he'd been trying to do that all along. Tom also felt, very firmly, that the onstage chemistry between him and brother Dick, when they played and joked together, was predicated on seeing them both at the same time, or at least, timing the close-ups for maximum effectiveness.

"While Tommy was talking," former Smothers manager Ken Kragen explains, "Dick's reaction was almost even more important than what Tommy was saying." Tom hated it when camera shots lingered on him alone, or when the composition of the frame wouldn't follow, and capture, the natural flow of the comedy. "Tommy had a specific way he thought it should be done," Kragen says, "and he was very adamant about it, and he was impatient with directors . . . He was just a very hands-on, total-control guy, not happy with a lot of stuff."

Tom also fought with his teams of writers, who were eager—too eager, Tom felt—to dip into the well of Smothers Brothers comedy bits honed in concert over the years. When the show premiered, those time-tested nuggets of comedy gold were a currency it made sense to spend. But once *Comedy Hour* was a hit and appeared to be settling in for a long TV run, Tom and Dick were much more protective of the material they had taken years to develop.

"The first thing the show had to deal with was, it had to be a show that had good ratings," recalls Mason Williams. "So believe me, all we wanted to do was be entertaining and funny. Fortunately, we had the Smothers Brothers comedy routines. Here's eight to ten minutes that's solid, that you know is really worked out. All you have to do is put them on camera. That freed you up to create material for them, because they had this huge database of material. There was nothing wrong with them putting a classic, ten of them, up in the first ten shows, to make Tom and Dick come off well." But after that, Tom and Dick, and managers Kragen and Fritz, were less accommodating. "We protected it with our lives," Fritz says of the brothers' back catalog. "Often, somebody on the show, if we were short," Fritz remembers, "would say, 'Well, why don't you do 'Boil That Cabbage Down'? No, we're not going to do that. You guys go back and write something else."

"We ran through our own stuff very quickly," Dick says. "We did seventy-two shows. We didn't come close to seventy-two Tom and Dick spots that we knew." And while the nightclub material was polished, the new pieces often were not even adequately rehearsed. "I really liked doing the new material," Dick says. "The only negative about it was Tom not spending enough time on it because he was busy producing the show, really . . . That's what happens when you wear too many hats."

Dick's own role in *The Smothers Brothers Comedy Hour*, on the other hand, was beginning to lessen as the series progressed. It was a reversal of the dynamics in the brothers' nightclub act where, over the seven years in which they worked clubs and recorded albums as a duo, Dick's role had become increasingly prominent. He had developed, by this point, into a consummate straight man, effortlessly setting up his partner, leading or following as they veered off into unexplored terrain, and milking silence for additional laughs, all while singing and playing. *Comedy Hour* writer-producer Allan Blye assessed Dick's straight-man skills in raw, enthusiastic terms ("He was absolutely fucking brilliant"), and even occasional guest star Carl Reiner, the consummate straight man to Sid Caesar on *Your Show of Shows*, says, "Dickie is as good a straight man as you can get," and calls him "one of the best ever." On the show, especially in season one, Dick also got to team with such freewheeling comics as Jonathan Winters and Carol Burnett, and more than held his own. "Dick's very good—a very good straight man," Tom says. "When I do look at these old shows, I see how solidly—normally, ninety percent of his performance—is just *solid*. And although, at the time, we used to think he overacted or something, it was *me* who was overacting!" Blye remembers Dick, when the series began, popping into writers' sessions just to listen to sketch ideas or offer ways to rework a line or an idea. "His insights and his ideas were as brilliant in the writers' room as they were on camera," Blye says. However, Blye's appreciation wasn't shared by everyone, and Dick began to offer input less and less.

"When I wanted to get in with the writing, I wasn't taken seriously," Dick recalls. Like Tom, Dick had artists he was keen on booking on *Comedy Hour*, but most of Dick's suggestions were rebuffed from the start, and he soon gave up trying. "If I could harbor a resentment," Dick says now, "I would say that whenever I wanted someone on the show, I didn't get enthusiastic support." He'd been similarly frustrated when trying to get his acting coach hired as a director on the sitcom, but this was different: Tom had a lot more input and control this time around, yet little brother Dick wasn't given an equal amount of latitude. He remembers pushing for Nino Tempo and April Stevens, the singing duo of "Deep Purple" fame, to appear on the show. When they finally did, it was not until one of the last shows of the last season. "When you do it once or twice, and it doesn't happen," he says, talking about having his guest star ideas rejected, "why subject your friends to it?"

Adding to his sense of rejection was the show's frantic pace of production, which introduced and intensified other elements of tension. One was that, when programs were taped and ran over the allotted hour, the easiest element to remove, in most cases, was Dick's solo musical number. "The Dickie solo was the first thing to get cut if the show was long. They used me as a buffer," Dick says, laughing. "They said, 'Cut Dickie's song!' It got to be a joke. I didn't mind." Tom, in retrospect, suspects otherwise ("It's got to hurt his feelings, you know?") but also recalls other, more obvious sources of conflict.

One was that Dick increasingly devoted time to such pursuits as car racing and motorcycling and became less of a presence around the office and on the soundstages unless he was specifically needed. "I wasn't really very important to the production aspect," Dick says, "but they had to give me an office and a secretary. It just wouldn't look right. I was busy playing with my cars, and I really think, had I worked harder with the writers and stuff . . . I'd have got in Tommy's way. And I probably would have wanted to do my stuff more, and then we'd get conflict." Often, when Dick did hang out at the studio, he had little to do. "Lots of times," he says, "I would end up going out and waxing my car. How many times," he asks with a laugh, "can you lie down and take a nap in a dressing room with no windows?"

His distancing, Dick says now, was kind of a "defense mechanism," but also a prioritizing of interests ("I liked my family life, I liked my hobbies"). On occasion, he would book red-eye flights on Fridays, the day of taping, to participate in a weekend racing event, and push to keep things moving swiftly so he could make his plane. "And I think that stuff made me perform better," Dick rationalizes, "because I focused—because there was a *need* to be good, to make it right." Dick would get upset when Tom wasn't as prepared, while Tom bristled for the opposite reason. He was keenly aware of Dick's stealth approach to the show—get in, get it right, get out—and it grated on Tom tremendously. Not because Dick wasn't prepared, or effective, or polished, but because he *was*.

Dick's ability to memorize lines, songs, and routines more quickly had frustrated Tom ever since they started performing together. Tom's undiagnosed dyslexia put him at a tremendous disadvantage when it came to reading scripts and cue cards. (He wasn't diagnosed until age thirty-one, when the series was almost over.) Tom also was spread thin, working on every aspect of the production from first drafts to final edit, so whether or not Dick intended his in-and-out, casual perfectionism as a form of passive-aggressive revenge, Tom often read it that way at the time.

"Midway through the second season," Tom says, "we fought constantly. On the stage, backstage." Dick, Tom recalls, would be "the first one at rehearsal" for a 2:30 p.m. call for going through a musical or sketch piece, but if the next bit was scheduled to begin rehearsal at 3:15, when that time arrived, Dick would look at the clock and say, "I'm done," and leave. "It used to irritate the hell out of me," Tom admits. Even more annoying, he adds with a laugh, was Dick's habit, when they were about to perform, of ignoring Tom until the very last moment.

"Dickie *still* does it to me," Tom complains, both amused and flustered. "He'll stand there, and they say, 'Okay, ten seconds.' He'll be talking to the boom man. 'Nine, eight . . . ' I'm standing on my mark, I hardly know my lines anyway, and I say, 'Dick! Dick!' And he's there chatting away until the last second, and he steps right in on the mark. He hardly ever had a false move, and he pretty well had his stuff down. It used to drive me fucking crazy." Tom remembers one TV taping, as he and Dick were making a rapidfire costume change just offstage between scenes, when they just started yelling obscenities at one another. "We were sitting there screaming, 'Fuck you, you son of a bitch!' 'You goddamn fucker!' 'You're fired!' 'No, you're fired! . . . We forgot we were three feet from the set, where the audience was sitting!'"

As the second season began, there were signs of a temporary truce, as least concerning Dick's on-air prominence as a solo singer. His September 1967 solo LP, *Saturday Night at the World* (the title song a Mason Williams composition), had just been released, and *Comedy Hour* featured it prominently. The first four shows taped for season two, including the high-profile season premiere with Pete Seeger, made room for a solo number by Dick and promoted the album. Tom, meanwhile, had plenty of other places to focus his interest and vent his frustration.

Producer Saul Ilson remembers a late-night confrontation, near the end of season one, between Tom and Ilson's partner, Ernie Chambers, over an editing change demanded by the network. This was during the poststrike, two-day turnaround period, when shows were taped on Friday and broadcast on Sunday, necessitating an exhausting overnight editing session after each taping. CBS was demanding an excision of something—no one involves remembers what—and Tom refused to comply. Ilson and Chambers took a break from the editing room to decide what to do next, and when they returned, the master tape—which, once edited, had to be flown to New York to be approved for broadcast and relayed nationwide—was gone.

"We finally figured out that Tommy took the videotape," Ilson says, swearing that what happened next was so vivid he recalls it verbatim. "The master. And we said, "Tommy, we've got to have the master.' And he wouldn't budge. He said, 'It's never going to go to New York. We're not going to do it!' And Ernie Chambers grabbed him, grabbed him by the throat, and put him up against one of the bins. And says, 'Goddamnit, you gimme it!'—at four o'clock in the morning." Dick, who was asleep at home, was called in to mediate the argument, and the videotape eventually was found by the artists' entrance, hidden under one of the vans. Lafferty, in his memoir, confirms that account.

Despite such emotional and physical clashes, Chambers and Ilson would be rehired for season two, but not director Stan Harris. Actually, Harris had a two-year contract, but over the summer, Tom decided he didn't want Harris back and demanded he be replaced. Harris demanded full payment to walk, and Tom was so intent on hiring a new director that he agreed, replacing Harris with Bill Davis and paying Harris his full-season salary to *not* direct. Harris took that money, he told me, and built an addition onto his house, complete with a plaque commemorating it as "The Tommy Smothers Memorial Library."

Before the end of the second season, after hiring and firing Bill Davis and hiring another director, Sam Gary, Tom visited Harris out of the blue. "The doorbell rings at, like, nine a.m. on a Sunday," Harris said, "and there's Tommy standing at the door. And he says, 'Can I come and look at my library?' " Tom apologized for firing Harris, even with full pay, and asked Harris to come back for the final shows of season two—for even more pay. Which Harris did.

The most significant fights Tom waged during season two, though, weren't with his writers, producers, directors, or even his brother. It was with the censors, the CBS program practices department that, during season two, began interfering enough with the content of *The Smothers Brothers Comedy Hour* for Tom to chafe at their suggestions and defy and mock their authority. On one hand, he fought seriously and passionately for ideas and acts he thought deserved a voice. On the other hand, he and the other writers tweaked the network censors by peppering scripts with jokes and phrases they knew would never be approved. Some were inserted as leverage, as bargaining chips to sacrifice in order to protect other jokes or ideas. Others were included just for the rebellious fun of it—"fun" that would up the ante, and the emotional temperature, and eventually turn the negotiations with program practices, in season three, into all-out war. Nobody denies the behind-the-scenes brinksmanship that went on, and most recount it with impish glee, like adolescents talking about intentionally pushing the buttons of their frustrated parents.

"I referred to it as 'Two shits for a fuck,' " recalls former executive producer and manager Ken Fritz. "The horse trading would go on. It was basic salesmanship. You couldn't go in there and just say, 'I want this, it's this or nothing,' because they needed to get something. As we often said, these guys own the store. So if there's some little incremental, in their own minds, victory—which we didn't care about in the first place—okay, let them have it." Former management partner Ken Kragen concurs: "We got a lot of stuff by, by either putting obvious stuff in the script that they would focus on, which was one trick, or just because they had no clue. They didn't understand the double entendre. They got better as time went on, though, because they realized they were getting fooled."

The hierarchy at CBS began on the West Coast, where CBS Television City was based and *Comedy Hour* was taped. Perry Lafferty was the program executive in charge there, whose tenure began when the Smothers started production on their 1965 sitcom. Tom Downer, the West Coast director of program practices for CBS, took that post in the middle of 1967, just in time to deal with *Comedy Hour* on the Pete Seeger "Big Muddy" controversy. His staffers, Charles Pettijohn and Sam Taylor Jr.—his censors, though CBS called them "editors"—reviewed scripts, attended tapings, suggested changes, and reported at weekly meetings. Thanks largely to the Smothers Brothers, these meetings soon expanded to twice weekly. Notes and recommendations were relayed to the *Comedy Hour* producers and dispatched to the East Coast, where program executive Mike Dann paid a lot of attention—and William Tankersley, at least until season three, didn't, preferring to rely on the chain of command and defer, in large part, to his West Coast subordinates. By season three, Tom would rebel angrily against all these layers of input and interference, but for much of the time during season two, it was not only a battle, but a game.

"Often Tommy would stick in sketches with parts in them that he thought I would cut out," recalls Mike Dann, "or that program practices would cut out. So there were always arguments about what should go in or out." In the early second-season episode featuring the Who, the opening Tom and Dick musical spot, "Waltzing Matilda," is very funny—but was even funnier in its first draft, before CBS got to it.

Dick, trying to explain to Tom the foreign slang in the famous Australian folk song, digressed into a discussion of that country's unusual native people and creatures. Tom, trying to show off, says in the original script, "Hey, what about the natives that live in the wilds of Australia? They're the most uncivilized wild people in the world—

the Abortionists." "Aborigines, Tom," Dick corrects him. "Aborigines?" Tom replies. "That doesn't sound as wild." That didn't make the final cut. Sam Taylor, in one of the earliest official memos to circulate from program practices to the *Comedy Hour* producers, writes, "The use of 'The Abortionists' is unacceptable," but suggests an alternative: "Perhaps 'Abolitionists' would suit your purposes." Also not making the cut was Tom's description of a native Australian species as the "Duck-Billed Platypussys." (On air, Tom calls them "Duck-Billed Platitudes.") "In those days," Dann said, confirming the obvious, "they were very strict still."

By December 1967, Tom and his writers were intentionally, outrageously confrontational in their scriptwriting. In one show, in a Tom and Dick spot about French culture, the on-air routine ends after Tom reveals his ignorance about French wine, women, and song. The script, though, kept going, into wholly unacceptable territory. "Back to the subject," Dick tells Tom. "You've flunked French wine, you've flunked French women . . ." "Hold it," Tom says. "I've never flunked a French woman in my life." According to the script, Dick then says, "I said flunked, not fucked," and Tom replies, "So did I. You're the one that said fucked." Dick's next line is, "Well, now we've both said it, and I'm sure the censors will cut it out," and Tom's final line is, "Yeah, I guess we flunked up." Years later, when Tom and Dick sued CBS and were deposed for trial, Tom was asked specifically about that script and its "fuck" dialogue.

Q: Was that submitted to CBS?
A: *Yes, it was.*
Q: Was that seriously intended?
A: *No, it wasn't.*
Q: What was the reason for doing that?
A: *Try to insert a little sense of humor into the program practices department and see what their reaction would be.*

Those tests extended not just to naughty words, but also to ris-qué and risky ideas. According to Mason Williams, Tom wanted to do a skit about a typical A. C. Nielsen family, satirizing the ratings system used to estimate TV viewing patterns and set advertising rates. The joke was that the TV being monitored in this typical American family home was downstairs, turned on but abandoned, while the family was upstairs, secretly watching what it wanted on a second, secret television set. "They wouldn't let us touch that with a ten-foot pole," Mason recalls. "They said, 'No, no, this is part of our market-ing mechanism. It's not up for grabs for you to talk about in any way, shape, or form.'" According to both Tom and Mason, every time the censors said no to something, the writers pushed back and filled the next script with even more. "A lot more," Tom admits. "If they hadn't been so hard on me, I probably would not have been so intractable. And pretty soon I became *very* intractable. We started putting little red herrings in—things we knew they would take out, or things that meant nothing at all, but which they'd fear was the newest slang."

Mason chuckles deeply, recalling this playful period of dueling with the CBS censors. "I wrote a 'good night' once," he says, refer-ring to the end-of-show spot where the brothers come on their Tif-fany stage to end the show, "where Tom comes out and says, 'Dick, you're not going to believe it, but Jesus Christ has just showed up, and he wants to say something to the audience!' And Dick says, 'Sorry, we're out of time.'" Mason erupts with a hearty belly laugh. "Believe me," he says, "that one didn't make it."

Most of season two can and should be looked at through two sets of prisms: what didn't get on the air and what did.

One thing *The Smothers Brothers Comedy Hour* maintained through season two was the show's cross-generational appeal, an ap-proach that continued to work beautifully. Veteran vaudevillian Jimmy Durante, who had delivered the highest audience for the first season, did it again for season two, in a show also featuring young singer-songwriter Janis Ian. According to Nielsen estimates, that *Comedy Hour* was seen in an estimated 24.8 million TV homes, earning a 36.8 percent share of that hour's viewing audience. The brothers ushered in 1968 by doing something truly astounding: one January 1968 show, featuring actress Patty Duke, comedian Don Rickles, and the Association, marked the first time the series had beaten an original, non-repeat episode of *Bonanza*. In February, an original *Comedy Hour* beat an original *Bonanza* installment once more, with another show that proved the wisdom of appealing to all ages: that hour's eclectic guest list included Golden Age of TV star Arthur Godfrey, "chitlin' circuit" comedienne Jackie "Moms" Mabley, and a relatively new Australian singing group, the Bee Gees.

Even with all the infighting and censorship squabbles behind the scenes, what made it on the screen pushed the boundaries of TV in several directions, most notably regarding who was seen and what was said.

Musically, comically, satirically, politically—everything seemed to build and feed on itself. The more the show spoke the language, played the music, and expressed the opinions of the counterculture, the more it was embraced and utilized as a potent, and an important, platform. Simon and Garfunkel returned for season two, singing not only their old hit "Homeward Bound," but unveiling a brand-new song, "Overs," which wouldn't be released until the duo's *Bookends* album six months later. ("We finished it about a week ago," Paul Simon said, before he and Art Garfunkel presented its first public performance.) The Bee Gees made their US television debut on *Comedy Hour*, singing "Words," which entered the record charts the following week. On other shows, the Byrds, the Hollies, the Temptations, Nancy Sinatra, and a two-week-old band named the First Edition, led by Kenny Rogers, all proudly performed, but so did such genre-challenging artists as Ravi Shankar and the Juilliard String Quartet.

At the same time, and sometimes in the same show, there was room for showbiz singers as well—everyone from veteran vocalists Kate Smith, Mel Torme, Shirley Jones, and Jane Powell to such younger entertainers as Nancy Wilson, Nancy Ames, Robert Morse, and Diahann Carroll. And finally, among the show's most significant musical imports that season were Glen Campbell and John Hartford, the singer and composer, respectively, of "Gentle on My Mind." Tom and Mason both took to Hartford immediately and hired him for the writing staff. Campbell, though a TV neophyte, was such a natural that Tom shrewdly hired him, within a month of his first *Comedy Hour* appearance, as the host of the program's summer replacement series, *The Summer Brothers Smothers Show*.

In terms of pure comedy—comedy, that is, not layered with political commentary or satire—season two had only a pair of true standouts. One was "Me and My Shadow," in which Dick performs in front of an illuminated screen, throwing a "shadow" which turns out to be Tom, behind the partition, breaking lockstep to go his own way—and, long before Steve Martin even arrived on the show as a fledging writer, sporting a pair of goofy bunny ears. The other, timed for a Christmas Eve telecast, was Nanette Fabray's inspired, manic performance of "The Twelve Days of Christmas." She sings the song while pointing to, and whirling her way around, an increasingly overpopulated stage full of everything up to and including "ten pipers piping" (on bagpipes), "eleven ladies dancing" (Fabray joins them), and "twelve lords a'leaping" (on pogo sticks). All performed, and shot, in one whirlwind take.

The satire and political humor were a lot less rare, and in season two popped up in almost every element of the series. The cold openings were great places to aim at selected targets. In one, Dick notes that, because of political unrest abroad, the US government is asking citizens to refrain from visiting foreign lands. Tom, hearing this, looks into the TV camera and shouts, "Okay, all you guys in

Vietnam—come on home!" In another cold open, Dick points out that President Lyndon B. Johnson is asking people to refrain from traveling overseas and spending money abroad, and asks Tom what LBJ could do to make people want to stay in this country. "Well," Tom replies, "he could quit."

The show closings, the good-byes, were another natural platform for Tom and Dick to express themselves and their views. "I'd like to say hello to all the Americans up in Canada—all the young men who went to Canada to avoid the draft," Tom said, ending the already explosive September 1967 show with the Who. "Take it easy, fellas. We hope to have you home—if not by this November, maybe next." The next November, of course, was a presidential election year. Sometimes, when signing off, Tom and Dick were deadly serious, as when they urged viewers to join the Peace Corps. ("They don't want your money," Dick says somberly, "they want you.")

Not many musical selections during season two were overtly political, but there were a few. The Association presented a very strong antiwar song, "Requiem for the Masses," early in the season, and Tom, Dick, and guest George Segal teamed as a trio on Phil Ochs's "Draft Dodger Rag," in which the lyrics are a litany of excuses for avoiding of active duty ("I'm only eighteen, I got a ruptured spleen, and I always carry a purse . . .").

But most of the political points were made during the skits, and nowhere were they more prevalent, or more amusing, than during Pat Paulsen's continuing series of mock editorials, which really hit their stride in season two.

On the topic "Should We Be Spending Billions to Reach the Moon?" (this was two years before Neil Armstrong planted his footprint there): Pat notes the plan has its detractors: "They say we'd be better off spending these billions on slums. Personally, I think we have enough slums."

On the topic "Are Our Draft Laws Unfair?": Pat begins by saying, "A good many people today feel our present draft laws are unjust. These people are called soldiers." He goes on to say that the draft is accused of being unfair and immoral, that it discourages young men from studying, and that it ruins their careers and their lives. Pat's response: his trademark catchphrase "Picky, picky, picky."

On the topic of "Social Security": "It's time to reexamine this whole Social Security program," Pat says. "We've been paying into it all these years, thirty-five years, and what good has it done? There are more old people now than when it started!"

And on the hot-button, inside-baseball topic of "Should TV Be Censored?": "We're not against censorship," Pat deadpans, "because we realize there is always the danger of something being said. Censorship is not unconstitutional. The Bill of Rights says nothing about freedom of hearing. This, of course, takes a lot of fun out of the freedom of speech," Pat says, laughing wickedly.

"We are allowed to say Ronald Reagan [then the governor of California] is a lousy actor," he adds, "but we are not allowed to say he's a lousy governor. Which is ridiculous. We all know he's a good actor." Pat concludes this particular editorial by saying, "There's a place for censors, and we only wish we could tell you where it is!"

Leigh French was another *Comedy Hour* talent who got more exposure, and courted more controversy, in season two. After making one brilliantly improvised appearance in season one as an audience plant, she returned early in season two to pull the same trick. Tom, once again, finds her in the studio audience and invites her to step forward and chat. She identifies herself as Goldie, a hippie visiting from San Francisco. "Thanks for coming down," Tom says. Goldie replies, "I didn't come down. I *never* come down," and the audience erupts with a loud, knowing laugh.

From that point, she was worked into the show as a recurring player, appearing in sketches playing everything from the Mona Lisa to the biblical Eve. Finally, on the same January 1968 show that introduced Glen Campbell, she got her first "Share a Little Tea with Goldie" slot and found her career role as TV advice giver Goldie O'Keefe. "I'd like to greet you ladies as I usually do—hi!" she says, hitting the last word to emphasize its "high" drug connotations. In one sketch, Don Knotts plays a nervous guest dropping by, offered tea but wary of drinking it. "It's just regular," she says, reassuring him, then asks, "Like a little sugar?" When he sees it's a sugar cube— a popular method of dispensing LSD at the time—he panics and says, "No, thank you." This sort of thing just wasn't seen on TV at the start of 1968, and the studio audience loved it.

The nationwide TV audience was another matter. Some viewers, along with certain pressure groups and various local CBS affiliates, were less approving of "Share a Little Tea" and other controversial *Comedy Hour* skits. One lengthy finale sketch, a particularly overt political tract, was on the subject of guns. Tom introduces the finale by announcing, "More Americans have died from privately owned guns than in all the wars this country has fought." A series of short sketches and blackouts follow, including a TV game show, "The Shooting Game," in which contestants are giving the chance to shoot celebrities, and even spouses, for insurance-money prizes. Finally, to the tune of "Seventy-six Trombones" from *The Music Man* (but with lyrics changed to "a hundred and six shotguns in the big parade"), a group of gun-toting "criminals and out-and-out nuts" march for their right to bear arms—while actual magazine ads for mail-order and department-store guns, and headlines about gun violence ("Sniper Kills 2") are superimposed over the action. The effect is striking, and so is the timing: within six months, both Martin Luther King Jr. and Robert F. Kennedy would be shot and killed.

"That was one notch more serious than the show had ever been, over this issue," says Mason, who didn't write it but recognized the bluntness of its message. So did the National Rifle Association, whose public relations director, John R. Hess, fired off a letter to producer Ken Fritz. "The pathetic performance I viewed last Sunday night," he wrote, "most certainly will not do much to inform the American public of the pro's and con's [sic] of the proposed firearms legislation now pending in the Congress of the United States which you not so subtly tried to influence." The letter also included, not so subtly, the threat of a boycott: "The 50 million people you portrayed as idiots also purchase your sponsors' products and, as you are well aware, it is these purchases which make or break television programs."

Affiliates, by this point, were threatening to pull out also—not many, but it doesn't take many to get a network's attention. The vice president and general manager of WISH-TV in Indianapolis was so upset by the second-season opener that he wrote to protest its "extremely poor taste"—not because Pete Seeger was appearing on CBS, as scores of angry viewers had written the network to complain, but because a comedy sketch with Tom and guest star Janet Leigh revolved around Tom getting a tablecloth caught in his zipper. If the show didn't present material of "a more wholesome nature," this executive threatened, "we might have no choice but to cancel its showing in Indianapolis." It wasn't the only affiliate letter on that subject, and the number of complaints increased, over the season, in both frequency and intensity. *Comedy Hour*, though, was interested in reflecting and exploring the times, not shying away from them.

Dick anchored a series of "Smothers Polls," in which he asked cast members and guest stars about the issues of the day. One installment has him interviewing Fidel Castro, played by Sid Caesar, about the US boycott of Cuba. "Do you miss Americans on the island?" Dick asks Caesar's Castro. "We try not to," the ersatz Cuban dictator replies, and shrugs. "We shoot. If we miss, we miss."

Also, a series of fairy tales and fables were enacted and updated, using colorful costumes and clever subtexts, to make some rather serious points. This, too, was a continuation from season one, and hit a second-season high point with a sketch featuring Tom and guest star Nancy Wilson, a beautiful black singer and actress, as frogs. The twist is that she's a green frog, he's a red one, and she's prejudiced. "You know what happens," she complains, "when you let one red frog in."

In the show's biggest and boldest political commentary of all, Pat Paulsen was elevated to presidential candidate (more on that later). Both Richard Nixon and segregationist Alabama governor George Wallace announced their candidacies within weeks of Paulsen's campaign unveiling, giving him more competition to joke about (this was decades before Stephen Colbert tried a similarly headline-stealing campaign to get on the South Carolina presidential ballot).

One other newly arrived competitor, though, was a threat of sorts to *Comedy Hour* itself. The same week Pat Paulsen first announced—or, rather, denied—his candidacy, NBC launched *Rowan & Martin's Laugh-In* as a series. The two shows didn't compete directly, and the two sets of hosts were friendly enough to appear on each other's shows. Yet *Laugh-In,* which wouldn't have existed without the ground broken by *The Smothers Brothers Comedy Hour,* very soon would steal some of its thunder and attract millions more viewers. But as the Smothers Brothers were a few shows away from closing out their second season, they weren't quite ready to relinquish the media spotlight to *Laugh-In* or anyone else. Tom and Dick had one more ace up their sleeve.

15

Wading Back into "The Big Muddy"

September 10, 1967, on the opening show of the second season of *The Smothers Brothers Comedy Hour*, Pete Seeger's performance of his new antiwar song, "Waist Deep in the Big Muddy," was censored in its entirety by CBS. Five months later, on February 25, 1968, Seeger returned for one of that season's final shows, sang "Big Muddy"—and it was broadcast without objection by CBS.

What happened in the interim to reverse the network's once-fervent position? Part of it was Tom's tireless battle to keep the issue alive in the press, but most of it was due to nothing more, and nothing less, than current events.

In January alone, the news from overseas was particularly disheartening. The USS *Pueblo* was seized by North Korea in the Sea of Japan, and in Vietnam, the North Vietnamese launched the Tet Offensive, a massive, deadly military assault on American and South Vietnamese forces that, at least temporarily, surprised and embarrassed the US military. As American troop levels and casualties rose, with neither a clear path to victory nor a clear exit strategy in sight, opposition to the Vietnam War rose fractionally but measurably each month. On the home front, in the first week of February, both Richard Nixon and George Wallace announced their intention to run for president.

Another measure of the changing times was reflected in two letters written by program practices head William Tankersley. Both dealt, in part, with Pete Seeger and the "Big Muddy" controversy—and while they were only four months apart chronologically, they were worlds apart in terms of tolerance and temperament.

"Our touchstone should be that we accept material which is obviously designed for the primary purpose of entertaining rather than to advance a point of view on a controversial subject," Tankersley wrote in one internal CBS memo. He later added, ". . . nor can we ever ignore taste considerations such as that present in Pete Seeger's 'Big Muddy,' in which there is metaphorical reference to the President as a fool."

That was in September 1967, two weeks after Seeger's first, censored CBS broadcast. By January 1968, answering a sponsor's complaint about the *Comedy Hour* content, Tankersley sounded much more tolerant. "Their material," he argued, "expresses to a great extent the concerns of a large segment of today's youth, and to suppress it entirely could be said to contravene the postulate that television should mirror life around us. In fact, it is almost impossible to present contemporary popular songs which do not contain some comment directly or indirectly on issues of public importance: war, peace, civil rights, patriotism, and the like."

The Smothers Brothers, meanwhile, were pushing the envelope, topically and musically, as much as they could, while still clinging to the show's generation-gap-crossing approach that had served them so well. And every week, in almost every media interview opportunity, Tom kept venting his anger about how CBS had censored Pete Seeger.

"Every time they were interviewed anywhere," Seeger said of Tom and Dick, chuckling, "they'd bring up that incident. And, sure enough, in February, CBS said, 'Okay, okay, he can sing for you.' On six days' notice—in fact, on twenty-four hours' notice—I canceled whatever else I was doing throughout the West Coast and recorded the song for [the second] show."

It was, truly, as sudden as that—and it was big news. The *New York Times* ran a news story on February 15, in which Tom Smothers enthusiastically announced that Seeger was being invited back with permission to sing his once-banned number: "I just heard from Mike Dann in New York and he told us to go ahead. Mike's really on our bandwagon." The article went on to say, "By allowing Mr. Seeger to sing the ballad, which some critics have interpreted as being critical of President Johnson's conduct of the Vietnam War, CBS appeared to be reversing its long-standing policy of not permitting controversial material on prime-time entertainment programs."

The very next day, Seeger was onstage at Television City, taping a solo set, and another set with Tom and Dick, as part of an hour that looks a lot less rushed than it must have been to produce. Because there were nine days between the program's taping and its February 25 broadcast, all CBS executives had plenty of time to see and approve its contents—and there was enough time for the contents themselves, and the controversy surrounding them, to generate even more publicity and headlines.

Comedy Hour got a coveted *TV Guide* "Close-Up" that week, with a picture of Seeger and a half-page highlights description that began, "The Brothers' guest is folksinger Pete Seeger, whose appearances on the show last September sparked a censorship row that raged for months." After describing "Big Muddy," *TV Guide* went on to promise: "Tonight, Pete is scheduled to sing the song, as well as others that 'get the history out.'"

The show itself was a triumph, one of the most significant hours of the three-year run, and arguably the one in which Tom, tilting against the network windmills, scored his greatest and tastiest victory.

Unlike the previous Seeger appearance, which broke the blacklist against him and was otherwise rather tame, this particular *Comedy Hour* pushes a lot of hot-button issues. It pokes fun at politics, with Pat Paulsen coming on to deny, once again, he was running for president. (When Tom shows him a clip, from Paulsen's appearance on a rival network, in which Paulsen describes his candidacy, he sheepishly insists he was "misquoted.") It salutes the other hot new show on TV, the month-old *Laugh-In,* by having Dan Rowan and Dick Martin on tape interrupting, and remarking on, certain segments. It complains about the lack of minority representation on TV, in a "Smothers Poll" segment in which Scoey Mitchell, a black cast member, complains that the only star of color on TV is Smokey the Bear. And on another delightful, envelope-pushing "Share a Little Tea with Goldie" segment, Leigh French offers advice on how to decorate gas masks ("As sure as you live and breathe, we know air pollution, in its own small way, is going to wipe us out"), and promises, "Next week, we'll discuss how to get rid of roaches." The implication, entirely missed by the censors, is that she is *not* talking about bugs.

All this was prelude to, or overshadowed by, Seeger's amazing return appearance. Dick introduces him proudly, noting that it's only Seeger's second major TV appearance in seventeen years—but without saying why (the blacklist). The scene shifts to Pete, lounging stretched out in a chair, playing his banjo.

His first song is a totally benign and cheerful rendition of "Get Up and Go" ("my get up and go has got up and went"). Then he stands, banjo in hand, and starts playing "a pop song of two hundred years ago"—an instrumental version of "Yankee Doodle." But before singing the words, he decides, instead, to offer "little bits of some other songs of other American wars." His war medley covers the war with Mexico, the Civil War, the Spanish-American War, and World War I—all leading up to World War II and "Waist Deep in the Big Muddy."

Without any introduction whatsoever, Seeger launches in. He

switches from banjo to guitar. The lighting dims so it's just the folk-singer against a black background. And he starts—strumming and singing like a man possessed, with his loudly tapping foot providing added urgency.

"It was back in 1942, I was a member of a good platoon," he begins, singing a tale of World War II soldiers on maneuvers in Louisiana, under orders to cross a river that is treacherously deep. The captain forces them forward, leading them until he drowns and the sergeant turns everyone around back to safety. The final verses are the ones that shift the tale from one war, and one leader, to another:

> *Well, I'm not going to point any moral;*
> *I'll leave that for yourself*
> *Maybe you're still walking, you're still talking*
> *You'd like to keep your health.*
> *But every time I read the papers*
> *That old feeling comes on;*
> *We're—waist deep in the Big Muddy*
> *And the big fool says to push on.*
>
> *Waist deep in the Big Muddy*
> *And the big fool says to push on.*
> *Waist deep in the Big Muddy*
> *And the big fool says to push on.*
> *Waist deep! Neck deep! Soon even a*
> *Tall man'll be over his head, we're*
> *Waist deep in the Big Muddy!*
> *And the big fool says to push on!*

It's a stunning performance. At the end, Seeger brings the guitar to his face, almost embracing it, and swallows hard. He's done it, and the look of satisfaction, pride, and accomplishment is unmistakable.

Later in the show, to close it out, Seeger joins Tom and Dick for another set that's thrilling, for different reasons. They start with "Old Joe Clark," a blisteringly fast song that has Seeger on banjo, Tom on guitar, Dick on bass, and all three of them trading vocal verses and clearly having a blast. Seeger serves up a wild solo on banjo—so good that when Dick then says "Take it, Tom," to throw it to his older brother, Tom laughs and says, "Not me." Great moment—and a great, vivacious number.

It's followed by the hour's closing number: the trio performing "Turn! Turn! Turn!" (To Everything There Is a Season)," the song with music by Seeger and lyrics adapted from the Book of Ecclesiastes. The Byrds scored a number-one hit with a folk-rock version of the song in 1965, but here Tom, Dick, and Seeger do it acoustically and totally straight. When Tom, taking his turn, stares straight into the camera and sings—"a time of love, a time of hate / a time of war, a time of peace"—he's no longer a comic who made his career acting silly and ridiculing folk songs. He's singing purely, without irony and with total conviction. And when all three of their voices combine, at the end, to sing "a time of peace, I swear it's not too late," it's a special, powerful moment.

"Singing on *The Smothers Brothers* was one of the high points in my long life," Seeger said. "I look back on it with pleasure." What they did, he insisted, was unprecedented: "It was one thing to criticize the establishment when you're just with yourself and a few friends," he said. "But to do it on prime time and get away with it— that was an extraordinary achievement. They did it by being extraordinarily honest."

The show was a triumph artistically and commercially. While the first appearance by Pete Seeger, earlier in the season, was seen in some 11.8 million TV homes, his triumphant return, with all the fuss about "Big Muddy," was seen in an estimated 13.5 million homes. And that's homes, not people, so those families add up. For the two-week rating period including the Seeger show, *The Smothers Brothers Comedy Hour* made the Top 10 of all prime-time TV shows, tied for tenth place. *Bonanza,* its time-slot competitor and old nemesis, ranked fourth. (*Laugh-In,* which the Smothers Brothers had boosted in the Seeger show with some rare, defiant cross-network promotional inserts, wasn't near the Top 10 yet, but that would soon change.)

The second Seeger show was a hit with viewers, a home run for the artists, and a surprisingly well-received show with the network affiliates.

"I used to sing 'Big Muddy' at every college I came to, and to cheers," Seeger told me. "The funny thing is, somebody, sometimes in the middle of the song, would boo. There would be one or two lonesome boos—but at the end of the song, it was just overwhelmed by the applause. I was laughing, because some poor guy is looking around saying, 'What's our country coming to, when traitorous songs like that are sung?' Of course, I didn't consider it traitorous, I suppose. In my own sense, I thought of it as patriotic."

Seeger added, "I'm deeply proud to have been a part of that whole period. I don't know who agrees with me, but my own opinion is, it was a tremendous victory for the American people to get out of Vietnam. It might have been a defeat for the Pentagon, or a defeat for the people manufacturing bombers and bombs, but I really look upon it as an historic victory for the American people."

He wasn't alone in that assessment. In the months since he had first tried to sing "Waist Deep in the Big Muddy," more and more people were seeing things his way. "Maybe the song helped to do some good," Seeger said at the time. "President Johnson decided not to run again a month after I finally got in on the air."

More to the point, on the same CBS network, only two days after Seeger sang "Big Muddy" on *The Smothers Brothers Comedy Hour,* Walter Cronkite appeared with a special prime-time *CBS News Special* called "A Report from Vietnam by Walter Cronkite." In it, he offered the conclusion that "it seems now more certain than ever that the bloody experience of Vietnam is to end in a stalemate" and that more troops would not affect the probable outcome. "It is increasingly clear to this reporter," said Cronkite, who at that more noble time in broadcast news history still held the unofficial mantle of "the Most Trusted Man in America," "that the only rational way out . . . will be to negotiate, not as victors, but as an honorable people who lived up to their pledge to defend democracy, and did the best they could."

Johnson saw that broadcast and remarked afterward that if he'd lost Walter Cronkite regarding support of the Vietnam War, he'd lost middle America as well. At that particular moment, it appeared the Smothers Brothers and CBS were on the same page, reaching the same conclusions, caring about the same things. Those appearances, though, were dangerously deceiving.

16

"Classical Gas"

T om Smothers had every reason to feel vindicated, even invulnerable, after the second Pete Seeger broadcast. CBS had come around to his way of thinking, just as public wariness and weariness with the Vietnam War seemed to be falling more in line with his own antiwar opinions. *Variety* reported that one CBS affiliate, WJBK-TV in Detroit, had faded to a public service announcement rather than broadcast the final, telling verse of "Waist Deep in the Big Muddy," but otherwise, the once-blacklisted Seeger, and the once-censored song, had been received well. Four days after the telecast, Robert F. Kennedy, not yet a presidential candidate, said there was not "any prospect" for victory in Vietnam. The voices and concerns of youth, it appeared, were beginning to be heard. Not just heard, but respected.

The Smothers Brothers Comedy Hour had long ago been renewed for a third season—its high ratings had seen to that. And by reaching that threshold, Tom and Dick's company, Comedic Productions, also had the option to provide, and executive produce, a separate summer series. Dick wasn't much interested in the prospect—he had other plans for spending his summer—but Tom relished the idea of steering things from behind the scenes. He had some bold ideas, including hiring an intentionally, perhaps unprecedentedly, young writing staff, and already had tapped Glen Campbell to star. But first there were two more *Comedy Hour* shows to complete, to wrap up the second season.

The first order of business, in the first of two shows, was to note that both Glen Campbell and John Hartford had won Grammys for "Gentle on My Mind," and that both of them would be appearing on Tom's new summer series. Later in the show, the two performed together—Campbell on guitar, Hartford on banjo—singing and swapping verses on Hartford's already hugely popular composition. In another spot, Tom and Dick chatted with Campbell, who expressed gratitude for being selected as the *Comedy Hour* summer replacement. "It's a big break for me," Campbell said, but Tom teased that there might be other surprises to come. "The ulcer," Tom said. "And, if you really make it big, the divorce." Then they all launched into "Thank You Very Much," a song listing a series of things that did, or didn't, deserve thanks. "Thanks a lot for censorship" was one line, with little doubt which category it represented.

On the same show, Pat Paulsen furthered his presidential ambitions, delivering a speech and identifying his political affiliation as the Straight Talking American Government Party—the STAG Party, for short. Yet the most notable segment of all, in this penultimate show of the 1967–68 TV season, was the national TV debut of Mason Williams's "Classical Gas."

Mason was seated in front of an unfurled copy of his *Bus,* a life-sized, folded-up photograph of a Greyhound bus, a copy of which, Tom explained in his intro, was on view at the Museum of Modern Art. Mason was holding an acoustic guitar, looking very elegant and serious, and before long launched into his instrumental composition, which, at that point, no one had yet heard. Well, no one but Tom.

"I got to hear that song at least a hundred times in the process of Mason's writing it," Tom recalls, "because we were roommates at the time. And he'd say, 'Oh, God, I've got to change something here.'

And he'd start again, right from the beginning. I'd miss the change. I'd say, 'Where's the change? Play the change!,' you know. But I had to listen to the whole thing. He was really hot on it."

Mason had written it, he admits, to have something impressive to play—and, with luck, to seduce women—when people were passing around the guitar at parties. Mike Post, later a very successful TV theme song writer (*The Rockford Files, Hill Street Blues, NYPD Blue*), arranged the song for orchestra and recorded it with Mason's guitar prominent throughout. "The arrangement turned out to be really wonderful," Tom says. "The minute they recorded it, as soon as we could, we put it on the show."

For the song's *Comedy Hour* debut, the bus background was lifted to reveal a full orchestra behind Mason—an "orchestra" made up of life-sized cutouts of Mason himself, holding and appearing to play various instruments. Director Stan Harris, rehired for the last few shows of the season, cut quickly among them all to give the illusion of movement. The song took four months to hit the charts, but then it made it all the way to number two—kept from the top spot by the likes of "Hello, I Love You" by the Doors and "Hey Jude" by the Beatles. Eventually, "Classical Gas" became one of the most unusual, and iconic, songs of the late 1960s.

The season's final show was a family affair, with much of the hour spent giving bits of screen time, and thanks, to virtually the entire company and backstage crew. Announcer Roger Carroll is seen as well as heard, and bits of comedy business are given to the prop man, the cue card holders, even to Smothers managers Ken Kragen and Ken Fritz, who pretend to split up the brothers' salaries unfairly. West Coast censors Sam Taylor and Charles Pettijohn aren't on camera, but they are saluted. "Even though we've had our fights, we've had some good times with them, too," Tom says. "We'd like to thank our censors, Sam 'Party Pooper' Taylor and Charlie 'Petty' Pettijohn.

Tom (*left*) and Dick in grade school military uniforms.

Jack Benny hosts Tom and Dick on the final
Jack Benny show in 1965.

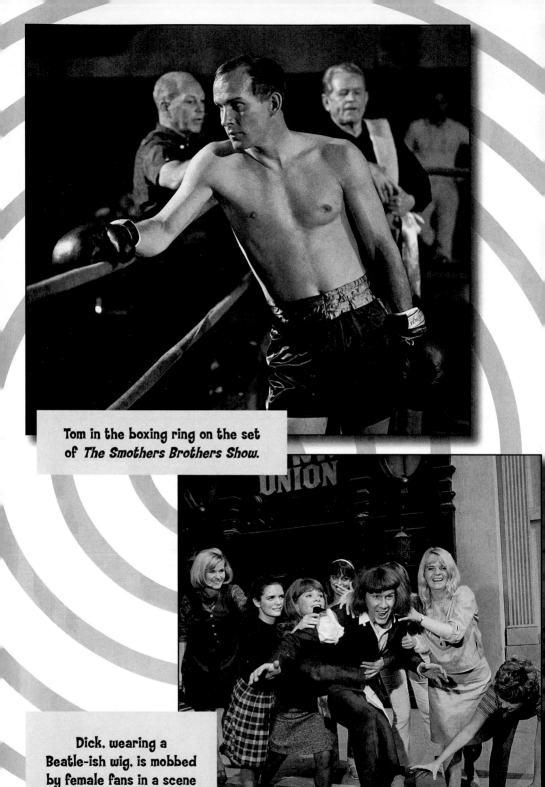

Tom in the boxing ring on the set of *The Smothers Brothers Show.*

Dick, wearing a Beatle-ish wig, is mobbed by female fans in a scene from *The Smothers Brothers Show.*

Dick and Tom in a private moment in January 1967 during production of the first installment of *The Smothers Brothers Comedy Hour.*

Tom and Dick on the Tiffany-styled stage for the opening scene of the February 5, 1967, premiere of *The Smothers Brothers Comedy Hour.*

Jack Benny and George Burns slip into the clothes and mannerisms of Tom and Dick, respectively, on episode three of the first season.

Tom and Bette Davis as Robespierre and Marie Antoinette in a first-season sketch that provided a template for later female movie star guest spots.

Tom, in costume for a first-season vaudeville number, checks the shot.

Elaine May and Tom play movie censors caught up
in the passion of the film they're censoring in a
first-season sketch that was banned by CBS.

Janet Leigh as a three-legged dancer in
"The Last Great Waltz," a first-season sketch
based on a song by staff writer Mason Williams.

Paul Simon and Art Garfunkel, as Western troubadours, flank Tom as Billy the Kid in a first-season sketch questioning television's acceptable levels of sex and violence.

Leigh French, in her first *Comedy Hour* appearance, emerges from the audience to have a long ad-libbed dialogue with Tom in this first-season show.

Tom and Dick perform in a second-season show with Bobby Blackmore, who was the third member of the Smothers Brothers in 1959.

Tom and Dick start their second season by welcoming blacklisted folksinger Pete Seeger, making his first prime-time TV appearance in almost two decades.

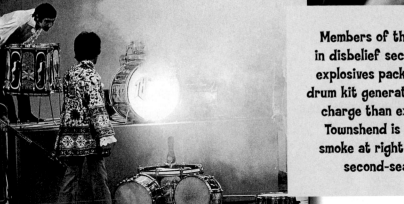

Members of the Who look on in disbelief seconds after the explosives packed into Moon's drum kit generate a much bigger charge than expected. Pete Townshend is caught in the smoke at right in this famous second-season show.

Staff writer Mason Williams and guest star Nancy Ames—who cowrote the *Smothers Brothers Comedy Hour* theme song—perform another collaborative composition "Cinderella Rockefella" in this second-season show.

Pat Paulsen delivers a second-season "editorial" about censorship.

CENSORED

Tom playfully musses Glen Campbell's hair as Tom and Dick announce that Campbell will host the brothers' summer 1968 variety series.

Pat Paulsen in a moment from the Pat Paulsen for President campaign in 1968 on *The Summer Brothers Smothers Show*.

Pat Paulsen records a comedy piece with Senator Robert F. Kennedy, who jokes about Paulsen's faux presidential campaign having "peaked too soon."

Tom and Dick open season three with a defiantly different look and sing an equally defiant "We're Still Here."

Tom, guest star Harry Belafonte, and Dick in a sp introduced as "Tom, Dick and Harry." It was broadca as recorded, but Belafonte politically charged solo "Carnival" medley was not

David Steinberg delivers a comic sermonette early in the third season. Reaction from viewers and affiliates was so heated that CBS bans Steinberg from delivering any more of them.

George Harrison makes a surprise appearance during the third season to support Tom and Dick's fights against the network censors.

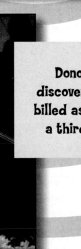

Donovan and *Comedy Hour* discovery Jennifer Warnes (then billed as Jennifer Warren) sing in a third-season concert show.

Jim Morrison sings "Touch Me," backed by the Doors and members of the *Comedy Hour* orchestra in this third-season show.

John Hartford, *Comedy Hour* writer and performer, plays guitar and sings in a third-season staff showcase.

Steve Martin, *Comedy Hour* writer, juggles and jokes in a third-season staff showcase.

Joan Baez with Tom and Dick in a third-season show.

David Frye does an impersonation of President Richard M. Nixon, who had recently taken office.

Mason Williams, whose "Classical Gas" instrumental had become a hit thanks to his many *Comedy Hour* appearances, returns late in the final season to perform one last song and to recite a poem, "The Censor," aimed at the audience as well as the network.

In the final installment of *The Smothers Brothers Comedy Hour*, staff writer Bob Einstein, as Officer Judy, sprays Mace at guest star Anthony Newley for allegedly pushing the limits too far in a comedy sketch.

THE WHITE HOUSE
WASHINGTON

November 9, 1968

Dear Messrs. Smothers:

I am very grateful for your kind and thoughtful
letter.

To be genuinely funny at a time when the world
is in crisis is a task that would tax the talents
of a genius; to be consistently fair when standards of fair play are constantly questioned demands the wisdom of a saint.

It is part of the price of leadership of this great
and free nation to be the target of clever satirists.
You have given the gift of laughter to our people.
May we never grow so somber or self-important
that we fail to appreciate the humor in our lives.

If ever an Emmy is awarded for graciousness,
I will cast my vote for you.

Sincerely,

Lyndon B. Johnson

Messrs. Tom and
 ' Dick Smothers
7800 Beverly Boulevard
Los Angeles, California 90036

Dick read portions of this letter from President Lyndon B. Johnson at the end of what proved to be the final *Comedy Hour*.

Months after the Smothers Brothers were fired by CBS, Tom was invited by John Lennon to visit him and Yoko Ono in their Montreal hotel room during their "Bed-in for Peace." John played one guitar, and Tom the other, as they led the day's guests, including Timothy Leary, in the recording of what became a generational anthem, "Give Peace a Chance."

In 2008, Tom and Dick serve as hosts of the Television Critics Association Awards in Los Angeles, where they are received very warmly.

That same year, Tom receives a special commemorative 1968 Emmy, honoring his uncredited writing for *The Smothers Brothers Comedy Hour*.

"We'd like you to meet these men," Tom continues, "but they're not here tonight. Because they're over at the bar across the street, entertaining the customers with the jokes they censored out of our show." (According to Tom, writer-producer Saul Ilson, and others, that actually was a fairly common practice.) And at the show's end, Tom gives a very memorable, and very telling, end-of-season salute: "It takes over one hundred twenty people, working strongly against each other, to get this show on the air."

The Smothers Brothers Comedy Hour ended the second season very powerfully. The Mason Williams "Classical Gas" show tied the program's season high, and the full 1967–68 *Comedy Hour* season was ranked in eighteenth place. That's a slight drop from the previous season's sixteenth place, but that was over only half a season. *Laugh-In*, with only half a season in its inaugural year, just missed the Top 20, finishing twenty-first, and the popularity of *Comedy Hour* had pushed *Bonanza* from number one to a tie for fourth. But things were about to change drastically, and not just in the Nielsen ratings.

One other segment in the final show of the second *Comedy Hour* season was a faux minidocumentary starring Pat Paulsen, on the campaign trail and with Tom Smothers acting as an intrepid reporter. It was a superb piece called "Pat Paulsen: The Making of a President" and included interviews with Woody Allen, Andy Williams, and others. The most noteworthy participant, though, was New York Democratic senator Robert F. Kennedy, who was interviewed by Tom about his opinion of Pat's presidential campaign. Gamely, and wittily, the senator provided one.

"I think he's a very nice man," Bobby Kennedy said of Pat Paulsen, "and I think that he's come forward and expressed himself on the issues. But I do think—looking at his campaign, watching carefully how he's moved—I think he has peaked a little early."

That program was broadcast on March 10, 1968. Six days later, RFK announced his own candidacy, and his intention to run for president. Lyndon Johnson, who had succeeded Bobby's assassinated brother, John F. Kennedy, in the White House, at that point was seeking another term. But a few weeks later, at the end of March, LBJ took to national TV—preempting a Smothers Brothers rerun—and told a stunned nation he would not seek reelection.

On April 4, less than a week after that, Martin Luther King Jr. would be dead, killed by an assassin's bullet. Two months after that, the same horrible fate would befall Robert Kennedy. If 1967 was the summer of love, 1968 was the summer of shock, grief, anger, and bitter divisiveness. And after all that, on the heels of the deaths of both King and RFK, the summer replacement program for *The Smothers Brothers Comedy Hour*, with an angry young gaggle of writers, tried to make sense of it all, and to find humor where so little seemed even remotely funny.

The Summer Brothers Smothers Show

Three months had elapsed between the March 1968 second-season finale of *The Smothers Brothers Comedy Hour* and the June 1968 premiere of its CBS summer replacement series, whimsically titled *The Summer Brothers Smothers Show*. During those three months, Martin Luther King Jr. and Bobby Kennedy were killed; more than one hundred students were arrested after a three-week sit-in at Columbia University; the Beatles fled their Indian retreat with the Maharishi Mahesh Yogi and soon denounced him; Vietnam peace talks began in Paris; LBJ decided not to seek reelection; *Hair* transferred uptown to Broadway; Simon and Garfunkel's "Mrs. Robinson" and Otis Redding's "(Sittin' on the) Dock of the Bay" had reached number one on the pop charts; and the movies released, in that three-month span, included Roman Polanski's *Rosemary's Baby*, the Beatles' *Yellow Submarine*, and Stanley Kubrick's *2001: A Space Odyssey*.

Also during that period, the Emmy Awards had honored the new kids on the variety block, *Laugh-In*, the variety series and writing awards over *Comedy Hour*, but had acknowledged Pat Paulsen's inventive and impressive comedy contributions by giving him an Individual Achievement Emmy for his work with the Smothers Brothers. And Mason Williams and Allan Blye, the *Comedy Hour* writers who had sung together on air as "The Cowboy and the Cantor," teamed to write an NBC variety special for Petula Clark, called *Petula*, with guest star Harry Belafonte. It became infamous for the uproar it caused, and fought, when Clark reached out and touched and held Belafonte's arm during a taping of one of their duets. It was her own composition, an antiwar song called "On the Path of Glory," they were singing, but it wasn't the message that incited a controversy—it was that a white woman had reached out and touched a black man on national television. The sponsor for the special was Chrysler, and a Chrysler executive present at the taping objected to the "interracial touching" and demanded another take, without the physical contact, be used instead. Clark refused, destroyed all other videotaped takes of the duet, and demanded the segment be broadcast intact or the entire special scrubbed. It was televised intact, after much national press attention about the backstage battle, and received high ratings and wide acclaim. It sounds absurd, but this was the first time a man and woman of different races had shared any physical contact on national TV. (The famous interracial kiss on *Star Trek* wouldn't occur until that fall.)

The summer show was loaded with veteran *Comedy Hour* talent, in front of and behind the camera. Produced at Television City in the familiar *Comedy Hour* studios and surroundings, it featured the same core support staff—the Louis DaPron Dancers, Jimmy Joyce Singers, Nelson Riddle and his orchestra—with Mason Williams and Allan Blye as supervising writers, and Ken Kragen and Ken Fritz as executive producers. On camera, Campbell and John Hartford already had been showcased on several *Comedy Hour* installments, and Pat Paulsen, Leigh French, and Mason Williams were signed on for the entire summer.

The real shift was in the production office and writers' rooms, where Tom was more determined than ever to reflect younger viewpoints and hire younger staffers. After two years as head producers for

The Smothers Brothers Comedy Hour, Ernest Chambers and Saul Ilson had quit, so Tom took up producing chores on his own, along with new hire George Sunga. "By then, we'd had enough," Ilson says. "All these fights for ridiculous reasons, and it just didn't make sense for Ernie and me to do it anymore. Two seasons was fine, and we felt that we were very proud of what we did." Tom and director Stan Harris also agreed to part ways, for the second time, after season two, and Tom hired a new director, Marty Pasetta, for *The Summer Brothers Smothers Show*. Youth and inexperience, in Tom's view, were assets, not liabilities, especially among the writing staff. Trusting Mason and Allan Blye to act as shepherds and guides, Tom wanted to hire a bunch of new writers—young people with little or no experience writing television—and give them a chance to experiment and learn, bringing fresh viewpoints and enthusiasm.

Tommy went to the Writers Guild of America and negotiated an innovative special arrangement for the summer show. "Scale was like $1,100 a week or something," Kragen recalls, "and Tommy wanted to have these writers, these new writers, in kind of a bullpen situation. And so he got an agreement, and made a deal with the union, that he would have six writers at $150 each a week, but each week, two of them would be paid full scale on a rotating basis."

The writers that began on the summer show made up the best bullpen of young writers since Mel Brooks, Carl Reiner, and Neil Simon collaborated on *Your Show of Shows*. Tom's eye for talent was never more evident, or more accurate. Steve Martin, Bob Einstein, John Hartford, Rob Reiner, McLean Stevenson—all of them, and others, got their start in the *Summer Brothers* writing room. And all but Stevenson, who eventually went on to play Colonel Henry Blake on the series *M*A*S*H*, were retained and elevated from the minors to the majors as writers for the third and final season of *The Smothers Brothers Comedy Hour*.

"That was great fun," Tom says. "I was paying more attention to that than to almost anything else." Almost every hire came with a story attached.

Before he gained fame as an actor as Archie Bunker's "Meathead" son-in-law on *All in the Family*, Rob Reiner was a twenty-one-year-old known to Tom mostly as the son of Carl Reiner, who had been on *Comedy Hour* a few times and was a critical component of *Your Show of Shows*, but that was enough. Tom saw Rob Reiner and Carl Gottlieb when they performed as members of the Los Angeles company of the improv comedy troupe the Committee, and hired them both. "It was my first writing job," Reiner says, and his passion about politics put Tom in the unusual position of arguing for moderation rather than instigation. "Reiner was *really* on my case as being soft," Tom says, and Reiner agrees. "I was a maniac," Reiner says. "I mean, I was the wildest radical lefty that you could possibly imagine." He would get into shouting matches with Tom, saying, "You're selling out!" In hindsight, though, today he credits Tom as being "on the cutting edge of TV."

Bob Einstein—who eventually got noticed as Officer Judy on the final *Comedy Hour* season, then went on to star as ill-fated stuntman Super Dave Osborne and as Marty Funkhouser on *Curb Your Enthusiasm*—was working at Grey Advertising in Los Angeles when he appeared on a local TV show and did a deadpan comedy spot pretending to be the person in charge of selecting stars for the sidewalk on Hollywood Boulevard. Tom called him the next day and offered him a writing and performing spot on the summer show—then didn't call back for months. "I don't hear from him for three and a half months," Einstein says. "So you go through the euphoria of 'Isn't this going to be unbelievable' to 'Fuck him, I'm not going to call him!' So I hear from him three and a half months later, and he says, 'We go to work next week.' I said, 'Let me tell you something, pal. I've been at this company for three years. You think I'm going to go in and give them a week's notice when I didn't hear from you? You are really something . . . ' I went on and on." Tom asked, a little sheepishly, "Well, how much time do you need?" and Einstein, who happens to be Albert Brooks's brother, was ready with his punch line: "Give me ten minutes."

John Hartford had been brought on the previous season of *Comedy Hour* as a performer, an impulsive but impressive decision shared by Tom and Mason when they were sharing something else: pot. "We started listening to Johnny Hartford's first album," Tom says, "while we were smoking some weed, and said, 'Hey, this is great! You want to invite him on the show?' 'Geez, yeah, bring him out!' So that was great. We could do that." And just as impulsively, they offered him a job on the summer show, serving as both on-air performer—backing Glen Campbell during the many concert segments—and as a staff writer. "I went back [to Tennessee] and got my wife and family," Hartford told me in 2000, "and we drove out there, and I started writing for them. My first project was the summer show."

Steve Martin was the strangest hire of all. At age twenty-two, he was a stand-up comic, but by no means a successful one. A young woman who had dated both Martin and Mason got Martin an audition as a possible guest performer near the end of season two. Martin, trying out in front of Mason, Tom, and other *Comedy Hour* writers and personnel, found a way to use his bad reviews to make a good first impression.

"He had a little case or something, and a music stand," Allan Blye remembers. "And he takes a bunch of papers out of this case and puts them on the music stand, and he starts to read from them, and they are reviews of his act. The worst reviews you could ever imagine . . . And while he's doing it, he is doing shit to himself like you cannot believe. He is breaking eggs, raw eggs, on his head, he is pie-ing himself, he is seltzer-ing his armpits and his crotch . . . Unbeliev-able. You can't see him anymore. There's just crap everywhere." He concludes by reading a long, glowing review of a concert by the Nitty Gritty Dirt Band. "And the last line of the review," Blye continues, "says, 'Opening act Steve Martin does nothing to be remembered by.' And he just looked out at everybody and said, 'I may not be very funny, but can you honestly say you won't remember me?' I was on the floor, it was so funny!" Tom and the others weren't sold on hiring Martin as a stand-up, but Blye suggested he showed promise as a writer. Mason agreed and was so supportive, he ended up hiring Martin for the last few shows of the second season of *Comedy Hour*—and providing his salary. "I was making three hundred dollars a week," Martin says, "and I found out later that Mason was paying me out of his own pocket." Martin was hired in time to contribute to, and witness, the show featuring Pete Seeger's return appearance. And when Martin was retained for the summer series, he benefited from the rotating-salary bullpen arrangement Tom negotiated.

Glen Campbell already had crossed paths with the Smothers Brothers, and with Mason Williams, before he was showcased as a guest star on *Comedy Hour* in season two and offered the job of summer show host. Campbell, an in-demand session musician whose guitar work can be heard on everything from the Beach Boys' 1964 hit "I Get Around" to Frank Sinatra's 1966 classic "Strangers in the Night," had been one of the musicians hired on the 1966 *Smothers Brothers Play It Straight* album. One of the producers of that LP was Mason, who, along with Campbell, had contributed to a pair of 1963 guitar album anthologies, *The Twelve-String Story*. Although he'd played guitar on lots of best-selling recordings by other artists (others in his résumé include the Righteous Brothers' "You've Lost That Lovin' Feelin'" and the first two albums by the Monkees), Campbell's first solo recording of note was "Gentle on My Mind," a John Hartford composition released in 1967 (reaching only number 62 on the charts), and rereleased a year later, after "By the Time I Get to Phoenix" made Campbell a crossover hit. In January 1968, Campbell performed both songs on ABC's late-night *The Joey Bishop Show*. Both Tom Smothers and Ken Fritz were watching, and both of them flipped over Campbell's material, his guitar, and his singing, and his affable, down-home, aw-shucks, casually comfortable personality as he interacted playfully with Bishop and his sidekick, Regis Philbin. Campbell was booked immediately on a *Comedy Hour* show for January. At that time, according to Fritz, others considered by Tom for the hosting job included Noel Harrison (who'd appeared on both *Comedy Hour* seasons to date) and singer Lou Rawls. But the *Joey Bishop* appearance made Campbell the instant front-runner.

"Tommy had called me after the Bishop show," Campbell says. "And out of the blue, he said, 'I think I would like you to host the *Summer Brothers Smothers Show*.' I said, 'Really?' And he said, 'Yeah—you can read, can't you?' " Before Campbell returned for his second *Comedy Hour* appearance in March, with "Gentle" composer Hartford appearing as well (and, surprisingly, meeting Campbell for the first time), Campbell already had been announced on-air by Tom as host of their upcoming summer series. Campbell had one stipulation, and insisted to Tom, "I can't do anything controversial."

Fat chance. Though Tom's intention was to make the summer series an intentionally lighter hour, there was no way to avoid controversy completely. Not with Leigh French doing drug jokes in almost every sketch. Or with Pat Paulsen continuing his sharp-edged satiric run for the White House. Or with a new stable of untested, unbroken TV writers—most of whom were well under thirty, and all of whom, except for Campbell, were decidedly liberal.

"There's nothing wilder than being . . . a team comedy writer on a weekly television show," Steve Martin says. "Because you lock yourself in a room and essentially go berserk. Our offices had no windows, and you have these guys who are mostly crazy, running around, and it's great. We would work long, long sessions into the night." Rob Reiner remembers that "everybody was high, smoking dope and doing stuff like that," but Einstein, Mason, and Tom all say any drug use was after hours, usually on weekends, because the production schedule was so grueling, no one could both imbibe and function. "It was not a stoned office," Einstein says. "But," he adds, with a smirk, "I believe that grass was smoked." Looking back on the experience of moving from Tennessee to Los Angeles and becoming a TV comedy writer, Hartford once told me, a bit ruefully, "I stopped behaving after I got out there, which quickly led to a divorce. I didn't know what it was like. I didn't know what it meant to really misbehave till I got out there."

In Maureen Muldaur's excellent 2002 documentary, *Smothered: The Censorship Struggles of The Smothers Brothers Comedy Hour,* Tom describes how he would take the next week's *Comedy Hour* or summer show script home, when he lived with Mason, and "torch a joint" before going through the scripts page by page, looking for inventive or funny material and crossing out the rest. Stoned or straight, Tom always was looking for the next thing, the fresh talent, the raw truth.

The Summer Brothers Smothers Show premiered in the summer of 1968, in what was a mostly bland prime-time TV lineup. Reruns dominated, topicality was frowned upon and all but nonexistent, and the major new variety-show competition that summer was NBC's *Dean Martin Presents the Golddiggers,* starring Joey Heatherton and a bevy of curvaceous chorines pretending to be flappers of the 1920s. (So much for topicality.) Actually, there was one stunningly original drama series imported during that period—Patrick McGoohan's *The Prisoner,* a CBS summer replacement for *The Jackie Gleason Show.* But truly, with *Laugh-In* off for the summer, nothing else on TV had the attitude, or the edge, of the *Summer Brothers* series.

Tom, coproducer George Sunga, and writing supervisors Allan

Blye and Mason Williams stocked their talent pool as aggressively as their writing bullpen. Some guests already had appeared on *Comedy Hour*: Nancy Sinatra, Bobbie Gentry, Judy Collins, Barbara Feldon, the First Edition. Some guests, like most of the summer show's new writers, would be brought back for season three of *Comedy Hour*; both George Carlin and Jennifer Warnes (then called Warren) were road-tested first on the summer series. And some very impressive guests would appear only on *The Summer Brothers Smothers Show*, including Flip Wilson, Johnny Cash, the Everly Brothers, Lulu, and an ultra-rare American TV appearance by Eric Clapton's supergroup Cream.

Tom's desire to be different was evident from the start. He and Dick introduce Campbell as the summer host, and Campbell's first solo number is performed against giant glittery letters spelling "GLEN." As dancers dance, Campbell sings "Once in a Lifetime," in what looks to be a standard variety-show production number—until it's interrupted, halfway through, by a drove of pigs wandering freely across the stage, surrounding and disrupting Campbell and the dancers. "I came up with that idea myself," Tom tells Campbell afterward, with mock pride. "One of the reasons I did this is because it's different."

That approach would explain a lot of the *Summer Brothers* features. Each episode opens with Campbell and John Hartford singing the opening verse of "Gentle on My Mind"—but from the audience, not the stage. And just the range of elements in the first of the ten summer installments shows how much these young writers were stretching things in ways that often would carry over to the final season of *Comedy Hour*. Pat Paulsen, performing in front of a white background as a spotlight shone brightly on him, performed a series of silly hand shadows ("This one won me a blue ribbon up at the Seattle Pottery and Marijuana Festival," he jokes), then uses two fingers to flash a "V" sign for peace. "We'd like to take it out of the shadows," he intones seriously. "Peace." Another segment, a film by Dan McLaughlin, presents almost subliminal images of artwork, with twelve different visuals shown each second, into a rapid-fire overview called *3,000 Years of Fine Art in Three Minutes*, set to Mason's "Classical Gas." ("We must have done seventy-two versions of 'Classical Gas,' " Bob Einstein jokes.) When it was over, Campbell announced, "You are now cultured." Nothing quite like it had ever appeared on TV, but *Comedy Hour* soon would return to the idea, making political as well as artistic statements with its rapid-fire film montages. Leigh French reported on the latest fashion statement, which she claimed was the unadorned naked body: "Not only is it wash and wear," she explains, "but it comes in a variety of colors."

And even when not resorting to a parade of pigs, that first summer show's musical elements are ambitiously original. The Beatles' "She's Leaving Home" is sung by Campbell, with string-section accompaniment, while being enacted comically by Tom, Dick, and Nancy Sinatra. They all sing "Squares Make the World Go Round," which segues into a dance performance of Dave Brubeck's famously (and literally) offbeat "Unsquare Dance," a very jazzy, risky number to present. And like other summer shows, this one carves out a large chunk for Campbell, Hartford, and other musicians to huddle near the audience and perform an intimate, casual mini-concert. "This is *my* thing, here," Campbell says, and he means it. The level of musicianship is first-class—and it's no accident that, when the summer was over, Tom staged a series of in-the-round concert specials on *Comedy Hour.*

Other unusually conceived musical highlights from *Summer Brothers* included a full-hour country concert, with Johnny Cash and the Tennessee Three performing "Folsom Prison Blues"; Barbara Feldon singing "After the Lights Go Down Low" while soaking in a bubble bath, with the camera swooping above and around her; an oldies revue of classic rock, conceived by Steve Martin and Rob

Reiner; and Cream's "Sunshine of Your Love," in a live performance, with a sizzling Clapton solo, that's jaw-droppingly great and different from most televised representations of a rock band: Clapton and bass player Jack Bruce face drummer Ginger Baker, rather than the audience, intently focusing on the music they were making.

The comedy, following Tom's mandate, was different also. Bob Einstein, playing an unethical auto mechanic in one comedy skit, displayed the droll, imposing persona that would earn him the role of Officer Judy on *Comedy Hour*. Leigh French played a weather reporter tracking the national climate, drawing high-pressure lines and other symbols that spelled the word HATE, then, by erasing and rewriting a few squiggles, projected a forecast of a change to HOPE. Pat Paulsen kept offering new presidential policies, including better ways to spend the defense budget. "It costs the government about $600,000 for every Vietnamese person killed," he noted, then suggested, "They can be bought off cheaper than that. In fact, *I* can be bought off cheaper than that." Guest star George Carlin appeared as guest host of a twisted comedy skit called "The Torture Game," a probable reaction to Firesign Theatre's "Beat the Reaper" audio sketch on their *Waiting for the Electrician or Someone Like Him* debut album, released earlier that year. (Firesign Theatre was a comedy troupe that recorded the LP equivalents of lavishly produced radio comedies.)

Tom recalls that during the summer, the CBS program practices department was easier to deal with, although there were occasional memos of objection from the West Coast, and even one William Tankersley–written memo from New York. As a producer rather than star, Tom was more willing to compromise, and he recalls turning the game of battle-the-censors into a *literal* game—of Ping-Pong. A table was set up outdoors, on the roof terrace, for staffers to unwind, and Tom once bet the status of a joke—left in, or cut out—on the outcome of a Ping-Pong game with censor Sam Taylor, who agreed to the duel. Tom's recollection has Tom winning, two out of three. "There were no hard-and-fast rules," Tom explains, noting that the network's acceptance of "Big Muddy" in the same season as its earlier outright rejection taught him to approach controversial material creatively and aggressively. "We had to push it," he says, "because sometimes when you push it again, they'll change their mind if you re-present it." Ironically, most of the hesitancy and conservatism that summer came not from the network presenting *The Summer Brothers Smothers Show,* but from its star.

On his final *Comedy Hour* guest appearance of the second season, just before shifting to the summer show, Glen Campbell was put into a segment in which Pat Paulsen, in his tongue-in-cheek role as a presidential candidate, remarked on politicians who had, or hadn't, entered the race. One of them was Ronald Reagan, and Pat's line about Reagan was that he was "a known heterosexual." At first, Campbell refused to have anything to do with that word, or that scene, until he looked it up in the dictionary. It was a moot point—CBS cut the line from the tape anyway, before it was broadcast—but Campbell, who was about to go off and star opposite John Wayne in the Western *True Grit,* wasn't interested in espousing any particular political viewpoint. Especially a liberal one.

"I was very sympathetic to Glen," John Hartford said, "because I kind of came from the same background that Glen did, although I got the joke." According to Mason, the summer host was alone in *not* getting it. "The only person who didn't understand the drift of the show was Glen Campbell," Mason says. "I'm serious . . .

"The summer show would have been gigantic if you'd have had a star that was with you. We used to call him Joe Palooka. That was his nickname. I like Glen as a person, but I never did understand how brainwashed he was by his position on things. He was so enamored of that establishment world. When he did *True Grit* with John Wayne and all those sorts of things—that was like the greatest day of his life, to be part of that world."

After *The Summer Brothers Smothers Show*, Campbell took the summer series and continued it as a renamed winter spinoff, called *The Glen Campbell Goodtime Hour*. Tom retained the title of executive producer but focused energies on his own series instead. *Goodtime Hour* premiered in January 1969 and continued until the summer of 1972—outlasting its parent program by three years. And Tom, though he had ownership of Campbell's TV series, didn't retain the rights. "Tommy gave me the show," Campbell said, somewhat incredulously, and very appreciatively. "Just gave it to me. He didn't even take any money. I said, 'Wow, you are generous!' "

Tom, at the time, had his eyes on a different prize. As he did with the season two opening show, by breaking the prime-time blacklist of Pete Seeger, Tom had something special in mind with which to begin season three that September.

In August, while *The Summer Brothers Smothers Show* was presenting its last three episodes, a lot was happening on the Republican side of the presidential ticket. Ronald Reagan, that "known heterosexual," announced his intention to run for the Oval Office, but to no avail: a few days later, Richard Nixon won the nomination at the Republican National Convention and named Spiro Agnew as his running mate. With Bobby Kennedy assassinated and LBJ refusing to run for reelection, Vice President Hubert Humphrey was the clear Democratic frontrunner. But with little more than two weeks to go before the Democratic National Convention, antiwar senator George McGovern announced his candidacy. Also that month, the Smothers Brothers released their first comedy LP in three years, titled and culled from *The Smothers Brothers Comedy Hour*. On August 25, they televised the final edition of *The Summer Brothers Smothers Show*. The next day, the Democratic National Convention, with thousands of antiwar demonstrators gathered around the site, convened in Chicago. Chaos and brutality festered inside and outside the hall. Dan Rather, reporting inside the convention center for CBS, was knocked to the ground and punched by security forces, men whom anchor Walter Cronkite characterized as "a bunch of thugs." Hundreds were arrested in battles between protesters and police, in bloody skirmishes filmed and broadcast nationwide by TV news crews. Humphrey got the Democratic nomination, Edmund Muskie was named his vice presidential running mate, and Mayor Richard Daley's brutal treatment of the protesters fanned the flames on both sides of the Vietnam War issue. "The policeman isn't there to create disorder," Daley said afterward in a famous slip of the tongue. "The policeman is there to preserve disorder."

With all that going on, Tom had his idea for a nifty season opener. He'd take CBS news footage of the Chicago riot and use it as background for a big musical number.

Welcome to season three, the year CBS declared war on Tom Smothers—and vice versa.

Season Three: "We're Still Here"

G oing into season three, Tom Smothers had plenty to say and was more determined than ever to say it. The Democratic National Convention in Chicago was a fitting metaphor for the tensions tearing the country apart: young versus old, hawk versus dove, conservative versus liberal. For the first *Comedy Hour* telecast of the 1968–69 season, Tom wanted not just a special guest star, but an ally, a fellow soldier in his war to influence public opinion as an entertainer. In that regard, he could hardly have chosen better than Harry Belafonte.

Belafonte, with his influential *Calypso* album and "Banana Boat (Day-O)" song, was one of the first artists satirized by the Smothers Brothers when they developed their act, back when they were a trio. A decade later, it was Belafonte's civil rights and political activism, no less than his music, that attracted Tom. Belafonte's entire career was a history of brave, bold stands against injustice. From 1954 to 1961, Belafonte refused to perform in the segregated South and, like Pete Seeger, once was a victim of the McCarthy blacklist. He was a cultural adviser to John F. Kennedy's Peace Corps, a friend and supporter of Martin Luther King Jr., and an organizer of King's 1963 March on Washington. In February 1968, when Belafonte was a guest host for Johnny Carson on NBC's *The Tonight Show*, his guests one night included Lena Horne and Bill Cosby (proudly showcasing other talented black entertainers), Robert F. Kennedy (not yet in the presidential race, but eager to talk angrily about cutbacks in the so-called war on poverty), and the Smothers Brothers. Tom and Dick discussed material that had been censored by CBS, and Jack Gould of the *New York Times* applauded Belafonte's defiant coup: "letting one network present what another network refused to carry, which could be a welcome amendment to video's prevailing mores." On the same show, Belafonte told Tom and Dick he'd be "honored" to appear on *The Smothers Brothers Comedy Hour*, to which Tom replied jokingly, "We don't allow any of that interracial stuff."

A month after that *Tonight Show* appearance, Belafonte stirred up trouble again, this time unintentionally, with the furor that arose after he touched Petula Clark's arm on her NBC special *Petula*, written by *Comedy Hour* writing partners Allan Blye and Mason Williams. "I loved working with Harry," Mason said—and now, to start season three, they'd all get to work with him again.

Belafonte was given the spotlight in four different segments for the third-season opener. One was a standard solo musical spot. Another was a trio appearance with the Smothers Brothers, where, yes, they playfully introduced themselves as Tom, Dick, and Harry. A third was a lengthy comedy spot, "Bonanzarosa," in which they all, along with guest stars singer Mama Cass Elliot and football star Rosey Grier, spoofed their NBC competition. That one had some lines of dialogue censored and might have generated more controversy, if not for the fact that Belafonte's fourth contribution proved so incendiary that CBS refused to air it at all—sparking the rapid, total disintegration of the relationship between the network and the *Comedy Hour* staff. In it, Belafonte sings a calypso medley built around "Don't Stop the Carnival," written originally about the frenzied madness of a Mardi Gras celebration, but with new lyrics added to refer to the Democratic National Convention—as footage from the convention, and of police dragging and arresting protesters outside the hall, is projected behind him.

"Since the Smothers Brothers' show was not only a format of music, but also a format of social and political satire," Belafonte explains, "it seemed to us the most appropriate thing to do would be to comment on the way the conventions were behaving, and the political situation in America was unfolding. So the idea that we do something to satirize the events of the day was on the table in general." He adds, "I specifically came up with the song, and when it was put before the group, we all had a hand in trying to rewrite the lyrics and to shape them, to be able to make political comment."

The first few verses of the song are sung by Belafonte underneath a warmly lit Tiffany-style overhang, with no news clips. It appears to be a standard variety number ("Lord, don't stop the carnival / carnival's an American bacchanal"), until the footage kicks in, with delegates screaming, police batons flying, and guns being drawn. "Let it be known," Belafonte sings, "freedom's gone and the country's not our own."

Sam Taylor, one of the members of the CBS program practices department on the West Coast, objected to the "Carnival" number before it was even blocked and rehearsed. Tom was warned that no footage could be shown depicting any violence whatsoever, or clearly identifying any individuals. Taylor's boss, Tom Downer, allowed the Smothers Brothers to proceed with the taping but warned that the number would not be accepted for broadcast. The season opener was taped on September 20 and televised nine days later. During those nine days, an increasingly testy series of memos, letters, and telegrams was exchanged—between coasts, from executives, producers, agents, lawyers, and others. The Smothers Brothers had been censored and had argued their case before. They even had reason to believe, given that the second season of *Comedy Hour* had ended with CBS capitulating on the Pete Seeger controversy over "Big Muddy," that they might win their case again by stating it forcefully and pursuing it passionately.

Season three, though, was a completely different battlefield. Tom had come out of the summer series with a new band of angry young writers and without original series producers Saul Ilson and Ernest Chambers, who served as elder-statesmen buffers between Tom and the network. By then, the image of Tom and Dick as either caustic troublemakers or censorship victims (depending upon your point of view) was so widespread that *Mad* magazine published a satiric memo, in rhyme, to "The Smothered Brothers" from CBS. Caricatures of Tom and Dick were shown gagged and chained, and the memo enumerated the many topics the brothers were to avoid in season three. "Don't kid the Blacks, don't kid the Whites / Cross out the Klan and Civil Rights," went one couplet. Another would prove amazingly prophetic, identifying the very third-rail topic that would help get the Smothers Brothers fired that very season: "Be funny, boys, but it's taboo / To clown with Catholic or Jew."

If people were expecting the Smothers Brothers to be combative, and to present material in their show that reflected the changing times, the 1968–69 season premiere certainly didn't disappoint. Instead of wearing their trademark colored blazers and ties, Tom and Dick open the show sporting stylized cranberry Nehru jackets and white turtlenecks—and mustaches, at a time when the network was oddly uncomfortable about facial hair. At a podium, Tom asks for a voice vote from the studio audience on whether they like the Smotherses' new appearance. Coached in advance on the gag, the crowd offers a smattering of unenthusiastic "ayes," then a resoundingly loud chorus of "nays." Tom hammers his gavel, confers with Dick, and announces, "In the true American Democratic conventional spirit, the ayes have it." Then, after the opening credits, they perform their opening number, a line-in-the-sand burst of defiance called "We're

Still Here" with new lyrics by Mason Williams and others, based on John Hartford's "I'm Still Here."

> *The war in Vietnam keeps on a-ragin'*
> *Blacks and whites still haven't worked it out,*
> *Pollution, guns, and poverty surround us—*
> *No wonder everybody's dropping out,*
> *But we're still here . . .*

It's an amazing opening, more of a mission statement or a manifesto than a peppy opening song, though it is that, too. And if the first verse stressed the current problems nationwide, the second verse, no less bluntly, took direct aim at the Smothers Brothers' more immediate problems with the network and even with the TV audience:

> *That weekly grind is stretching out before us,*
> *Beeping censors lurking in the wings—*
> *CBS would like to give us notice,*
> *And some of you don't like the things we say,*
> *But we're still here . . .*
> *You may not think we're funny,*
> *But we're still here . . .*

And then the capper, the final verse that addresses head-on how much they've changed—and how, at the same time, they haven't:

> *Both of us have grown a manly mustache,*
> *Blazers that we always wore are gone,*
> *Our clean-cut, all-American look is changing,*
> *But underneath, we're still old Dick and Tom,*
> *But we're still here . . .*

The CBS censors sitting at that taping couldn't have been comfortable with that opening song, but they had plenty of other troublesome segments demanding their attention. Pat Paulsen, bringing his presidential campaign into the fall, attacked the competition in ways that made CBS squirm. Responding to the bumper-sticker slogan "Nixon's the One," Pat Paulsen deadpanned, "I don't care if he *is* one." He also said, "The other candidates charge that when I speak, I often embarrass myself. At least I don't embarrass the whole country." And, in the show's first direct allusion to the Democratic National Convention in Chicago, Pat boasted, "Today, I have so many new major supporters that even Mayor Daley couldn't beat them off with a stick." Even the most innocently entertaining offerings caused the censors to write notes and voice objections. A Tom and Dick performance of "My Old Man," their old stage standby from the *Think Ethnic!* days, still was considered risqué enough to generate memos about the "chicken plucker" tongue-twister. And guest star Mama Cass Elliot's lovely vocal performance of "Dream a Little Dream of Me" was considered pushing the envelope—because she sang it while she and Tom were in bed together, with Tom falling asleep but being roused whenever Mama Cass raised her volume.

Then there was the closing sketch, "Bonanzarosa," taking aim not only at *Bonanza*—still the Smotherses' formidable time-slot competitor—but at the Nielsen ratings, which earlier was declared off limits as a subject by CBS. Satirizing a rival TV show in the same time slot was unusual, but not unprecedented: In the 1950s, Dean Martin and Jerry Lewis, when guest hosting NBC's *Colgate Comedy Hour,* had taken aim at their direct competitor, Ed Sullivan's *Toast of the Town,* by presenting a lengthy and very funny spoof, "Toast of the Colgate Town," starring Lewis as a very toothy "Ed Solomon." In the Smotherses' spoof of *Bonanza,* they were after more than just a Western parody.

"It had come from the scriptwriters first," Belafonte recalls, "and then it had been put before me, seeking my vote as to whether I found anything about the sketch offensive—and, if I did approve of it, would I be willing to play in it? And I wholeheartedly approved of it and *was* willing to play in it."

In the sketch, Pat Paulsen plays Ben Cartwrong, Belafonte plays Little Jerk, and Mama Cass is Hass. (Parodying, respectively, the patriarchal Ben Cartwright and his sons Little Joe and Hoss.) The spoof opens with a branding iron burning a map, as on the Western they're lampooning—but instead of "Bonanza," the branding iron reads "Censored." And the plot, quickly unveiled, involves the kidnapping of a local family—the Nielsens—by a pair of outlaws (played by Tom and Dick) known as the Smut Smothers. They arrive with bandanas covering their mouths—bandanas that read "Censored." The sketch includes several calculatingly naughty plays on the name Hass (as in "grab Hass" and "wise Hass"), one well-received Belafonte ad lib (when Tom strips Belafonte's Little Jerk of his fake mustache, Belafonte raises his gun and says, "Put my hair back, white boy!"), and a twisted sight-gag climax in which former Los Angeles Rams football player Rosey Grier, dressed in drag, emerges from hiding—literally, comes out of the closet—as the long-missing Ma Cartwrong. Belafonte's classic reaction, "Oooh, you a *big* mother!" somehow made it past the censors without complaint, as did the part where Rosey, as Ma, picks up "son" Little Jerk, hugs him, and plants a kiss on his forehead.

"Here comes this black woman, in a male form," Belafonte says, laughing. "It was so funny. It was so really, viscerally *funny*." Yet the kiss Rosey Grier planted on Belafonte's forehead, the singer continues, offered "a lot to be said to the homophobic men all over the world. It was a wonderful, wonderful thing that show did."

Equally wonderful, and no less daring, was the final capper to the skit, when Rosey, as Ma, kisses the forehead of Mama Cass's Hass.

("Now they'll *never* get the Nielsens back," says a mustache-twirling Tom.) Take away the gender-bending comedy play-acting of Rosey Grier playing a woman and Mama Cass playing her son, and what you have, on national television, is a white woman being kissed, albeit on the forehead, by a black man. This is only five months after the Petula Clark–Harry Belafonte incident. Yet the CBS censors were so concerned about the "Hass" puns in the sketch, and so infuriated by Belafonte's "Carnival" number, that the rest, for the most part, slipped on by.

The day the show was taped, the first interoffice CBS memo was sent, chastising the West Coast operation for allowing *Comedy Hour* representatives to screen and copy network news footage of the convention there. Then the real fighting began, with CBS standing firm on its rejection of the "Carnival" number and Tom standing equally firm on arguing for its inclusion. By September 25—four days before the season premiere was scheduled to air, and two days before the Smothers Brothers were set to tape their next show (for broadcast the following week)—West Coast CBS executives were getting their East Coast counterparts and bosses involved.

Programming executive Perry Lafferty sent a telegram to Mike Dann in New York, summarizing a lengthy, heated meeting he'd had with Tom and his personal managers. Tom, Lafferty said, had threatened to hold the master tape hostage and not return it "until the very last minute" in hopes that CBS would accept the program as is, with the "Carnival" number intact. Lafferty said CBS wouldn't change its position, but Tom argued that in the past, CBS already had, many times. "It is my opinion that we have two courses opened to us," Lafferty wired Dann. "First, we capitulate and run the Belafonte number, and thus will never again have any real control over the creative content of this program for the duration of its run. Or we take the strongest legal position possible in [an] attempt to establish the fact that the Smothers Brothers must live under the same rules as all of our other programs."

Tom took the issue up the chain of command to William Tankersley, who, to this point, had rarely gotten involved in any problems involving *The Smothers Brothers Comedy Hour*. Because the telecast was only days away, and the arguments between Tom and Tankersley's West Coast operative Sam Taylor had gotten so heated, Tankersley agreed to talk to Tom by phone. The appeal didn't help much, because Tankersley hung up and fired off a memo to Tom, listing the four items in the season premiere "which for reasons of policy and taste are not acceptable." Three of them involved the "Bonanzarosa" sketch, including the lines "grab Hass" and "wise Hass" (which ended up being bleeped)—and the fourth was Belafonte's "Carnival" medley.

It wasn't so much the issue of showing some violence, which Tom included despite warnings to the contrary, Tankersley explained to me in 2008. The issue was that Chicago mayor Richard Daley was clearly identifiable and shown in clips that were, to put it lightly, not at all flattering.

"It wasn't the Chicago convention stuff behind him," Tankersley said of the Belafonte number. "It was Mayor Daley behind him. That was the big problem . . . It was a direct attack on Daley."

Strengthened by the backing of Tankersley in New York, Tom Downer, head of program practices on the West Coast, went on the offensive. "If the tape is delivered to us containing these items," Downer wrote in a memo addressed directly to Tom, "we shall be forced to delete them." All this activity took place the same day. The next day, Tom tried a finesse play and listed the "Carnival" medley, a taped production number now deemed unacceptable for the season premiere, into the final draft script rundown for the following *Comedy Hour* show, which would be taped the following day for later broadcast. Sam Taylor, Downer's subordinate, caught the bait-and-switch, and fired off a memo of his own. "We must reiterate that, for reasons of policy," he warned Tom and the show's producers, "this material is unacceptable." Tom no sooner received the memo than he replied with a one-sentence missive of his own: "Contrary to your statements," he wrote curtly, " 'policy' has not been defined." Then Tom upped the ante by calling in the lawyers.

Jack Schwartzman, representing Tom and Dick's Comedic Productions, sent a letter on September 26, addressed to Tankersley. "This letter is a formal request," it said, "that we be furnished as soon as possible with a copy of CBS' Program Practices and Standards." He explained that repeated informal requests by his clients for such written guidelines had been ignored. He also requested, in the future, that "each and every CBS objection to program content be furnished in writing to our client, and the specific provision of CBS' Program Practices and Standards alleged to be violated be identified." Schwartzman also sent a letter to Perry Lafferty, CBS West Coast programming executive, to complain that "the threatened deletion of the Belafonte Carnival Medley . . . constitutes an unauthorized interference with Comedic's creative control of the program." The attorney, on behalf of his clients, agrees they themselves will make the requested deletions from the season opener, including a removal of the "Carnival" medley, merely to "preserve the artistic quality of the remainder of the program." But here, too, Schwartzman asked for a copy of the network's guidelines and threatened that without such information, "Comedic can only interpret this as an act of bad faith on the part of CBS."

Attorneys have no problem recognizing "bad faith" as a lawsuit-threatening buzzword, and CBS responded the same day. CBS lawyer Frederick C. Wing sent a telegram back to Schwartzman, informing him that if the Smothers Brothers carried through on their idea (threat?) to recycle the unapproved Belafonte "Carnival" medley tape into the second show of the season, "appropriate action" would be taken. The same day, West Coast censor Robert Tamplin provided CBS with a program status report on all shows taped at CBS Television City, including the season-opening show with the Belafonte number now removed. "Due to censoring problems," he writes, "the Sunday air show will be delivered to us on Saturday at noon."

Tom's solution to replacing the Belafonte number, for the short term, was to take a moment during the September 27 taping of the show scheduled to run October 6—the one featuring Nancy Sinatra and the Beatles—and do a Q&A with the audience, then quickly insert it into the tape for the September 29 season premiere. That segment survives, and it seethes with hostility. Tom says they have to fill time "for various reasons," while Dick suggests the audience "switch to *Bonanza*"—but only for a few minutes. Finally, Tom gets down to issues: "Who has the last say-so, the censors or you?" he asks, and also asks the audience to deluge the network with letters, to protest that TV isn't allowed to express itself in the same manner as other American mass media. Tom comes off as strident but sincere, and the studio audience applauds. The audience in their living rooms, however, never saw it. CBS had one more card to play—and it was a doozy.

"I would estimate that the show will be eight to eight and a half minutes short," Tamplin wrote about the "Carnival"-free season opener in his status report of September 27. That was the very day Tom and Dick were taping the next show, including the angry Q&A segment they intended to insert as a substitute in the Belafonte show, but Tamplin and CBS, obviously, already had other ideas. "Five minutes of the time," Tamplin wrote of that third-season opener, "will be filled by a political buy." At that point, Tom contacted Belafonte to let him know the song had been pulled from the opener. "He was very angry," Belafonte recalls. "And he said the battle was far from over—that this would have to be taken to other authorities, and the basis of its problem discussed on a broader playing field. And I thought that his point of view was valid, and one that should be supported."

On Sunday, September 29, season three of *The Smothers Brothers Comedy Hour* premiered on CBS, without Belafonte's "Carnival" medley. "It would have been one of the most electrifying moments in the hour," Mason says. "With 'Don't Stop the Carnival,' the original [song] was the madness of Mardi Gras, and this was the madness of the political machine." In Canada, the complete program, including the medley, was shown by CTV, and the only person it seemed to offend was an American citizen teaching in Canada who, in the era before VCRs and DVRs and TiVos, wanted to watch it twice. "I was very impressed by a biting medley sung by Harry Belafonte to the accompaniment of newsreels of the recent Democratic Party Convention," he wrote. "I was so struck and affected by this number that I decided to catch it again when the show was aired on CBS [in his area, from Cleveland] later the same evening. To my astonishment and horror," he continued, "the entire number had been completely cut, and as an American citizen I am fighting mad about it. Must Americans now watch Canadian television to see uncensored versions of American programs?" When it came to *The Smothers Brothers Comedy Hour*, yes.

Both Canadians and US citizens watching a CBS affiliate, however, saw the season premiere end with the same thing—the "political buy" referred to by Tamplin to replace the space opened with the deletion of the "Carnival" number. The five minutes were sold to the Republican Party, as a campaign spot for Republican presidential candidate Richard M. Nixon.

"I was furious," Tom says. "But that was pretty clever of them," he says of the Republicans, "buying that kind of time on a show that had a tendency to lean the other way." Mason Williams, in the less heated perspective of decades later, also credits CBS with winning that particular battle with a devilishly vindictive twist. "Selling a five-minute spot to Nixon—how was *that* for one-upsmanship?" he asks. "I have to admire that," he adds, laughing at the memory.

Ironically, Jack Gould's review of the season premiere in the *New York Times* complained that "Harry Belafonte had one solo, which was not nearly enough." And within days, Tom was back in the *Times* again, this time complaining about the CBS censorship. "They destroyed our first show," Tom said of the season opener. "We intend to insert Mr. Belafonte's song segment in this Sunday's program to force CBS to spell out its policy. But we don't expect to see it on the air."

Instead, after lawyers on both sides exchanged vitriolic letters, Tom and the show's producers backed down. Instead of trying to reinsert the "Carnival" medley in the following show, producer Allan Blye informed Bob Tamplin that the time would be filled with a new Q&A spot, this one including Pat Paulsen and centered on his presidential campaign. The return memo from Tamplin was, in its way, priceless: "Eight minutes is a long period for question and answers," he wrote. "Would it be possible to use a portion of this eight minutes with Tom and Dick performing a number together? They have no similar type number in the show, thus no conflict." The Smothers Brothers, from this point on, were in no mood to placate or play nice. They had met the enemy—and more and more, they perceived the enemy as CBS.

19

Meet the Beatles—
This Time on *Comedy Hour*

When the Beatles made their live American television debut on *The Ed Sullivan Show* in February 1964, breaking TV viewership levels, Beatlemania began in earnest. These polite but cheeky young men from England, dressed in matching suits with matching bowl haircuts, owed a large part of their global superstardom to their exposure on Ed Sullivan's show. Yet four years later, much had changed. The Beatles had stopped touring, stopped dressing alike, stopped cutting their hair—stopped doing anything they didn't want to do, which included making the usual rounds to promote a new record. When it came time to publicize the new Beatles single, a double-sided gem with "Hey Jude" on one side and "Revolution" on the other, the group decided to stay in the studio, invite a small audience, film themselves performing, and send out the videotape as a new method of promotion: a "music video." And to make it a TV event, the Beatles doled out the videos slowly, and exclusively. It's hard to imagine, in the internet era when everything seems to be available instantly, but it took a month before the Beatles videos crossed the Atlantic. Early in September, "Hey Jude" was unveiled in England on David Frost's Sunday program. A few weeks later, the video of "Revolution" was shown on *Top of the Pops*, that country's equivalent of *American Bandstand*. In America, the double-sided single hit number one—and the very next week, the video of "Hey Jude" was televised in America for the first time. *The Smothers Brothers Comedy Hour* had it (and, a week later, "Revolution") exclusively in the United States. Though *Comedy Hour* was on the same network and night as *The Ed Sullivan Show,* the Beatles saw the Smothers Brothers as kindred spirits, and *Comedy Hour* was where they wanted to be.

"We were the hot show at that time," Tom recalls. "We were against the war in Vietnam, and all about peace and love and everything. There was no point for the Beatles to put their stuff on Sullivan, when our show was where it was philosophically. They were in agreement with us, and we were knocked out by them." The Beatles contacted the Smothers Brothers, offered them exclusive American rights to the pair of videos, and that was that. And both videos were mesmerizing. On "Hey Jude," just as Paul McCartney's scream leads into the lengthy sing-along chorus, the group is surrounded by fans, who crowd right next to them and sing along. "Revolution" features a boisterous rock 'n' roll performance from the entire group—a fabulous, high-energy video—and John Lennon, singing lead, hedges his bet after singing "But when you talk about destruction / Don't you know that you can count me out" by adding a qualifying, contradictory ". . . in."

"It was a tremendous coup," Ken Kragen recalls. "When you become a hot show, a talked-about show, a written-about show, a lot of stuff starts to fall your way. You get momentum. It's always hard to get momentum, but once you have momentum, everything becomes a heck of a lot easier." Everything, that is, except the internal dealings with CBS.

The *Comedy Hour* with "Hey Jude," shown as the second program of the third season, drew a 25.1 Nielsen rating and a 37 percent share of the viewing audience—big enough to edge out *Bonanza* as the number-one show in the time slot. It was only the fourth time that the Smothers Brothers had beaten a first-run episode of the NBC Western, and it would be the last. At the time, the Smothers Brothers were riding at a creative and popular high, presenting ambitious, entertaining shows and delivering audiences that were very profitable for CBS. Had the relationship between the show and the network been less antagonistic, the show could have continued and flourished for years. Instead, at the same time Tom and Dick were delivering attention-getting exclusives like the Beatles, they were fighting— and losing—battles to present other things. Tom's on-air intro to the second Beatles video said it all, and said it plainly:

"If you watched our show last week," he said, "you saw the Beatles singing 'Hey Jude.' And if you also watched the show the week before, you *didn't* see Harry Belafonte singing 'Please Don't Stop the Carnival.' Which has nothing to do with the fact that the Beatles will now sing 'Revolution.' Or does it?"

Any doubts that Tom would refuse to go quietly were also va- porized by the opening of that "Revolution" show, which began with one of the most famously belligerent comedy bits of the entire series. Some of the show's writers—Murray Roman, Bob Einstein, Steve Martin, and Carl Gottlieb—are lined up onstage, passing a script to one another, laughing, then ripping pages from it as they go. Finally, a single surviving page gets to Gottlieb, who examines it closely and says, "There's nothing funny in this." Then he hands it to Tom and Dick and says, "Here you are, boys. We're through censor- ing your show."

Not everything clever, funny, or edgy in those early third- season shows was gutted. Politically, Pat Paulsen kept landing strong punches with his presidential campaign jokes. Even the Q&A spot featuring Tom and Pat, which Bob Tamplin had hoped would be replaced by a Tom and Dick musical number, was both ahead of its time and wickedly funny, in a way only the hangdog Paulsen could pull off without raising the ire of the censors. When asked about possible choices for a running mate, Pat said, "I'm thinking about a woman." When a woman in the audience volunteers to be his First Lady, he replies, "I guarantee you wouldn't be my First Lady. But you can be my next." And asked about his mismatched socks (one green, one blue), he explains, "It's a new trend I'm starting, along with honesty in government."

Racially, *Comedy Hour* made room for a black ventriloquist, Aaron Williams, who introduced a new dummy—a white one—into his act. "Some of my best friends are Negro ventriloquists," the new addition tells Williams, in an attempt to put him and the audience at ease. "That's good," Williams replies, "because some of *my* best friends are white dummies."

Most of the show's button- and envelope-pushing was not musical, political, or racial, but conceptual. The third season featured ideas and numbers that were unique for the time. *Comedy Hour* eventually would win special directorial awards for its technical innovations, but the innovations didn't stop there. Guest star Barbara Feldon sang "Lady Godiva," but *as* Lady Godiva, in an extended skit in which she actually sang, draped by floor-length white hair, atop a real white horse. Guest star Nancy Sinatra teamed with Tom and Dick and the Jimmy Joyce Singers on a production number built around the Beatles song "The Word," taking the lyrics "the word is love" and stopping to define the word according to the dictionary. The choir sang the definition aloud as it was superimposed on the screen: "A feeling of strong personal attachment, indicated by sympathetic understanding, or by ties of kinship; ardent affection." And a love ballet, done with stop-motion and slow-motion video back when such work was considered video art, to the tune of Mason Williams's "Sunflower." Not the sort of thing you'd see on, say, *The Red Skelton Show*, or even on *Laugh-In*—but that was precisely the point.

One unforgettable set piece, included in the same hour as "Hey

Jude," was "the 'Honey' house," a lacerating lampoon of "Honey," the maudlin Bobby Goldsboro ballad about a young widower that was one of the year's biggest hits. Dick, pretending to be the widower who was "the actual Honey husband," took tourists on a walk-through of the home "where Honey lived and Honey played," pointing out the various elements of the song. It was like Tom ridiculing "I Talk to the Trees" as "a stupid song," except here, they weren't just deconstructing it. They were destroying it.

"Tommy and I both thought 'Honey' was such a sappy song," Mason says. "I started doing a satire of it, not unlike the houses I'd seen in Oklahoma and Texas, like 'Jesse James lived here'—little shrines of small-town America, that always have a curio shop off to the side. I thought, there should be a shrine to this broken heart. And Dick's performance was fabulous!" It was a true group effort, with Mason turning over the concept to the set decorators, and to writers Roman and Einstein, who put themselves in the skit as two of the more prominent tourists. As the song ends, and the next group of people comes through, Dick begs off singing the song again, and Tom becomes the new "official" weeping widower. Harlan Ellison, then writing a TV column for the *Los Angeles Free Press*, praised it as "a scathing putdown of that saccharine Top 40 'hit' " and praised the brothers and their writers for "doing it in royally, exposing the tawdry sentimentality of it for the shuck it was." Within a few months, Ellison would be predicting in print that the powers that be would have to "kill" *The Smothers Brothers Comedy Hour*.

In the third season, Tom and his compatriots were on a different mission than before. The guest list changed from an intentionally balanced multigenerational mix to shows often dominated entirely by the young: George Carlin, the Committee, and the Doors in one program, for example. Sketches got more pointed and political, songs and singers got even more outspoken, and Tom, behind the scenes, fought more vociferously for every word, guest, and thought. A year before Woody Allen took time on an ABC special to sit and chat with the Reverend Billy Graham, Tom and Dick, in front of a *Comedy Hour* studio audience, recorded a ten-minute interview with Dr. Benjamin Spock, the respected pediatrician who recently had been indicted for protesting the draft. It was envisioned as the first in a series of *Comedy Hour* conversations with provocative, opinionated thinkers. Norman Mailer, Henry Miller, and William F. Buckley had been approached about visiting the series, but after the Spock interview was taped, CBS informed Tom and the producers it would never be broadcast, because convicted felons were not allowed on CBS entertainment programs. The planned interview segment, like many ideas generated by Tom and the *Comedy Hour* writers, never got past the drawing board. Or, at least, past the censors.

"What they *wanted* to do," Mason said of Tom and the rest of the *Comedy Hour* staff, "is a lot more interesting than what they *got* to do. What was it they wanted to get away with? It wasn't the chance to say 'fuck.' It was to present an idea."

A few shows later, George Harrison would show up on *Comedy Hour*—this time in person, making a surprise cameo appearance—to support the Smothers Brothers' fight to say on American television what they consider important. When Tom tells the visiting Beatle that saying anything important is likely to result in censorship, Harrison replies, "Well, whether you can say it or not, keep *trying* to say it!"

Tom took that advice very, very seriously.

20

Pat Paulsen for President

Suddenly, political hardball was the game of choice between CBS and *The Smothers Brothers Comedy Hour*. Network executives argued adamantly that political points of view had no place on television in an entertainment hour—despite the fact they had sold the five minutes of an entertainment hour to the Republican National Committee for a Richard Nixon campaign ad. Two weeks later, CBS sold another five-minute spot at the tail end of the *Comedy Hour* time slot, this time to the Democrats—specifically, to incumbent Vice President Hubert H. Humphrey, that party's pro-war candidate. This time, *Comedy Hour* writers learned about the encroachment on their air time in advance and prepared a special bit to be taped and inserted, at the last minute, at the very end of the show. In it, Pat Paulsen, in his guise as the Straight Talking American Government presidential candidate, offers a "disclaimer" in a spot intended to run immediately prior to Humphrey's campaign ad.

"This is Patrick Layton Paulsen, STAG Party candidate," he was to say. "The opinions expressed by the political commercials appearing after this show are not necessarily those of the show, and definitely not mine as a candidate." The remarks got no further than the script phase, when CBS censor Sam Taylor pounced on it.

"The above material is not acceptable for broadcast," he stated flatly in a memo that left little room for negotiation. "Commonsense business ethics would prohibit the demeaning of a product for which a commercial were to follow, and the same principle applies to political announcements or programs." It was another battle the Smothers Brothers would lose without recourse, but a proud victory was right around the corner. On October 20, just weeks before the 1968 election, the Smothers Brothers devoted their entire hour to a prime-time special called "Pat Paulsen for President." It was an absolutely brilliant piece of work, stunningly ahead of its time, mocking the documentary form, as well as politicians and the media, in a living-theater experiment that paved the way for everyone from the alter-ego antics of Andy Kaufman to the savvy commentary and posturing of Jon Stewart and Stephen Colbert.

The Pat Paulsen for President campaign was the *Comedy Hour* master stroke—the contribution above all others that makes it one of the most audacious and inventive series in TV history. It was, quite literally, a running gag: a joke that took more than a year to tell, targeting and lampooning the entire political process of campaigning. What had begun as a simple piece of abstract conceptual art wound up as an astoundingly well-informed, pitch-perfect attack on the process of running for office, with the media taking as many hits as the candidates. At first, though, it was just an idea. A "high concept" Mason Williams idea, like turning a life-sized photograph of a bus into a fold-out book, or hiring a skywriting plane to draw a stem and some petals in the sky, so that he could line up his camera and take a picture of a literal "sunflower." (The picture didn't turn out, but the book did.)

Paulsen's spot on the *Smothers Brothers* editorial desk had started out as an accident. "I want to do serious editorials," Tom had said at the start of his show. "I want to take a stand." Back in season one before any of the show's ratings had come in, and neither Tom nor the program had any clout, Chambers said no. "You're not going to do the serious editorials," he told Tom. "This is a comedy show." Whereupon Tom, according to Chambers, replied, "Well, then, the hell with it. Let Pat do it."

"I recall my feeling at the time," Pat said, "was that I just wanted to do something every week and score every week. And there was a lot of esprit de corps on the show, with everybody working together. We worked very hard, and I'd bring in things, and I'd work with the writers." He worked intensely with writers Al Gordon and Hal Goldman on the early editorials, then took them to his old stomping grounds, at the Ice House in Pasadena, to try them out in front of a crowd and "find out what was funny," before returning to reshape the scripts with the writers and perform them on TV. "I always wanted to work with writers," Pat said. "I understood that's where it's at." And with his editorials, just as with the *Comedy Hour* series itself, what began purely as an entertainment vehicle began to gather both momentum and purpose. Allan Blye, Mason's writing partner on the series, agrees that "Those little lectures, in the beginning, were based on double-talk," but notes that the focus soon widened, other writers began contributing, and before too long, "They *were* editorials."

The acceleration of the satire—what Mason calls a change of focus from form (ridiculing TV editorialists) to content (making actual points through comedy)—was rapid. In season one, Pat's second editorial, on the issue of firearms restrictions, has him brandishing a handgun while supporting relaxed regulations ("Let's preserve our freedom to kill") and accidentally shooting and killing the announcer. Poverty, divorce, police restrictions by the courts—during the first season, Pat tackled them all and won. What no one knew at the time was that, by pretending to be espousing the official Smothers Brothers Corporation position on various issues, he was molding an image tailor-made for a pretend presidential run.

In season two, Pat addressed such topics as legalized gambling, health care fees, sex education, government spending, draft laws, the long-term viability of social security, and TV censorship—all with increasing flair and insight. He also, early in the second season, appeared in a sketch as Tarzan, who claimed to be running for president and quoted his political adviser, Cheetah, as saying, "You can fool some of the apes all of the time, and some of the apes some of the time, but you can only make monkeys out of the voters every four years." And then, in the twentieth show of season two, the two ideas—Pat as comic spokesman and running a presidential candidate for comedy—were merged.

"The Pat Paulsen campaign for the presidency," recalls Ken Kragen, "came out of Mason wanting to run the *Mona Lisa*, and then the Statue of Liberty, for president. He was going to run an inanimate object, and then it sort of morphed into the idea of Pat Paulsen for president." Mason's original plan was to promote Leonardo da Vinci's famous portrait as a write-in candidate. "Who's not going to vote for the *Mona Lisa*?" he asks. "I mean, it's a great work of art, and it should be president." But then, according to Pat, Mason and Nancy Ames came up with the concept of turning Pat's station editorials into a political platform, allowing them to do an extended satire of the entire political process. Tom loved it, and the rest is political, and satirical, history.

Pat recalled, "Tommy and Mason came to me and said, 'We're gonna run you for president.' And I said, 'Might as well, I can't dance.'" The difference—what really made this faux campaign so brilliant—is that, as Pat put it, "We did our homework." Mason suggested that *Comedy Hour* hire an actual political consultant, someone with solid experience as a campaign manager, to guide them on how to unfold a campaign as realistically, and yet as sarcastically, as possible. Like the campaign idea itself, it was an out-of-the-box suggestion, but it paid big dividends from the very beginning.

Tom ended up hiring Don Bradley, at the time one of the most influential men in California politics. Bradley had worked in Northern California for the John F. Kennedy campaign in 1960, and was Pat Brown's campaign manager in 1962, when Brown ran against Richard Nixon for the governorship of California and won (leaving a defeated Nixon to address the press corps and snarl, inaccurately, "You don't have Nixon to kick around anymore"). Bradley, in other words, helped defeat Nixon twice in two years. Bradley also was Brown's campaign manager when Brown ran for reelection in 1966 but lost to actor Ronald Reagan. Both Reagan and Nixon would campaign for president in 1968, and Bradley was more than happy to offer his expertise. Eventually, Bradley was one of Robert F. Kennedy's advisers as well, but the Smothers Brothers got to Bradley and started their Pat Paulsen for President campaign earlier than Bobby Kennedy, and earlier than most.

"The thing we learned from this consultant," Mason remembers, "was, how do you stretch out a campaign to get the most out of the press? The denial is one part of it. That way, you get a profile for several weeks. It was us following his lead. He's telling us what a *real* candidate would do." Mason smiles. "That's when I realized this whole presidential campaign was going to become a way for the general public to get a broader sense of the political process. You're illuminating what goes on, but also attempting to make people interested in the political process by demystifying it." This was, it should be emphasized, a full five years before *The Boys on the Bus*, Timothy Crouse's seminal account of the press corps covering Nixon's 1972 reelection campaign, would get credit for exposing the uncomfortable, symbiotic dance between politicians and the media. The "Pat Paulsen for President" campaign did that, brilliantly, in 1968.

It wasn't the first time an entertainer had mounted a pretend presidential bid. Satirist Will Rogers did it in 1928, running as the

"Anti-Bunk" candidate, getting the playful support of Henry Ford and Babe Ruth and a weekly campaign column in *Life* magazine, all built around the single campaign pledge, "If elected, I will resign." Vaudeville star Eddie Cantor ran in 1931–32, trying to find humor, and offer some, during the Depression. In 1940, the same year W. C. Fields published his "Fields for President" comic essay, Gracie Allen used her platform as a radio star to run as a candidate representing the "Surprise" party—a running gag supported by *Time* magazine, which warmed up to the comic idea of a woman running for president as a "candidette." In 1948, a candidate whose strings really were pulled— Howdy Doody, the marionette star of NBC's *Puppet Playhouse Presents*—ran as "President of All the Kids." Free campaign buttons were sent to anyone who wrote in, and the show received sixty thousand requests, at a time when the number of US homes equipped with TV sets was only triple that.

Pat Paulsen, though, approached his assignment in a way that would later inform the Jon Stewart playbook: by imitating and lampooning the process and, on occasion, interacting with its real-life participants. It was an audacious, ambitious extended joke, a pioneering piece of performance art at a time when politics was getting not only deadly serious, but deadly. And Pat, whose pre–*Comedy Hour* days included highly unusual work as a street performer and improv comic (Mason recalls him gathering a crowd for an hour promising to walk on water, then taking one step forward and falling in), was the perfect fake politician to take the joke as far as it could go. "Paulsen was an original," producer Ilson says admiringly. "He had the confidence in how to play the piece, and he added to it, too."

The campaign unspooled beautifully, absurdly, and hilariously. On the twentieth show of season two, Pat gives an editorial on congressional ethics ("Of course, there are abuses," he says, "but usually there are reasons"), after which Tom enters to ask about "rumors that have been circulating" about Pat's intention to run for public office.

"Absolutely not," Pat replies flatly. Then, after a beat, he adds, "What office, I am not at liberty to say." Another beat. "Therefore, I wish to say, with regard to the presidency of the United States," he says, as the studio audience erupts with laughter, "I will not run if nominated. And if elected, I will not serve." The remark, a paraphrase of Civil War general William Tecumseh Sherman's famous refusal to run for president, came straight from Mason's journal ("Use this statement"). Paulsen said it on national television on January 28, 1968. Two months later, in an astounding example of life imitating art, President Johnson went on national television to tell the country, "I shall not seek, and I will not accept, the nomination of my party for another term as your president."

Paulsen, meanwhile, was moving from reluctant noncandidate to reluctant candidate. His initial "campaign denial" appearance ended with his shaking hands with people in the studio audience and thanking Tom for allowing him to make his position clear "this early in my campaign." And so it begins. The following week, Pat takes questions from the audience, once again denying his candidacy ("It's all hearsay"), but taking political potshots ("As a comedian, I think I'm just as effective as President Johnston," he says, intentionally mispronouncing the name of the chief executive) and sounding somewhat presidential in offering solace ("We have nothing to fear but fear itself . . . and the boogeyman").

In the next show, airing February 11, 1968, both Pat and the show's finale poked fun at the many candidates who, at that point, either had or had not declared. Nixon and Wallace had just declared themselves, but Ronald Reagan and Bobby Kennedy had not.

"There are so many other candidates denying their candidacy," Pat complains when Dick asks about his status as a candidate, "that it's hard for me to find equal time to deny mine." Ticking off the names of others who have yet to declare, Pat asks, "Why should *they* get all the publicity for not running?" Then, once again, he denies he is running for high office. "The fact that I have a surefire plan of action to lower taxes, solve our civil rights problem, obliterate the national debt, and put an end to war in Vietnam obviously disqualifies me as a presidential candidate." The studio audience applauds with delight, but Pat waves off the obvious show of support. "I don't want to be any more than I am today," he tells them. "A common, ordinary, simple savior of America's destiny."

The same show ends with a finale built around hats, and one blackout sketch within it shows a boxing ring in which various hats are being thrown—Dick narrates from off-screen as hats are tossed in one by one. A regular black hat for McCarthy. A pointedly white one for Wallace. A dunce cap for Nixon. A crown for Johnson, who had yet to abdicate his reelection bid. And finally, a gray hat for Bobby Kennedy—a hat that is attached to a hidden string, and keeps popping in and out of the ring. "Come on, Bobby," Dick says with some exasperation, "make up your mind!"

The day after that show aired, the *Comedy Hour* staff fielded a call from Ethel Kennedy, Bobby's wife. "She said, 'Bobby's a big fan of the show, and that [the skit] was just way out of line,'" producer Saul Ilson says. "My thought at the time," he adds, "was, God! We're just doing *comedy* here!" Manager Ken Fritz spoke to her directly and remembers her beginning the conversation by saying, "You made me cry last night." When Fritz asked why, Ethel Kennedy replied, "You were making fun of the senator." Fritz defended the segment, saying it was meant only to convey how much they wanted her husband to run, and asked if Bobby Kennedy had seen it himself. He had, she said—at which point she admitted, "He laughed."

It was the beginning of a behind-the-scenes relationship that blossomed into a brief but memorable routine, with Ethel Kennedy calling Fritz most Monday mornings to talk about the political jokes in the previous night's show. But after complaining about the hat joke on that first call, Ethel Kennedy offered an olive branch that paid unexpected dividends immediately. Because Tom and Dick had met Bobby Kennedy and gotten along well with him (they all were guests on NBC's *Tonight Show* when Harry Belafonte was guest host), she invited the Smothers Brothers to be among the guests performing on a local five-hour WTTG-TV telethon the following Saturday—a benefit for Junior Village Orphanage, a Kennedy-supported charity for mentally challenged youngsters. Jack Paar, who had given the Smothers Brothers their first big break and who had featured Bobby Kennedy on his own show, was the emcee, and other guests flying in for the benefit performance included Jefferson Airplane and Woody Allen.

For the Smothers Brothers, attending would mean flying from Los Angeles to Washington, DC, right after taping a Friday night show—the show on which Pete Seeger sang "Waist Deep in the Big Muddy." Tom decided to attend, and wisely brought along Pat Paulsen and a camera crew, with plans to gather footage for a special filmed piece about Paulsen's first visit to Washington. Many of the guests at the Junior Village event agreed to be interviewed, and part of the footage from that trip—including Pat's visits to the White House (outside the gates), the Washington Mall, and the Lincoln Memorial—was shown two weeks later on the second-season finale.

"Pat Paulsen: The Makings of a President" was the name of the eight-minute film, and it includes several celebrities and politicians talking about Pat Paulsen's candidacy, including David Frye, former JFK press secretary Pierre Salinger, Woody Allen ("The truth is, I don't really know Pat Paulsen, because I've never seen the show"), and Bobby Kennedy himself, interviewed by Tom.

Another filmed Kennedy piece, in which Bobby spoke directly with Pat, was saved for later—for use in a planned full-length "Pat Paulsen for President" special. Their tongue-in-cheek chat ended with Pat saying to Bobby, "To get the country moving ahead, we need optimism, most of all," then quickly adding, "even though I don't think I can get elected." Bobby Kennedy, hearing that, cracked up and walked off camera, muttering with a smile, "Oh, God, have *I* got to go through this?" But that footage was never shown. Before Pat Paulsen had a chance to resume his comic candidacy on *The Summer Brothers Smothers Show*, Bobby Kennedy was dead.

But as season two ended and *The Smothers Brothers Comedy Hour* went into reruns, Bobby Kennedy, like the political turmoil of 1968, was very much alive. President Johnson was still the presumptive Democratic candidate—and he, too, reached out from time to time to let CBS, if not the Smothers Brothers, know how he felt about their jokes aimed at him. Johnson's close friend at CBS was Frank Stanton, the longtime executive just below Chairman William S. Paley in the network hierarchy. Stanton, by his own account, was so close with LBJ that he was "practically living at the White House" in the days after the John F. Kennedy assassination. Stanton also was the person who provided LBJ with his famous three-screen TV console, from which the president could watch all three network newscasts simultaneously at the White House. "I wanted somebody else to catch the brunt of his complaints, rather than just me," Stanton once explained. And while President Johnson would complain to Stanton about some of the material on *The Smothers Brothers Comedy Hour*, the president of the United States was not above calling Paley directly to register his personal, and presidential, displeasure.

Yet Pat Paulsen, who wasn't a politician but who played one on TV, drew few if any complaints from any real politicians. Pat was someone everybody seemed to like. Even more significant, and a bit more surprising, the "Paulsen for President" bits were not opposed by CBS censors, at least in theory. Oh, cuts were made—and as the campaign resumed that summer, those cuts became increasingly jarring. But as CBS program practices chief William Tankersley explains, "That was understood to be pure humor . . . That was a laugh!"

. . .

Politics itself, though, was no laughing matter.

On March 12, 1968, with LBJ still expected to run for reelection, Eugene McCarthy won the influential New Hampshire Democratic primary, claiming 42 percent of the vote. Paulsen, for the record, got a total of fifty-one write-in votes in that same primary and complained about his minuscule showing: "I have conducted my campaign thus far in the true American political tradition," he grumbled. "I lied about my intention to run, I have been consistently vague and evasive on all the issues, but this apparently has not been enough."

Four days later, Bobby Kennedy finally threw his hat into the ring, doing what that *Comedy Hour* sketch had begged him to do the month before. And on March 31, only three weeks after the second-season finale in which Tom interviewed Bobby Kennedy about Pat Paulsen, a rerun of *The Smothers Brothers Comedy Hour* was preempted for a prime-time address by LBJ. The president, who at the time (according to a just-released Gallup Poll) had only a 26 percent national approval rating for his Vietnam War policy, announced he would not run for reelection. Watching that telecast, Tom Smothers felt "the big shock" of President Johnson throwing in the towel, and a moment of rebellious, antiwar pride in which Tom thought, "Wow! Man, all right! We're *getting* to him!" But as the speech went on—"the best speech," Tom says, "he gave in a long time"—Tom felt sufficiently moved to declare his intention to write the president a letter.

Four days after Johnson's speech, the Reverend Martin Luther King Jr. was shot and killed. A month later, in May, Bobby Kennedy won his first presidential primary (in Indiana), and Pat Paulsen won an Individual Achievement Emmy for his work on *The Smothers Brothers Comedy Hour*. (Art Carney also got one, for his second-banana work on *The Jackie Gleason Show*.) It was the first Emmy

Award for anyone associated with *Comedy Hour:* the Variety Series and Variety Writing Emmys that year both went to *Laugh-In.*

With Paulsen and his "candidacy" given a big push at the Emmy Awards, and with the summer series due to begin in a month, all signs looked good for a big summer push on the campaign trail. And there was one: Pat took his show on the road, with a *Comedy Hour* film crew capturing all the action in mock-documentary form. He descended on states holding caucuses and primaries just as real politicians did, and began engaging in all the familiar behaviors: eating regional and ethnic foods, kissing babies, passing out bumper stickers, begging for votes, and holding rallies. Crowds grew so quickly, and were so responsive, that Ken Kragen insists Pat turned to him at one rally and said, "You know, I could maybe win this thing!" On the campaign trail, Pat engaged in fund-raisers, but of an absurdist, low-rent variety. He sold lemonade for a nickel; went door-to-door selling cookies for a dime; set up a kissing booth, offering to kiss women for money ("25 cents plain, 50 cents fancy"); and, a few days before the California primary, invited a gaggle of celebrities to an 89-cents-a-plate cafeteria-style dinner. Guests who showed up ("The important thing is, I got their money") included Groucho Marx, Steve Allen, Phyllis Diller, Carl Reiner, Dick Martin, Jill St. John, Debbie Reynolds, Robert Morse, Martin Landau, and Barbara Bain. All this was filmed and banked for future use in a special. And then, on the night of the California primary, just after announcing his victory on the Democratic ticket, Bobby Kennedy was assassinated.

The tragedy stalled the comedic Paulsen campaign for a while— Ken Fritz, who was producing the "Pat Paulsen for President" special with Ken Kragen, recalls a tough period of everyone being "stunned." (The entire *Comedy Hour* troupe had gathered at the Aquarius Theatre to support Paulsen on "his" big night.) Elements recorded for the special, including Bobby's individual conversations with Tom and Pat, had to be eliminated, but no one recalls having so much as a conversation about halting the bogus campaign in the wake of the unthinkable tragedy. Tom, when asked why the decision was made to keep going, said simply, "You *had* to!" And so they did.

On the campaign trail, they resumed filming, banking more and more material for the special, and even filming at the Democratic National Convention. On TV, the campaign resumed officially in July, on the third episode of the *Summer Brothers* show. Before the summer was out, Pat was plugging his *Pat Paulsen for President* book—and in the first shows of the third season, Pat's weekly speeches became more prominent, more forceful, and more memorable. "A female running mate is not as strange as it sounds," he insisted, after the studio audience laughed at his announcement that he was considering a woman on his presidential ticket. "I say it is time we restored some glamour to our own White House. If I get a woman for a running mate," he reasoned aloud. "all the women of this country will come over to my side—bringing all the men with them."

On the heels of all that, the "Pat Paulsen for President" special finally arrived. With Henry Fonda providing sublimely grave narration, this October 20 *Comedy Hour* program skewers the documentary format, pioneering a new satirical form a full year before Woody Allen's landmark 1969 mockumentary *Take the Money and Run*. It contains well-selected snippets from Pat's *Comedy Hour* editorials and speeches, including his perfectly calibrated initial nonentry into the race. ("True, all the present candidates once denied they had any intention of running," Pat says. "But the fact that I am *also* a liar doesn't make me a candidate.") The special, however, also unveils all that footage stockpiled throughout much of 1968.

At each campaign stop—Jacksonville, Denver, Texas, California—Pat tells the local TV and radio interviewers that when the campaign is through, he wants to return to their state and live, rather than be stuck where all "the phonies" are. As the cities pile up, so does the hypocrisy. He unveils his campaign slogan, "We Can't Stand

Pat." In his native state of Washington, Pat asks, "The Depression was over a long time ago for most people. Why does the state of Washington continue to have to sell apples?" His stump speech, routinely mispronouncing the names of his rivals and attacking them by style if not substance, contains one well-aimed zinger after another.

On LBJ's decision not to run for a second term: "Most people do not really vote for someone for the presidency as much as they vote against the other candidate, and I think President Johnston's decision was unfair to these people."

On making campaign promises: "I ask you—will I solve our civil rights problems? Will I unite this country and bring it forward? Will I obliterate the national debt?" After a pause: "Sure, why not?"

On his chances for election, with a sideswipe at Richard Nixon's running mate, Spiro Agnew, and his fondness for alliteration: "Many political experts have told me that nobody will vote for me because America is not ready for such decisive and dynamic leadership. They tell me these things, and I say nay to the negative nincompoops who never nourished the nihilistic nerve to name a novice to nail down the nomination."

On gun control, claiming a punch line decades before Chris Rock: "Guns are not the real problem. The real problem is bullets."

He gets entrée, and so does his camera crew, into the National Press Club in Washington, the political conventions and caucuses, and just about anywhere he wants to go. It's a great performance, a great stunt, a great hour of television—and Pat Paulsen isn't quite through yet.

Two weeks later, on the last *Comedy Hour* to be televised before the election, Pat makes one last appeal to the national viewing audience. "Please don't waste your vote if there really is a candidate you support," he says, promising that he won't try to "sway you with emotional appeals." Then he says, "Ignore my war record, and that I've invested my fortune in this campaign," and begins crying on cue. "Don't waste your vote on me, America! Just remember which candidate stood *up* for America!" he sobs. Then he half-cries, and half-sings, "God Bless America," backed by a choir, and finishes the bit by being cast in shadow, walking toward a projection of the White House.

In the 1968 election, Republican candidate Richard M. Nixon, with running mate Spiro Agnew, beat the Democratic ticket, Minnesota senator Hubert Humphrey and Maine senator Edmund Muskie, by just over half a million popular votes. Nixon got 43.4 percent of the national vote, Humphrey got 42.7 percent, and American Party candidate George Wallace got 13.5 percent of the vote, with just under 10 million ballots cast. That left about 0.3 percent of the national tally, a total of 242,258 write-in votes, going to such write-in candidates as black comedian Dick Gregory and Pat Paulsen. One such write-in vote for Paulsen came from an army soldier named Len Feiner, who explained his protest vote by saying, "Nixon versus Humphrey: enough said!" Most sources credit Paulsen with amassing 200,000 votes, which was Pat's claim as well, though that seems a little high. In any event, he didn't win, and his 1968 campaign for the presidency was over—except for one final appearance.

In the first postelection edition of *Comedy Hour*, Pat returns, looking much less presidential than in his previous appearance. In fact, he looks like he's been on a lengthy bender: disheveled, weary, hungover. "I have sent a telegram to Mr. Nixton promising support," he says, playing the mispronunciation card one last time. And, with one last political bull's-eye, he adds, "I harbor no resentment towards the voter. For in the long run, he is the real loser."

David Steinberg Finds Religion

A fter "Pat Paulsen for President," the next installment of *Comedy Hour* opened with a taped piece featuring a montage of headlines of global student unrest. Writer Murray Roman was shown wearing a different military or police uniform in each, playing authority figures from Mexico, France, Japan, and Russia— and, finally, from the United States, where headlines told of the uprising at Columbia University earlier that month. In every guise, in every accent, Murray blamed the problems on "outside agitators." Then, to cap off the skit, Tom and Dick showed up and said, "Hi! We're the outside agitators!"

It was a prophetic opening, because this episode, more than any other to this point, ending up agitating CBS, and a portion of the country in rural counties and what was called the Bible Belt, tremendously. It wasn't because the show featured veteran comic Jack E. Leonard, who played against type—and made a strong contribution to the show—by singing the Beatles' "Fool on the Hill" completely straight, as opposed to going for laughs, while photographs of Charlie Chaplin, Laurel and Hardy, W. C. Fields, Buster Keaton, and others were projected behind him. It wasn't because the Everly Brothers, who had appeared on the *Summer Brothers Smothers Show*, returned for another guest spot, sporting much longer hair than Tom and Dick.

And it certainly was not because of the New Day Singers, eight clean-cut young men from the seminary training to become Jesuit priests. No, it was the young man with whom the New Day Singers, in their starched white collars, shared the stage: a Chicago Second City comedian named David Steinberg.

Steinberg was there to perform, in the words of *TV Guide*, "a satirical sermon on 'the lack of communication.' " Just as Pat Paulsen had taken aim at the then-common TV fixture of local station executives offering poorly reasoned, poorly delivered editorials, Steinberg was poking fun at an equally familiar small-screen sight: the late-night TV sermonette. Religion was one of the big third-rail issues in prime time. Entertainment shows avoided it religiously, so to speak, and here was Steinberg—preceded by singing seminarians, and surrounded by Tiffany-style stained-glass panels—taking it head on.

Steinberg, a Canadian whose father was a rabbi, grew up in Winnipeg before moving to Chicago and settling in with the Second City improv troupe. One of the things he started doing there was a mock sermon. Audience members would shout out a name or story from the Bible, and he would take it from there. When Tom, at the start of season three, told Allan Blye that he wanted to "take another few steps" in pushing the prime-time envelope, Blye thought of, and suggested, Steinberg. Blye, too, was raised in Winnipeg, and Steinberg was an old friend, but it was the idea of a comic sermonette that got Tom excited. Steinberg, who had studied religion himself before switching to comedy, had a firm grasp of the subject he was satirizing, which made it both hysterical and volatile. "It's kind of dangerous," Blye warned Tom. "People of the cloth really find it funny, but the public may find it tough." Bill Cosby's 1963 debut LP, *Bill Cosby Is a Very Funny Fellow Right!*, had reenacted a biblical story from the point of view of Noah, with Cosby going so far as to supply the booming voice of God, but Cosby was considered playful, not irreverent. Steinberg's approach—pretending to lecture as though a man of the cloth himself—was received much less warmly by some.

"Tommy went crazy for it," Steinberg says. "Tommy loved anything that was irreverent. Besides actually having a political point of view, he just loved being against someone big, someone over him. So he loved the irreverence of the sermon. And the sermons, which now seem tame by comparison . . . just never had been done [on TV in that way]. And it shocked people." Steinberg adds, "When I look at it now, it just seems so safe, and so *nothing*. But I remember the tension, the tension in the audience."

As the New Day Singers finish their "How I Rejoiced" song (sample lyrics: "My soul can sing any time of year"), Dick Smothers steps into frame and says, "As far as the television industry is concerned, God seems to have no rating. So tonight, for a change, we'd like to give religion prime time—and present, for the first time on our show, the *Smothers Brothers* version of a television sermonette."

"The only reason the priests were there," Steinberg recalls, referring to the singing seminarians, "is we didn't want to scare the audience. We wanted to show that even theologians, who were secure with the Bible, didn't feel that I was sort of making fun of God . . . Even *priests* liked me. That was the point."

"Our topic for tonight," Dick continues in his introduction to the bit, as the New Day Singers continue to hum, "is, 'The Lack of Communication in Our Changing Times.' And here, speaking on this ever-increasing problem and how it relates to Scripture, is David Steinberg, MA, DHL." (DHL stands for Doctor of Humane Letters, which Steinberg didn't possess, despite spending years of his youth at the Chicago Theological Seminary.)

Behind a Tiffany-illuminated podium, Steinberg, in blue suit and tie, leans forward and intones, "Today's sermon deals with the exciting personality of Moses, who had a wonderful rapport with

God, whom I'm sure you'll remember from last week's sermon."
Steinberg got his first laugh from the studio audience, and kept
going—weaving a story about *The Sound of Music* into his sermon
before launching into his version of Moses and the burning bush:

> Moses was wandering in the wilderness, when he saw a
> bush that was burning, yet it would not consume itself. A
> voice came out of the heavens. "Moses, take off your shoes
> from off of your feet," God said in His redundant way. "For
> the land that you are standing upon is holy land." Well, Moses
> took his shoes off, approached the burning bush, and burnt
> his feet. God went, "Aha! Third one today!"

That all got televised, but the next part did not. CBS objected to
it even in script form, but Tom insisted Steinberg's bit be taped in
full, and a final decision made only after the network could see how
it was received by the studio audience. In Los Angeles, Sam Taylor
stood by his opinion that the joke went too far, and Tom asked that
a tape of the show, with the sermonette intact, be reviewed in
New York by programmer Mike Dann and head censor William
Tankersley. Both of them agreed with Taylor, and the disputed joke
was deleted from the final tape broadcast on the CBS network. Here
was the joke considered too offensive to run, coming right after
Moses was hot-footed by a mischievous God: "We're not sure what
he said," Steinberg said of Moses, "but there are many New Testament scholars who, to this day, believe it was the first mention of
Christ in the Bible."

That was the only deletion in the segment by CBS censors. The
rest of the sermonette, which CBS approved and broadcast, contains
jokes both religious and secular. When God orders Moses to go to
the pharaoh and demand the release of his people, in Steinberg's account, "Moses says, 'Who shall I say sent me?' God said, 'Whom!'"

(That always makes me laugh.) Later, when the pharaoh ignores Moses' pleas to let his people go, Steinberg says, "And so God destroyed all of the land with that mystical sense of humor that is only His." The sermon concludes as Steinberg claims to have witnessed, that very day, an "old man being beaten to a pulp by four little children"—and after noting that the four youths were of different races and ethnicities, he adds, "Now if these little children can learn to play together, certainly we can. Thank you."

"The Bible Belt didn't think it was funny, I'll tell you," program practices chief William Tankersley says. The complaints about that sketch, he adds, were more numerous than anything else in the history of CBS television—and also generated an unprecedented number of complaints from the network affiliates. CBS executives responded to the affiliate concerns by instituting a network first: a closed-circuit telecast of each week's *Comedy Hour* sent in advance so local stations could see, and approve, the program before televising it.

"At this time," CBS executive Bob Tamplin wrote the Smothers Brothers and their managers and producers, "we are subject to possibly losing from 15 to 40 affiliates on your program. They now demand a closed-circuit telecast of your show on Friday prior to its airing on Sunday, and will decide at that time whether or not they will carry the show on Sunday, depending upon material on the show. If they do not see a closed circuit, they will not carry the show."

This memo, dated October 30, 1968 (three days after the Steinberg show was broadcast), was a newly introduced demand, found nowhere in the contracts between CBS and the Smothers Brothers. Immediately, it changed the rules in two important ways.

First, it introduced a new layer of approval—or censorship—in addition to the West Coast and East Coast offices of program practices. Now the affiliates, every one of them, had a voice in whether what the Smothers Brothers were doing was acceptable in their respective markets. Eventually, that practice became the status quo for all network-delivered programs, but *The Smothers Brothers Comedy Hour* was the first to be subjected to such scrutiny. Before David Steinberg's sermonette, if something was good enough for the network, it was good enough for the affiliate.

Second, this new ruling required the Smothers Brothers to deliver a finished tape to CBS in New York days earlier than they had been doing previously. This meant less time for postproduction—and less time for Tom to argue with censors on either coast. "Until further notice," Tamplin informed the *Comedy Hour* team, "we will have a closed-circuit telecast of the show on Friday for [the affiliates'] appraisal. Consequently, the show must be delivered to us in time to have it arrive in New York before 6:00 a.m. Friday morning. Please plan your editing accordingly."

Both issues, along with network hypersensitivity to the furor caused by Steinberg's routine, led eventually to the end of *The Smothers Brothers Comedy Hour*. The extra layer of interference from affiliates caused Tom to fight even harder against the network censors, shunning those on the West Coast and alienating those in New York. The failure to deliver tapes on time for closed-circuit screening was the excuse used, in the end, to fire the Smothers Brothers. And in the network's CBS eye, David Steinberg's sermonette act was too controversial—which made the combative Tom Smothers determined to both defend Steinberg and invite him back. In the end, he did both. But from this point forward, every shot fired between CBS and the Smothers Brothers staff was far more serious than it had been before, part of an escalating arms race that demonstrated precious little humor behind the scenes, and sometimes on the screen.

"Because of the surprisingly large negative response to David Steinberg's sermonette broadcast on *The Smothers Brothers Comedy Hour* October 27," Tom Downer wrote in a memo to the show's producers one week later, "we are obliged to ask that Mr. Steinberg, should he make return appearances on the show, avoid material based on religious themes or references." He added, "Please understand this is not an objection to Mr. Steinberg as a performer. In light of reaction to the sermonette from viewers and affiliated stations, however, we must advise that similar material could not be accepted for future broadcasts."

To show how heated the conflict between CBS and the Smothers Brothers had become, a new installment was taped the day after the receipt of that memo that addressed the Steinberg furor both indirectly and directly. The show begins with that surprise appearance by George Harrison, who encourages the brothers to keep trying to say things on American television, even if it's difficult. More pointedly, the show ends with a short speech delivered by Tom—written by Mason Williams—that amounts to a very caustic "apology" for the Steinberg sermonette.

"We try to do new things on our show, things that haven't been done before," Tom says, defending Steinberg's sketch. "In the case of the David Steinberg sermonette," he adds, "we got the approval of many theologians, and priests and things, before we put it on the air.

"We're sorry that some of you out there didn't see the piece as we did. Because it was not our intention to offend anyone. To those of you who were offended, we apologize, but we don't regret having done it . . .

"We feel that God has a sense of humor," Tom says, and the studio audience applauds spontaneously. "We were made in His image. And if we have a sense of humor, and we were made in His image, God must have a sense of humor also.

"We figure that God will forgive us," Tom concludes with a smile, "even if some of you don't."

Hair Today, Gone Tomorrow

The *Smothers Brothers Comedy Hour* and *Rowan & Martin's Laugh-In* were kindred spirits: the only prime-time entertainment series of their era that dealt overtly and irreverently with politics and current events. They had much in common: both shows were fronted by comedy duos, were launched at midseason against formerly indomitable competition (*Laugh-In* was scheduled opposite CBS chairman Bill Paley's favorite son, *Gunsmoke*), built their own stars from a talented repertory company of supporting players, and were their respective networks' most controversial programs. But there were differences as well, which led to the rapid acceptance and ascendance of *Laugh-In* and the simultaneous polarization and eventual silencing of *Comedy Hour*.

The two variety shows began the 1968–69 TV season ratings race on fairly equal footing (Tom and Dick's show was ranked eighteenth for the previous season, while *Laugh-In* finished twenty-first). That equality didn't last long. By the second Nielsen ratings book of the new season, *Laugh-In* was the number-one TV offering for the two-week period, drawing 28.4 percent of all TV households—even more than that week's telecasts of the World Series. *Comedy Hour*, during that same period, was ranked in eleventh place, a very impressive showing, but it was clear which show had the momentum. *Laugh-*

In would be the number-one show in all of television that season, and the next season as well, while *Comedy Hour* would finish in twenty-seventh place for the 1968–69 season—and then be finished, period.

Tom could see the writing on the wall—on the *Laugh-In* joke wall, that is, where cast members finished each show by peering through miniature doors and spouting one-liners. He had embraced Rowan and Martin early by featuring them, as unbilled guest stars, on the second Pete Seeger show, only a month after *Laugh-In* had premiered. On the last show before the 1968 presidential election, *Comedy Hour* featured them again, this time with Rowan and Martin appearing at the end, dressed in the Smothers Brothers' familiar burgundy blazers and white turtlenecks. As Rowan and Martin start to close the show, hidden doors open in the background set, and the heads of Tom and Dick pop out in a *Comedy Hour* approximation of the *Laugh-In* joke wall. Tom spouts a bunch of popular *Laugh-In* catchphrases, rapidly but without any inflection or enthusiasm: "Look that up in your Funk and Wagnalls. Sock it to me. Very interesting. Here comes the judge . . ." Dick interrupts him and complains, "That's not funny." "I know it's not," Tom replies wryly. "But it sure is successful."

Where *Laugh-In* had more viewers, the Smothers Brothers had more teeth. They not only bit the network that fed them—repeatedly and defiantly—they also satirized politicians and their positions, especially regarding their respective stances on the Vietnam War. The Smothers Brothers made fun of Richard Nixon as he ran for president. *Laugh-In* never did. In fact, the biggest difference between the two shows may well be this: where *Comedy Hour* used Nixon as a punch line, *Laugh-In* let Nixon *deliver* the punch line. The September 16 season opener of *Laugh-In,* less than a month before the election, presented Republican candidate Nixon as a very special but very fleeting guest, capping a series of celebrity blackouts by looking straight into the camera with mock incredulity and saying, "Sock it to *me?*"

The impact of that five-second appearance is impossible to

gauge: on one of the most popular TV shows in the nation, Nixon managed, in a single sentence, to convey more of a good-sport persona, and a sense of humor, than during most of the rest of his campaign. With only half a million votes deciding the election, Nixon's *Laugh-In* appearance, and all the positive media attention it gained, may well have been an influential factor. Hubert Humphrey had been offered the same guest appearance but had turned it down as unseemly for a presidential candidate. Nixon, on the other hand, had a reason to be less suspicious. *Laugh-In* head writer Paul Keyes not only was a personal friend, but also had provided material for some of Nixon's speeches. Keyes also protected Nixon from suffering the barbs of other *Laugh-In* staff writers: Lorne Michaels, who went from *Laugh-In* to *Saturday Night Live*, recalls Keyes excising his one-liners whenever they took direct aim at Nixon.

A key difference between the two shows, *Laugh-In* executive producer George Schlatter concedes, was the format itself. *Laugh-In* was all about quick edits, sight gags, and high-speed punch lines, following the trail blazed by TV pioneer Ernie Kovacs in the 1950s and running the whole concept at a higher gear. *The Smothers Brothers Comedy Hour* evolved to be more about ideas, about giving new talent a place to shine, and about attempting to say something. "*Laugh-In* was not a variety show," Schlatter says simply. "*Laugh-In* was a comedy show." The difference between the two shows, Schlatter adds, "was that with the Smothers Brothers, you were aware of intent. We tried to not take a position as obviously as Tommy."

Laugh-In, for example, never would have presented much of what *Comedy Hour* served up on the show just before Nixon was elected, even though Rowan and Martin themselves made an appearance. Pat Paulsen, presented in close-up in vertical split-screen, answering political questions by literally talking out of both sides of his mouth? That was a perfect modern extension of an Ernie Kovacs video trick, but too arty for *Laugh-In*. Leigh French's Goldie, wiping away the raisins from her raisin bread recipe out of solidarity with striking grape pickers? Too on-the-nose political for *Laugh-In*. Glen Campbell, showing up to sing a song so new that it wouldn't even enter the pop charts for another two weeks? Not the *Laugh-In* style—though the song in question was "Wichita Lineman," which Campbell credits his *Smothers Brothers* appearance as the reason for it becoming an instant hit.

There was one other segment on this particular *Smothers Brothers Comedy Hour* that hovered above all others, and showed why it stood alone as the bravest, boldest entertainment series of its age. It was a short film called *American Time Capsule,* and its genesis, like its prime-time unveiling, owes everything to Tom Smothers's eye for talent, eagerness to champion new artists, and increased insistence upon slipping meaning into *Comedy Hour* whenever possible. Chuck Braverman, a young man who had just graduated from film school at USC and still lived with his mother, was the unlikely auteur behind *American Time Capsule,* and his entry into the Smothers Brothers orbit was even more unlikely. Tom was shooting pool one night at the Factory, a Hollywood nightclub, when Braverman's mother, playing at a nearby table, introduced herself and said he should take a look at her son's student movies. "I met Tommy Smothers tonight, and he wants to see your films," Braverman says his mother told him—and to his amazement, when he called the number Tom had given her, Tom picked up and invited the young Braverman over. After seeing his films, which included images presented in rapid-fire, almost subliminal jump cuts, Tom suggested maybe he should do something about history. Braverman left, and Tom forgot about it, but Braverman didn't. He and some friends, following the mandated three-minute limit, decided on a film about American history, and assembled a fast-moving piece he called *American Time Capsule*. When he showed the finished product to Tom, Tom rushed it onto *Comedy Hour* the very next week—just before the election.

"It's a real mind-blower," Tom said as he introduced the film. "Two hundred years of American history compressed into just two minutes and fifty-three seconds." It's an astoundingly powerful compilation, and one of its regrettable but unavoidable recurring themes is violence: massacres of Native Americans, assassinations of American leaders, bloody world wars, and, at the end, current bloodshed at home and in Vietnam. The film concludes with a swift parade of presidential faces, from George Washington to LBJ, and comes to a halt with an ominous question mark. (When *Comedy Hour* repeated the film due to popular demand a few weeks later, it replaced the question mark with the face of President-elect Richard Nixon, which seemed, somehow, even more ominous.) Tom had presented a fast-paced montage by another filmmaker before, on the summer series, but that was a rapid romp through the history of art. *American Time Capsule*, by contrast, was an artistic sprint through our country's history, so potent it still stuns college students when I show it to them in a TV history class forty years later. Today's *Saturday Night Live* may present viral videos about "Dick in a Box" and "Laser Cats," but forty years ago *Comedy Hour* presented a piece of film—a piece of art—that really meant something.

George Harrison, visiting the United States, happened to be visiting Tom Smothers and having dinner at Tom's place that Sunday night. They turned on the TV to that evening's preelection *Comedy Hour*, and Harrison was impressed by what he saw, especially the Braverman piece. "He went crazy," Tom remembers. "He was asking, 'Who put that together? What was that?' He really was excited." So excited that Harrison agreed, for the next *Comedy Hour* show, to slip in and appear as a special unannounced guest.

Most of these third-season shows, even after the election put an end to the Pat Paulsen presidential campaign, included something cutting, something rebellious, something fresh. Not a lot, necessarily, and not the sort of thing that may sound daring and outrageous so many decades later. But in a TV season when the most popular shows in the nation included *Family Affair, Gomer Pyle, U.S.M.C.*, and, once again, *Bonanza,* anything at all was tantamount to revolution. What the Smothers Brothers got on the air, at that time and in that context, was crucial. Most shows boasted at least one element that managed—musically, comically, or politically—to experiment somehow and enhance the show's reputation as *the* place on network television for young people to gather. Older and less liberal viewers, especially in the rural South and Midwest, may have begun gravitating back to the Ponderosa, but younger viewers, especially those who had rejected TV as a waste of time altogether, were making *Comedy Hour* an early form of appointment television. What they saw, more and more, was being made for them. The original *Comedy Hour* mandate of appealing to all viewers equally, like the show's original team of producers, was gone. Youth was to be served, which made the show a political lightning rod, inside and outside CBS.

The show on which Harrison appeared was the first of three concerts in the round staged on *Comedy Hour*—a setup that broke the standard mode of variety-show presentation that had been in place at CBS Television City since the earliest Jack Benny and George Burns shows in 1950. Instead of standing onstage and performing to an audience in front of them, in the manner of Broadway shows, the Smothers Brothers constructed an intimate environment in which audience members surrounded them on all sides, like spectators at a sporting event. In look and feel, the setting borrowed from both the relaxed coffeehouse atmosphere of the time and the up-close-and-personal Beatles videos. "Center stage" was a raft-sized Tiffany-style platform, and audience members were present in every shot, smiling, nodding, or singing along appreciatively.

In the first in-the-round show, when guest star Donovan sits in a cross-legged lotus position and sings a gorgeous acoustic version of "Lalena," members of the audience respond by pelting him with flowers. Another guest, Dion, sings "Abraham, Martin and John," a powerful song mourning the assassinations of Abraham Lincoln, John F. Kennedy, Martin Luther King Jr., and Robert Kennedy—merely a week after it first entered the charts. Tom and Dick sing with Donovan, as does Jennifer Warnes (billed, then, as Jennifer Warren). Because of a musicians' strike, Nelson Riddle and his orchestra are absent, so all the incidental and background music, even the show's theme song, is provided a cappella by the Jimmy Joyce Singers. The comedy troupe Committee provides comic relief, highlighted by a hilarious waiting-room percussion duel by Peter Bonerz and staff writer Carl Gottlieb. The feel of it all, from the playful sing-along on Donovan's "Happiness Runs" to the poignant topicality of Dion's composition ("Didn't you love the things that they stood for? / Didn't they try to find some good in you and me?"), is pure, undiluted '60s. It's not a stretch at all to see this show, and the other concert shows that followed, as an extension of what Tom witnessed and experienced at Monterey, or as prime-time precursors to Woodstock, which would follow four months after the Smothers Brothers were thrown off the air.

But the Smothers Brothers weren't just about peace and love, flower power, and rock 'n' roll—and certainly weren't just about making people laugh. The next show they recorded, featuring Nanette Fabray and Steppenwolf, was taped in November but held for broadcast as the first show of 1969. It begins with Tom complaining about not feeling funny. They switch parts, with Dick holding the guitar and Tom cradling the bass and adopting the role of the straight man. Dick tells him to think seriously, and Tom says there's nothing he wants to think seriously about, either—whereupon Dick responds with a litany of serious topics that, even with a two-month shelf time, turns out to be more current and pointed than most things in prime time. "Think about the race problem, Tommy," Dick tells his brother. "Think about higher taxes. Think about the war in Vietnam. Think about Richard Nixon trying to *solve* all those problems." Tom's eyebrows shoot up. "*That's* funny," he replies.

Even with President-elect Nixon only a few months from assuming office, the Smothers Brothers still felt secure enough to make jokes at his expense. The postelection Thanksgiving week show had tied the ratings for the "Hey Jude" program with the Beatles, making it one of the season's most-watched installments. Elsewhere on CBS, a new prime-time series, an ambitious and controversy-seeking newsmagazine called *60 Minutes*, had decided to send Harry Reasoner and a camera crew to do a story on *The Smothers Brothers Comedy Hour* for the first *60 Minutes* report of 1969. At that point, there was every indication that *Comedy Hour* would be renewed for a fourth season. Moreover, the brothers' summer series, starring Glen Campbell, had proven so popular that a spinoff series, *The Glen Campbell Goodtime Hour*, was scheduled to launch on CBS in late January. The Smothers Brothers were on a roll, but not for much longer.

Their very success had caused a thinning of the ranks. Mason Williams, after becoming a popular and bookable entertainer in his own right thanks to "Classical Gas," was on the road instead of in the writers' room. He would, quite literally, phone in ideas from time to time or contribute occasional introductions or comedy or concept pieces if he felt so inspired. This is why, that third season, his on-air writing credit was given as the highly unusual, probably unprecedented "And Sometimes by Mason Williams."

Pat Paulsen, the biggest *Comedy Hour* star, left the nest also, in a high-concept stunt worthy of anything dreamed up by Andy Kaufman or Stephen Colbert. During the good-byes of that same Fabray show, Tom utters a respectful farewell to Paulsen, whom Tom explains is leaving to become a regular on *The Glen Campbell Goodtime Hour*. Pat enters and begins with a mock-sincere show of gratitude ("Thank you, Tom and Dave"). Then he starts talking about his accomplishments on the show, and his fond memories, and he gets more and more emotional. His voice cracks, and he so deftly accomplishes the illusion of uncomfortable sadness that the audience watches, for a while, in dead silence. "I didn't even want to leave," Pat says, sobbing, and finally the studio audience, quite relieved, gets that Pat is putting them on. "I want my Tommy!" he finally shouts, burying his head in Tom's chest. Pat Paulsen would make only two more appearances on *The Smothers Brothers Comedy Hour*, including an unbilled cameo, the perfect coda to his *Comedy Hour* career.

Another member of the Smothers family made an appearance in the Fabray-Steppenwolf show—Tom and Dick's mother, coming up from the audience to join her sons onstage. It was just after Fabray had played the Smothers Brothers' mother in a skit fleshing out the duo's now-classic "Mom Always Liked You Best" routine, a sketch that had Fabray, as Mrs. Smothers, doting on young Dick and constantly berating poor young Tom. Their real mother was called onstage and introduced to the studio audience. "You are our real mom, aren't you?" Tom asks her. "Sadly enough, I am," she replies. She gets a big laugh, followed by an even bigger one when she kisses Dick, then playfully slaps Tom on the face.

At least that's what happened in the afternoon taping. Between then and the evening performance, their mother asked Tom if she could do something else, as a surprise ("Just let me do it," she told Tom, "and don't tell Dick about it"). Instead of kissing Dick and slapping Tom, she kisses both siblings, then slaps Dick, hard—catching him completely unawares. Dick is stunned, Tom is delighted, and the audience howls. Tom loved it so much that, later in the show, he explained what had happened and showed videotape of both versions. He even reran his mother slapping Dick, repeatedly and in both slow-motion and sped-up motion, and identified it as his favorite moment all season.

The next show taped was the one that *60 Minutes* was visiting backstage to observe and film. The fledgling newsmagazine had lucked into a potential gold mine: the show broadcast December 8 included the West Coast cast of *Hair,* singing and performing in a way that was quite controversial for its time. There was a big backstage story brewing about the *Hair* company's appearance on *Comedy Hour,* but *60 Minutes* missed it. Instead, Reasoner was focusing on writers' meetings, a rehearsal of a musical comedy sketch, the relationship between the brothers and CBS (and between the brothers themselves), and polarized reaction from members of the audience. It's all a very revealing, very reliable trapped-in-amber look at *Comedy Hour* at the end of 1968, just as the show was heading into its biggest controversies and its final months.

Reasoner began his report by quoting letters to CBS about the Smothers Brothers, both pro and con. The con pile in the sample was larger, and more heated. "You seem to have joined the lower element who have dirty long hair beards [and] low morals . . . [It's] like seeing your own son going hippie," one viewer wrote to complain. Another wrote, "We all have hopes that this program will be taken off the air before they do any more damage with their kind of talk." *60 Minutes* then showed comedy clips from the concert-in-the-round show, including Tom and Dick pretending to be network censors. To contrast the show with a less controversial era of radio and TV comedy, *60 Minutes* showed a vintage backstage clip of Jack Benny conferring with his writers, without noting that two of Benny's writers had been members of the *Smothers Brothers* staff the first two seasons.

Interviewing the brothers separately gleans some insight about their relative passions, and passion, as 1968 was coming to a close. "I want something that makes a statement, and has humor in it," Tom says, to which Reasoner's narration adds, "The question becomes, *Whose* statement?"

Dick, in a solo interview, explains, "Tommy's the one who's the crusader. He crusades, and to be a crusader, you have to overreact—because underreaction doesn't get any results. And I'm the one, generally, who says, 'Well, I think this is too strong. I think if we temper it, and we bring it down maybe twenty percent, we'll get a little bit better mileage out of it.' And he's the one," Dick adds, laughing, "that says, 'Forget it, I'm running the show.' We do it that way. And chances are, he's right."

When *60 Minutes* visits a planning meeting of the writing staff, run by writer-producer Allan Blye, we see a lot of young (and now familiar) faces, a lot of blue denim shirts and open collars, and quite a few dilated pupils. The crowded room includes, among others, Bob Einstein, Steve Martin, Murray Roman, Carl Gottlieb, and Rob Reiner. Roman begins to describe a sketch about an ineffectual minister. Through his bumbling sermon, Roman explains, "you show how innocuous Christianity is, and how it has no relationship to the world today."

"It's not true, though," Steve Martin, shaking his head, speaks up to complain. Others back up Martin, and Tom explains that the problem of being too outspoken, especially about religion, is that there are now close to twenty affiliated CBS stations that won't broadcast the show if they disapprove of its content in advance.

"Every Friday," Tom tells his staff, "our show is shown, through a closed line, to all the affiliates, which is unheard of. They demand that they have to see the show before they will air it. So it's not like we can just do [it] the way we want to do. If we're going to change anything, we have to cop out a little bit to adjust." The newsmagazine showed some of those adjustments, including a closing series of blackouts and one-liners called "What would happen if . . . ? ," which included such inoffensive silliness as Steve Martin embodying the sound, and sight, of one hand clapping—by smacking himself in the face repeatedly with his own palm. Yet other hypothetical questions, and their answers, were more pointed and meaningful. To the question "What would happen if crime paid?" Tom's answer is, "The same people would have all the money." Another hypothetical imagines a black man as president of the United States—a concept, at that point, exactly forty years ahead of its time.

It was a bit brave of *60 Minutes* to air that segment—like the Smothers Brothers, *60 Minutes* was heightening the awareness of its own network's censorship merely by discussing it. It also, however, was a canny attempt to widen its own viewership and demographic. *60 Minutes* wouldn't become a Top 20 show for another eight seasons. *The Smothers Brothers Comedy Hour* already was one.

Not many prime-time stars or producers, before or since, fought as hard to stretch the boundaries of prime-time television as Tom Smothers, even at that very moment. Had *60 Minutes* trained its cameras in a different direction on a different day, it would have captured one doozy of a battle. Not between Tom and CBS, but between Tom and one of his own crew members. It was a fight, and a physical one, with fists flying and bodies wrestling on the ground as a soundstage full of people watched. It was a fight about *Hair*.

Hair, billed as "the American Tribal Love-Rock Musical," opened Off-Broadway in October 1967 as the first production of Joseph Papp's Public Theater. It moved uptown to the Biltmore Theatre in April 1968, and established a West Coast company at the newly opened Aquarius Theater that summer in Los Angeles. One of the investors who brought the show to Los Angeles was Tom Smothers, who, as a pot-smoking showbiz kindred spirit, was approached repeatedly to help finance the show's California company and theater.

Tom admits it wasn't exactly love at first sight, even though the original cast included then-unknowns Diane Keaton and Melba Moore.

"I went and saw it in New York," Tom recalls, "and I went back and said, 'I don't want to be involved. There's a lot of naked people running down the aisle, and their butts are hanging out and stuff.'" He laughs at the memory. "And then they said, 'No, you've got to see it again!' I went back, and saw it again, and liked it a little better. And then they just kept pushing me, and I said okay . . .

"I fell in love with the show later on," he continues, "but it was a slow take for me. I had a good eye for talent. I didn't have a good eye for music," he says, laughing at his own turn of phrase. "I never thought any of the songs from *Hair* would be a hit."

It turns out there would be several hits, all of them cover versions by other artists. First was a medley, by the vocal group the 5th Dimension, of "Aquarius / Let the Sunshine In," which reached number one and eventually won a Grammy as Record of the Year. Then came the pop group the Cowsills, with its version of the Broadway show's title song; a singer named Oliver, with his rendition of "Good Morning Starshine"; and, finally, rock group Three Dog Night, with a gritty version of a *Hair* ballad, "Easy to Be Hard."

All of those records reached the Top 10, but not until the spring or summer of 1969. In the winter of 1968, when the West Coast cast of *Hair* was showcased on *Comedy Hour*, there were no hits, and there was no mainstream airplay. *The Ed Sullivan Show*, which preceded *Comedy Hour* on CBS and specialized in showcasing the latest from Broadway musicals, didn't feature *Hair* and its music until March 1969, four months after Tom presented them first. In prime time, on *Comedy Hour*, the songs from *Hair* were fresh and startling, and the three selected for performance, in an intense miniset, all were future hits: "Aquarius," "Hair," and "Let the Sunshine In." The original coauthors, lyricists, and stars of *Hair*, James Rado and Jerome Ragni (the composer was Galt MacDermot), had moved west in time to reprise their roles for the *Comedy Hour* performance. The West Coast company also included a face familiar to *Comedy Hour* fans: Jennifer Warnes, whom Tom had gotten a job with the California cast. (On *Comedy Hour*, she positively wails on "Let the Sunshine In.")

There were some concessions made for the performance of these three songs on network TV—no nudity being the obvious one. Other parts, though, demonstrated remarkable fidelity to the original stage version. The lyrics to the title song included a couplet cut from the subsequent Cowsills rendition yet presented on *Comedy Hour* intact, despite the show's history with offending many religious viewers: "My hair like Jesus wore it. Hallelujah, I adore it!" And elsewhere in the same song, a cast member sits in a yoga lotus position, draped in an American flag and pretending to sew Betsy Ross–style, as his fellow "tribe members" sing, to the tune of "The Star-Spangled Banner," a brief, irreverent anthem: "O say, can you see my eyes? If you can, then my hair's too short!"

"For Tom to invite such revolutionary stuff to be on national TV was a real risk," says Jennifer Warnes, who credits Tom with having "a revolutionary heart" and lots of bravery. "It took someone like Tom, who was absolutely unafraid, to break the barrier," she adds. "To say, 'Absolutely, why not? This is great!' . . . He was very definitely a patron of the arts, a cross-pollinator, and a catalyst."

A catalyst, indeed—in more ways than one. The afternoon taping of the *Comedy Hour* show that Friday went without incident, but in the hours between that performance (the "dress" version) and the evening taping (the "air"), one member of the tech crew rebelled angrily and others backed him. Word got out to Tom that the union crew refused to do the evening show if that kid from *Hair* intended to repeat the "desecration" of having the American flag touch the ground. What *60 Minutes* missed—but enough witnesses described in enough detail to qualify as an action scene with R-rated dialogue—was the one time on the *Comedy Hour* set where the generation gap, and the political divide between hawks and doves, manifested itself in a full-blown physical fight.

Everyone gathers in a circle on Stage 43, like Sharks and Jets at a knife fight in *West Side Story,* as Tom confronts this "big old burly guy" who runs the boom microphone.

"What's the problem?" Tom demands.

"Why do I have to put up with that shit, man?" the boom operator snaps back, referring to the *Hair* sequence with the flag touching the ground. This, Tom later points out, was before the flag became an acceptable fashion statement, incorporated into shirts, bandanas, and so on.

"Come on," Tom says, waving him off. "It's not a big deal."

"*You* come on," the man snarls. Suddenly, he and Tom are on the ground, wrestling and punching, arms flailing, legs kicking, both men grunting and groaning as they work in and out of a series of headlocks and bear hugs. Tom, as wiry and strong as in his days as a college gymnast, finally had an ideological opponent at whom he could lash out physically. It was a fierce fight, erupting from all the tensions of the show and the era, but it didn't last long.

"The big crowd around us," Tom recalls, "started laughing their asses off. It diffused everything. We got up, huffing and puffing, and I gave him one last shot, and he gave me a shot, and we went and did the show. And that was the last time we ever had a problem." Most of the crew members, Tom says, were veterans and blue-collar types ("They were not the hippie 'peace and love' people"), but that was the only time, he insists, that a problem with the production crew ever surfaced. Over matters of politics, that is. When it came to the show, Tom was just as demanding as ever with his directors and managers, demanding more and becoming satisfied with less. All season long, he had been wooing Tim Kiley, director of *The Ed Sullivan Show,* to come to California and work on *Comedy Hour* instead, to give the show more of a "live" feel and capture the action better.

Kiley, Tom was certain, would make things run more smoothly—and Kiley eventually accepted, showing up in time to direct some of the best and most ambitious episodes of the entire series.

Other things were happening behind the scenes, though, that made things run less smoothly. Tom was fighting someone all the time, it seemed—and not one-on-one in a wrestling match that ended genially. He was fighting censors, executives, affiliates, and increasingly his own managers and staff members. At the end of almost every battle, the amount of rancor was increasing, not dissipating. And every show, it seemed, hit its chosen subjects harder and more directly, and paid less attention to trying to please, or appeal to, all ages in the demographic spectrum.

"I felt that Tommy was getting too obvious," admits Blye, who coproduced with George Sunga that final *Comedy Hour* season. Tom himself admits to being too intense and losing his sense of humor in his passion to get his and other viewpoints across, as the third season progressed. Looking at the individual shows, that progression is obvious. So, however, is the quality, and singular outspokenness, of some of those same programs. Seen in sequence, as they were at the time, the determination to speak out is clear.

The following show, taped December 6 and broadcast nine days later, featured George Carlin (returning from the summer show), the Doors, and yet another visit by the Committee. Carlin, the Doors—this was younger-generation fare all the way, with no concessions to the over-thirty crowd. Not unless you count Nelson Riddle's orchestra, brought onstage to back Jim Morrison and company in an impressive live performance of "Touch Me." But even that Doors' mixture of rock and big band was new—so new that "Touch Me" wouldn't hit the charts for another month.

Politically, this *Comedy Hour* was feisty from start to finish. It started with Tom, in the opening bit with Dick, fumbling to put on a gas mask and police helmet. When Dick finally asked him why,

Tom replied, "I'm getting ready to go to college"—a punch line aimed at all the student unrest and clashes with police.

One lengthy sketch featured Dick interviewing *Comedy Hour* players, much as Steve Allen used to in his "Man on the Street" pieces, in a new feature called "The Smothers Brothers Minority Report." This was a new way to build comedy around topical issues of the week, a function formerly served by Pat Paulsen's editorials. The opening "Minority Report," in which representatives of various minority groups were asked their opinions, was on how their taxes were being spent. Among the characters, and the zingers, is Murray Roman as a Mexican American, who is told by Dick, the interviewer, that the government spends only two cents of every tax dollar on education. "How come, in a presidential election," Roman asks, "it is possible for one man to get less votes than his opponent and still get elected president of the United States?" (The question applied, in the '60s, to Nixon versus Hubert Humphrey—and, decades later, to George W. Bush versus Al Gore.) When Dick explains they're not dealing with that topic on this particular program, Roman replies, "Excuse me, Mr. Smothers, for showing my lack of education—but when you only spend two cents, you get what you pay for." (The studio audience actually "oohs" at that one.) And to close the show, Carlin and the Committee joined with the others on a finale built around the daily newspaper—more excuses for topical yet still relevant humor. George Carlin, setting it up, tells viewers at the end of 1968, "Newspapers all across the country are closing because they haven't any readership." He, Tom, and Dick then break into a sympathetic song: "Television's stealing all their thunder / newspaper companies are going under." (Substitute "the internet" for "television" and here we go again. Sigh.)

George Gobel, Tom's original stand-up hero and influence, was a guest on the next program. It was the Christmas show, broadcast on December 22, and was appropriately wholesome and well behaved.

Even it, though, had some spark to it. Tom complains about the hypocrisy of the Vietnam War's Christmas truce ("Only two days, and it's back to killing") and, for the holidays, offers President-elect Nixon a solution to stop the fighting permanently. "We can end it with dignity and honor for our country," Tom says of the Vietnam War, then reveals how: "We declare a victory, and pull our troops out." And in the same show, during a "Share a Little Tea with Goldie" spot, Leigh French scores points on three different fronts. She slips in some slyly open-ended jokes by answering viewer mail without reading the questions ("Answer number one: 'Yes, I do' . . . Answer number two: 'Twice a day is not too much' "); she uses the subject of Christmas trees, and their source, to make a point about conservation ("You remember forests—they used to cover the Earth"); and, at the end of her Christmas report, she signs off by saying, "And don't forget whose birthday this is. Peace."

The first newly taped show for 1969 wasn't very topical: it was another writers' showcase, a loose, silly talent show featuring various members of the Smothers Brothers' onstage and offstage family. About the only political element in the entire hour was the opening, in which Tom raves excitedly, and supportively, about Nixon, whose inauguration was only weeks away. Dick questions why his brother would consider Nixon's ascension to power so "out of sight," and Tom tells Dick to think back to Nixon's history as vice president under President Eisenhower. "Every single country he ever went to," Tom said of Nixon's international travels in the late 1950s, "he got stoned."

By now, viewers tuning to *Comedy Hour* expected such controversy: the January 12 writers' show was the first one to air after CBS, earlier the same week, had televised the *60 Minutes* report on the Smothers Brothers. Most of this *Comedy Hour* writers' show, though, was nothing more than a nationally televised party, a chance for everyone to show off and goof around. John Hartford sang a song, and so did Mason Williams, but both of them displayed other talents as well. Mason recited one of his comic "Them" poems, "Them Toad Suckers," while Hartford and Carl Gottlieb performed a musical duet—playing their faces. (Full disclosure: I played my face, in the same ridiculous manner, in high school. Until seeing tapes of this show decades later, I had no idea where I'd gotten the inspiration.)

Steve Martin, in his biggest showcase in the entire series, got two solo bits, both of them funny. In one, he did an intentionally inept magic act, including a "napkin trick" in which he covered his face with a paper napkin and pushed his tongue through it. In another, he juggled—well, but with lots of comic bits of business between tricks. Bob Einstein and Gottlieb did a violent circus act called "The Pain Brothers," throwing bowling pins at each other rather than juggling them, and Einstein and Murray Roman did a failed-escape magic act that may as well have been the prototype for Einstein's "Super Dave" character. That, and more—all delivered in a casual, good-natured manner.

The next show was different. The more traditional, but still wonderful, entertainment is provided by Ray Charles, who plays saxophone on one number and piano on another. Another guest star is comedian Jackie Mason, who would prove almost as controversial a comic as David Steinberg—and whose *Comedy Hour* appearance is all about equality. He teaches Ray Charles how to sing what he called "the Jewish blues," which ends with them harmonizing on the phrase "Oy, vey!"—and in his stand-up routine, Mason insists that "people are all the same." He singles out a white man in the audience and tells him, "A man is born black, does that make him worse than you?" Then, after a single beat, the comedian adds, "There's *nobody* worse than you." The show includes a second "Minority Report," this one on the military draft, about which a member of the African American minority interviewed by Dick notes an unusual level of racial integration. "I believe the black man," he tells Dick straight-faced, "has an even better opportunity to be drafted than the white man."

The hour also includes a second film by Chuck Braverman, a four-minute film called *1968* that wraps up one of the most volatile years of the twentieth century in Braverman's incessant, incisive, subliminal style. The assassinations of Martin Luther King Jr. and Bobby Kennedy, the police brutality and Democratic National Convention footage banned from the excised Harry Belafonte "Carnival" segment—it's all here, fast and furious, quite literally on both counts. And CBS could hardly censor Braverman's *1968* film, since it had premiered, twelve days earlier, on the same network's *60 Minutes,* on the very episode featuring the Smothers Brothers. It's a stunning film, and ends with the image of a peace sign, which remains projected behind Tom and Dick as they deliver their very pointed wrap-up. "Let's hope 1969," Tom says, "will allow us to make a film that has nothing but beautiful things in it."

It also was an example of the type of thing that, in those days, only the Smothers Brothers would attempt—as was the highlight of the following week's show, in which folksinger, actor, and former blacklist victim Burl Ives played the stage manager in an "updated" version of Thornton Wilder's *Our Town.*

The set piece, nearly eleven minutes long, has the Stage Manager still looking down on Main Street from above and seeing familiar sights after all the intervening years—the barber shop, the pharmacy, the dance hall, and so on. But the closer he looks, the more differences he notices. The barber complains about the long-haired kids ("those commie pinko long-haired peacenik pre-verts") and longs for "the good old days, when a kid used to come in here every two weeks and get a crewcut." At the pharmacy, the Stage Manager watches a matronly customer load up on cough syrup and tranquilizers while railing against drug use by the young. At the dance hall, the Stage Manager peers in and sees the Chambers Brothers, the week's other *Comedy Hour* guest stars, singing "Time Has Come Today." What, he asks, have they done to the waltz? Then he talks to a priest, played by Tom, who fills him in on some other recent events. Finally, he points to the shadows, where a young couple, in silhouette, are embracing each other.

"They look like they're in love," Ives, as the Stage Manager, says with quiet satisfaction. "Now there's something that doesn't change. As long as people love each other, and as long as there's love in the world, there's hope for all of us." The lights come up, and it's Steve Martin, holding the hand and embracing the shoulder of a beautiful young woman. He's white, she's black. The Stage Manager stares silently for a second, then turns to Tom.

"Is there anyone who hasn't changed?" he asks. "What about Fred Hanson?"

"Oh, he hasn't changed," Tom the priest replies. "He's dead."

"And Ed Wilkie?"

"He hasn't changed, either."

"So he's dead, too," the Stage Manager sighs.

"No," the priest replies. "But he might as well be. You see, he's never changed."

Ives steps forward, fills the screen, and begins singing Bob Dylan's "The Times They Are A-Changin,' " slowly and very, very pointedly. Soon, the entire town joins in, and the lyrics are superimposed so they, like the message of the piece, can be understood clearly. "Your sons and your daughters are beyond your command," they sing. And warn.

"Effective skit?" asked Harlan Ellison in his February 21 TV column for the *Los Angeles Free Press*. "You bet your ass it was. Simple, direct, eloquent, and enormously well-done because it was all underplayed, with just the right touches of comedy and not a cornball note in the entire production." Ellison was smart enough to know groundbreaking television when he saw it—and, more than most people around at the time, including the Smothers Brothers themselves, he understood both the game and the stakes. In terms of the ratings, *The Smothers Brothers Comedy Hour* had done a good thing by attracting young viewers who didn't watch much television, and a very good thing by continuing to draw large audiences in the major cities. But when it came to the outlying rural areas, where CBS was so strong with such shows as *Gunsmoke* and *Gomer Pyle, U.S.M.C.,* the appeal of the young-skewing, taboo-puncturing *Comedy Hour* dropped off precipitously, and ratings in the country's heartland were starting to tank. As Ellison put it: "Oh, sure, in the Thirty Cities Ratings, the Smothers clan does well, but in the outlying regions, where most of the soap-suds are bought, they die. And the network notices this, make no mistake."

Ellison doesn't blame the audience, necessarily—just their in-ability, in those pre-cable, pre-computer, pre-internet days, to get enough information to make an informed decision, even when fil-tered through entertainment. "They haven't been given the opportu-nity for weighing one side against the other," Ellison insists. "The entrenched forces rule the mass media, in ways they deny because they don't conceive of them as being misused." The content of *Com-edy Hour*, he adds, is too threatening to the status quo, especially of the network—and when the Stage Manager sings of a battle outside raging, one that will "soon shake your windows and rattle your walls," the network doesn't want to hear it, much less relay it nation-wide.

"So, inexorably," Ellison concludes with amazing prescience, "they will kill a show like *The Smothers Brothers Comedy Hour*. They have to. It threatens them too much." Six weeks after that column was published, *Comedy Hour* was dead.

Beeping Censors Lurking in the Wings

T he Burl Ives show, with the stinging *Our Town* update, arrived two-thirds of the way through season three of *The Smothers Brothers Comedy Hour*. Ratings, at that point, were beginning to slip a little, but not that much: the Ives hour had drawn an estimated 31 percent of the viewing audience. The following week, *Comedy Hour* would be preempted so CBS could present an imported Royal Shakespeare Company film version of *A Midsummer Night's Dream,* receiving its American premiere on TV rather than in theaters. Directed by Peter Hall, it boasted what, in retrospect, clearly was a *Dream* cast: Diana Rigg, Judi Dench, Ian Richardson, Ian Holm, David Warner, and others. Yet, as a replacement for the Smothers Brothers, it attracted only 21 percent of the available viewing audience. So on the surface, Tom and Dick still had clout, visibility, and support.

The duo had just released a new LP, a compilation of classic bits ("Cabbage," "My Old Man") that were newly recorded, reflecting the comedy pieces' evolution over the years. The album was titled *Golden Hits of the Smothers Brothers, Vol. 2*, a typically twisted Smothers prank (there never was, and never would be, a *Vol. 1*). *TV Guide* continued to feature *Comedy Hour* in profiles and detailed "Close-Up" listings, and *The Glen Campbell Goodtime Hour*, with Pat Paulsen and Leigh French aboard, had opened to good ratings and positive reviews. But politics, both nationally and within the CBS hierarchy, were about to change, quickly and significantly.

President Lyndon Baines Johnson delivered his final State of the Union address in mid-January. One week later, on January 20, 1969, Richard Nixon was sworn in as the thirty-seventh president of the United States. The shift from Democrat to Republican, and to a politician already wary and resentful of the media and vengeful in a manner embodied by the creation of an "enemies list," would bring a new level of heat on CBS and the Smothers Brothers. CBS wanted to avoid controversy, while Tom Smothers was equally determined to pursue it. On the first show after the Shakespeare special, one of Tom's special guests was master impressionist David Frye, and among the sketches being prepared was one that skewered Nixon scathingly.

What Tom had no way of knowing was that, like the country itself, CBS was about to get a new president, one just as conservative, obstinate, and combative as Nixon himself. Tom didn't want to play by the rules at CBS and was frustrated by never being told exactly what those rules were, even when he asked, specifically and repeatedly, to see them.

Tom already had taken his fight to every level of CBS, starting at the very top. Chairman William S. Paley, who had made CBS a radio and TV powerhouse by fostering, backing, or outbidding for such broadcast greats as Jack Benny, George Burns, Edward R. Murrow, and Lucille Ball, enjoyed occasional interaction with his talent. But Tom quickly went to that well too often and soon was told that both Paley and Frank Stanton were off limits.

Tom Dawson, CBS network president, had, to this point, involved himself with the *Comedy Hour* controversies only once. During the show's first season, he made the unilateral decision to stop the Elaine May sketch on censors from being broadcast. Under Dawson, in the New York office, was William Tankersley, the veteran vice president for program practices, who thought Dawson's Elaine May decision was a mistake but hadn't been involved in it. Tankersley, too, up to this point in 1969, had dealt with the Smothers Brothers very infrequently, sending a memo regarding the summer show, and getting involved by phone during the Harry Belafonte "Carnival" controversy. Tankersley, like CBS senior vice president of programming Mike Dann, preferred to let his West Coast lieutenants handle day-to-day operations. With the gauntlet Tom Smothers was about to throw down, though, the East Coast was about to get a lot more involved.

In Hollywood, Dann's vice president of programming on the West Coast was Perry Lafferty, who had come from producing *The Danny Kaye Show* and assumed the job just in time to work with the Smothers Brothers on their short-lived sitcom. He, like Dann, was in Tom and Dick's corner, as the show's success had reflected on them both. But Robert Tamplin, Lafferty's assistant, was more of a functionary and clearly more on the side of network management. It was Tamplin who fired off the memo right after the David Steinberg sermonette show demanding that all future *Comedy Hour* shows be delivered in time for an advance closed-circuit screening to CBS affililates.

Then there were Tankersley's Hollywood operatives, responsible for approving every script and attending every taping of every show emanating from CBS Television City. Tom Downer was the West Coast director of program practices, and had gotten that job just in time to play a part in the initial veto of Pete Seeger's performance of "Waist Deep in the Big Muddy" at the start of season two. He also was the CBS executive who wrote the memo, following Steinberg's appearance, that should the comedian appear on the show again, a similar sermonette sketch would be strictly forbidden.

Downer's primary West Coast assistants—censors, really, though they were given the more benign title of "editors"—were Charles Pettijohn and Sam Taylor Jr. They did the day-to-day viewing, script vetting, set visiting, and note taking, and were familiar faces at Television City, and not unliked. Red Skelton, when taping his weekly variety shows, would load the afternoon rehearsals with obscenities just to fluster Pettijohn, then, when the evening performance was taped for broadcast, giggle at all the dirty jokes he *wasn't* saying.

The first two seasons, the Smothers set exuded a similar good-fun atmosphere for the most part. There were occasional high-stakes battles with censors, but both sides, for a while, found ways to enjoy the escalating behind-the-scenes gamesmanship. Ernie Chambers, producer of those two *Comedy Hour* seasons, remembers slipping through some drug references or double entendres by erasing the studio audience's laughter from the master sound track. Instead of "sweetening" the show's sound track by adding canned laughter, Tom and the producers intentionally would "sour" it. "You could do something off-color," Chambers explains, "as long as it didn't get a laugh . . . We would erase the laugh, then they [the censors] would leave it in."

The CBS side made its share of sneaky moves as well. After NBC premiered *Rowan & Martin's Laugh-In* as a weekly series, Tom began complaining about that network's seemingly freer standards. Downer attempted to appease Tom by adding to his program practices staff a new hire—a recent college graduate named John Kaye, part of the "under thirty" demographic Tom so treasured. When Kaye came aboard, Tom enthused about him to the *New York Times*, saying of CBS, "They gave us a much younger and more sympathetic man from program practices to pass on our material." Smothers manager Ken Fritz recalls Kaye as "a real Joe College, Ivy League-y kind of button-down guy," and that both CBS and the Smothers Brothers hoped Kaye would be "the guy who would bridge the generation gap." Instead, he proved so stuffy and out of touch that Tom engineered an elaborate prank designed to embarrass him.

Tom and the writers set a trap for the censors by instructing everyone—dancers, singers, even the camera operators and costumers—to roar with delight whenever anyone at rehearsals uttered the nonsense phrase "rowing to Galveston." Sometimes it was slipped into scripts, and sometimes it was ad-libbed onstage, but it always was edited out by the CBS censors, who were unhinged by the "dirty laughter" it invariably elicited from the cast and crew. Mason Williams explained it was a nonsense phrase, and everyone was in on the joke except for program practices. "So they were running around like crazy," Mason says, "trying to figure out what 'rowing to Galveston' really meant in 'hippie-ese.' " Fritz remembers Kaye coming over to him, finally, and saying, 'That's got to go—'rowing into Galveston.' And we said, 'Why?' And he said, 'You *know* why!' " Tom tried to get the objection in writing, but before that happened, Fritz says, Kaye realized he "had gotten his chain pulled."

"We liked them individually," Dick says of the censors. "They just had to play the corporate game, or they didn't have a job." Tom agrees. But each season, the players in the game changed, and the game, and the rules, changed accordingly.

The first two seasons, Ilson and Chambers served as buffers between the CBS censors and the *Comedy Hour* stars and writers. When memos first began trickling down from, as Ilson puts it, "the Kremlin upstairs"—specifically, from Bob Tamplin, Perry Lafferty's assistant—one of the producers would call Lafferty to object. "Some of them were really absurd," Ilson says of the objections, and sometimes Lafferty would give in. Other times, they would negotiate, but only up to a point. "Everything was a negotiation until it got to Tommy," Ilson says, "and then Tommy just wouldn't budge. We'd have to sit there and go through it all. And sometimes he was right, and sometimes it was ridiculous, because he'd fight the wrong battles."

Chambers says of the West Coast program practices team, "The truth was, they weren't bad guys. They were guys who were supporting their families and they had a job to do, and their job was to keep the sponsors from being bombarded by offended listeners. That doesn't matter anymore, but it mattered in 1967." What is now called the Religious Right, Chambers says, was then called the Bible Belt.

"If the Bible Belt organized their constituents, boy, and started bombarding General Motors or General Foods," he explains, "CBS heard about it, and then CBS said, 'We don't want any trouble with our sponsors, so get that stuff out of there' . . . That's ultimately what it came down to, was the sponsors being upset that they would alienate their customers."

And with the Smothers Brothers, what it came down to, ultimately, is that Tom kept firing, losing, or leapfrogging over those who served as intermediaries between him and the powers at the top. Ilson and Chambers left after season two. Tom, at this point in season three, had just dismissed manager Kragen and soon was to do the same to comanager Fritz, leaving himself more directly involved, and less shielded, when it came to fighting his battles. Going directly to Paley and Stanton no longer was acceptable, but Tom's zeal for wanting to deal directly with those in charge had not diminished. He had successfully managed to go above the head of Tom Downer, and thus all the West Coast censors division, by establishing direct contact with William Tankersley, who ran the program practices division out of New York. Tom's next move, in trying to standardize this new line of communication, would bring him into direct contact with another powerful CBS executive, Tom Dawson—and, after Dawson was replaced, by Bob Wood. By dealing directly with Tankersley and Wood, especially, Tom thought he was solving his problems with the network. In reality, he was adding to them and threading his own noose.

The *Comedy Hour* staff was continuing to get detailed memos from Sam Taylor, objecting to such items as "the toilet flush sound effect" and "a blackout involving the sudden deflating of an inflatable brassiere." Tom objected to the heavy-handed censorship, and phoned Tankersley directly to plead his case. Tankersley supported most of Taylor's objections, overruled a few, and added some additional objections of his own, which added to postproduction editing time. Tom, however, was pleased to deal with one person who had the power to say yes or no, rather than argue his case to a string of often contradictory network and affiliate voices. On January 30, 1969—after the Ives show was taped and edited, but before it was broadcast—Tom sent a memo trying to make it official. Sent to Dann, Lafferty, and Downer, and complaining of indecisiveness and a lack of cooperation and clarity from Downer's West Coast staff, it was less a memo than a gauntlet.

"We will no longer deal with the people in the Continuity Acceptance Department here in Los Angeles," Tom wrote, "regarding any changes or deletions. All requests for changes or any problems regarding taste etc. will be expected to come from Mr. Tankersley in New York."

The stunning memo continued: "We do not wish to have Sam Taylor or anyone else from the department in Los Angeles in our control booth, at the script readings or run-thru [sic]. All memos will be returned and we wish to formally sever our relationship with the people in the Continuity Acceptance Department here in Los Angeles." Justifying the new policy, Tom added, "We on the SMOTHERS BROTHERS COMEDY HOUR do not feel that it is correct or proper that we be subject to three (i.e., Los Angeles, New York and general affiliate approval) opinions, oftentimes countermanding and contradicting each other regarding our show content." The memo concluded by saying the *Comedy Hour* staff had been instructed not to deal with anyone from Continuity Acceptance at Television City in Los Angeles in any way, "except on a personal or friendship basis where that exists." In his memo to the *Comedy Hour* staff, Tom was even more blunt: "An Iron Curtain now exists between us and them."

The CBS memo Tom received in reply came not from any of its recipients, but from the president of the CBS Network, Thomas H. Dawson. Dawson was taking the liberty to reply, he explained, not only because of his business association with Tom, but because "the procedure you have outlined is totally impractical and unacceptable." Dawson argued that the only time New York had reviewed a *Comedy Hour* tape was when it had failed to meet West Coast standards, and that providing a master tape in time for affiliate review was mandatory. "The standards of CBS must be maintained," Dawson wrote. "And I ask you to respect them and to cooperate with the people whom we have designated to administer them." Dawson ended with a personal aside: "As I have said to you many times—let's use our energies for the development and promotion of better SMOTHERS BROTHERS *COMEDY* HOURS." Tom Smothers may have strained whatever personal relationship he had with the CBS president, but things were about to get a lot worse. One month after Dawson wrote his letter, Tom and the rest of the *Comedy Hour* staff would be dealing with a new, much less patient CBS president: Robert S. Wood.

At Television City, Tom's memo was the talk of the building. Joe Hamilton, executive producer of *The Carol Burnett Show,* sent out a parody memo of his own, claiming that the staff of the *Burnett* show no longer would deal with, recognize, or eat the food from the CBS cafeteria there in Hollywood, and demanded that all meals be flown out from New York. ("I thought it was pretty funny," Tom says, laughing.) But Tom was dead serious. He tried to use the next show, which featured guest stars David Frye and Liberace, as a test case and ignored Dawson's rejection of his suggested new policy.

At Tom's behest, *Comedy Hour* producers George Sunga and Allan Blye sent a telegram to Tankersley in New York, saying, "Since we have not heard from you after completion of videotaping, we assume that the program is approved for broadcast. We would like your confirmation of this fact at which time the tape will be delivered to CBS." Tankersley wired back, telling them the acceptability of their program would be judged, as always, by the West Coast office, and to "please contact Tom Downer or Sam Taylor." Sunga and Blye wired Tankersley again, this time reiterating Tom Smothers's "no West Coast" position and threatening, "Unless our show is adjudged by you, we will not deliver the tape to CBS." This was on February 12, only four days before the show was scheduled to be broadcast nationwide. Tankersley referred them to Dawson's letter, and its rejection of Tom's proposal—at which point Tom himself stepped in, with his own telegram to the New York program practices executive.

"During the past six weeks," Tom wrote, "the Smothers Brothers shows have been censored, approved, rejected, etc., out of New York by you, Mr. Tankersley. As long as this seems to be your working policy, I will continue in this manner." The wire concluded, as was common in Tom's correspondences with the network, by a barely disguised final jab: "When you have allowed your West Coast department to have autonomy in its dealings, we will be prepared to deal with them."

Tankersley was not a person to trifle with. His history with CBS was so long, and his relationship with Paley so solid, that his position within the company was unusually and unquestionably unshakeable. His tenure predated both the construction of the network's Black

Rock headquarters in New York and, before that, Television City in Los Angeles, which was built in 1950. "I was there when they laid the first stone," Tankersley told me. A former broadcaster himself—like many on-air pioneers in radio's early days, his duties included imaginatively re-creating entire baseball games from brief wire-service accounts—Tankersley wound up working for CBS in Los Angeles, finding theater spaces for live broadcasts until CBS built its own television studio facility, which he helped design.

Tommy, who had just turned thirty-two, was dealing with a man who, when he was precisely Tom's age, literally was establishing the broadcast standards for CBS Television. Before the quiz show scandals, advertisers sponsored entire shows and enjoyed fairly free rein, but Tankersley and CBS set a more stringent standard. When plugs for Carnation Milk consistently went over the allotted commercial time on *The George Burns and Gracie Allen Show*, Tankersley got the backing from Paley to insist that Carnation stop the overruns or void its contract and lose the show. Red Skelton, one of the early inhabitants of CBS Television City—and still starring in his decades-long hit variety series while *Comedy Hour* was on the air—used to be vetted by Tankersley long before that job went to Charles Pettijohn. Other broadcast icons who learned to both respect and like Tankersley included such normally feisty creative types as Rod Serling and Alfred Hitchcock.

By and large, Tankersley had a strong working relationship with his CBS stars, especially the truly creative ones. He appreciated, and did not fight, Hitchcock's cleverness in skirting the network's established moral codes. (Hitchcock would include the requisite crime-doesn't-pay moral in an epilogue he would deliver himself, but the filmed part of each week's story would conclude with what Hitchcock considered the "true" ending.) And Serling, whose scripts Tankersley had to wrangle back in the days of live TV's *Playhouse 90*, long before *The Twilight Zone*, is considered by Tankersley to be his all-time favorite responsibility. Serling fought hard for what he believed, Tankersley says, but always wisely. Tankersley recalls of Serling, "He said to me, 'They're only words, Bill. If we accept the theme, if we accept the thesis, we're dealing with words. I'm not going to change words.' He was a delight."

Tankersley spent twenty-two years at CBS, sixteen of them in program practices. Serling, Hitchcock, Skelton, Burns, as well as Jack Benny, Carol Burnett, and others—over the years, Tankersley worked with them all. In 1967, just as *The Smothers Brothers Comedy Hour* arrived on the CBS schedule, Tankersley moved to CBS in New York and turned over West Coast operations to Tom Downer.

As years passed, and Tom Smothers began reaching out to Tankersley to overrule decisions by Downer and his staff, the passionate comedian found a friendly and rational ear. But what Tom also found, to his eventual downfall, was an executive who had stood his ground firmly for decades, had a great respect for the chain of command, and had dealt directly and firmly with so many celebrities for so long that young Tom Smothers's aggressive gamesmanship was neither imposing nor impressive.

"I'll tell you one thing for sure," Tankersley says. "If I'd been on the ground out there [in Los Angeles], there would have been no problem with the Smothers Brothers. I guarantee it." Tankersley admits he didn't pay that much attention to the series until Tom began insisting upon involving him directly. He wasn't even aware, until I asked about it, of the "Beeping censors lurking in the wings" lyric in the show's third-season opener. "I didn't have time," Tankersley says of his responsibilities in New York, "to concentrate on one lousy show in California, you know?"

Yet Tankersley respected Tom as both a comedian and a producer ("He had a tremendous staff"). He admired the way Tom plowed all his increased production funds from CBS into the hiring of bigger guest stars and additional writers. "You know, most people won't do that," Tankersley told Tom. "You're very sincere, and I appreciate it." What Tankersley didn't appreciate, and wouldn't tolerate, was Tom's intended avoidance of the West Coast branch of Tankersley's operation. "I personally got along with him," Tankersley says—but adds that when Tom refused to submit scripts to Tom Downer on the West Coast, "That's when they should have fired him . . . That's grounds for firing right there. You can't decide whom you deal with. That's not procedure."

When Red Skelton learned of Tom's defiant stance (like Carol Burnett, he taped on an adjoining Television City soundstage and had heard the gossip), he offered to intercede on behalf of the West Coast office and "talk to these boys." It was a sweet gesture, but Tankersley vetoed it ("It would be embarrassing for Red; they'd poke fun at him"). Instead, Tankersley held his ground, demonstrating the easy, flinty confidence of a man born in a Texas town named after his own grandfather. The way William Tankersley dealt with the flurry of proclamations from the *Smothers Brothers Comedy Hour* staff, and from Tom himself, was to do what Tom had threatened to do. He ignored all memos—and eventually, Tom backed down.

However, Tom did not stop appealing to Tankersley. Once Tom reopened lines of communication to the East Coast, Tom Downer still found himself second-guessed and his authority undermined. "It was not our intention," Downer said in his court deposition, "nor did we have the time, to play all the games that Tommy wanted to play. He seemed to have an unlimited appetite to do that." Downer also said, more admiringly than grudgingly, "Tommy used every means at his disposal, including his great popularity and his appeal to the press, to get his way, and I don't object to that at all. Every producer who feels strongly about his product should do that. Perhaps Tommy was more inventive than most."

Tom got Tankersley's home phone number somehow and began calling—nights, weekends, oblivious to the time-zone differences.

"Nobody did that. Nobody *ever* did that," says Tankersley, who eventually had his teenage daughter Marcie screen calls and not put Tom through. But Tom was persistent and friendly. He twice invited Tankersley to come visit his California house (the middle-aged executive demurred, telling Tom, "I wouldn't go to your house—I'd be afraid to use the sugar, or anything else"), and sought details of Tankersley's birth so he could commission an astrological chart. "He was going to try and understand this man who was always stopping him from doing things," Tankersley said, laughing. "Whether he ever figured it out or not, I don't know." What he certainly figured out, for what it's worth, is that he and Tankersley shared the same astrological sign: Aquarius. In the '60s, for someone who coproduced a production of *Hair*, that may indeed have meant something. For Tankersley, it was just one more endearing yet unusual quirk. "He's charming and likable," Tankersley said, "but he drove me nuts."

"Offhand," Tankersley also says, "I don't remember anybody giving us problems like the Smothers."

Those problems were beginning to take an obvious toll. Affiliates in rural areas were complaining, and some were dropping the show entirely. Ratings, too, were dropping, as older viewers who once adored the sweet, clean-cut young comics were put off by the liberal political messages, rock music, and drug jokes. Advertisers were jittery, the sales department was unhappy, and the relationship between the CBS censors and the Smothers Brothers, while reestablished by Tankersley's iron hand, was more tenuous and fractious than ever. The next program, featuring David Frye and Liberace, would be the third season's lowest-rated *Comedy Hour* to date, beaten handily by both an NBC *Ice Capades* special and an ABC showing of *The Carpetbaggers*. Within a few months, ratings would drop even lower. As controversy increased, ratings continued to spiral slowly downward.

Despite all the backstage fighting and posturing with Tankersley and his staff, the *Comedy Hour* writers had gotten away with a lot, particularly in its "political fable" finale, and also had presented plenty of helpings of pure entertainment. While the Smothers Brothers were fighting their toughest battles offstage, and even fighting at times with each other, they were succeeding impressively at presenting some of the best, and most meaningful, installments of their entire series.

Classics and Controversies

The February 16, 1969, edition of *The Smothers Brothers Comedy Hour*—with Liberace and David Frye—was the representative episode submitted for the Emmy Awards that season. Though beaten by *Rowan & Martin's Laugh-In* in the overall Variety Series category, it won in the category of Outstanding Writing Achievement. A quick clip reel was put together to show as part of the Emmy presentation that night, but the snippets—containing only material already approved and televised by CBS—were further censored and edited for the Emmy telecast. Which network broadcast the Emmys and thought the nominated Smothers Brothers needed even more pruning before being fit for national consumption? CBS.

A quick recap of the show explains why—and explains why the Smothers Brothers were so proud of this particular hour. Instead of the usual Tom-and-Dick opening, the program begins with a comedy blackout. Tom plays a preacher with a Southern accent presiding over the interracial marriage of a black man and a white woman. The couple exchanges vows, after which Tom reaches out his hand and asks for something other than the wedding rings. "The rope, please," he says—and as the audience laughs loudly but nervously, the show cuts to the *Comedy Hour* bass drum and the opening credits.

Even the musical elements of the show had subtext to them.

Hedge and Donna, a folk duo, made points not by what they sang, but by who they were: he's white, she's black, at a time when such pairings on TV still were controversial, especially in the South. And while it's overreaching to interpret Liberace's appearance as a similar statement for gay rights, he was used cleverly in comedy bits, including one in which Bob Einstein, as the not-yet-named Officer Judy, pokes fun at hard-helmeted, hard-headed motorcycle traffic cops. Partway through Liberace's performance of Chopin's rapidfire *Waltz in D Flat Major* (better known as the "Minute Waltz"), Einstein's gruff cop enters on a motorcycle, dismounts, pulls out his traffic ticket book, rests one foot on Liberace's piano bench, and asks, deadpan, "You know how fast you were playing?" On one level, it's pure absurdist comedy; on another, it's slipping in a gentle but clever commentary on the invasiveness and abuse of police authority.

Without doubt, though, what earned this show the Emmy was the political finale, "A Fable for Our Time," in which the recent transfer of presidential power is reflected through an Arthurian-era tale. Liberace and Dick play wandering troubadours; Tom, a court jester; Steve Martin, a court juggler—and Frye, in various wigs and costumes, plays almost everyone else. He's the king who has to give up his crown to a qualified contender and who looks and sounds exactly like LBJ: "I come here tonight because I no longer have any place to go." Various contenders try to remove a sword from a stone to claim the throne. Frye plays them, too, including Sir George of Wallace ("I call a spade a spade," he says, to which Tom the fool replies, "Methinks he sounds like a bigot"); Hubert H. Humphrey as a friar who fails to extricate the sword ("So I lost? So what? What does it mean? Just everything . . ."); and, at last, Richard Nixon.

"I don't know, frankly," Frye's Sir Richard of Nixon says, "if I should stay on the sidelines and watch the kingdom go down the drain or to go right in there and blow the whole thing myself." Tom asks him to try to pluck the sword, and Nixon replies, "I've been called many things. I've been called a loser. I've been called a bad sport. I've been called an opportunist. I've even been called Tricky Dicky. Just don't try calling me a sword plucker!" He tries, and fails, but the townspeople are out of options: "Either we crown him as king," Dick tells Tom, "or say the old king must serve for four more years." Sir Richard is crowned King Richard as the townspeople sing: "Rejoice, rejoice, there's no other choice . . . For now, he's the best we could find . . ." And after they all exit and the lights dim, Pat Paulsen—who's been absent from the show for weeks—makes an unbilled appearance as a janitor, cleaning up afterward. He sees the sword in the stone, removes it easily from its stony scabbard, and sneaks away. Pat Paulsen could have been his country's leader after all . . .

It all sounds benign enough, but making such direct fun of Richard Nixon, who'd been in office less than a month, was treading on thin ice. The sketch contains at least one obvious, network-mandated edit, and though the first written proof of Nixon's targeting of Tom Smothers doesn't appear until years later, this "Fable for Our Time," quite likely, was the sketch that put the Smothers Brothers on Nixon's radar. The skit also received support from an editorial in *TV Guide*, published February 22, which began, "We occasionally receive letters from readers who take affront at *Laugh-In* and the Smothers Brothers for poking fun at high government officials. We cannot agree with this point of view; it smacks too much of the atmosphere of the tyrannies which man has spent the last few centuries trying to destroy." The editorial added, "We cannot agree that 'entertainment' or 'comedy' is some innocuous thing that produces laughter but must have nothing to do with the real issues of living." *TV Guide* soon would reverse that position, just as the magazine's publisher, Walter H. Annenberg, was openly seeking a political appointment by President Nixon.

Attacks on authority figures, in punch lines and sketches, became more frequent on *Comedy Hour* once Nixon, the "law and order" candidate, took office. Einstein's tall, imposing officer became a familiar presence, used in sometimes surreal ways. When Judy Collins guest stars and sings a song, Tom introduces another number by saying, "Ladies and gentlemen, here's Judy!" We hear the opening strains of Randy Newman's "I Think It's Going to Rain Today" and Collins singing the opening verse—but the camera pans back to reveal not the gentle female folksinger, but Bob Einstein's leather-jacketed cop, leaning against his police cycle to mouth the words to the entire song. Afterward, Tom explains to Dick that "Officer Judy" (the Collins bit was how Einstein's character got his name on the show) had given him a speeding ticket but voided it in exchange for an appearance on the show. Unpredictable ad-libbing comic Jonathan Winters, playing an army sergeant examining his troops, throws out one male recruit after he greets the sergeant not with a salute, but with a kiss. "You're out!" he tells the soldier, then adds, "but you're not bad." And in the same show, Tom takes on religion, the most taboo of TV topics, by staging a finale in which warriors from various eras and cultures pray to God or to Allah for victory in battle. "God can't be on *all* your sides," Tom says—a simple, but very volatile, declaration for prime time.

The next two shows, a marked departure from the program's usual staging and format, sound tame and noncontroversial on the surface. Yet they proved to be anything but.

On March 2 and 3, Tom decided to tape back-to-back concert editions of *Comedy Hour,* returning to the theater-in-the-round staging from the earlier show with Donovan. It was a cost-saving measure that reduced production costs near the end of the season, but it also was a way to program, even more precisely, for the younger, more liberal viewers. Donovan returned for the first of these concert hours, which also included Peter, Paul and Mary and veteran stand-up comedy troublemaker Mort Sahl. The second hour was headlined by Joan Baez and featured John Hartford, comic Jackie Mason, and the brother-sister singing duo Dick Smothers long had fought to have on, Nino Tempo and April Stevens. A lineup that sounds relatively trouble-free, however, led to some of the most heated off-air exchanges and clumsy on-air edits—and some of the boldest television—in *Comedy Hour* history.

The first of the two shows began with Tom and Dick leading the studio audience, which surrounded the in-the-round stage and was clearly visible on camera, in the Pledge of Allegiance. The entire audience had been coached, though, and enlisted as coconspirators to recite the pledge with one phrase missing—the "under God" part, which President Dwight D. Eisenhower had added to the nineteenth-century pledge in 1954. On this occasion, *Comedy Hour* removed it, and that bold secular statement led directly into Donovan's "Atlantis," which hit the charts a month later. No time for applause, no time to react—and, for CBS, no easy way to edit.

This particular *Comedy Hour*, from start to finish, is one of the best. Jennifer Warnes, who appeared with Donovan on the last concert show, returns, singing a lovely "Easy to Be Hard," her solo number from *Hair*. Peter, Paul and Mary sing "Too Much of Nothing" and other songs, and comedian Sahl performs a free-form stand-up act that targets, among others, Nixon, J. Edgar Hoover, and the FBI. A decade ago, Sahl had headlined at San Francisco's hungry i, across the street from the Purple Onion, where the Smothers Brothers had gotten their start as a trio. When Tom began envisioning the series *Comedy Hour* would become, Sahl's raw topicality was one of his inspirations. Finally, he had Sahl on the show, and just getting him there was a victory, even if his set was uncharacteristically tame. "You don't get the chance to see Mort Sahl on national television very much," Tom says in his introduction, "and you can draw your own conclusions from that." The closing concert segment is built around the Smothers Brothers' recent receipt of their first gold record, *Live at the Purple Onion*—awarded after "only" eight years. The duo boasts of this, comically and sheepishly, and challenges Donovan and Peter, Paul and Mary to a "goldies but goodies" duel, performing pieces of their most popular recordings. It's a delightful contest: one round alone covers "Puff the Magic Dragon," "Sunshine Superman," and "John Henry." At the end, everyone, including Jennifer and Sahl, teams up for "Day Is Done," with the audience not only singing along but streaming peacefully down to the stage, as the crowd had done in the "Hey Jude" video. Tom, strumming his guitar alongside the crowd and the other artists, looks as happy as at any point on any show.

The next day, March 2, *Comedy Hour* mounted another concert show—and CBS considered this episode especially problematic. The comedy of Jackie Mason, in the opinion of CBS censors, had gone too far, discussing sex in a way that was improper for prime time. Decades later, the "objectionable material" seems laughably tame and tamely laughable. (Describing sexual curiosity as perfectly natural, Jackie Mason says, "I never see a kid play accountant. Even the kids who want to be lawyers play doctor.") And while the musical selections and performances by Joan Baez presented no problems (her version of Bob Dylan's "I Shall Be Released," sung with Tom and Dick, was especially lovely), the introductions did. After Dick cited Joan Baez's early appearances at the Newport Folk Festival, Tom noted, "She's been on the cover of *Time* magazine, and in *Life* magazine, and in jail in Oakland, California. And tonight she's on our show. We admire her very much, and her individuality, and her integrity." Tom didn't mention that she was in jail for participating in a sit-in protest against the draft and the Vietnam War, so CBS let that comment stand. Baez's own preface to one of her songs, though, was another matter.

The song, "Green, Green Grass of Home," was a selection from her brand-new LP, *David's Album,* released the day after the *Comedy Hour* concert. David, she explained, was her husband, "a sort of California hillbilly," and the songs on the album were all country and western, compiled and recorded especially for him. While she didn't identify her husband as antiwar, antidraft activist David Harris, most viewers knew to whom she was referring, and she made her motivation behind the album, at least, quite clear.

"It's kind of a gift for David," she explained, "because he's going to be going to prison, probably in June, and he'll be there for three years. The reason he's going," she continued, in a very calm and warm tone, "is because he refused to have anything to do with the draft, or selective service, or whatever you want to call it—militarism in general. And the point is, if you do that, and you do it up front, and 'overground,' then you're going to get busted, especially if you organize, which he does. So this song is called 'The Green, Green Grass of Home.' " Then, strumming her guitar, she sang it, plaintively and proudly. Dick Smothers says of her performance and her visit, "I didn't have the maturity or the sensitivity at that point, when I saw it originally, to know how absolutely precious and sincere and womanly and beautiful and compassionate her music was. It was everything." To the CBS West Coast censors, however, there was no way that introduction could stand. Almost as soon as the taping was over, the memos and posturing began. But this time the higher authority to whom Tom would be appealing was different and less sympathetic. William Tankersley stayed out of this fight. Instead, a new player—just-installed CBS president Robert S. Wood—stepped in, adopting a much tougher approach.

The day after the Baez-Mason show was taped, CBS and the *Comedy Hour* staff agreed to move the show up in the broadcast order. Instead of running as intended on March 23, it would now be televised on Sunday, March 9, just six days away. With yet another show being prepared for taping on Friday, March 7, this made postproduction a daunting task as it was, especially since the two concert programs ran about thirty minutes overtime and had to be edited down into smoothly packaged hours. Sam Taylor, one of Tom Downer's West Coast assistants in program practices, fired off a memo instantly, informing Tom Smothers he had observed both taping sessions, had noted plenty of "problem areas," and was ready and eager to discuss them and work with Tom during the editing process. "As you know," Taylor told Tom, "it is our function to work with programs on a step-by-step basis rather than acting merely as final arbiters of finished tapes." That memo was dated March 3. Tom waited until Thursday, March 6, to respond officially. "We will begin editing the Jackie Mason spot today," Tom wrote, "and try to complete it by Friday if our show now in progress allows for this to be done. We will try to finish the editing in time for affiliate viewing, per the network's request."

There was a lot of cutting to be done for time constraints alone. Jackie Mason had done twenty minutes of stand-up for an hour show, and segments from both the dress rehearsal and air tapings were intercut for the final edited performance. (Mason changed his tie between sets, so sharp-eyed viewers can follow those edits.) But when Tom's memo reached Wood's desk, the new CBS president got on the phone with Tom's recently appointed attorney, Ed Hookstratten, and followed up a blistering conversation with an equally forceful telegram that same day. "This is to re-emphasize our need," Wood wrote, "to have the Smothers Brothers tape delivered to us in New York Friday morning, March 7, in order that we can 1) screen it and make whatever modifications are necessary, if any, and 2) preview it on closed circuit for the benefit of those CBS affiliates that carry the show. The latter is a responsibility which we will not abdicate." If the tape isn't received by the Friday deadline, Wood threatened, "it will not be broadcast," and CBS would feel no obligation to pay for it.

Tom, responding to the toughness of tone, worked with his producers and finished assembling a polished cut of the show by Thursday night—only to be informed by Taylor that additional edits were required, including in both the Jackie Mason and Joan Baez spots, and that "the tape as it stood was not acceptable." Tom sent a pleading memo to Perry Lafferty, the West Coast programmer who was one of his last sympathetic CBS bosses, explaining his difficulties in making the deadline while dealing with last-second objections, but also promising to try his best to comply and make the edits himself "so as to avoid a repeat of the heavy-handed censoring of the show in previous weeks." (Even when asking for mercy, Tom seems to look for opportunities to land another punch.)

Lafferty set aside two editing machines for Tom to finish his work Friday morning, with the final tape due no later than 12:30 p.m., in time for a specially scheduled afternoon feed to New York and the country's CBS affiliates. Tom missed the deadline, blaming the lateness of the new changes demanded by Taylor, but attempted to cover his bases. On Friday, after missing the deadline, Tom's attorney cabled Bob Wood, claiming "Tom Smothers physically exhausted," and that "Tom will edit at first available date for delivery not later than Sunday as in past weeks." The attorney, Hookstratten, then countered with a threat of his own: "If said show not broadcast Sunday, March 9, we feel network repudiating our agreement, and thus reserve all rights at law and equity with respect to payment thereof."

Tom worked into the night after the Friday taping of the next show (which featured return appearances by David Frye, Leigh French, and Glen Campbell) and delivered his version of a broadcast-worthy tape of the Jackie Mason–Joan Baez show. It was flown out and hand-carried Saturday morning, and arrived at CBS in New York at 5:05 p.m. ET. Hours before that, however, Bob Wood had pulled the plug, or the trigger—pick your metaphor—and given the order to replace the Mason-Baez show with a *Comedy Hour* rerun from January.

"The content of the broadcast is not at issue," the CBS press release emphasized. "As broadcast licensees, the stations affiliated with the CBS Television Network have the right to preview on request any program before it is presented on the air. Stations have requested that each episode of the Smothers Brothers show be previewed. Because a tape of this Sunday's program was not made available to the network in time for closed-circuit preview to our stations, we were obliged to substitute another Smothers Brothers program previously previewed." That Sunday, viewers in the United States saw a rebroadcast of the Nanette Fabray–Steppenwolf show, while viewers of Canada's CTV saw the Mason-Baez show intact, preserving Tom's final cut.

Many factors played into CBS's drawing a line in the sand, and the unyielding stance of Bob Wood—who as a CBS station manager had written and delivered editorials suggesting that student protesters be expelled from college—was only one piece of the puzzle. As candidates, Nixon and his running mate, Spiro Agnew, already had targeted the media. In February, *Laugh-In* producer George Schlatter had created an ABC variant on the same formula, a new series called *Turn-On* that was so poorly received and so roundly attacked for being too crude and unfunny that ABC canceled it after a single episode. Senator John O. Pastore, a Rhode Island Democrat, seized on the issue immediately and scheduled a round of hearings on Capitol Hill to explore not only "crime and violence," but the sexy model in Noxzema shaving cream commercials ("Take it off, take it *all* off!") and shows that are "getting a little more risqué." He didn't name *Comedy Hour* but may as well have: "*Laugh-In* and *Turn-On*, things of that kind . . . That's why we're here. That's what this is about."

The network heads, including CBS's Frank Stanton, were summoned to Washington the week after the controversial Mason-Baez show was to air. ABC and NBC agreed to Pastore's proposal of previewing questionable shows before a National Association of Broadcasters review board, but CBS balked. It would police its own standards, thanks, Stanton told Pastore—and, as TV critic Kay Gardella pointed out in the New York *Daily News,* pulling the Smothers Brothers show just before attending the hearings gave CBS the chance to provide "a perfect example of how cautious it is about making certain that programs are shown to its owned-and-operated licensed stations and affiliates, even if it means canceling a show."

The hard-line approach was adopted by the censors as well, who worked together on both coasts to enforce it. Two days after Leigh French appeared on *Comedy Hour* playing an old country singer who lived her whole life enjoying bluegrass ("A couple of weeks ago, I started smoking it"), Tankersley sent a memo to all program and program practices personnel citing the National Association of Broadcasters' television code: "The use of hallucinogenic drugs shall not be shown or encouraged as desirable or socially acceptable." Tankersley's interpretation of this, he explained in framing a newly specific CBS policy, was that "material of any nature, including comedy, which would mislead youthful viewers as to the serious consequences of drug usage, is not permissible." Tom Downer, at Television City, eagerly distributed a copy of his boss's memo to all West Coast producers, including the *Comedy Hour* team. Tom Smothers's response was to ignore Downer and send a memo instead to West Coast programmer Perry Lafferty and his assistant, Bob Tamplin, inviting them to see a finished tape of the forthcoming show—and signing it, with sarcastic informality, "Love, Tom."

Tom's sarcasm would continue, and escalate, with almost every interoffice correspondence. When Tom got a memo reminding him of the deadline for expected delivery of an edited tape of the next show, Tom not only challenged the deadline, but also made fun of the memo's legalese by imitating it. The memo to Tom begins, "Without waiving any of our rights or remedies, this is to advise you that in accordance with the agreement between us, we are expecting you to make delivery to us in Hollywood no later than commencement of business on Thursday, March 13 . . ." The memo from Tom, written the same day, begins, "Without waiving any of our rights or remedies, this is to advise you that I would like to see the contractual papers regarding the agreement between us, of which I am unaware. To my knowledge, there is no agreement to produce a tape on the commencement of business Thursday."

Another fight was waged, on Tom's behalf, by attorney Ed Hookstratten and others, who balked at CBS's refusal to allow an on-air mention that the various directors of *The Smothers Brothers Comedy Hour* had won the first Excellence in Electography award from the 3M company. This new process, of which *Comedy Hour* clearly was a pioneer, included blue-screen effects, superimposed visual gimmickry, and other fresh TV tricks. In this case, CBS relented, allowing the award to be noted and a montage of the winning effects presented, but wiping any mention of 3M from the sound track.

Battles were breaking out on almost every front. Network executives were testifying before Senator John Pastore's communications subcommittee in Washington. Tom was not only resisting prescreening deadlines and writing sarcastic memos, but also fighting network-mandated edits in the Baez-Mason show. Jackie Mason, informed of the excisions demanded by CBS, went public with his own demands, asking that his appearance be deleted from the show entirely. "I think it was ridiculous censorship," he told the press, "and I don't want to be castrated by CBS."

Both Mason and Tom would fail to carry the day. When the program finally was televised, Jackie Mason's stand-up routine was included but chopped in all the places Sam Taylor had marked for exclusion. That was bad enough. What was worse—"heartbreaking," according to Dick Smothers—was the way CBS treated Joan Baez. The network didn't just edit her remarks about her husband, David Harris. CBS butchered them. Her entire explanation about why he was going to jail, as a pacifist war protester, was lopped off, so that her second song's introduction, seen on nationwide TV that evening, conveyed a very incomplete and misleading message.

"It's a kind of a gift to David," Baez is shown saying, talking about her husband and her new album, "because he's going to be going to prison." There's a jarring, obvious edit, after which Baez says, "So this song is called 'The Green, Green Grass of Home.'" David Harris might as well have been going to prison for murder or child molestation as for draft evasion.

"I remember them saying, 'Do what you have to do,'" Baez said later, recalling the support she got from the Smothers Brothers to deliver her intro. They all were aware that censorship might come into play. When Baez appeared on NBC's *Tonight Show*, she was told not to say even the *name* Nixon—but, she added, "They knew I said what I *had* to say, or I didn't want to be on." In the end, her remarks were censored in a way that seemed not only heavy-handed, but vindictive. One of the biggest surprises uncovered in researching this book was learning that William Tankersley, the head censor for CBS, agreed with that assessment.

"Yeah, that was a pretty messy deal," he told me. "The cutting was terrible."

According to Tankersley, the editing was done on the West Coast without his knowledge or approval, at a time when both sides were provoking each other. "It was botched up," Tankersley says of the Joan Baez edit. "It would have been much better if they'd left it in."

The day Jackie Mason went public about his disgust at CBS's censorship, two other events occurred that, even in this show's roller-coaster history, were rather amazing.

One is that CBS—despite the censorship battles, the leaks to the press, the combative memos, the slowly sinking ratings, the increasing complaints from certain affiliates and advertisers—notified the show's producers that it was picking up the show's option for the 1969–70 TV season.

Meanwhile, also on March 14, there was another *Comedy Hour* to tape. Guest stars included Ike and Tina Turner, Pat Paulsen (his farewell appearance), Biff Rose, and Mason Williams, returning after a long hiatus, and just after winning a pair of Grammy Awards for "Classical Gas." Mason has a heavy beard at this point and is dressed in a burgundy jacket and an early prototype of the "puffy shirt" from *Seinfeld*. He plays a guitar instrumental, "Greensleeves," as ballet dancers pirouette in the background. Then, still cradling his acoustic guitar, Mason grabs a giant pair of scissors, and delivers an introduction, and a spoken-word poem, that are nothing short of remarkable. That they were ever broadcast on prime-time network TV is remarkable. That they were broadcast in 1969, in the midst of constant battles to say anything of substance at all on television, borders on unbelievable. It's a cry of defiance and a call to battle that dares not only to call the censors by name, but also to call them out. Early in season one, *The Smothers Brothers Comedy Hour* had incurred the wrath of CBS censors by doing a sketch about censors. Late in season three, Mason Williams says this about censors—and somehow gets it *past* the censors.

"As Tom said a little earlier," Mason says, speaking softly and staring directly into the camera, "I have been a writer on this show since it began. And I've really loved working on this show, because the people are beautiful, and talented, and they have a lot of integrity. And they do have a sense of responsibility about what they present to you as entertainment."

He continues, "We've done good things on this show. We have done some *great* things, but you haven't seen them because of—*The Censor.*" He strums a single chord on his guitar and thrusts the scissors forward, open, so that they fill the screen and frame his face, as he recites "The Censor," a poem from his just-released book, *The Mason Williams Reading Matter.* Afterward, he snips shut the scissors forebodingly, and the screen cuts to black. The poem, read in its entirety, goes:

The censor sits
Somewhere between
The Scenes to be seen
And the television sets
With his scissor purpose poised
Watching the human stuff
That will sizzle through
The magic wires
And light up
Like welding shops
The ho-hum rooms of America
And with a kindergarten
Arts and crafts concept
Of moral responsibility
Snips out
The rough talk
The unpopular opinion
Or anything with teeth
And renders
A pattern of ideas
Full of holes
A doily
For your mind.

Fired, Not Canceled

T om Smothers was about to go too far—and, with new CBS president Robert Wood, provoke an adversary who had no intention of backing down. But as Wood flew west to meet Tom and discuss the future of *The Smothers Brothers Comedy Hour*, Tom had every reason to be cocky, plenty of reasons to be distracted, and few indications of how quickly his fortunes at the network were about to turn.

After all, despite the increasingly antagonistic tone of the dealings (or lack of them) between the CBS censors and the *Comedy Hour* staff, Tom approached that March 17, 1969, meeting with Wood—his first official conversation with the new CBS president—with what looked like a strong hand. *Comedy Hour* had been picked up for a fourth season, its renewal approved by Wood himself. *The Glen Campbell Goodtime Hour*, the offshoot of the previous summer's *Summer Brothers Smothers Show*, was an established hit (it would end the 1968–69 TV season in fifteenth place). Even while waging, and sometimes losing, battles over program content, Tom was shaping *Comedy Hour* into a show that spoke more directly to the young.

Tom's own attitudes and lifestyle, at age thirty-two, reflected much of what was happening with youth culture. Drugs, while never an issue during the weekday production schedule, were a common part of Tom's weekend scene. Smoking pot was the usual activity, but Jennifer Warnes recalls one road trip on which she and Tom dropped acid before he drove her around San Francisco to visit his grandfather, and Mason Williams remembers mistakenly eating a batch of Leigh French's specially enhanced brownies. Judy Marcione, Tom's secretary, had become his girlfriend as well, which lent a conspiratorial air to the dictation of memos aimed at his CBS censors and bosses—and could well explain some of the aggressive and sarcastic posturing he adopted in them.

Letters, though, were being dictated and sent elsewhere, too. It was Judy to whom Tom dictated the letter he sent to Lyndon Johnson—and, much later, to members of Congress, whose support Tom was hoping to solicit in the creation of a Department of Peace. Among the surviving letters received in response are from Indiana senator Birch Bayh ("I support the concept") and, notably, Donald Rumsfeld, then a representative from Illinois ("This proposal has been referred to the Committee on Government Operations, of which I am a member, and you may be sure that your expression of support will be kept in mind as we proceed with deliberations on this legislation"). Lobbying for peace, like scouting for new talent, producing TV shows, and starring in them, was a full-time job. Tom's attentions were spread thin, his passions were high—and his ulcer was back.

Brother Dick was better at delegating, compartmentalizing, and letting go. He, too, was carrying around lots of stress, but he was better at hiding it. Dick wasn't into drugs and seldom indulged, but had no such qualms about alcohol. Away from the show, he relieved stress by indulging his passion for auto racing, which got him both mentally and physically away from the series, its problems, and his brother. Dick remained involved in his segments of the show—Tom says now that Dick, in the third season, had much more presence as a performer than he did—and on occasion would shine, as when Dick harmonized with Joan Baez or played straight man to Jonathan Winters. But when it came to fighting for the show's content, Dick was a noticeably silent partner. He never signed memos, seldom got involved (except as a peacemaker), and mostly trusted Tom to pick and fight the necessary battles with censors and management. Everyone knew that Dick was happiest speeding around a race track. What not even Tom knew then was that Dick's marriage was in trouble and heading for divorce.

"I was torn between two things," Dick says. "I was torn between my selfish desires and my desire to be a good husband and a parent. And I guess my wife didn't want to go out and drink and ride motorcycles and hit all the clubs like I did," he adds, laughing. "She was a hell of a lot more mature than I was!" Dick moved out, separating from his wife and three children, and lived in an apartment. "And he never told me that!" Tom says in amazement. "All during that time, there was an edgy edge to him that I never understood. He never shares that kind of stuff. So it was pretty abrasive between the two of us," Tom admits, but not because of any of the issues with CBS. "Our argument was never over that issue," Tom says. "It was always—just attitude. We had attitude problems with each other. We could clear the room!"

The third-season fight everyone seems to remember occurred while preparing for the Burl Ives show, which was scripted to begin with a three-minute film showing Dick doing off-terrain stunts on a motorcycle, driving to CBS Television City and onto Stage 43 just in time to drive through a big mockup of the *Comedy Hour* bass drum head and join brother Tom onstage for the show's opening. The payoff was that Tom would get on the bike and restart it, and—by running the videotape in reverse—go backward into the drum head, which would miraculously reassemble into one piece.

"Dick got the first Honda 350 in the country," recalls staff writer Bob Einstein. Tom's drive from the drum head had to be taped beforehand and reversed, so it was staged in advance, without an audience present. Dick begged Tom to be careful, because the new bike was such a collector's item, but both brothers had ridden motorcycles for years, so Tom told his brother to stop worrying, and Dick walked offstage to watch from a video monitor. Einstein laughs when describing what happened next: "When we're blocking, Tommy drives the bike right off the stage—four, five feet off the ground—and he crashes into the seats. Dick comes running down. He runs over to the mess and says, 'My *bike!*' And Tommy, from the ground says, 'Your *bike!* What about your *brother?*' "

Dick says he was only kidding: "I already thought that out on the way down, just for Tom," Dick insists, adding, "I wasn't worried about the damn motorcycle. I was doing it for the laugh." But Einstein, Mason Williams, and other witnesses remain unconvinced—or *too* convinced. "We had to separate them," Einstein recalls.

Dick, by his own admission, was at this time spending occasional weekends in Puerto Rico, visiting a German model, but the lure of a racing event led Dick to ask for what was, in effect, a week off, with two shows to go until the season was over. Dick wanted to enter a twelve-hour endurance race at Sebring, Florida (he would finish first in his class and eighth overall). Tom decided to write Dick's absence into the show, "firing" him at the opening and replacing him with Dan Rowan, his straight-man counterpart on NBC's *Laugh-In,* the most popular TV show in the country. (The argument, and firing, was recorded during the previous show's taping, on March 14, to allow Dick the maximum time away from the studio.) In addition, the show Dick would miss would feature two returning guest stars whose prior appearances had been memorably controversial: Nancy Wilson, who had appeared in the season two "red frog/green frog" sketch that attacked prejudice, and David Steinberg, whose comic sermonette earlier in season three had created a firestorm of angry reaction. Tom stayed behind to oversee the production of the show—and to meet with CBS president Robert Wood.

. . .

Wood had been out of college twenty years when he assumed the presidency of CBS—long enough to identify with the previous, rather than current, generation of students. He had graduated in 1949 with a BS in business from USC—the same college attended by Richard Nixon's White House chief of staff, H. R. Haldeman (though Haldeman transferred to another California college, UCLA, before graduating in 1948). Haldeman later recruited from campus a group of younger graduates, nicknamed "the USC Mafia," who had engineered and rigged student elections and pulled all manner of dirty political tricks . . . and who were encouraged to do the same years later in a series of White House–sanctioned illicit and illegal activities that became known collectively as "Watergate." Ron Ziegler, Donald Segretti, Dwight Chapin—all were part of "the USC Mafia." (Segretti, when interviewed for the *Washington Post* about stuffing ballot boxes and other student pranks, colorfully described the pranks as "ratfucking.") In retrospect, both Tom and Dick Smothers suspect Wood of being tightly allied with the Nixon White House as well. But Wood's concerns didn't need to be partisan to be political.

Wood and CBS had plenty to worry about. Under newly elected President Nixon, there was a fear that the formerly rubber-stamped renewals of affiliate licenses by the FCC might be more closely scrutinized. And a storm was brewing with Democratic senator John Pastore (who was in the headlines for proposing new regulations to combat TV's alleged permissiveness). If Pastore had his way, network content might require government approval, which Frank Stanton of CBS, one of Wood's most senior bosses, vehemently opposed. Stanton was determined to keep his own house in order and to keep his affiliates happy.

Wood's agenda in meeting with Tom Smothers, especially since

Comedy Hour just had been renewed, was to ensure the weekly pre-screening schedule for the series—unprecedented at *any* network—would be rigidly followed. Tom's agenda in meeting with Wood was to demand *looser* restrictions, not accept tighter ones. Plus, Tom admitted later, it was fun: dealing with a corporate giant, he said, was "a stimulating experience." The two met on March 17, 1969, in West Coast vice president of programs Perry Lafferty's office. Lafferty, too, was in attendance, as was Tom's new attorney, Ed Hookstratten. The meeting lasted two hours but was largely unproductive and noncommittal. Wood pushed for Tom to promise to deliver shows for affiliate preview by the Wednesday before their Sunday telecast. Tom said he would try but made no promises. Tom asked for "younger cats" to be hired to censor his show, or to allow the programs to be approved or edited by the individual affiliates directly, without any prior CBS interference or censorship ("Let the affiliates be the arbitrators," Tom suggested).

Tom also asked that if the network were going to keep objecting to the show's content the same way, the Smothers Brothers would rather be released from their contract and allowed to take their show to another network. Wood said he couldn't provide any immediate answers. And then the meeting deteriorated. Lafferty remembers Tom saying to Wood, "You are a square," but saying it "not ungracefully." Tom admits to saying many other things, a lot less gracefully—including getting red-faced and yelling about "people dying in Vietnam" and "babies burning," and shouting, "How can you possibly have a show when you cannot say what's going on?" Tom ended up walking out of the meeting. "I was very, very stressed at that time," he says. He admits that Wood "sure pushed my buttons."

So Tom, true to form, pushed back. Whether deliberately or coincidentally, he began loading the show currently in production—the one with Nancy Wilson, Dan Rowan, and David Steinberg—with elements guaranteed to push Wood's buttons. Nancy Wilson, a beautiful black singer, was cast in an interracial sketch with Tom, singing a duet of the love song "Will You Remember (Sweetheart)," then talking, in character, about how their love can overcome all obstacles—despite the fact that she even is richer, smarter, a divorcée with children, and even, he points out finally, "the fact that I'm white and you're black." "I'm *what?*" she asks, pretending to be surprised. At that moment, a black waiter returns with their drink order, and she immediately turns and begins singing the love song to him instead. The waiter looks at Tom and says, "Here, boy," hands Tom the drink tray, embraces Nancy, and joins her in song.

"One thing I liked about them," Nancy Wilson says about the Smothers Brothers, "they were *way* ahead of the game."

That was strike one. Strike two was using Rowan's appearance as an excuse to import and utilize the most potent comic weapon from *Laugh-In:* the Flying Fickle Finger of Fate. It was a mock award the series gave out regularly, and sarcastically, to "deserving" candidates, from the Ku Klux Klan to the Pentagon. With Dan Rowan as his straight man, Tom planned a running *Comedy Hour* gag in which they would debate whether Rowan, who had brought along a Fickle Finger of Fate statuette, could present it to Senator John Pastore—the very politician about whom CBS executives were so concerned. In effect, Pastore was everything that Tommy Smothers was fighting against . . . and Tommy wasn't going to let the audience forget that for a moment. In the sketch, Rowan claims he doesn't know enough about Pastore and begins calling around trying to learn more—pretending, at one point, to phone President Nixon directly ("Sorry to interrupt you right in the middle of *Bonanza*"). It was a gesture sure to give the network the kind of attention and scrutiny from Pastore they were hoping to avoid.

And then, most daringly and impudently of all, there was David Steinberg. Steinberg was booked to appear with Tom in a straightforward comedy sketch: Tom would play a nervous philosophy student taking an unusual oral exam from Steinberg's crazy college professor, who would greet every incorrect answer with a loud blast from a horn. But Steinberg also was invited to do a stand-up routine, and the first draft of the week's script—which West Coast CBS censor Sam Taylor acquired the same Monday Tom met with Bob Wood—included a five-minute space for an unidentified, as yet undetermined Steinberg solo routine. Taylor flagged it immediately in his program notes, fearing that Tom might be trying to slip in another sermonette. Both Tom and David Steinberg insist they had no such plans, at least not initially. But the lure of the forbidden proved too hard to resist. Early in the week, so many *Comedy Hour* staffers asked Steinberg if he were doing another sermon that Tom asked casually if Steinberg wanted to do one, and Steinberg just as casually agreed!

They knew it was a rebellious move. After Steinberg's first sermonette (on Moses), head West Coast censor Tom Downer had dispatched a memo declaring that, should Steinberg make a return *Comedy Hour* appearance, "similar material could not be accepted for future broadcasts." Tom was aware of that edict but didn't see fit to honor it. "We had artistic and creative control," Tom insisted afterward, and, still incensed by his unfulfilling meeting with Wood, decided to try to exercise it.

On Wednesday, two days before the show was to be taped, Tom and Steinberg showed their hand at a blocking rehearsal, but only barely: Steinberg performed only three lines of the routine. "That was probably to protect myself and protect us," Steinberg says. "The game was always to get everything past standards and practices. Tommy loved the game, very frankly. He loved to taunt the censors, the network. They were the Establishment." Three lines were enough for the West Coast contingent to identify it as a sermonette and cry foul. West Coast programmer Perry Lafferty warned Tom that program practices on the West Coast wouldn't accept another Steinberg sermon, but Tom included it in the final script anyway, determined to tape the show as he saw fit. His plan was to charge ahead, present the complete show in time for prescreening, and allow the affiliates to make their final judgments on an individual basis. "The controversial aspect of doing a religious piece of material satirically at that moment in time—it's very hard to remember how bold that was," Steinberg says, adding that the same went for the political humor presented regularly on *Comedy Hour.* "It looks so tame by comparison to today—but it was so bold, it's unbelievable."

Tom was well aware of the risks. He asked Steinberg to base his sermon on a topic he had road-tested onstage before, rather than risk improvising completely. Even so, to the conservative Christian audience, just presenting another comic sermonette was like waving a red flag in front of a bull. On Thursday, the day before taping, Taylor acquired a copy of the final script and called producer Allan Blye to intercede. The Steinberg sermonette, Taylor insisted, was "unacceptable," and giving a Fickle Finger Award to Senator Pastore was "highly questionable." Tom ignored the warnings, and the penultimate episode of *The Smothers Brothers Comedy Hour* was taped as intended—by Tom, anyway—on Friday, March 21, 1969.

Tom piled on the defiance by ad-libbing his introduction to Steinberg's piece, thereby denying program practices the opportunity to dilute his intro before it was performed in front of a studio audience. "Last year, we had a young man named David Steinberg on the show, who did a sermonette," Tom begins. He adds, "We had a great deal of problems from that telecast. It was all intended in fun. Well, we have Mr. Steinberg back with us again. We think he's one of the truly fine comedians and writers in the business—and he's going to do, now, another sermonette." Tom's proud stubbornness seemed aimed not only at CBS, but also at the previously outraged viewers and network affiliates. "Now, we don't want to offend anybody out there," Tom adds, "but if you get offended, that's the way the cookie crumbles . . . None of us are happy here in America anyway." The studio audience is amused and applauds. CBS, not so much. When Tom edits together the tape of this show, the "none of us are happy" remark is excised, but the network still doesn't like what's left.

This time, Steinberg's sermon was devoid of the trappings designed to protect it before: no Jesuit singers around for support, no official-looking pulpit. Just Steinberg against a black background, telling the story of Jonah, who got onto a ship commandeered by Gentiles ("A bad move on Jonah's part," Steinberg notes, to the raucous laughter of the studio audience). "And the Gentiles," Steinberg continues, "as is their wont from time to time, threw the Jew overboard." Steinberg, a former seminary scholar, then breaks the biblical story down into Old and New Testament concepts. The Old Testament scholars, Steinberg says, believe Jonah indeed was swallowed by a whale, while New Testament scholars—"the Gentiles"—say otherwise. "They literally grab the Jews by the Old Testament," Steinberg says, flashing an impish smile. The studio audience reacts tentatively but positively—on the tape, you can hear gasps, laughs, and claps, almost as a three-step reaction. It's amazing how uncontroversial the religious humor plays today, but Steinberg remembers the air of nervous expectation in the studio as being unlike any time he had performed a sermon, even on *Comedy Hour*. "It felt big," he said simply. So far as CBS was concerned, it was *too* big. Steinberg's routine was not only strike three, but may have been the entire ball game.

Neither the show nor Tom was quite through yet, however. To close the program, Dan Rowan returned with his *Laugh-In* Flying Fickle Finger of Fate statuette, claiming that he's been researching John Pastore for the entire hour and ascertained that he may indeed be a worthy nominee. "So Senator Pastore," Rowan says, looking into the camera, "whoever you are—wherever you are—keep up the good work." Rowan exits, and Tom, rather than ending the show on that sarcastic note, concludes on a somber one with special commemorative remarks keyed to an event from the same month a year before.

"Ladies and gentlemen, I've got something a little bit serious to say," Tom says, with neither absent brother Dick nor stand-in cohost Dan by his side. "We live in a time that has its own troubles, but history has proven that difficult times breed great men. And our time has its own great men. Tonight, in a moment of seriousness, we'd like to take this moment to remember a man who had a dream—Dr. Martin Luther King. Let us all hope his dream will someday come true. Good night." King had been murdered on April 4, 1968, and *Comedy Hour* was the only prime-time show to acknowledge the anniversary of his death. Or would have been, had CBS televised this particular show. But CBS did not. Not then. Not ever.

After witnessing the Friday taping, censor Sam Taylor ruled that the toned-down, more vaguely rewritten Fickle Finger award to Pastore was acceptable and indicated he had no specific objection to the Nancy Wilson sketch. Steinberg's sermonette was another matter entirely, but since this particular show wasn't scheduled for broadcast until April 13—more than three weeks away—there was no urgency in fighting this battle. Not when CBS had a much more serious foe to face on another front: John Pastore, the Flying Fickle Finger of Fate winner himself.

The senator from Rhode Island was a keynote speaker at that weekend's National Association of Broadcasters (NAB) convention in Washington, DC, and was widely expected to use that pulpit to try to bully the affiliates, and the networks, into establishing more rigorous standards and a different method of censoring programs. Without the network's knowledge, though, Tom Smothers had decided to use the weekend to make some political contacts and points of his own. Tom told CBS program executives Perry Lafferty and Mike Dann he was going to Washington but didn't say why. To CBS, this was an even more unprecedented, and less forgivable, transgression. For a performer to run to the press with complaints of internal censorship was bad enough, but to appeal to or argue with lawmakers in Washington—that was simply unacceptable. "He went public," explains CBS program practices head Bill Tankersley. "The public fight against the network was worse than the show itself. That became an out-and-out war, you know."

Tom, eager to fight for his "creative control," was so determined to eliminate the CBS middlemen and deal directly with the network's affiliates that he went public. The day after taping the show with the intentionally volatile Steinberg sermonette, Tom met with two of Pastore's fellow Democratic senators, California's Alan Cranston and visiting Massachusetts senator Ted Kennedy. He regaled both with tales of having his viewpoints being deliberately suppressed by CBS and then flew to Washington to take the same message there. Tom's celebrity made him a very effective lobbyist: he met with Federal Communications Commission members Nicholas Johnson and Kenneth Cox, who assured Tom that if affiliates, rather than a network, approved the content of a network program, no FCC rules would be broken and no local station licenses in jeopardy. Tom met with any senators and congressmen who would see him, held a press conference, and also corralled a few local broadcasters. He offered to address the NAB attendees as a last-minute speaker or to gather and meet with CBS affiliates in attendance, but he was rebuffed. Pastore, meanwhile, was very vocal—and so was Frank Stanton, also in Washington that weekend representing CBS.

"Clean up the filth!" Pastore yelled at the NAB attendees. Pastore's solution to the increasing amounts of sex and violence on TV was that the NAB's own Code Review Board be given the responsibility of prescreening and approving or censoring "questionable" shows. NBC and ABC executives, fearing increased government in-

tervention as the alternative, had agreed, but CBS refused c.
Pastore called the CBS decision "unfortunate," but Stanton held
firm, arguing that a centralized arbiter of TV tastes and morals would
be "harmful, indeed dangerous." Stanton then made a public statement seemingly supporting everything for which Tom Smothers had
been fighting within CBS itself. "An outside agency wielding the
blue pencil," Stanton said, "would throttle the creative impulses
which are essential to the continuing improvement of TV. The creators of our programs need encouragement and stimulation, not the
reverse."

Tom was thrilled. None of the CBS brass would meet with him
in Washington, but he returned to Los Angeles elated anyway. Tom
had fought hard for change and thought he had won. He told *Daily
Variety* that he and Dick now wanted to continue with the show, "to
stay on and continue to push for new standards of broadcast content."
He fired off a congratulatory telegram to Robert Wood thanking
CBS for "the courageous stand which Dr. Stanton took," and promising to work in partnership with CBS "to help broaden and raise
[broadcast] standards." In addition, an unexpected ally had joined in
the fight against CBS censorship. Jackie Mason, informed of the deep
cuts made in the tape of his *Comedy Hour* stand-up act, filed a
$20 million damage suit against CBS, charging the network with
"wrongfully, recklessly, arbitrarily, unreasonably and capriciously"
deleting material from his TV appearance. Mason asked that the material be restored or the entire appearance removed before the program was televised.

Meanwhile, Tom was pleased by the *Comedy Hour* installment
that had premiered over the weekend while he was lobbying in
Washington. It was the first of the two recently taped in-the-round
concert shows, the one with Donovan and Peter, Paul and Mary. It
was a show with a decidedly "hip" look and with one aggressive message that had gotten past the censors: the recitation of the Pledge of

Allegiance by the performers and the studio audience, but with the intentional omission of the words "under God."

After the *Comedy Hour* telecast with the Pledge of Allegiance was televised, CBS switchboard operators logged 305 viewer calls. Of those, 205 were against the show's removal of "under God" in the pledge, and 90 were against the entire program itself, which left 10 calls in support. With CBS ignoring Pastore's call for an industry review board, this was exactly the sort of controversy—accusations of being both sacrilegious *and* un-American—CBS wanted to avoid. On March 25, Wood sent a telegram to Tom with an undisguised tone of sternness and disapproval. Instead of acknowledging Tom's acceptance of the network's renewal offer, Wood ignored it and pointed out that in their face-to-face meetings, Tom had asked to be exempted from CBS's standards and practices or be released from his contract. "We are presently considering that request," Wood wrote chillingly, "and I assure you that my answer will be in your hands not later than April 4." The telegram closed with another icy salvo: "I appreciate your candor in stating your position. I assure you I will be equally frank in my reply."

Apparently, Wood felt that he needed an even wider and deeper paper trail, and he sent Tom a follow-up telegram the same day. "Much of this will be repetitious," Wood wrote, but much of it wasn't. Instead, it spelled out the network's position regarding the Smothers Brothers as being less of a generation gap than a possibly unbridgeable chasm. Tom, Wood warned, "may have misconstrued" Stanton's opposition to Pastore's call for an independent censorship authority. "You would be misleading yourself," Wood wrote, "if you believed that CBS has any intention of diminishing our program standards, or narrowing the application of those standards in the slightest degree." The CBS standards, he insisted, "are simply not negotiable," and Wood scolded Tom for his giddy quote in *Daily Variety*. "You are not free to use *The Smothers Brothers Comedy Hour* as a device to 'push for new standards.' If you cannot comply with our standards—whether or not you approve of them—*The Smothers Brothers Comedy Hour* cannot appear on CBS." The lengthy wire also emphasized the need for Tom to agree to deliver a final tape of each week's show by the Wednesday before, to ensure that each tape conformed to acceptable CBS standards, and to cooperate with network censors as shows were planned, rehearsed, and performed. "You now seem to be having second thoughts," Wood concluded, finally acknowledging that Tom had rescinded his threat to void the contract renewal for fall, "and I am happy that you are. But we are approaching a point beyond which decisions cannot be revoked, and contracts cannot be remade . . . If you think your principles and ours are oil and water, say so now." The network's final answer, Wood added in a foreboding postscript, "can be in your hands by April 4."

When Tom got the memo, he phoned programmer Mike Dann, his most sympathetic CBS contact in New York, to get a sense of where Tom really stood. Where Tom stood, he had no way of knowing at the time, was on very thin ice. Even Dann, who genuinely liked Tom and was protective of even the reduced ratings *Comedy Hour* still generated, was wary enough to secretly record their phone conversation. That's why we have this verbatim account of Tom's enthusiasm, and his justified paranoia, and his temperamental combativeness. Mike Dann knew the recorder was on, Tom Smothers didn't, but it's hard to say who was being more sarcastic or tongue-in-cheek.

> *Tom:* Am I still the fair-haired boy back there?
> *Mike Dann:* Yes, you are the absolute love of our life.
> *Tom:* I figured that.
> *Dann:* Only . . . your understanding [of broadcasting]
> could enable me to go forward as a
> programming executive.

Tom: I'm trying to do it for you, Michael. You're part
of the Establishment in the company, but I
know you really care about pushing forward for
more meaningful broadcasting.

Dann: I certainly do.

Tom: Hey!

Dann: What?

Tom: Is everybody pissed off?

Dann: No.

Tom: You're lyin' . . . Hey, by the way. There's some
pretty good guys back there in Washington.
Those FCC commissioners are groovy . . . as
[far as more permissive] content [is concerned],
I think we can really move forward now.

Dann: Tommy. Hand in hand, we will overcome.

Tom: That's right. I want to be part of this great new
resurgence. As Dr. Stanton said, No further
restrictions, but more broadening and really
exercising our responsibilities to the American
public. Okay?

Dann: All right. I hear you, and I got the message.
We will overcome.

Tom: You're so full of shit.

In the midst of all this, amazingly, Tom continued to forge
ahead, overseeing the final *Comedy Hour* of the third season and completing his proposal for a summer replacement series. The comedy-
variety show, as Tom outlined it, would be performed in the round,
in the manner of the currently televised *Comedy Hour* concert installments. Astrology would be "the motif and the glue to hold the hour
together," and, like *Comedy Hour*, there would be a regular orchestra
and a corps of singers and dancers. Each show would feature one

major guest star and a troupe of regulars. (This was an especially enticing list, and included John Hartford, Jennifer Warnes, and singer-songwriter Biff Rose, who had guest-starred on a *Comedy Hour* that hadn't aired yet.) According to Tom's proposal, Donovan had agreed to appear as cohost on five of the episodes. It was a potent pitch, and getting the internationally popular Donovan to participate as a semi-regular on a network show, in 1969, was quite a coup.

On Friday, March 28, the day after Robert Wood's telegram to Tom and Tom's phone call to Mike Dann, lots of things happened that affected the future of *Comedy Hour* directly or indirectly. Former president Dwight D. Eisenhower died, which dominated the news and eventually would be cited by Robert Wood as an excuse for shelving an episode of *Comedy Hour*. That same day, somewhat surprisingly, Tom's summer show was provisionally approved by Robert Wood and Mike Dann, with the caveats that astrology "may never be treated seriously or as even a pseudo-science" and that "no professional or amateur astrologer may appear on the program at any time." (Tom, predictably, would balk at those restrictions.) And finally, in a coincidence that was to have unexpectedly far-reaching consequences, the *Comedy Hour* producers were informed of an unforeseen scheduling conflict regarding one of their future shows.

The remainder of the *Comedy Hour* TV season was scheduled to televise four episodes in as many weeks. Except for the season finale, all had been taped, though not all had been assembled. First up was the once-postponed, choppily edited Joan Baez–Jackie Mason show—the one that Jackie Mason was suing, unsuccessfully, to affect—which finally was due to be broadcast on Sunday, March 30. The Easter show, loaded with bunny costumes and human Easter eggs (and including guest star Biff Rose and Mason Williams's "The Censor" poem), was next, fittingly scheduled for Easter Sunday, April 6. The

Dan Rowan–David Steinberg show would follow on April 13, and the season finale would wrap up the year on April 20.

The *Comedy Hour* folks were then told that Dan Rowan was slated to be a guest star on NBC's upcoming Dinah Shore special, scheduled for April 13—the same night and time Rowan's *Comedy Hour* guest appearance was intended to run. Since long-established cross-network guest-star courtesy held that no network would program an appearance by the same performer on a competing network, Rowan's *Comedy Hour* show had to move. Tom immediately suggested that the Rowan show be moved up a week to April 6, and be swapped with the Easter show, which now would run on April 13. It was an awkward solution, because it meant running an Easter-themed show a week *after* Easter. However, showing the season finale out of sequence, given all the special good-byes Tom had planned, would be even worse. CBS agreed, and the switch was made. The fatal ramifications of that simple decision, though, put the Dan Rowan–David Steinberg show on a more accelerated postproduction schedule, inadvertently scheduled a comic sermonette on Easter Sunday, and threw a powder-keg controversy into the mix just as Tom Smothers and Robert Wood were fighting like pit bulls over which of them had the right to dictate content. If it wasn't a perfect storm, it was a perfect nightmare.

That weekend, the postponed Joan Baez–Jackie Mason show, already seen in Canada, finally was shown by CBS to viewers in the United States. This time, the calls logged by the CBS switchboard reflected a virtual tie: There were 125 calls against Joan Baez, but 97 calls in protest of the choppy censoring of her remarks, and another 18 calls supporting the program in general. The president of CBS was silent on this particular weekend, but the president of the United States was not. Richard Nixon, a Republican, chose it to come out in support of Pastore, a Democrat, and his call for further study of TV's content. "I share your deep concern," Nixon informed Pastore, "and strongly applaud your vigorous criticism of what you regard as a misuse of this great medium." Back at CBS, vigorous criticism was precisely what Tom Smothers was about to experience.

Though most *Comedy Hour* staffers were gone and celebrating the end of a season's rigorous production schedule, a few remained hard at work at Television City, preparing the next show for broadcast. Because of the scheduling shift caused by the Dan Rowan conflict, that next show was now the Nancy Wilson–David Steinberg program, with a second Steinberg "sermonette." On Wednesday, April 2, 1969—the day of the week on which CBS was demanding finished copies of the upcoming episode—postproduction work on the episode was visible on Television City's closed circuit. It was an otherwise normal day—West Coast programmer Perry Lafferty already had sent a letter to Tom discussing some compromises regarding the summer astrology series—until Lafferty and censors Tom Downer and Sam Taylor all saw the closed-circuit feed, freaked out, and mobilized immediately. Lafferty's assistant, Bob Tamplin, called Tom at home on Wednesday afternoon and informed him that both the program and program practices divisions of CBS considered the sermonette unacceptable. Tom told Tamplin he preferred to keep the piece in the show and let individual affiliates decide whether to broadcast or delete it. Otherwise, Tom insisted, he would make the cut only if CBS provided him with a detailed memo explaining why Steinberg's sermonette was unacceptable, and would not supply filler material to account for the excised minutes. Once Tom got the memo, he told Tamplin, CBS would get Sunday's show.

Then Tom left for San Francisco, to scout locations for his plan to relocate the show there for season four and claiming to take the contested tape with him. (Actually, he left it in the trusted hands of *Comedy Hour* producer George Sunga.) Sam Taylor called Tankersley in New York, in a panic, reaching him at 10:00 p.m. Eastern time to tell him that Tom had fled town with the unedited Steinberg tape.

Tom, meanwhile, sent a brief telegram to Robert Wood, mentioning nothing about the Steinberg flap but expressing pleasure that CBS had exercised its option for a fourth season of *Comedy Hour.* Alluding to the date given by Wood as the deadline by which the network's intentions would be made clear, Tom signed his April 2 telegram, "Happy April 4th. Love, peace and progress, Tom Smothers."

Back at CBS, two of those three ingredients—love and peace— were in short supply. Progress, though, was in evidence, as several East Coast CBS executives unhappy with Tom's shenanigans began to mobilize, pouncing on Tom's failure to deliver a preview tape for affiliate prescreening on Wednesday, as promised by both Frank Stanton and William Tankersley. Stanton, at this point, was staying above the fray, as was William Paley, but Tankersley—after getting the panicked phone call from the West Coast—was outraged enough to make a phone call of his own. He called Wood and laid out his case for swift action against the Smothers Brothers.

"As you know, Bob," Tankersley reminded Wood, "I thought at renewal time that the time had come to let them go. Mike [Dann] and I argued like mad, and I lost. Well, I don't lose this time, Bob. You turned the network over to the Smotherses, but I'm not." Tankersley concluded with some advice that Wood heeded to the letter. "Get the lawyers tomorrow," Tankersley said, "and let's sit down." At the meeting, CBS programming vice president Mike Dann still supported the Smothers Brothers, but at New York's Black Rock headquarters, he found himself increasingly, overwhelmingly outnumbered.

"It was always kind of a cliffhanger," recalls Fred Silverman, who at the time was a CBS programmer for daytime TV and present at most executive meetings, "whether the tape would even get there. Those were irritating ploys. And I will say one thing, and this I can say firsthand. The executives in New York really got angered. I mean *really* angered. They said, 'We don't need this aggravation. This is just one lousy show. We're a major, major institution in this country, and we just are not going to put up with it. We've got to be in control of this network, and this schedule, and not a couple of kids in Los Angeles. This is just not acceptable.' "

With this latest impudent controversy, the irritation level quickly reached critical mass. Wood and Tankersley hated that the Smothers Brothers refused to play by the CBS rules—even if those rules sometimes were fluid or elusive. West Coast CBS censors felt ignored—which, for the most part, they were. Affiliates in the Southern and smaller communities, the ones most upset by the first Steinberg sermonette, weren't going to appreciate another. ("The Smothers Brothers were antithetical to our Southern affiliates," Silverman recalls. "They were like Martians.") And at Black Rock, the network sales representatives commuting the Eastern corridor, and the many conservative network executives who lived in Connecticut, were tired of having to field questions each week, from friends as well as colleagues, about the latest Smothers Brothers controversy. "The moment Bob Wood and his contingent . . . started getting static at their country clubs," Silverman says, "with people saying, 'Who are those young Turks you have on there?' it started to become a personal embarrassment. And it became a personal embarrassment to Frank Stanton and William Paley." A month into his tenure as the new president of CBS, Robert Wood wanted the Smotherses out, and the Steinberg stunt, and the nondelivery of the tape, looked like a good enough excuse to cancel the renewal and void the brothers' contract.

"All I knew was, it wasn't delivered," says Tankersley, who said he never saw the Steinberg show before calling the meeting. "That's all I knew. That's the only point of issue with me, was if we can't get the tape to show to our affiliates. It had nothing to do with the content of the show. I had no idea." Tankersley and Wood resented the disrespectful gamesmanship, while Tom continued to relish it. On Thursday, April 3, as CBS in New York was having a meeting to discuss his insubordination, Tom phoned from San Francisco and reached Perry Lafferty at Television City in Los Angeles. Lafferty asked for the tape, and Tom asked for the memo: a standoff. After hanging up, though, Tom backed down, yet still tried to snatch some sense of victory amid defeat. He authorized Sunga to remove the sermonette but leave Tom's introduction intact, and to cut directly to the end of the routine, where Steinberg takes his bows and receives applause. Tom considered the idea of the jarringly obvious edit to be "hilarious" and justified it as fair-play turnabout regarding CBS. "When they deleted something which I thought should stay in," Tom once explained, "they deleted it with obvious cuts. I was only following the policy of cutting the show the way they did when they eliminated something they wanted out."

Tom, still in San Francisco, wrote a memo to CBS in Los Angeles, explaining to programmer Lafferty and censor Downer that the Steinberg show tape would be delivered for affiliate viewing as requested, with the sermonette removed. Tom repeated his wish to have a written statement from CBS regarding justification for the deletion and closed with another jab: "I appreciate your feeble attempt to cooperate on our request." Sunga delivered the sermonette-free tape to Lafferty and Tamplin late Thursday afternoon, and set to work on a final tape that would include noncontroversial substitute material. Flight and shipping records show that the first tape was received by CBS in New York at 10:00 a.m. Friday, April 4, and that the second, broadcast-ready tape was hand-delivered to CBS at 9:00 a.m. on Saturday, April 5. Given that when affiliate prescreenings of *Comedy Hour* were instituted after the *first* Steinberg sermonette, they had been scheduled for Fridays, and sometimes fed on Saturdays, this master tape actually had arrived in New York in plenty of time for broadcast, had CBS executives been so inclined. They, however, had already made up their minds.

"John Appel was the lawyer for CBS at the time," Dann said,

recalling the marathon April 3 meeting, "and he said to me, 'Mike, do you have the tape for the affiliates?' And I said, 'I do not.' And Appel, at that point, jumped up to Wood and said, 'We *got* them now. We can cancel them!' And Wood agreed.

"I looked at them as if they were both crazy, because what show did they have? I didn't have any show to put in! I wasn't being noble. I was worried for my life—my *broadcast* life. I said, 'What are you guys so excited about? We just renewed them for good reason—[without them] we don't have a show!' And they both said, 'Well, we made an agreement. You can't break the agreement.' "

A telegram was written, under Wood's name and sent to Tom Smothers late Thursday night, April 3. ("Eight o'clock at night," Tankersley recalls, "we sent them the wire.") Tom, in San Francisco, received it the next day. Robert Wood had been true to his promise: regarding the show's status with CBS, Tom would have his answer by April 4. This, in part, was that answer:

> As we have advised you on several occasions, most recently in my wire of March 27, your obligations to us require you to deliver an acceptable broadcast tape to us no later than the Wednesday preceding the scheduled broadcast date of each program in *The Smothers Brothers Comedy Hour*. We hereby notify you that by reason of your failure to make such delivery yesterday (Wednesday, April 2), we are forced to treat this failure of delivery of an acceptable program as a substantial and material breach of your obligations to us, and as conclusive evidence that you have no intention of performing those obligations in the future . . .
>
> On the basis of our information about parts of that program, we believe that the program in its present form would not be acceptable under CBS's standards because, at the very least, it contains a monolog which in our opinion would be

considered to be irreverent and offensive by a large segment of our audience and, therefore, unacceptable even if this were not the week of the Eisenhower funeral rites and even if Sunday were not Easter Sunday.

Therefore, we hereby notify you that the agreement between you and us is terminated . . .

Wood pulled the Steinberg show from the schedule and substituted it with a *Comedy Hour* rerun from the previous November (notably, one featuring super-patriotic singer Kate Smith as guest star). He waited until late Friday afternoon to issue a CBS press release, relegating the news of the contract termination, for most newspapers, to a rather buried holiday weekend for news coverage. Yet the news was big enough to be noted by CBS's own Walter Cronkite on that night's evening newscast and to make the front page of the next day's *New York Times.*

"*The Smothers Brothers Comedy Hour* has been canceled for next season by the Columbia Broadcasting System," wrote Jack Gould, "bringing to a climax months of argument over the program's content." Tom was quoted in the story, complaining that the "inappropriate" Steinberg sermonette already had been "voluntarily deleted in advance," that network censors had seen the rest of the program days before, and that the network's complaints were just a pretext "to get us off the air." Tom, who had received a fourth-season *Comedy Hour* renewal notice weeks earlier, would read the opening sentence of Gould's story and voice the same insistent correction he has uttered for the past forty years.

"Fired," he says, "not canceled."

26

The Aftermath, the Bed-in, and the Trial

The Smothers Brothers, with their very different personalities, had markedly different reactions to news of their show's sudden removal by CBS. Dick, in New York to host an auto show, was phoned by the *New York Times* and stirred from a deep sleep to ask what he thought of his show's "cancellation." Since Dick knew nothing about it, his reply was a mumbled "Not much," and he went back to sleep. "It didn't upset me at all," Dick says now, recalling his feelings when the facts finally became clear. "I was tired [of doing the show], and it probably took a couple of days before we knew we were *really* fired. But we were financially secure . . . I knew we could always do work."

Tom was much less accepting of the sudden CBS pronouncement and didn't think they *had* been fired. The complaints in the telegram, to Tom, sounded bogus: He *had* agreed to delete the Steinberg sermonette and had delivered an edited tape in plenty of time for broadcast. What he'd done, and what CBS considered the last straw, was to miss a Wednesday delivery deadline for affiliate preview—but that was a requirement, Tom knew, that was nowhere in the original *Comedy Hour* contract and was a recently added edict that the Smothers Brothers never agreed to formally or in writing. "There was no contractual arrangement, ever, of what time the tape should be delivered," Tom says, in what became the pivotal argument in the eventual lawsuit against CBS. "Only in time for broadcast."

Tom treated it like any other major showdown with CBS and took it to the media, mobilizing his battle plan with a vengeance. While CBS was sending out a press release, Tom was contacting TV reporters and critics he had befriended over the years, inviting them to a Monday press conference in New York at the Four Seasons, where he'd show a tape of the allegedly offensive show. He booked a suite at Toronto's Park Plaza Hotel for Easter Sunday, and flew there in time to host reporters who watched him watch the show that was too hot for the United States yet was shown, unedited and with the Steinberg sermonette included, on Canada's CTV network. The *New York Times* reported on that, too, and noted the rueful irony of a blackout in which Tom and guest cohost Dan Rowan compare backstage woes. "I said, 'You can't censor an entire show!'" Tom complains to Dan. "And they did!" That punch line, seen that night in that Toronto hotel suite, carried the added punch of being powerfully prescient.

Reacting to the story over and after the Easter holiday weekend, much of the press came down on the side of the Smothers Brothers. The *Times* story from Canada quoted the president of the privately owned CTV network, who said he had prescreened the Steinberg-Rowan *Comedy Hour* and found it "tasteful." *The Hollywood Reporter*, on Monday, made the firing of the Smothers Brothers the lead front-page story and led with Tom's insistence that the complaints against them were "lies, lies, lies." The *New York Times* reflected the seriousness of the CBS action by printing a Monday editorial in support of the Smothers Brothers, calling the debacle "the latest example of how the networks profess their right to freedom of expression but fail to exercise it in defense of their own programs." The *Times* also dispatched its TV reporters and columnists to weigh in on the issue, and all proved similarly supportive of the fired comedians. "The brothers managed to present a rather impressive case for their side," John J. O'Connor wrote after covering the New York press conference, while Jack Gould, under the headline "Mavericks and How to Smother Them," called the unaired Steinberg-Rowan hour "one of the best programs the Smothers Brothers have done this season." The influential TV critic added even more praise in its defense: "It was an eminently enjoyable outing, with ample entertainment, bite and laughter. It was not distasteful." And it wasn't just the *New York Times*. Over at the *New York Post*, Murray Kempton saluted the bravery of the brothers in bringing on guests Pete Seeger and Joan Baez, and quoted Tom's self-effacing but accurate assessment of the blandness of 1960s television: "We stand out," Kempton quoted Tom as saying, "because nothing else is being said. We'd be moderates anywhere else." And *Variety*, also present at the New York conference, reported that the *Comedy Hour* program yanked by CBS "was well received by the press, who, a fair sampling disclosed, found its taste virtually unquestionable."

David Steinberg learned about the firing by catching the name "Steinberg" on the front page of the *New York Times*, and curiously reading the story in case it was about a relative. ("Who is this Steinberg who's making the news?" he wondered. "And it was me!") Bob Einstein heard the news through the media, too, but was reassured at a meeting held by Tom after his return from New York. "Tom told us not to worry about it," Einstein recalls. "I didn't really think we were canceled." Einstein and the rest of the staff, at that point, mostly were ignoring the furor and spending more energy worrying about whether to follow the show in its planned move to San Francisco for season four. (Almost everyone, according to Einstein, opted to head north.) Even after Robert Wood sent his memo, his program underlings Mike Dann and Perry Lafferty were counseling patience to Tom. "They kept saying," Tom recalls, " 'Hold on, guys. I think this is just a little bump in the road here.' "

After his weekend of press conferences and screenings, Tom believed the same thing. He announced at his New York press conference that he had no intention of filing a breach-of-contract lawsuit against CBS and went back to work doing postproduction on the next *Comedy Hour* in the production schedule, the show originally intended for Easter. That show and the Anthony Newley season finale, both of which were taped before CBS pulled the plug on the Smothers Brothers, still were in the pipeline and on the schedule, despite the outright deletion of the Steinberg-Rowan program. On April 9, Tom alerted Perry Lafferty that a finished tape of the show for April 13 was ready for CBS approval and signed the memo with the hopeful phrase "Peace, love and progress." He undercut that conciliatory gesture, though, by adding one of his usual disrespectful postscripts: "P.S.," Tom wrote, "Any further requests regarding any of the shows will only be accepted if put in writing. If you need any help in spelling, contact my staff."

Tom's tone may have been different had he understood the severity of his situation. West Coast censor Tom Downer did reply in writing, to let Tom know the episode was acceptable as assembled "except for a question regarding the [Mason Williams] censor poem and its introduction." In the end, Mason's poem was allowed to stay, most likely because Downer and CBS could afford to relent on that particular battle. Tom didn't know it, but CBS already had won the war.

Contrary to what Dann and Lafferty were telling Tom, other CBS executives didn't see Wood's firing memo as "a little bump in the road," but as the land mine it was. Saul Ilson, producer of *Comedy Hour* for the first two seasons, says he was contacted by Wood even before the Smothers firing became public and asked if he and producing partner Ernie Chambers would run a new CBS variety series to replace the Smothers Brothers in the fall. (Wood gave them a choice of Tim Conway or Leslie Uggams; they chose Uggams.) According to Ilson, Wood phoned to tell him, "I'm going to drop the Smothers

Brothers next week. I'm going to announce it. They're gone." If this chronology is correct, Wood had made up his mind just after Mike Dann fought successfully for the renewal and jumped on the Steinberg sermonette as the first available excuse. "As you started to see an attrition in the ratings," Fred Silverman points out, "the network became much more vocal in its opposition to . . . political humor on the show. As the numbers started to drop, I guess the network figured, 'Well, we have less to lose here.' " Ken Kragen, pointing to NBC's more forgiving attitude with its top-rated *Laugh-In* series, insists, "There's just no question that if we were a show bringing in major revenue, with no problem with the revenue source, they [CBS] would have figured out a way to make it work."

Instead, when the April 13 installment of *Comedy Hour* was televised—the first fresh episode after the Steinberg show was yanked and a week's worth of front-page headlines and controversy—it drew the lowest rating in the series's three-year history: Nielsen estimated the audience at 16.5 million TV households, attracting some 26 percent of the viewing audience. Since the show, in its prime, had drawn nearly 40 percent, that was quite a slip, and it made it much easier for Wood to be firm in his resolve. The next day, CBS delivered news that, to the Smothers Brothers, was a personal insult as well as a death blow. The summer replacement for *The Smothers Brothers Comedy Hour,* instead of Tom's idea of an astrology-themed variety show, would be a country-western version of *Laugh-In* called *Hee Haw,* followed in the fall by a new Leslie Uggams variety show. With their season finale yet to be televised, the Smothers Brothers were watching their real estate sold out from under them.

One last gasp of support, from several angles, tried quixotically to reverse the tide. David Steinberg went on *The Tonight Show* to perform the now-infamous Jonah sermonette for Johnny Carson, who cackled appreciatively and ran the routine in its entirety. Simon and Garfunkel, who had appeared twice on *Comedy Hour,* ran a full-page ad in *Billboard* saluting the brothers and showing the dictionary definition of "satire" being cut in half by a censor's scissors. Two powerful national newsmagazines, *Time* and *Life,* came to Tom and Dick's defense. "CBS's stated reason for canceling the *Smothers Brothers Comedy Hour,*" said *Time,* "was one of those rationales distinguished by the fact that just about nobody believed it." The banned episode, it asserted, "was one of the Smotherses' best-produced shows," and "David Steinberg's retelling of the story of Jonah was more in the vein of Mark Twain than Lenny Bruce." John Leonard, in *Life,* saluted *Comedy Hour* as "one of the few programs on television with an independent and irreverent political point of view," and noted wryly that "Canada has been telecasting Smothers Brothers programs uncensored for a couple of years without any perceptible increase in the incidence of rapes and assassinations."

One national magazine, however, did an about-face and printed a caustic editorial in defense of CBS. It was *TV Guide,* whose articles and editorials on the Smothers Brothers, up to this point, had been overwhelmingly favorable. Yet under the headline "Smothers Out: A Wise Decision," a full-page "special editorial" on April 19, 1969, hit the brothers with one harshly critical body blow after another.

"The Smothers Brothers have been saying plenty to arouse a substantial part of America. Where does satire end—and sacrilege begin?" And: "Shall a network be required to provide time for a Joan Baez to pay tribute to her draft-evading husband while hundreds of thousands of viewers in the households of men fighting and dying in Vietnam look on in shocked resentment?" And, most bitterly of all: "At this writing, neither of the other two networks has said it will pick up the show. We applaud this judgment." Dick Smothers recalls being surprised not only by the tone of the *TV Guide* editorial, but also by the swiftness of its publication, given the magazine's lead time. "I think we found out, really, the big boys don't play fair. We thought they would," Dick says.

The "big boys," in this case, had an obvious political motive. Even though *TV Guide* had championed the brothers in the past, and Frank Stanton of CBS had opposed John Pastore's calls for an overall broadcast censorship panel, both *TV Guide* publisher Walter Annenberg and CBS chairman Bill Paley were actively courting something that only President Nixon could grant: an appointment as ambassador to the Court of St. James, the cushy and highly coveted post of serving as the United States ambassador in Great Britain. Neither Paley nor his chief lieutenant, Frank Stanton, claimed any involvement in the Smothers Brothers firing ("The network and the group made the decision," Stanton said in a rare comment on the matter, "but I suppose I could have vetoed it if I had wanted to—but I did not participate in that decision"), but the *TV Guide* editorial unquestionably would have been overseen by Annenberg, who was the publisher. If the Smothers Brothers, as they themselves firmly believe, already were marked as media troublemakers by Nixon, that editorial should have pleased Nixon tremendously. If Nixon had yet to become annoyed by Tom and Dick's political comedy, the editorial may have led him in that direction. In any event, Annenberg, not Paley, won the ambassador post, and served from 1969 until 1974, when Nixon resigned the presidency in disgrace.

The day after the *TV Guide* editorial ran, CBS broadcast the final installment of *The Smothers Brothers Comedy Hour.* The program, intended as the third-season finale, had been taped three weeks earlier, but Tom was using this last opportunity to spar with the CBS censors to, at least, go down swinging. He threatened to insert the Harry Belafonte "Carnival" medley, which CBS had yanked in its entirety from the third-season premiere, into the final show, which drove censor Sam Taylor to write a curtly dismissive memo ("If inserted in the tape, [it] will not be broadcast"). Other memo wars, this last time around the track, concerned the show's special guest, musical theater star Anthony Newley (*The Roar of the Greasepaint—the Smell of the Crowd*), who was there to plug his new movie by discussing it with Tom and showing a clip. The problem for content-wary CBS—and, at the same time, the joy for troublemaking Tom—was that the movie, a comedy costarring Joan Collins and Milton Berle and titled *Can Hieronymus Merkin Ever Forget Mercy Humppe and Find True Happiness?* was X-rated.

Back then, though, an X rating carried a slightly different connotation. The Motion Picture Association of America had established its new ratings system only five months previously. In 1969, a movie rating of X meant only that people under eighteen were not admitted. Later that summer, *Midnight Cowboy*, starring Dustin Hoffman and Jon Voight as New York hustlers, would be released with an X rating. Two years later, so would Stanley Kubrick's *A Clockwork Orange,* starring Malcolm McDowell as a futuristic thug. Newley's film was "legitimate," but CBS wanted no part of it. Eventually, a few seconds of a commonplace beach scene were shown, but without audio, and the term "X-rated" was forbidden. Instead, Newley described it as "a very raunchy movie," and Bob Einstein's Officer Judy called it "poetry—dirty poetry" and retaliated by squirting Tom in the face with what he claimed was Mace. Later in the show, Newley offended Officer Judy's sense of propriety and Newley, too, was "maced."

The end of that last show turns out to be a fitting coda. To conclude the season, Tom and Dick thank the cast and crew by gathering everyone on camera to say good-bye. Tom and Dick had many scripted remarks that didn't make it to air, including a recap of their biggest censorship problems with CBS over the years, and a proud announcement by Dick that no longer was true, and which was edited out of the final tape as clumsily as Joan Baez's salute to her husband had been. "CBS has shown great faith in the *Comedy Hour* by picking up our show for next season," Dick had said. "We are thrilled to be part of the great CBS family."

What did survive, as closing remarks, were Tom and Dick's gratitude to viewers for their continued support and one last effort to defend their show and its content. "We have a certain point of view on *The Smothers Brothers Comedy Hour*," Dick says. "And we feel that entertainment should contain *some* opinion, social comment, and should mirror the social changes that are happening in this great country." They quote proudly from the letter of support they had received from then-president Lyndon Johnson. Dick reads two paragraphs from it, verbatim, which are met with supportive applause from the studio audience, and from the *Comedy Hour* family assembled in camera view behind the Smothers Brothers:

> *To be genuinely funny at a time when the world is in crisis is a task that would tax the talents of a genius; to be consistently fair when standards of fair play are constantly questioned demands the wisdom of a saint.*
>
> *It is part of the price of leadership of this great and free nation to be the target of clever satirists. You have given the gift of laughter to our people. May we never grow so somber or self-important that we fail to appreciate the humor in our lives.*

Dick doesn't go on to read the letter's concluding paragraph, in which Johnson writes to Tom and Dick Smothers, "If ever an Emmy is awarded for graciousness, I will cast my vote for you." And on the show broadcast that April 20, an abrupt CBS edit, skipping over the duo's talk of network censorship and interference, cuts straight from the LBJ letter to Tom's ironic closing plea: "Please keep those cards and letters coming, if you have anything good to say." By then, of course, any show of support would have been too little, and definitely too late.

"When you have George Harrison on the show, how can you be canceled?" Bob Einstein asks in bewilderment. "And Harry Belafonte! That was a different kind of star altogether! When you can get all those people on [as guests], and the show was reaching an audience that no other show was reaching, how could they get rid of it?" Yet they did. *The Smothers Brothers Comedy Hour* was no more. Seventy-two episodes had been produced from 1967 to 1969, one of which, the Steinberg-Rowan hour, never was televised by CBS. The series ended its third and final year ranked twenty-seventh for the season—still in the Top 30, but a sizable drop from the more than 30 million viewers who watched seasons one and two, when *Comedy Hour* was ranked sixteenth and eighteenth, respectively. To the end, though, the Smothers Brothers program ranked high in newly factored demographic categories: one of the five largest in terms of viewers under thirty-five, college graduates, professional workers, and high-income families. The young, affluent, and aware audience that *Comedy Hour* attracted, and the controversies it generated, wouldn't be anathema to CBS for long.

One season after CBS fired the Smothers Brothers, Robert Wood made the dramatic and risky decision to cancel many of the network's most popular programs, which drew most of their support from rural areas and elderly viewers, and replace them with programs aimed at attracting a younger audience and reflecting more topical content. Mike Dann was replaced by Fred Silverman, and Top 10 shows such as *Mayberry R.F.D.* and *The Red Skelton Show*, as well as such still-popular series as *The Beverly Hillbillies* and *Hee Haw*, were gone. Pat Buttram, who played Mr. Haney on *Green Acres*, another victim of the network's 1971 "rural purge," said memorably, "It was the year CBS killed everything with a tree in it." Bill Paley, in his memoirs, explained the programming flip-flop another way: "The time had come to catch up with some of the developments that had taken place in the United States," Paley wrote, explaining the sudden appearance of such provocative series as *All in the Family* and *M*A*S*H*. "We came out and said, in effect, we'll do it the way it is and not be afraid of the complaints we expected." If only the Smothers Brothers, who proved that a young and issues-oriented audience base was there for the taking, had received similar support from CBS.

These were tumultuous times for the Smothers Brothers—and, from a current-events and popular-culture standpoint, for everyone. Within a month after CBS televised the final episode of *Comedy Hour*, President Nixon instituted a draft "lottery" system to provide more soldiers for the Vietnam War, Timothy Leary's drug conviction was overturned by the Supreme Court, the Who unveiled its rock opera *Tommy* in a live concert in England, and the Beatles' "Get Back" topped the charts in the United States. On the personal front, Dick was fired by CBS and divorced by his wife, Linda Ann (whom he later remarried and divorced again), the same week, while Tom dealt with court proceedings of his own. In May 1969, he hired two attorneys to represent the Smothers Brothers in a string of lawsuits against CBS—suing the network not only for breach of contract, but for constitutional denial of free speech and freedom of expression.

A week later, Tom accepted an invitation by John Lennon to join him in Montreal, where John and his new bride, Yoko Ono, were capitalizing on the media storm surrounding their recent marriage by staging the second of two "Bed-in for Peace" events. (They figured, since reporters and photographers were hounding their every move anyway, they may as well use their celebrity to get across a message—a strategy copied, many years later, by the likes of Brad Pitt and Angelina Jolie.) As John and Yoko had in Amsterdam, they invited the media to pop in as they stayed in bed for a week "for peace," this time from room 1742 of Montreal's Queen Elizabeth Hotel. This time, they immortalized the occasion by bringing recording equipment into the suite, plastering a giant poster of John's handwritten lyrics on the wall, and recording a new song called "Give Peace a

Chance." The song was recorded on June 1, 1969—two years to the day after the Beatles released *Sgt. Pepper's Lonely Hearts Club Band*—and released a month later, as Lennon's first solo recording with the Plastic Ono Band. Among those joining John and Yoko on the hotel-room sing-along recording were Timothy and Rosemary Leary, New York disc jockey Murray the K, members of the Canadian Radha-Krishna Temple—and Tom Smothers, who is name-checked by Lennon in the song's final verse ("Everybody's talking about John and Yoko, Timmy Leary, Rosemary, Tommy Smothers . . ."). John, sitting cross-legged on the bed with Yoko by his side, strums one guitar heard on the record. Tom, perched on a folding chair at bed-side, strums the other.

Tom's favorite memory of that "bed-in" recording session was when John taught him the chord structure of the song. Tom began filling in little grace notes, doing chord inversions, and showing off his guitar technique. Lennon didn't notice at first, because he was into singing the lyric, but eventually he stopped and looked straight into Tom's eyes.

"I thought maybe he was going to say, 'Man, that's really good, Tom,' but he didn't," Tom recalls, laughing. "He said, 'Tom, I don't like what you're playin'. Don't play it that way. I want you to play it like me. Exactly double it. Double what *I'm* playin'.'" Tom laughs again. "Two guitars doing the same thing, it gives a certain sound, I guess. But I thought I was doing something really special." In truth, he was. With its chorus of "All we are saying / is give peace a chance," Lennon's hit song became yet another generational anthem to spring from the pen of a Beatle—and put Tom, once again, right at the center of pop culture, coconspiring with one of the Fab Four.

For a while, it seemed as if the voices behind *The Smothers Brothers Comedy Hour* would continue to be heard in a big way, even though the show itself was gone. *Comedy Hour* won the Emmy for Outstanding Writing Achievement in Comedy, Variety, or Music that summer, a posthumous award to a dead but still respected show. Allan Blye, Bob Einstein, Steve Martin, and Mason Williams were some of the writers taking home statuettes that night, but Tom's name wasn't listed among the writers of that winning show. "I was very uncomfortable," says Tom, who had kept himself off the list of writers out of fear that his name would cost the show some votes. "I was not a relaxed warrior who'd won something. I felt conflicted, and very self-conscious." Most celebrities in the audience seated nearby, he recalled, would avoid eye contact. It was the sort of uncomfortable feeling that prompted Tom to move north to Marin County near San Francisco, where he had wanted to move *Comedy Hour* anyway. "I just couldn't stand being around LA," Tom admits, "because of the feeling I had of being out of the game." At least one person in the crowd was supportive: Lorne Michaels, a young writer for *Rowan & Martin's Laugh-In* that year, remembers expecting to win the writing award but accepting the loss to *Comedy Hour* easily because he respected that show's work. "I felt badly, but not *too* badly," Michaels says. "Which is as nice a compliment as you can give to another show."

Tom was invited that summer to write a guest editorial in *The New York Times*, and used his print pulpit to question Senator Pastore's propriety in offering local TV station owners lifetime licenses if they would agree to advance censorship by an NAB board. "I can think of no suggestion by a legislator in recent history which was so clearly against the public interest," Tom wrote, "as to tell businessmen—whose rate of return is already exceeded only by the petroleum industry—that they might be eligible for a perpetual franchise if they would promise never to offend a sixty-two-year-old senator who admits that some television shows make him blush if he views them in the same room as his married daughter."

• • •

Mason Williams, like Tom, was granted a prominent platform to speak his peace, if not to sing in support of it. Mason was the final witness at a two-day Federal Communications Commission hearing on proposals to limit network control over prime-time TV programming—and whether reading from his handwritten notes or playing notes on his guitar, Mason charmed the committee while making his points about TV, creativity, and censorship. He later collected his testimony into a book called *The Mason Williams FCC Rapport,* which is full of handwritten, quotable statements about television and *The Smothers Brothers Comedy Hour.*

"It was the most American show on television," Mason insisted of their program. "We were a bunch of Americans who believed in something, and when the networks wouldn't let us express it, we fought back." Writing for TV, he said, was like being a kid and being told, "Here's a ball, don't bounce it." On network executives: "The wrong kind of people are in charge of television, and until they are replaced or at least balanced, it will not improve." And finally, an entry titled "To Tom," which goes: "You can't have your heart in one place and your head in another. Jesus Christ was not a businessman."

It seemed possible, in the summer of 1969, that singing about peace might bring it about, and singing to FCC commissioners might charm them into doing the right thing. Neil Armstrong walked on the moon that summer, and 500,000 people gathered in Bethel, New York, for the Woodstock Music and Arts Fair, the counterculture zenith of the good-vibe musical happenings Tom Smothers had witnessed at Monterey and mounted on his own *Comedy Hour* in-the-round concert shows. At almost the same time, however, the peace-and-love era was unraveling as surely as the decade was closing. The same month that Woodstock demonstrated peaceful coexistence on a grand scale, Charles Manson demonstrated the opposite when his followers slaughtered actress Sharon Tate and other innocent victims. And before the year was out, a Rolling Stones concert at Altamont, California, would end with the stabbing death of a concertgoer by the Hells Angels security forces, symbolically signaling the end of an era.

Tom tried to regain ground, and the spotlight, by making his own syndication deal with close to one hundred local stations around the country. He offered stations the right to show, in September 1969, the never-broadcast *Comedy Hour* episode with David Steinberg and Dan Rowan, and offered it to them for free—making every minute of commercial time they sold translate to 100 percent profit. The deal was that each station would then buy rights to show a new special he was planning for December, featuring Simon and Garfunkel and, according to one report, Bob Dylan. The special never materialized, though, so Tom essentially gave away the biggest asset in his library of shows. And since the TV critics who reviewed it now were seeing it five months later, having not attended one of the spring screenings that drew such rave reviews, the response was less laudatory. Ben Gross of the New York *Daily News* grumbled, "I thought it came over as a so-so, rather tepid hour of entertainment." Even Dan Rowan, who saw the infamous show for the first time when he appeared at a September press conference with Tom, suggested it wasn't that particular program's content that got the Smothers Brothers fired. "Dinah Shore did stiffer shows," Rowan joked. And when Tom complained about network interference by saying, "It's not their candy store," Rowan assessed the situation differently. "But they're in there licking the lollipops, and you're sitting out here looking in the window," he told Tom. "So it's *got* to be their candy store." When Tom stubbornly said, "I want to change that," Rowan's rejoinder was neither optimistic nor unfair. "You and Don Quixote," Rowan replied.

For the next couple of years, as the Smothers Brothers prepared for their trial against CBS, their media appearances were minimal. They did one NBC special in 1970, *The Return of the Smothers Brothers*, featuring David Steinberg, Glen Campbell, David Frye, Bob Einstein, and *Easy Rider* star Peter Fonda, but it was met with mixed to negative reviews. An ABC summer series that same year, *The Smothers Brothers Summer Show,* fared no better. "I had lost my sense of humor," Tom says simply. Jobs began to dry up, and the trial loomed. So, in those early years in the 1970s, did the creeping shadow of President Richard Nixon.

Finding a smoking gun connecting Richard Nixon directly to the demise of *The Smothers Brothers Comedy Hour* was a task at which I proved unsuccessful, but not for lack of effort. Either Nixon covered his tracks well—as many, many people in the inner circle of *Comedy Hour* stars and staffers believe—or it was out of concern about what Nixon and his administration *might* do next regarding station licenses and political influence that led others to act in ways that might be interpreted, in retrospect, as White House influence. The April 4 firing of the Smothers Brothers took place within Nixon's first one hundred days of office, so it's likely his attentions were elsewhere. Certainly, the secret taping system he installed in the White House was not yet in place, so there are no "Watergate tapes" from the era to provide any clues.

What makes the concept of presidential interference in early 1969 impossible to dismiss, however, is the amount of evidence that piles up immediately following. In October 1969, presidential aide Jeb Magruder (later convicted and jailed as one of the Watergate co-conspirators) wrote a memo to Nixon's chief of staff, H. R. Haldeman (also convicted), suggesting an official monitoring system to watch network news—and, presumably, entertainment—programs for "bias against Nixon," leading to official complaints filtered through the FCC. If the Nixon White House has the idea of using government agencies such as the FCC as a harassment tool that early in his presidency, it might be more than coincidental that, in February 1970, the Smothers Brothers were hit by back taxes claims by the Internal Revenue Service. Especially since, in 1974, Senate Watergate committee member Senator Lowell Weicker introduced evidence that the Nixon White House, for years, had used the IRS and other federal agencies "to move against so-called political enemies."

In 1970, Vice President Spiro Agnew attacked the news media as "nattering nabobs of negativism," launching a frontal assault on newspapers and TV news operations and putting the White House in direct opposition to media outlets and, by extension, Hollywood. Also that year, Elvis Presley toured the FBI headquarters in Washington, hoping to be deputized as a federal agent (he wasn't). During that visit, Elvis volunteered the names of some showbiz celebrities he considered suspicious—names that were forwarded up the FBI chain and beyond. According to an FBI memo, Elvis advised that "the Smothers Brothers, Jane Fonda, and other persons in the entertainment industry of their ilk have a lot to answer for in the hereafter for the way they have poisoned young minds by disparaging the United States in their public statements and unsavory activities." Elvis met Nixon that same month in 1970, which makes it reasonable Elvis mentioned the Smothers Brothers then, too.

The closest and most persuasive link to a Nixon-versus-Smothers vendetta, though, involves former New York City policeman Anthony Ulasewicz. According to a sworn deposition by Herbert Kalmbach, Nixon's personal lawyer, Nixon assistant John Ehrlichman directed Kalmbach to pay $100,000 in campaign funds to Ulasewicz, between 1969 and 1971, for "work of an investigatory nature." Kalmbach testified he was unaware of the nature of those investigations, but in 1973 two *Washington Post* reporters, Bob Woodward and Carl Bernstein, cracked that part of the story. Ulasewicz, in more than twenty "secret probes" ordered by the White House and instigated by Haldeman and Ehrlichman during that three-year period, investigated such targets as Dick Dixon (whose only offense was imitating the president in satiric fashion, as David Frye had done on more than one occasion on *The Smothers Brothers Comedy Hour*) and Tom and Dick Smothers.

Unlike LBJ, who reassured the brothers, "It is part of the price of leadership of this great and free nation to be the target of clever satirists," Nixon's skin was a lot thinner. In 1972, Woody Allen wrote, directed, and starred in a brilliantly funny ersatz documentary for PBS, *Men of Crisis*, in which he played a powerful member of Nixon's inner circle. Actual news footage and outtakes were used to incorporate real politicians into the story line, and the editing was crafty enough to make it a forerunner of Allen's *Zelig*—yet the special, which poked direct fun at Nixon, Henry Kissinger, and others, was never shown. Like the Steinberg-Rowan *Comedy Hour*, it was precanceled by its nervous network. Steinberg tells a story from that same era of having a mysterious voice phoning a club where he was doing a stand-up act, warning him not to make fun of Nixon in his routine that night. Steinberg didn't heed the warning—comedians seldom do—but nothing happened.

Tom, though, remembers getting a warning of a much more serious nature. After *Comedy Hour* was through, and as the NBC and ABC attempts at reviving his TV career proved unsuccessful, Tom busied himself, in part, by coproducing a comedy short called *Another Nice Mess,* eventually released in 1972. Written and directed by Bob Einstein, who appears in the film as a secret service agent, the political comedy stars Rich Little as Richard Nixon and character actor Herb Voland as Spiro Agnew. "They looked exactly like Nixon and Agnew," Tom recalls, "but they acted like Laurel and Hardy." Tom dismisses it as "a terrible film," but says it was the reason, according to an ex-Marine friend of his, that "a drug bust was being set up." Tom's friend was tipped by another friend, a former CIA agent, that someone Tom knew had been turned by a federal prosecutor and plans were in motion to descend upon Tom and make an arrest. The ex-agent's advice to Tom was to wash his car twice a day (keeping it "clean," inside, in more ways than one) and never travel alone. Tom mailed a registered letter to the attorney general of California, and another to himself, saying he was afraid he was about to be set up. He cleaned all evidence of drugs out of his workplace and home, and stayed clean, just in case the warning was true. Within two weeks, Grandpa Remick, who was staying with Tom at his place near San Francisco, phoned while Tom was in Los Angeles editing and said, "Hey, Tom! There's a bunch of cops here, tearing up the house!" They found nothing—but only because Tom, like Woodward and Bernstein, had gotten an inside tip.

To Dick, all this harassment suggested the early equivalent of the White House mischief-making group known as the Plumbers, and the paranoia and retribution that resulted in the actual compilation of Nixon's "enemies list." If Nixon's Plumbers (as the White House Special Investigations Unit came to be known) had indeed targeted the Smothers Brothers early in Nixon's first term and succeeded in silencing and harassing them, Dick Smothers suggests, "It looks like a pretty good prototype of the enemies list . . . They got rid of this potential irritant." Dick suspects that once he and Tom were pushed off the media, the Nixon White House may have considered it such a successful operation, they looked around for other targets.

Was this really the case? Or were Tom and Dick merely part of an equally improper vendetta conducted *after* the brothers already had been fired by CBS? Either way, the Plumbers, CBS, Nixon's enemies, and the Smothers Brothers soon would find themselves defending their respective actions in the same federal building.

Nothing exemplifies the paranoia or audacity of the Nixon White House operation, or the Plumbers, more than their determination to discredit Daniel Ellsberg, who in June 1971 had leaked a series of classified documents to the *New York Times*. Ellsberg, a former Pentagon worker who was a civilian State Department expert on Vietnam, had been charged with adding to the government's classified dossier on the Vietnam War. These documents, which collectively came to be known as the Pentagon Papers, told in the clearest and coldest terms what the government, at that time, was keeping from its citizens: that the war was most likely unwinnable, would cost a staggering number of additional casualties, and that many operations were mounted with what appeared to be a callous disregard for the safety, even the lives, of US soldiers. After trying unsuccessfully to get parts of the documents read into the Congressional Record by an elected official, Ellsberg copied the Pentagon Papers and leaked them to the *Times*, which began publishing them. Attorney General John Mitchell ordered the newspaper to stop publication; the newspaper refused, sparking the landmark 1971 freedom-of-press case *New York Times Co. v. U.S.* Meanwhile, in order to discredit and build a case against Ellsberg, Ehrlichman authorizes the Plumbers to break into the office of Ellsberg's psychiatrist in late 1971, looking for damning information. The burglary eventually comes to light, and the damning backfires: one of the men participating in the Ellsberg "fact-finding mission" later was caught in the June 1972 break-in of Democratic National Committee headquarters in the Washington, DC, hotel known as Watergate.

When Ellsberg went on trial for espionage in 1973, nothing about the break-in of his psychiatrist's office was known. When it was revealed that April, along with evidence of illegal government wiretaps ordered by the White House, all charges against Ellsberg were dismissed because of the government's egregious conduct. The Watergate spiral began to widen, and most of Nixon's closest aides went to prison. The actions against Ellsberg proved, almost shockingly, just how far (or how low) the Nixon White House would go in pursuing and punishing an enemy.

· · ·

Coincidentally, at the same time Ellsberg was being tried and freed in California's U.S. District Court, another case was taking place in the same building: the case, finally arriving to court, of *Tom Smothers et al. v. Columbia Broadcasting System, Inc.* "Ellsberg had the trial right above us," Dick says. "The Pentagon Papers. And outdrew us, too. By then, we were so passé." The thought of it, though, is somewhat remarkable. Both of them, Daniel Ellsberg and the Smothers Brothers, found themselves in the same federal courthouse, at the same time, defending their actions because they had used the media to speak out against what they felt was an unjust, unwinnable war. Both had been targeted by the same illicit White House investigative unit, and subject to invasions of privacy and abuses of power. And most important, both Ellbserg and the Smothers Brothers emerged from the courthouse as victors.

The Smothers Brothers initially filed four suits against CBS, covering everything from antitrust and copyright infringement to censorship and breach of contract. Tom was most interested in arguing First Amendment rights, but was advised not to bring their claims before Los Angeles Ninth US District Court Judge A. Andrew Hauk. By the time the case got to trial in 1973, the key issues were copyright infringement and breach of contract, and the Smothers Brothers had to prove two things to win. One, that they had not invalidated their contract with CBS by producing material inappropriate for broadcast. Two, that the reason CBS gave for terminating the Smothers Brothers—a failure to deliver tapes in time for a Wednesday preview by affiliates—had no contractual grounds for enforcement, because that never was part of any written agreement between the two parties. Proving the second issue was easy: a paper trail, or lack of it, showed that the prescreening demands by CBS had come only in the final season, had changed deadlines more than once, and had never been mutually agreed upon. Proving the first part, as it turned out, was easy, too.

To demonstrate how often the Smothers Brothers had gone too far or how much leeway the network felt it had given them, lawyers for CBS brought a TV monitor into the courtroom and showed excerpts from various *Comedy Hour* shows to the jurors. The only problem was that the jurors thought the clips were entertaining, not offensive—and thought the same of various witnesses, including the now-infamous David Steinberg. "I remember the lawyer for CBS, with me on the stand," he recalls, "saying, 'When you said, "Grab the Jews by the Old Testament," were you insinuating *testicles*?' And I said, 'Of *course*! Otherwise it wouldn't be *funny*!' And the jury laughed."

Nancy Nolan, the youngest of those jurors, was eighteen when *The Smothers Brothers Comedy Hour* was launched in 1967, and watched it with her parents until she got married and moved out. She remembers "enjoying the social issues as well as the entertainment," which made her a good person for the Smothers Brothers to have on the jury. And she was a big fan of Leigh French's "Tea with Goldie" sketches, which made her an even better one—unlikely to be outraged by the show's more cutting-edge humor. Asked if she got all those drug jokes while watching as a teenager, she replied, "Oh, yeah! California-grown girl? Are you kidding?"

Independently, various people at the trial—including Nolan the juror, Steinberg the witness, and Tom and Dick Smothers the plaintiffs—described two of the main courtroom figures in the same TV terms. Judge Hauk, as Dick insisted, "looked like Archie Bunker," and acted like him, too—saying to Tom and Dick, "Are you the dirty boys from television?" The brothers' attorney, a former two-time mayor of Beverly Hills named George Slaff, reminded Dick of "the Columbo of the law," and had the same rumpled demeanor and disarming appearance of being scatterbrained. Lawyers and firms with clients in show business were reluctant to oppose CBS, but Slaff, with his proud history as an attorney with the American Civil Liberties Union, was happy to do battle. "CBS had this lineup of high-powered Wall Street lawyers sitting there," recalled Perry Lafferty, enjoying the contrast even though he was supposed to be on the network side of the case, "and there was George, with the rumpled hat, who kept dropping his pencil. He was a character like somebody wrote it for television, and this lawyer just put the jury in his pocket."

Jurors enjoyed themselves, applauding their favorite TV clips and even laughing at some of the testimony. For the brothers themselves, though, it was an emotional drain as well as a financial one. "Two months in that courtroom, it went on and on," Tom complained afterward. "Dickie and I were there five days a week, every day. He read books on vegetables to stay awake." Dick hated missing most of his ski vacation to be there, and even at the end, when the Smothers Brothers won a settlement for breach of contract, Tom denied that being vindicated in court made it a wonderful day. "It was a mediocre day," he said. The jury awarded the Smothers Brothers $776,300 in the breach of contract case; and the judge, focusing on the copyright aspect of the same case, awarded an additional $140,000. That made the total verdict an award of $916,300, plus one dollar in punitive damages. Even so, Tom would rather have followed his instincts and fought the battle over freedom of speech, even if he and Dick had lost. Perhaps he knew, now that the case was over, that he would never again fight as big a battle, on as big a stage, with as much at stake, as he did when it was Smothers versus CBS not in a California courtroom, but over the airwaves of America.

27

After the Fall, and Couples Therapy

Between their first failed attempts at a TV comeback in 1970 and the conclusion of their trial against CBS in 1973, the Smothers Brothers weren't very active and didn't necessarily look to work together. Despite his bad experience syndicating the "unseen" episode of *The Smothers Brothers Comedy Hour*, Tom tried again by offering, to local independent TV stations, a half-hour 1971 syndicated series called *Tom Smothers' Organic Prime Time Space Ride*. Only fifteen stations televised it, and it lasted only thirteen weeks.

Tom also flirted with acting in movies during this period, and had some opportunities that could have turned out big, but didn't. In 1972, he worked for director Brian De Palma, costarring opposite Orson Welles, in a dark comedy about magicians, titled *Get to Know Your Rabbit*. But this was just before De Palma began attracting notice as a young director, and the film bombed. Tom also was offered the lead role in another film, and he admits now it's one he should have taken—the one that got away. George Roy Hill, fresh off *Butch Cassidy and the Sundance Kid*, wanted Tom to star as Billy Pilgrim in his screen adaptation of Kurt Vonnegut's *Slaughterhouse-Five*. Distracted by preparations for the trial, Tom passed, so the role in that excellent movie, eventually released in 1972, went to a little-known but effective actor named Michael Sacks. "That's the one thing, in my whole career, I regret not doing," Tom says now. "I could have been really good in that." (Much later, in 1995, brother Dick landed his own solo film role of note, playing the senator in Martin Scorsese's *Casino*.)

After the trial, the brothers struggled, separately and together, and tried other things, then decided to write some new material and hit the clubs again. Working at a small club in Georgetown just to get the rhythm back, Tom remembers a time when Harry Nilsson ("a dear friend of mine, I loved his music," Tom says softly) showed up as a surprise to offer moral support. Nervous and rusty, and working solo, testing new jokes and songs to add to the act with Dick, Tom burned through his new material so fast that the entire planned forty-minute set took only about twenty minutes. To fill time, Tom asked for questions from the audience, and Nilsson, to help out, began heckling—and saved the night. So in 1974, when Tom and Dick decided to revive their stage act, they booked their first shows at a nightclub that had long been friendly to them: the Troubadour in West Hollywood. Nilsson, being a good friend, decided to surprise Tom again, and this time to bring along a friend who was in town having a very long "lost weekend": John Lennon. The results were disastrous.

"It was horrendous," Tom recalls, laughing at the memory. "They came in pretty ripped to see our show, and, as Harry later explained to me, he told John, 'He needs some heckling to make this thing work.' He didn't think I had an act. Well, they start heckling, and it was some of the worst language I've ever heard—and they had a real buzz on. Cognac and toot, I guess. And it was a mess." Lorne Michaels was writing for Lily Tomlin at the time, and they decided to support the Smothers Brothers because of the way they'd lost their TV show ("Uncompromising," Michaels says, "was an enormously attractive thing to be"). Michaels and Tomlin showed up the same night as Nilsson and Lennon, and saw the fireworks, which started with heckling and ended with Lennon returning from the bathrooms with a sanitary napkin on his head and with a few punches thrown. "It wasn't like *witty* heckling," Michaels recalls. "It was just a drunk . . . And they couldn't put him down," he says of the Smothers Brothers. "They had the microphone, but he was a Beatle." Lennon's antics drew national attention, but drew it away from Tom and Dick.

"A lot of people had come out to see if the Smothers Brothers were still okay and healthy, and if their timing was right," Tom says, "and we were working great until they started heckling." But for Tom, who after all had sung "Give Peace a Chance" with his inebriated heckler, there were no hard feelings, just another surreal moment in the spotlight. "I know that if they'd have thought clearer about it, they wouldn't have done it," Tom said, adding that afterward, "I got flowers from John Lennon and an apology from Harry Nilsson." Ken Fritz, who was there, laughs at Tom's generously forgiving account. "They were not there to help," he says of Lennon and Nilsson. "That was not a 'beneficial heckle scenario.' " Fritz had gone to them three times to ask them to quiet down and let the brothers do their act, but to no avail. The third time, Fritz says, Lennon grabbed Fritz's tie, pulled him forward, and rattled the tie back and forth, telling Fritz it would be okay. "Then," Fritz continues, "he grabbed a glass and broke it on the table and threw it, and that's when I came up swinging. It was only one punch. Good enough to knock him backwards."

Despite the well-publicized heckling, the Smothers Brothers' comeback effort worked well enough for them to get a new network series: *The Smothers Brothers Show*, presented by NBC in 1975. Enough time had passed, and the Smothers Brothers had been so low-profile for so long, that curiosity had built. Their return to television, the first time out, grabbed a massive 55 percent share of the viewing audience. That was the good news. The bad news is that the show was horrible, and ratings plummeted quickly week by week. "That was my fault," Dick says. "I pushed Tommy into doing it."

In order to get a contract with NBC, Tom and Dick had to sign over all creative control, and virtually all the decisions about the show, to producer Joe Hamilton, who had run *The Carol Burnett Show* back when the brothers were doing *Comedy Hour* at the same CBS Television City studios. Two months before NBC's *Smothers Brothers Show* premiered, Tom asked to be released from the contract—just as he had a decade earlier with the brothers' CBS sitcom, which bore the same *Smothers Brothers Show* name. "I was crying, I was begging," Tom says, but to no avail. As performers for hire, doing material with which they had no connection, Tom and Dick merely went through the paces—while behind the scenes, Tom needled and complained and intimidated at every opportunity, even to the press. "Some people think we got this show by making concessions and copping out," Tom told the *Washington Post.* "Nothing could be closer to the truth."

Eventually, all the friction got to Hamilton, who finally stepped away. The show, by that point, was canceled, but Tom was allowed to take control of the final four shows, and they're the ones in which the Smothers Brothers really blossomed, calling in favors and, once again, stretching boundaries. Two years before Steve Martin did his classic short comedy film *The Absent-Minded Waiter,* he performed the piece here, with Tom and Dick as frustrated but well-compensated diners. A Beatle showed up here, too (Ringo Starr—but still), and Lily Tomlin dropped by (post-Troubadour) for some delightful comic nonsense with Tom and with Pat Paulsen. Paulsen, like Bob Einstein, was back, and Tom had found a new regular talent to nurture: Don Novello, who created the character of Italian-accented Vatican correspondent Father Guido Sarducci. The program also introduced an early prototype of Tom's Yo-Yo Man, the alter ego that became a featured part of their stage act in later years.

. But without a TV platform, opportunities were a lot less plentiful. They tried working separately for a stretch, then teamed up for a Broadway and regional tour of the stage comedy *I Love My Wife*, which helped. But even after that, it was a long slog of doing club dates wherever, whenever they could, paring things back to basics. "We were pretty dead in the water," Tom told one reporter bluntly. "It was like starting from the beginning. We were the opening act for everybody." In the early 1980s, TV work was slim and not too impressive. A pair of variety specials for NBC went nowhere, and a 1981 "comedy-adventure series" called *Fitz and Bones,* in which Tom and Dick played a TV news crew in San Francisco, *deserved* to go nowhere. They picked up a pair of guest hosting spots on *Saturday Night Live*, from that show's creator, Lorne Michaels—but mostly, what they did was perform, and hone, their stage act. And a funny thing happened, literally. Just as in the earliest days of their career, when they recorded albums and only afterward shaped their bits of comedy into a coherent routine, Tom and Dick found that, with the repetition of an ongoing national tour, their interaction as a duo was much better than it had ever been when they had their hit TV show in the '60s. By the time they got their next opportunity to star in their own television program, they had learned the importance of eye contact to their comedy. "The tension can hold much better," Tom discovered, "when two people are staring at each other. It's palpable."

The opportunity, which surfaced after they reunited with former manager Ken Kragen, was a one-shot reunion special for CBS. It was titled *The Smothers Brothers Comedy Hour 20th Reunion Show*, and was scheduled for February 3, 1988—even though that wasn't the twentieth anniversary of anything. The show had begun in 1967, and was thrown off the air in 1969. What mattered, though, wasn't the timing, but the opportunity. This time, the Smothers Brothers were ready. Their mother, Ruth, died the day before rehearsals began, which made it bittersweet, but other loved ones and familiar faces were in abundant supply.

Tom and Dick invited all the old *Comedy Hour* gang to show up—not to sit through a lengthy parade of vintage clips, but to perform new material. And almost all of them showed up. Steve Martin, now a major star, was there for the special. So were Glen Campbell, John Hartford, Mason Williams, Pat Paulsen, Leigh French, Jennifer Warnes, and Bob Einstein. The show started with the brothers returning to their old CBS Television City studio by helicopter—and getting fired upon. The special employed the same marching-band opening credits, a similar Tiffany motif, but used nostalgia only as a jumping-off point for new comedy and music, and to show that the Smothers Brothers, as they firmly believed, were better than ever.

"Once upon a time we were on TV / Every Sunday night we knocked 'em dead," the brothers sang to the tune of "Those Were the Days," with new lyrics for the occasion by Mason Williams. "We stirred up trouble, so the network fired us / I guess that it was something that we said / Those were the days, my friends . . ."

The one-hour special was received very warmly by TV critics. Arthur Unger in the *Christian Science Monitor* pronounced the Smothers Brothers "as relaxed, relevant, and irreverent as ever." Tom Shales of the *Washington Post* called it "delightful" and "sweet revenge," and wrote, "The boys were right, the network was wrong; it was clear then, and it's clear now." This one-shot special grabbed not only the critics, but the ratings, finishing in a virtual tie with the time slot's dominant show, ABC's *Dynasty*. CBS Entertainment president Kim LeMasters, the new generation's Mike Dann, immediately ordered a small weekly run of new shows.

The high quality of the show was one factor, and the ratings were another. A third key element, however, was that between the time the Smotherses' reunion show had been televised February 3 and the series was set to premiere March 30, the Writers Guild of

America had gone on strike. The March 7 action halted most TV production in Hollywood, as it would do two decades later with its 2007–08 strike—but the Smothers Brothers, with all their residual goodwill and stick-it-to-the-man street cred, were given a waiver to permit them to stay on the air and produce shows. When it premiered as a series, *The Smothers Brothers Comedy Hour* (the creation of original titles, apparently, never was a big priority) saluted the striking writers by presenting them on camera—100 of them, each protecting his or her identity by wearing a pair of Groucho Marx glasses. Simultaneously, the song sung by Tom and Dick, to accompany and honor the anonymous striking scribes, was the Western classic "(Ghost) Riders in the Sky"—with its lyrics altered to the ultra-appropriate "Ghost Writers in Disguise." I'm sorry, but 1968, 1988, 2008, whenever—that's damned funny.

These were, indeed, the best TV shows the Smothers Brothers ever presented. Performances were sharp, segues between acts became seamless, and, not incidentally, Tom and Dick had their timing down and their humor back. The first show of the new series featured Harry Belafonte, who sang with Jennifer Warnes; Andrea Martin, who re-created the three-legged "Last Great Waltz" with Tom; and another special guest, Jack Lemmon, who recited a century-old anti-war poem. Later shows in the series's run supported new talent (Michael Davis, Jim Stafford), showcased talent rarely seen elsewhere on TV (Peter Schickele as P. D. Q. Bach), and embraced everyone from Linda Ronstadt and Phyllis Diller to Martin Mull and Shelley Long. Some sketches, like a barroom brawl built around wine tasting, rank as career-best efforts. But CBS, programming and renewing the shows in scattershot fashion (there were eighteen in all, in addition to the reunion special), did it no favors and ended up hastening its demise. "CBS has mistreated them for more than a year now," one critic (me) wrote in 1989. "As specials and as mini-miniseries (four weeks here, two weeks there), *The Smothers Brothers Comedy Hour* has been on and off more often than a light switch." Without the proper treatment by CBS (nothing new there), it soon was off for good, and Tom and Dick Smothers lost their last chance that century to work from their own regular TV platform.

But they've kept working, and kept growing, which is one of the amazing things about the Smothers Brothers. They introduce new material into their stage act cautiously, concerned that it'll compare unfavorably with their honed-to-classic routines, but their act does keep mutating and maturing. "Your fame gets you laughs for five minutes," Dick says. "After that, you better be funny." And as much time as they devote to their act, they now devote additional time to their relationship. In their personal lives, especially with wives, there has been ebb and flow. Tom married Rochelle Robley, a woman he knew from high school, in 1974; she came to the marriage with seven children, and the couple divorced two years later. In 1988, while working on the twentieth-anniversary special, Tom fell in love with one of the show's associate producers, Marcy Carriker, and she became his third wife in 1990. They have two children, Riley Rose and Bo. Dick, meanwhile, who could claim the lengthier, more stable marriage when the two brothers were younger, has found stability harder to maintain later in life. After two unsuccessful marriages to the same woman, Linda Miller, Dick married Lorraine Martin in 1986, then Denby Franklin in 1997, with both relationships ending in divorce.

Yet the Smothers Brothers, as a professional duo, have lasted longer than any act in the history of show business, save one: Smith and Dale, the vaudeville team whose longevity was the inspiration for Neil Simon's *The Sunshine Boys*. Smith and Dale, whose real names were Joseph Sultzer and Charles Marks, were together for seventy years—but they weren't brothers. Despite their obvious personality differences, Tom and Dick Smothers may have lasted so long precisely because younger brother Dick took the initiative to talk

Tom into something that sounded, on the face of it, absurd: couples therapy.

Dick, in his ongoing quest for self-improvement, had attended some group meetings and was convinced that a pair of counselors, who worked with big businesses and, in Dick's words, "make personal and corporate breakthroughs, allowing people to function," would be perfect for the Smothers Brothers. Dick was certain they would let Tom know how inconsiderate he'd been throughout their professional partnership, while Tom was certain it would be a waste of time. They were both wrong.

"Tom and Dick are totally different people, in every way," says Ken Kragen, who has been in and out of their lives several times as a personal manager. "Attacked from the outside, they close ranks and will defend each other adamantly. However, they always have complaints with the other . . . Tommy's totally consumed with career and business. Dick is consumed with outside activities." Dick agrees with this basic assessment, revealing that his standard line to Tom is "You save the world. I'll enjoy it."

When these very different brothers went to what Kragen said was "essentially marriage counseling," the results surprised everyone. Having an objective third party to listen and analyze as they voiced their respective grievances made all the difference. "Dick's own story," Kragen recalls, "is that he came out [of therapy] and said, 'I had no idea. I thought it was Tommy, and I found out it was me.' "

Tom's recollection is one of similar surprise. "I've never seen this work, you know," he says, "but I went with it, and these people came up, and we had a very productive time. It cleared out a whole lot of things, and both Dick and I looked at each other and said, 'Why didn't we do this ten years ago? *Fifteen* years ago? . . . Because we had legendary fights. Our fights were over timing, and over material. And we are exact opposites, which is our little edge onstage because we don't have to assume too much of a persona difference." The initial twelve-hour session convinced them both it was something they should do every few years—and since then, they have.

"One time," Tom says, "Dick was asked, 'Isn't it difficult working with your brother for thirty-five, forty years, like this?' And he said, 'Well, it's like an old marriage. A lot of fighting, no sex.' I thought, That's a funny line, coming from the straight man."

Thanks in part to couples therapy, Tom and Dick Smothers have reached the golden anniversary of their start as professional performers. The year 2009 marked the fiftieth anniversary of their debut as a trio—the Smothers Brothers and Gawd—while 2010 marks fifty years since they first performed as a duo, as the Smothers Brothers, in Colorado in 1960. Yet no matter how tenuous the relationship over that half century of showbiz teamwork, Tom is very aware of one of his brother's attributes for which he's extremely grateful. It has to do with the fact that when Dick went away to race for a week at Sebring, he came back to find that because of what happened in his absence, they were about to lose their show.

"Dick *never,* in all the time we've had our relationship," Tom says, "has blamed me, or said, 'You screwed it up!' That never happened, to this day. Never. Never. Which is kind of nice, because I was the one that *did* take it to the brink. My brother never second-guessed me on it.

"And during the big crises that we had, during that last season [of *Comedy Hour*], Kenny Kragen or someone would go to Dick and say, 'You know, he's out of control. Your brother's got this *position,* and he's not abandoning this one.' He'd come to me and say, 'You right or wrong?' I'd say, 'I'm right.' He'd say, 'Okay.' And that was it. That was *always* it. I don't know how he recalls it, but that's how I recall it. So as far as the brother thing went, the trust—that was perfect."

"He would always want me to agree with him, or know what was going on," Dick recalls. "And I never disagreed." His best advice, which Tom rarely heeded, was to string out the more controversial material over a greater number of shows, so the same message would get out, but at less of a risk. "Stay employed, basically!" Dick says, laughing. When he told that story in 2000, at the Aspen Comedy Festival in a panel saluting *The Smothers Brothers Comedy Hour,* fellow panelist Steve Martin looked at Dick and asked something as true as it was funny:

"How's it feel to be right?"

The Smothers Brothers Legacy

As the Smothers Brothers approached their golden anniversary in show business, they seemed to have settled in a good place. Instead of being forgotten, they were being increasingly remembered and saluted. In the middle of 2008, with a crucial election on the horizon, an unpopular and seemingly unwinnable war abroad, and a vocal young generation at home, it was hard not to think of a similar confluence of events back in 1968. Tom and Dick Smothers, for raging against the machine in the '60s, were being applauded and honored, more and more frequently, for the very things that generated thousands of angry letters, and got them fired, four decades earlier.

The Television Critics Association invited the Smothers Brothers to host its 2008 awards ceremony and perform a miniset in front of veteran critics who watched them as youngsters, as well as younger ones who had never seen them perform. The evening was a smashing success. Also in the room that night were such TCA Award winners as Tom Hanks, Tina Fey, the *Mad Men* cast and creator Matthew Weiner, and Lorne Michaels, who found himself once again in the same orbit as the Smothers Brothers. Tom and Dick, entering after their introduction, got a lengthy standing ovation and opened with the same reworked "Those Were the Days" song with which they had returned to CBS in 1988. In one couplet, before this nontelevised audience, they needlessly, playfully censored themselves—"Back in those days gone past / We didn't kiss their . . . *hey!*"—but the point was clear. Censorship had played a big part in their undoing, as had their defiance. "That was fun," Dick said afterward. "I was amazed that that was such a warm evening . . . They were like comrades." Tom's reaction was a beaming, appreciative smile: "Wasn't that nice?" And it was.

The same goes for the sixtieth annual Emmy Awards ceremonies, which took place six weeks before the 2008 election, at the tail end of eight years under Republican president George W. Bush. Steve Martin strode onstage to salute "one of my comedy heroes," and identified that hero as Tommy Smothers. Correcting a forty-year-old oversight that had denied Tom a well-earned writing credit as part of the Emmy-winning 1968–69 *Smothers Brothers Comedy Hour* writing team, Martin explained, "When it came time for the writers to submit their names to the Television Academy, Tommy, thinking that his name was too volatile, refused to let us include him on the list. The truth is, Tommy deserved the writing award as much as we did." By the time Tom arrived onstage to receive his special commemorative Emmy, the black-tie crowd was giving him a hearty standing ovation, which he clearly enjoyed. The academy presented Tom with a special commemorative Emmy—"a brand-new Emmy from 1968"—and Tom saluted the show's other writers and producers immediately, and creatively.

"I want to thank them for all the great writing that got me . . . ," Tom said, letting a long pause hang in the air as he held his Emmy aloft. Then he finished the sentence with a perfectly timed ". . . fired."

Even on this occasion—especially on this occasion—Tom had a message or two to deliver. The ABC Emmy telecast didn't have nearly the reach of the Smothers Brothers' old prime-time variety series (the Emmys drew an estimated 12.3 million viewers that year, about 20 million fewer than the average *Comedy Hour* forty years earlier), but it was the largest TV audience Tom Smothers had enjoyed in decades. Plus, the show was live. Tom could say what he wanted, or try to, and opted to speak out against the current administration, just as he had in the show for which he was accepting a very belated award. He never mentioned President Bush by name, but didn't have to.

"It's hard for me to stay silent," Tom told the black-tie crowd and the live TV audience, "when I keep hearing that peace is only attainable through war—and there's nothing more scary than watching ignorance in action.

"I dedicate this Emmy," he continued, "to all people who feel compelled to speak out, and are not afraid to speak to power, and won't shut up, and refuse to be silenced." He then looked into the audience for his younger sibling, who was seated next to Tom's wife, Marcy. "And I thank my brother, Dickie Smothers—for fifty years my partner, and all my life my brother." His parting words were a memorable definition: "Truth," Tom said with a smile, "is what you get other people to believe."

The truth of the Smothers Brothers' career is this: The longer they lasted, and the more they stayed true to their beliefs and styles, the more that mainstream America came to respect and even revere them, for stubbornly fighting for principles and ideas that, over time, were acknowledged as the right ones. The same happened to controversial *Comedy Hour* guests Pete Seeger and Joan Baez—but arguably, the Smothers Brothers, by risking, losing, and never again regaining the massive and influential popularity they had as outspoken young TV stars, may have suffered, and sacrificed, the most.

Rehabilitation, in the form of the introduction of their programs and story to a new generation, began in 1993, when E! Entertainment Television presented trimmed-down episodes of *The Smothers Brothers Comedy Hour,* complemented with new interviews with writers and performers. Tom and Dick cohosted these showings—the first time their infamous *Comedy Hour* series had been televised since they were tossed off the air—which included some material never before shown on TV. Almost a decade later, another cable network, Bravo, presented the TV premiere of Maureen Muldaur's 2002 *Smothered: The Censorship Struggles of the Smothers Brothers Comedy Hour.* Most recently, in 2008, Time Life released the first of Paul Brownstein's DVD compilations of their work, *The Smothers Brothers Comedy Hour: The Best of Season 3,* and followed with *Season 2* in 2009. (It was Tom's idea, with his usual disdain for established rules, that *Season 3* should come first. I should also add that I was interviewed in the *Smothered* documentary and wrote the liner notes for the DVD set—but that doesn't influence my opinion that both Muldaur's film and the Time Life DVD are excellent pieces of work.)

In terms of television history and evolution, what Tom and Dick accomplished in those three *Comedy Hour* years was important, and what they attempted was even more so. Within two years, Norman Lear's *All in the Family* sitcom would usher in a new style of television, one so intentionally confrontational that the first episodes were preceded with network disclaimers. But just as *Laugh-In* protected itself with the machine-gun speed of its one-liners, *All in the Family* made sure to balance various points of view (for every bigoted Archie Bunker remark, there was a liberal counterargument from his "Meathead" son-in-law), and to use Archie's venom-spewing yet cuddly character as a double-barreled weapon. Liberal viewers could get and enjoy the show's overall message, and laugh *at* Carroll O'Connor's Archie; conservatives could miss the message entirely and laugh *with* Archie. Yet when Tom made an antiwar joke on *The Smothers Brothers Comedy Hour,* he wasn't hiding behind a character. In the end, that cost the show viewers, just as the variety show's topicality threw, and offended, a few dozen CBS affiliates.

And that's another telling point, and crucial part of the brothers' legacy: Pre–*All in the Family,* pre–*Laugh In,* they strove for topicality at the very time the networks were scrambling to avoid any whiff of it. CBS wanted established stars from its own network to appear, while Tom was more interested in showcasing and nurturing new talent. CBS wanted performers to sing their hit songs, while Tom wanted them to sing new songs *before* they were hits. For CBS, almost every mention of religion, sex, drugs, politics, and war was anathema; for *Comedy Hour,* addressing such topics made the show unique. And it was. In some respects, it still is.

It's easy to trace the lineage of many of the best and boldest of today's TV troublemakers and iconoclasts to this three-year experiment from the late 1960s. Pat Paulsen's brand of comedy not only predated and prefigured Andy Kaufman's grand antics, but provided a blueprint for the mashup of real and fake politicians that would inform Garry Trudeau and Robert Altman's brilliant HBO series *Tanner '88* twenty years later. Paulsen also was a clear inspiration for *The Colbert Report* star Stephen Colbert's short-lived attempt to run for president *forty* years later.

With its emphasis on music and comedy, *The Smothers Brothers Comedy Hour* paved a lot of ground for *Saturday Night Live,* where Lorne Michaels emerged as the massively influential TV producer and generational talent scout that Tom Smothers was for a time—and could have remained had he kept his show. Tom and Dick mined current events for humor before HBO's *Not Necessarily the News,* just as the interviews with newsmakers that Tom planned for *Comedy Hour* but was forbidden to televise (like his chat with Dr. Benjamin Spock, finally released on the *Season 3* DVD collection), were '60s prototypes of Bill Maher's informal talks on *Politically Incorrect* and *Real Time with Bill Maher.* Similarly, there's a lot of the Smothers

Brothers chemistry, anarchy, and silliness in the songs and comedy of the New Zealand guitar-duo team showcased on HBO's *Flight of the Conchords*. It's not even pushing credulity too hard to suggest that *Comedy Hour,* in showing everything from its groundbreaking short films to its US exclusives of Beatles videos, included some of the early ancestral strands of MTV.

Besides owing a debt to Tom and Dick Smothers, all of those shows and networks mentioned have something else in common. They, like the daringly topical *South Park,* all reside on cable TV, or are nestled safely in late-night slots. When the Smothers Brothers lost their bid to be substantive in prime time, on a commercial broadcast network, that patch of battleground that was lost has seldom been fought over again. *M★A★S★H* had some clear messages to impart, as did *Lou Grant,* on CBS, in the 1970s and '80s. In the '90s, both NBC and Fox gave Michael Moore some rope, then hanged him with it, in *TV Nation.* NBC permitted Aaron Sorkin to address political themes, but in a fictional alternate universe, on the brilliant *West Wing.* And in the first decade of the new century, ABC's *Boston Legal* allowed David E. Kelley to get away with biting social comment by mixing serious courtroom debates with outlandish characters in equal measure, and NBC moved its "Weekend Update" ersatz newscast from *Saturday Night Live* into its own 2008 prime-time spinoff. And that's about it. Forty years after the Smothers Brothers were silenced, and you can take the subsequent attempts by push-the-boundaries, tackle-the-tough-topics shows on broadcast TV, and almost count them on one hand. Well, one hand and two fingers, if you count Fox's *The Simpsons*—which you should.

The Smothers Brothers Comedy Hour not only was on broadcast TV, it was hugely popular, presented on television's most-watched viewing night, with a weekly audience of between 30 and 35 million viewers. The only marginally comparable show reaching that sort of audience today is *American Idol,* and its influence on the record charts, and on the number and makeup of TV reality shows, is inescapable. So imagine, say, if Ryan Seacrest suddenly came out on the air and railed against the war in Iraq, rather than merely sniping at judge Simon Cowell. That's the sort of jarring disconnect Tom and Dick Smothers risked, on their show, by going from the "Mom always liked you best" jokers to some of the most vocal and opinionated performers in prime time.

"It's so important, and so hard for people to remember how big it was," David Steinberg says of *Comedy Hour*. "It was certainly the *Seinfeld* of its time. It was *the* premier show—*the* show to do. There'd never been anything like it."

Underscoring his point, Steinberg continued. "Somewhere along the way, I read this word 'present-ism.' It's very hard to judge the past from the [point of view of the] present, because you just don't know what was going on at the time. In context, *The Smothers Brothers Comedy Hour* was as irreverent in its own way as Lenny Bruce was in his time. It was *that* irreverent to do that on the air. As tame as it looks now, it was that incredible for someone to have had that following, which means you weren't *counter* to the establishment, you *were* the establishment. You were making the most money for CBS, and for them to do that—for the brothers to use their platform to speak out against the war—was as bold, and as courageous, and as self-destructive as you could get."

Kate Kahn, a *Comedy Hour* dancer who got her start on the show as one of the milkmaid extras in Nanette Fabray's 1967 "Twelve Days of Christmas" number, recalls the whirlwind energy of being swept up by what people on the show were saying and doing. "I arrived at the Smothers Brothers show gung-ho for the Vietnam War," she says, and was converted into a passionate antiwar person in three weeks." (Passion figured in other ways as well: Twenty-five years to the day after they first met, Kate and Mason Williams got married. Ten years later, they got divorced.)

You didn't have to work on the show, though, to be impressed or affected by it. *Comedy Hour* had a huge audience—and if you were of the right age, either an impressionable young child or teen or a forward-thinking adult in your twenties or thirties, its impact was enormous. When Tom and Dick appeared as guests on *The Late Late Show with Craig Ferguson* in 2008, they were led afterward on an impromptu tour of what remained of their old Television City offices and soundstages. One of the stages has been taken over by *The Price Is Right*—and when host Drew Carey learned the Smothers Brothers were in the building, he rushed down to the stage to let them know how much he had loved their show and their albums.

"I've heard more and more over the past two years," Smothers manager Ken Fritz says, "way more than I did twenty years ago, from young people who remember, so distinctly, being at home as children with their parents on Sunday night, watching the show. Remembering the musical acts, of course, but they remember seeing Pat Paulsen and the editorials, 'A Little Tea with Goldie,' Officer Judy . . .

"These are people in their forties and fifties, looking back and realizing the impact, and wondering, Why were my parents so tuned into it? And it's because they were the *contemporaries* of the Smothers Brothers, and they were looking at them as their leaders of a generation—really speaking out against the establishment, and against the Vietnam War, and so many things that to this day still resonate with people of that generation. Who would have ever thought that a variety show was going to take on issues like that? Young people now remember that show so clearly, and now realize why it was so important to their parents."

David Simon, who would grow up to be a newspaper reporter in Baltimore before creating such boldly opinionated, socially challenging TV series as HBO's *The Wire*, recalls watching *The Smothers Brothers Comedy Hour* with his parents, on their black-and-white Zenith, when he was seven to nine years old. "Even at that age, you could tell something was different," he says. While he admits he didn't get some of the jokes at the time, he also remembers, quite specifically, Tom and Dick daring to "poke the president," taking direct aim at Richard Nixon. "Being from a good, 'New Deal' Democratic family, it was to the great surprise and delight of my family.

"They were dangerous," Simon says of the Smothers Brothers. "My parents looked forward to them every week." So did Simon, who enjoyed not only the program, but its effect on his parents. "Here were two guys who were doing things that were raising my parents' eyebrows. I didn't think TV could do that."

The Smothers Brothers did, and raised a lot of eyebrows weekly. Jon Stewart, who watched it growing up in New Jersey, was asked by Tom Brokaw (in his *1968* History Channel documentary), "How much of what you're able to do, do you think, is the result of people like Tommy and Dickie Smothers?" Stewart's reply: "If I was going to trace my ideology, if I looked down the tree—that's, for me, where it ends." Then he points out that while the Smothers Brothers had 30 million viewers back then, *The Daily Show with Jon Stewart* averages 1.4 million. Yet the audience for both shows, in their respective eras, was described by Brokaw, quite accurately, as "young, hip, and politically engaged."

When I was a teenager, my father and I watched *Comedy Hour* together as a weekly ritual. My dad gave up *Bonanza* to do so—grudgingly, at first, because we had only the one TV set—but very quickly, he looked forward to the brothers' variety show as much as I did (Pat Paulsen was my dad's particular favorite). And I'm not the only boy in the '60s whose mother died young, and who bonded with his father while watching *Comedy Hour* each week. Another is Ken Burns, who grew up to be TV's premier documentary filmmaker. "My mom had been dying from cancer from the moment I was an aware human being," said Burns, whose mother died in 1965, when he was twelve. "I remember in 1962 and '63, when the height of a great deal of the civil rights stuff happened, that I would hear the TV set in the other room talking about fire hoses, or dogs in Selma, or missing New Englanders and four little girls in this church. And I would stay up all night worrying about that—and I trace my own interest and preoccupation with race in America to that. I think what I was doing—in retrospect, perhaps, with some dime store psychology mixed in—was transferring to the cancer that was killing my country all of my anxiety about the cancer that was killing my family. And the Smothers Brothers were not telling me anything new. They were just telling me that what my dad said, and what I was feeling inside myself, was right. And that was really important, because you didn't get that from television."

Burns used a metaphor I especially like, about how time can change value—how a grain of sand, which begins in the oyster as an irritant, eventually transforms, layer by layer, into something "extraordinarily valuable": a treasured pearl. To CBS in the '60s, *The Smothers Brothers Comedy Hour* was an irritant. Today, it's a pearl. "I think that this *is* the metaphor of it," Burns says. "That we ended up with this pearl, however difficult their passage was. And I'm sure, in a kind of wonderfully perverse, potentially hypocritical way, CBS is hugely proud of it."

It's easy to imagine, looking over the pop-culture landscape and singling out some of the more outspoken and independent artists and other voices, the inspiration and influence *The Smothers Brothers Comedy Hour* may have provided. But you don't need to imagine. If you want an impressive sampling of what Tom and Dick Smothers and their 1960s variety show meant to people, and to television and pop culture, all you have to do is ask. So I did. Their answers serve as a fitting way to end this salute to Tom and Dick Smothers and their groundbreaking variety show—especially fitting, since the brothers get the very last word.

Matt Groening, creator of *The Simpsons*, was weeks from recording a Smothers Brothers guest appearance on his show when we talked about his early comic heroes. "I was a fan of the Smothers Brothers from the moment I saw them on *The Ed Sullivan Show* as a little kid," he recalled. "They just seemed to have an emotional reality that was a little bit more immediate and alive, compared to most other comedy in the early 1960s—at least television comedy. I loved their albums. They were always in the record collections of older brothers of my friends. That's how I got to know the Smothers Brothers . . . before I bought records myself."

Groening loved "these amazing rock bands" the show would present, rattling off an accurate list of who (including the Who) appeared, and remembers when Mason Williams unveiled "Classical Gas." Groening recalls, "I bought the single the next week, and I've been a fan ever since." As for the show's humor, the *Life in Hell* cartoonist says, "As they got more political, I did, too. In thinking back about that time, there was just nothing else on television where you felt that there was criticism of the way things were going. It was considered outrageous, some of the stuff that they said, which is very mild by today's standards. But they really fought battles [in prime time] that no one else was fighting." Asked whether he considered *The Simpsons* a subversive comedy show in the *Comedy Hour* vein, Groening agrees, but also gives a nod to the fast-paced *Laugh-In*. "We do jokes very fast," he says, chuckling, "so if you're mad about a joke, it's too late."

Michael Moore, activist filmmaker and creator of *TV Nation*, said, "My earliest memories of watching television as a child, and being compelled by it, were the things I saw on the *Smothers Brothers*, from David Steinberg's rant on religion and the Bible, Moses and all that. I remember Simon and Garfunkel, I remember there was this antiwar thing. Between the skits, and the kind of pretaped stuff, and the music, and then the stand-ups that would come on, the political comedians who, again, believed in something. Because the best comedy is the flip side of really incredible anger."

Bill Maher, who moved on to HBO's *Real Time with Bill Maher*, remembered, "The Smothers Brothers were saying the Vietnam War was the wrong war to be in, it was unwinnable, and we shouldn't do it. By 1979, it was hard to find someone who would disagree with that, right? And I've noticed in the . . . years since what I said after 9/11, how that completely has faded . . .

"For something that, at the time, seemed like they were going to put me on a stake and light the pyre, it's funny. I either get 'Well, did you?' or I get 'I remember what you said, and I agree.' It just shows you that the truth, to most people, is like wine—it gets better with age. But to some of us, it's not like wine. It's something you want right away. I always think of that line in *The Godfather* where Tom Hagen says, 'Don Corleone is a man who insists on hearing bad news immediately.' Well, yeah, and I'm like that, too."

Maher says he wasn't censored, though, and that he was more fortunate in his travails than were Tom and Dick. "People said that was censorship, what happened to me," Maher says. "Not really. Because I was able to come back and get another show, and I went on a book tour, I wrote a book, I did the show on Broadway. All you've got to do is fight back. This country does give you that opportunity. It really does. Tommy and Dickie, I think they should have fought harder after. Of course, there were fewer outlets. There wasn't cable then, there were only three networks. So it was harder then. I was lucky. I came along at a better time."

David E. Kelley, the writer-producer whose *Boston Legal* on ABC was one of the few modern series on prime-time broadcast TV to address issues regularly and aggressively, says, "I *so* loved the Smothers Brothers! I grew up watching that show, every Sunday. When I was young," he continues, "probably much of their humor went way over my head. I was laughing just at the silliness of Tommy Smothers and the bickering of brothers. I have two brothers myself, and we used to bicker and argue over ridiculous things as well. But I always considered Tommy Smothers a hero," he adds, because of Tom's antiwar stance and artistic integrity.

"I've never sat down in the writers' room and said, 'Okay, we need to do what the Smothers Brothers did.' But I wouldn't be surprised, if you pulled back the wiring on my end, the influence could be in play." He was thrilled to see Tom get his honorary Emmy and compares him, in terms of the medium's importance, to *All in the Family* producer Norman Lear. "I always will think of those kinds of people, and how noble television can be, and how you can still say something. And when that day comes that you can't, that's when you fight even harder." Yet despite the battles those men fought, Kelley says too little has changed. "I'm not sure the goal for the networks and studios, and for most producers, is to either inspire or provoke," he says. "It's just to get a broad enough audience so you can sell your widgets."

Doonesbury cartoonist Garry Trudeau cocreated *Tanner '88*, the HBO series that ran an ersatz candidate for president. Of Paulsen he says, "He was there well before us." Trudeau attended Yale University at a time when there were only a couple of TVs around and not much interest in what they were showing. *Comedy Hour*, though, was a memorable exception. "When I saw it, I was just enormously impressed," he recalls. "And, of course, it just seemed incredibly unfair when they were yanked off the air." Part of the blame, though, he places on the combative spirit of the times, from both sides of the generational divide.

"It seemed that Tommy was so in-the-face of CBS," Trudeau recalls, "that he kind of made it hard for them to keep him. If he had said, 'Okay, look, we're on the same side. You want a hit show, we want to be on a hit show, let's see what we can do to keep this thing going'—they could have worked things out. But he declared his bosses the enemy. So you have to take that into account. You can't just say, well, the government forced the Smothers off the air, there was too much pressure, too much heat. People still talk about it as censorship. Of course, it *isn't* censorship, unless the government gets involved. It's just [the network] trying to decide whether it's worth it. Now if Tommy had gotten them on his side . . . But I don't know if that was possible. Maybe not."

At any rate, decades later, Trudeau remains impressed. "They're such huge talents," he says. "I saw them at a benefit a couple years ago, and they killed! They blew everybody else away. There were a half a dozen other acts, and they just *killed*. And without becoming something they haven't always been. It's that same wonderful brother humor—there's a slyness to it that's just irresistible. Plus the musicianship is actually at a rather high level."

Lorne Michaels, *a Laugh-In* writer who went on to create *Saturday Night Live,* observed, "What I learned from what happened to the Smothers Brothers, as much as anything, was that when it came to fights with the network, I would never get into a position where I would be seduced into losing the show over it. [Over the years on *SNL*] there were lots of censorship battles, and there was lots of brinksmanship—but somewhere, some healthy part of me knew that the bigger thing was that you were on the air."

Harry Belafonte says of the show's social impact: "I think it not only shaped minds and was able to move things forward, it also said something else. America was moving into a deadly serious time on the issue of race, and it was at the threshold of a huge struggle on the ideological front, politically, with the Soviet existence and the socialist bloc. And in this atmosphere, a lot about what America was doing was moving into the world of extremes. Extreme behavior, extreme response, and extreme anxiety about it.

"And I think . . . [the brothers] said to America: These issues which for so long have appeared to be taboo cannot only be approached, but they can be approached with humor, they can be approached with challenge, they can be approached with analysis and concern. But at no time can they be approached without dignity and respect for what it is that we're trying to say here . . . So here we were, not just a black man up there making a statement about, or satirizing his social environment and his own social and political experience, but white people were saying, 'Yeah, we not only see your point of view, but here's a few of ours.' So there was a sense of purpose, and camaraderie, and togetherness, in trying to do things in a way that would not alienate people. One of the biggest ways to do that, of course, is to do what Charlie Chaplin did, which was to put every serious issue on the table before you . . . [Comparing *The Smothers Brothers Comedy Hour* to the films of Chaplin] is high praise, but it's also highly factual."

Interestingly, even among the network suits with whom Tom clashed, the brothers are respected. Mike Dann, who was CBS Entertainment president while *Comedy Hour* was produced, stated, "The loss of the Smothers Brothers was a blow to freedom of expression." And Fred Silverman, the programming executive who took over CBS Entertainment after Dann left and later programmed ABC and NBC, said, "It was a very significant show, *The Smothers Brothers*. It was in the variety form what *All in the Family* was in comedy. And it is kind of ironic that *All in the Family* came along about a year and a half after they were canceled and made *The Smothers Brothers* look like a nursery rhyme . . . But the only thing on the air right now, on the networks, that would compare to *The Smothers Brothers* is David Letterman, in tone. And Conan O'Brien. I think that Letterman, when he was on NBC, when he first started out, was much, much closer to Smothers."

"What the Smothers Brothers' show did was, it brought people to television who normally would not watch," Perry Lafferty, West

Coast CBS lieutenant to Mike Dann, pointed out. "That's what it did. All these people you and I know who say, 'I don't look at television.' It brought those people to television—like, I suspect, *The West Wing* and *The Sopranos* did more recently."

Perhaps surprisingly, William Tankersley, the CBS head censor who was instrumental in getting the Smothers Brothers fired, observed, "What a good show it was. It was a well-mounted show. That thing was just perfect, and the guest stars were excellent. But with the battles, you know, they just wouldn't stop. It's a shame."

Smothers Brothers manager Ken Fritz said of the show's time and impact: "Sunday night at nine o'clock—what a platform we had! That's something that no one has now [to say something of substance, to an audience that large], and that's a pity." Manager Ken Kragen adds, "You have to look at the context of the culture . . . It's just critical that you do that. And I think we were in a different kind of time. The time fed the Smothers, and the Smothers fed the time."

Mason Williams, writer and musician who is credited as the "conscience" of *The Smothers Brothers Comedy Hour: "Saturday Night Live* picked up on a certain aspect of what we did, and wanted to do, but *SNL* went hip. We didn't even want to be hip, because we *wanted* Kate Smith and Jimmy Durante. We wanted the broadest palette. That was what was unusual about this show. It had a point of view, but it tried not to narrow down to some little demographic focus of who your audience was."

It's impossible not to wonder what could have been. Bob Einstein, the *Comedy Hour* writer who played Officer Judy, said, "It just would have been fascinating to see what would have happened had the show gone on, because I think it could have had a very long run. Tommy really, really could have had an unbelievable influence, because his thinking was really right. His thinking was right, and he loved discovering people and pushing them, giving them their shot.

He loved that. And how many performers do you know that love that?

"Tom and Dick realistically risked their career, they lost their career—*forget* about millions and millions of dollars. And also having a voice, having the other shows, losing your summer replacement for both Campbell and you . . . You remember how big Norman Lear became? Well, the Smothers could have had four hours of television on, and I think they would have used those hours to such a good end. It just would have been so good because Tommy really enjoyed finding new and different people, and new ideas."

"I always find gold in people that other people miss," Tom said. "You know what I'm saying?" He disagrees, though, that continuing to produce a string of shows as the 1960s ended would have been that good an idea.

"Thank God we were fired! Truly!" Tom says. "Because I look at where I was at that time . . . I was worn out, and I had no sense of humor, and I was out of whack. So, it's a good thing *I didn't* have those four shows. I don't know *what* would have happened."

"We almost quit," Dick recalls [during the dark '70s period]. "But then we saw *The Sunshine Boys*, the movie [about Smith and Dale, the only comedy team to have outlasted Tom and Dick in showbiz tenure], and said, 'No, this won't happen to us.' But then, Dick answers the question much more candidly than expected.

"It could have been the firing," Dick says. "It could have been the fact that when we did separate things, we weren't rip-roaring successes, but were just okay. It could be Tommy's responsibility, that he's worried about me. Traditionally, he's worried about me because I've been more foolish than he has. He's way more wealthy than I am, but I got married differently, and not as well . . . I spent more money, and enjoyed my life a lot more. Maybe he's just worried about me a little bit. It's not the main thing, but that could be part of the stew."

Of how he'd like to be remembered and what he'd like to happen next, Tom says, "I'd like to be remembered as a pretty good comedy team who, on a couple of occasions, refused to be shut up—refused to shut up when told to. And that's about it. We were a pretty good comedy team, and had a moment in time where a spark happened.

"But you know what?" he says, his eyes twinkling. "I'm enjoying it much more now than when I did it, and particularly *after* we did it, when we were really pariahs."

And, finally, about his future with brother Dick:

"I would love to do a show," Tom says. "I'd like to do one more show, because we've got our skills, and I could more easily raise a family doing a television show than being on the road. But the Smothers Brothers, Dick and I—there are a lot of good people out there. We'd like to do one more observational, comedic look at things." Surprisingly, Tom says, given the choice of doing it unfettered on cable, where all of the comic descendants of *The Smothers Brothers Comedy Hour* seem to dwell, or on broadcast network TV, he'd still opt for the latter.

"I think that Dick and I are good for broadcasting instead of narrowcasting," he explains. "I think we could capture a lot of people on the network and be successful that way—catch a couple of generations in the families. I think the censorship problem, the freedom you get on cable . . . you could have on network. We never did deal in dirty words or expressions like that. They were generally ideas. And I don't know if we would have any problem whatsoever. It depends on how precise and how astute we are at telling the truth and making people think. Not just thoughtless routines, but with a thought behind them. So that's what I'd like: I'd like to exercise my television muscles again."

Acknowledgments

F irst and foremost, thanks to Tom and Dick Smothers, for asking me to write this book, then waiting fifteen years and sitting through dozens of interviews, while I didn't.

This book wouldn't exist without them. Nor would it exist without Laurie Fox of the Linda Chester Literary Agency, who waited a decade without complaint before I delivered a salable proposal; Michelle Howry, senior editor for Touchstone Fireside at Simon & Schuster, who believed in the project enough to buy it, then refrained from murdering me as I missed one deadline after another; and Patricia Romanowski, who not only worked with Michelle to edit the manuscript but also to reshape and improve it. I'm very, very grateful to all three very, very patient ladies.

Mason Williams was especially generous of his time, watching old episodes with me and sending old journal entries and other materials. He and then-wife, Kate Kahn, opened their home to me, as did William Tankersley, Stan Harris, Perry Lafferty, and David Carroll, while Allan Blye and Bill Maher saw me in their offices.

Then there are the many dozens of interviewees, some of whom endured my calls and questions several times. These include Sherry Smothers, who provided key insight into her beloved brothers; Fred Silverman, who provided a corroborative smoking-gun perspective from within CBS; Ken Fritz and Saul Ilson, whose memories from inside the Smothers camp proved more accurate and detailed than many; and such key players in the *Comedy Hour* drama as David Steinberg, Harry Belafonte, Pete Seeger, John Hartford, Pat Paulsen, Roger Daltrey, Mike Dann, Ken Kragen, Bob Einstein, and Ernie Chambers. Thanks also to others who talked eagerly to me about the Smothers Brothers, including Carol Burnett, Ken Burns, Matt Groening, Hal Holbrook, David E. Kelley, Dick Martin, Lorne Michaels, Michael Moore, Bob Newhart, Nancy Nolan, Tony Randall, Carl Reiner, George Schlatter, David Simon, and Garry Trudeau.

Linda Donovan, who transcribed almost all those and other interviews, gets a huge pile of gratitude. Without her, I'd still be on chapter two. The pile of transcripts is so high that it includes ancient work by two of her predecessors, Nancy Simon and Chris Sandell, who deserve thanks as well.

Wendy Blair, the ever-patient Smothers Brothers office manager at Knave Productions, provided copies of every Smothers Brothers telecast and allowed access to all their files, including court transcripts and depositions, which proved an amazing treasure trove. Wendy died just as I was completing the manuscript; and it's one of my true regrets that she's not alive to receive a copy of what she worked so hard to help me produce. Others who gave me invaluable primary research materials include Paul Brownstein, who provided access to transcripts of his unedited interviews with *Comedy Hour* personnel taped for use as part of the repackaging for the *E!* rebroadcasts; Anne Elliot, then of A. C. Nielsen, who dug down into the hard-copy archives and duplicated weekly ratings for every *Comedy Hour* telecast and its competitors for the show's entire three-year run; Jane Klain, of what's now called the Paley Center for Media, for allowing me to do the same with old *TV Guide* issues; Mason Williams, for sending loads of contemporaneous material and detailed chronologies; Maureen Muldaur, for sharing materials from her 2002 documentary *Smothered: The Censorship Struggles of the Smothers Brothers Comedy Hour* (and for putting me in that documentary); and Gil Schwartz, executive vice president and chief communications officer of CBS, who made good on a decade-long promise. He and David Lombard at CBS Photo Archive let me dig through dusty boxes of negatives to select most of the photos reproduced in this book, and were as generous with their rates as they were patient with my glacial pace of operation.

Speaking of patience, this topic deserves a paragraph of its own. Completion of this book required me to be absent from several other places, or to have others step up and shoulder a lot of my load. At National Public Radio's *Fresh Air with Terry Gross*, that meant a six-month hiatus, during which time Terry Gross; executive producer Danny Miller; and my own producer, Phyllis Myers, all held off on firing me, while Dave Davies did all the guest hosting I wasn't there to do and so many other producers (thanks, all!) did without my services. At Rowan University, during my first full year of teaching, I benefited from the generosity of many who allowed me to stretch the boundaries of usual academic deadlines—president Donald Farish; dean Lorin Arnold; committee members (Ned Eckhardt, Joseph Bierman, and Keith Brand); even coteachers Mike Donovan and George Back, who allowed me to miss a class or two; and Mary Gifford, whose office-management skills kept me afloat. On my website, www.tvworthwatching.com, Diane Werts took over editing duties to help me during my final crunch. It worked; so did she.

Specialized research for this book was aided by Barbara Schmidt, who located several unpublished theses on the Smothers Brothers; David Sicilia and Ira Chinoy, who unlocked the secrets of various educational websites tapping into the records of vintage local newspapers; and Lance Rudzinski and my own daughter, Kristin Bianculli, who as law students tracked down hard-to-find court documents and rulings. Kris and my son, Mark, provided encouragement and sympathy during the entire fifteen-year writing process—and so did two friends who have provided some of the best guidance throughout the lengthy writing and editing phases, Mark Dawidziak and Michael Naidus. Two other dear friends, Ron and Paula Wengerd, kept me company and sane. Dave Olsen was invaluable in helping me secure rights to Pete Seeger's lyrics, Harlan Ellison kindly let me quote his columns extensively, Robert Haxby provided specifics about Television City's 1960s soundstage schedules, and Amy Grey helped me track down recent photos. Even my ex-wife deserves thanks, and knows why.

Finally, thanks to my father, Virgil Bianculli, for keeping me company each Sunday as we watched *The Smothers Brothers Comedy Hour*. That was an important show to me—and watching with my dad made it an important gift.

Bibliography

A mong the primary sources for this book were the original and air-check videotape recordings of *The Smothers Brothers Comedy Hour* and *The Summer Brothers Smothers Show* (CBS, 1967–69), and, from the same period, internal CBS memos; CBS press releases; national audience rating estimates from A. C. Nielsen; and weekly listings and highlights from *TV Guide*. Also primary were various transcripts and depositions regarding Tom Smothers, et al., vs. Columbia Broadcasting System, Inc., et al., United States District Court, Central District of California. Cases 69–1898-AAH, 69–1899-AAH, 69–1900-AAH.

Many clips described in this book can be found in the Time Life DVD season-by-season releases of *The Smothers Brothers Comedy Hour*. In addition, TV performances by the Smothers Brothers can be seen at the dedicated Smothers Brothers internet channel—www.youtube/smothersbrothers—and at Paul Brownstein's TV archive channel, www.youtube/tvclassics.

Detailed chapter-by-chapter notes can be found at www.dangerously funnythebook.com.

Albert, Eddie. Interview transcript for E!, November 2, 1992.
Allen, Steve. Interview transcript for E!, November 17, 1992.
Baez, Joan. Interview transcript for E!, December 18, 1992.
Baker, William Franklin. *Power and Decision Making in American Television*. Cleveland, OH: Case Western Reserve University, PhD thesis, 1972.
Belafonte, Harry. Interview transcript for E!, December 21, 1992.

————. Interview with author, September 21, 1998.

Bianculli, David. *Dictionary of Teleliteracy: Television's 500 Biggest Hits, Misses, and Events.* New York: Continuum, 1996.

Blecha, Peter. *Taboo Tunes: A History of Banned Bands & Censored Songs.* San Francisco, CA: Backbeat Books, 2004.

Blye, Allan. Interview transcript for E!, November 17, 1992.

————. Interview with author, July 18, 2001.

Bodroghkozy, Aniko. *Groove Tube: Sixties Television and the Youth Rebellion.* Durham, NC: Duke University Press, 2001.

Bonerz, Peter, and Howard Hesseman. Interview transcript for E!, November 7, 1992.

Braverman, Chuck. Interview transcript for E!, November 6, 1992.

Bruns, Marilyn Terese. *Suppression of Controversial Material by Corporate Interests: The Smothers Brothers, A Case Study.* Madison, WI: University of Wisconsin, 1977.

Buhle, Paul, and Dave Wagner. *Hide in Plain Sight: The Hollywood Blacklistees in Film and Television, 1950–2002.* New York: Palgrave Macmillan, 2003.

Burnett, Carol. Interview with author, August 25, 2006.

Burns, Ken. Interview with author, August 22, 2002.

Buzenberg, Susan, and Bill Buzenberg, eds. *Salant, CBS, and the Battle for the Soul of Broadcast Journalism: The Memoirs of Richard S. Salant.* Boulder, CO: Westview Press, 1999.

Camp, Hamilton. Interview transcript for E!, November 6, 1992.

Campbell, Glen. Interview transcript for E!, October 24, 1992.

Carpenter, Humphrey. *A Great, Silly Grin: The British Satire Boom of the 1960s.* Cambridge, MA: Da Capo Press, 2003.

Carr, Steven Alan. "On the Edge of Tastelessness: CBS, the Smothers Brothers, and the Struggle for Control," *Cinema Journal* (31, no. 4, summer 1992), 3–24.

Carroll, David. Interview with author, November 24, 1998.

Carruth, Gorton. *The Encyclopedia of American Facts and Dates.* New York: HarperCollins, 1993.

Castleman, Harry, and Walter J. Podrazik. *The TV Schedule Book: Four Decades of Network Programming from Sign-on to Sign-Off.* New York: McGraw-Hill, 1984.

Chambers, Ernie. Interview with author, February 18, 2009.

Coffey, Frank. *60 Minutes: 25 Years of Television's Finest Hour.* Los Angeles: General Publishing Group, 1993.

Coleman, Ray. *Lennon.* New York: McGraw-Hill, 1985.

Collins, Judy. Interview transcript for E!, October 28, 1992.

Daltrey, Roger. Interview with author, November 5, 1998.

———. Interview with author, August 7, 2001.

Densmore, John. Interview transcript for E!, November 5, 1992.

Draper, Robert. *Rolling Stone Magazine: The Uncensored History.* New York: HarperPerennial, 1991.

Eden, Barbara. Interview transcript for E!, November 18, 1992.

Editors of Rolling Stone. *Rolling Stone Rock Almanac.* NY: Macmillan Publishing Co., 1983.

Einstein, Bob. Interview transcript for E!, January 12, 1993.

———. Interview with author, December 19, 1999.

Ellison, Harlan. *The Glass Teat.* New York: Pyramid Books, 1975.

———. *The Other Glass Teat.* New York: Pyramid Books, 1975.

Epstein, Lawrence J. *The Haunted Smile: The Story of Jewish Comedians in America.* New York: Public Affairs, 2001.

———. *Mixed Nuts: America's Love Affair with Comedy Teams, from Burns and Allen to Belushi and Aykroyd.* New York: Public Affairs, 2004.

Erickson, Hal. *"From Beautiful Downtown Burbank": A Critical History of Rowan & Martin's Laugh-In, 1968–1973.* Jefferson, NC: McFarland & Co., 2000.

Finton, Thomas Edward. *A Historical Analysis of the CBS-Smothers Brothers Controversy.* College Park, MD: master of arts dissertation, University of Maryland, 1977.

Fleishman, Stanley. "Smothering the Smothers Brothers," *Censorship Today* (Aug./Sept. 1969), 25–30.

Free Speech Tribute, U.S. Comedy Arts Festival. Honorees: George Carlin, Tom Smothers, Dick Smothers, Bill Maher, Dick Gregory. March 2, 2002.

French, Leigh. Interview transcript for E!, December 12, 1992.

Fresh Air. Tom Smothers interview by author. National Public Radio, August 11, 1997.

Fritz, Ken. Interview with author, October 1, 2008.

———. Interview with author, October 3, 2008.

———. Interview with author, June 5, 2009.

Frost, David. Interview with author, October 7, 2003.

Gitlin, Todd. *The Sixties: Years of Hope, Days of Rage*. New York: Bantam Books, 1993.

Golenpaul, Dan, ed. *Information Please Almanac, Atlas and Yearbook, 1967*. New York: Simon and Schuster, 1967.

Gottlieb, Carl. Interview transcript for E!, November 20, 1992.

Groening, Matt. Interview with author, May 27, 2009.

Halberstam, David. *The Powers That Be*. New York: Knopf, 1979.

Hale, Lee, with Richard D. Neely. *Backstage at the Dean Martin Show*. Dallas, TX: Taylor Publishing Co., 2000.

Harris, Stan. Interview with author, April 19, 2001.

Hartford, John. Interview transcript for E!, November 10, 1992.

———. Interview with author, March 24, 2000.

Holbrook, Hal. Interview with author, July 19, 2001.

Ian, Janis. Interview transcript for E!, November 10, 1992.

Ilson, Saul. Interview with author, February 19, 2009.

Jones, Shirley. Interview transcript for E!, December 23, 1992.

Kahn, Kate. Interview with author, June 7, 2009.

Kaiser, Charles. *1968 in America: Music, Politics, Chaos, Counterculture, and the Shaping of a Generation*. New York: Grove Press, 1988.

Kelley, David E. Interview with author, November 18, 2008.

Kloman, William. "The Transmogrification of the Smothers Brothers," *Esquire* (October 1969): 148–153, 160, 192–194, 199–202.

Kragen, Ken. Interview transcript for E!, November 20, 1992.

———. Interview with author, November 20, 2003.

———. Interview with author, December 11, 2003.

Kurlansky, Mark. *1968: The Year That Rocked the World*. New York: Random House, 2004.

Lafferty, Perry. Interview with author, April 19, 2001.

———. *We Can Put the Laughs in Later*. Unpublished manuscript, 2001.

Landau, Martin. Interview transcript for E!, November 3, 1992.

Leigh, Janet. Interview transcript for E!, November 13, 1992.

———. Interview with author, July 12, 1997.

Lewis, Richard Warren. "St. Thomas & the Dragon," *Playboy* (August 1969): 142–143, 179–191.

Lewisohn, Mark. *"Radio Times" Guide to TV Comedy.* London: BBC Worldwide, 1998.

Long, Luman H., ed. *The World Almanac and Book of Facts, 1968.* New York: Newspaper Enterprise Association, 1968.

Maga, Timothy. *The 1960s (Eyewitness History series).* New York: Facts on File, 2003.

Maher, Bill. Interview with author, July 19, 2004.

Martin, Dick. Interview with author, June 6, 2001.

Martin, Steve. Interview transcript for E!, December 4, 1992.

———. *Kindly Lent Their Owner: The Private Collection of Steve Martin.* Las Vegas: Bellagio Gallery of Fine Art, 2001.

———. *Born Standing Up.* New York: Scribner, 2007.

Mason, Jackie. Interview transcript for E!, November 17, 1992.

Metz, Robert. *CBS: Reflections in a Bloodshot Eye.* Chicago: Playboy Press, 1975.

Michaels, Lorne. Interview with author, September 16, 1999.

Miles, Barry. *Hippie.* New York: Sterling Publishing Co., 2005.

Moore, Michael. Interview with author, October 16, 2000.

Moyers, Bill. Letter to author, April 19, 2005.

Nabors, Jim. Interview transcript for E!, October 25, 1992.

Neuwirth, Allan. *They'll Never Put That on the Air.* New York: Alworth Press, 2006.

Newhart, Bob. Interview transcript for E!, December 11, 1992.

———. Interview with author, July 13, 2005.

1968 with Tom Brokaw. History Channel, 2007.

1969 Reader's Digest Almanac and Yearbook. Pleasantville, NY: Readers Digest Association, 1969.

1970 Reader's Digest Almanac and Yearbook. Pleasantville, NY: Readers Digest Association, 1970.

Nolan, Nancy. Interview with author, July 17, 2006.

Noone, Peter. Interview transcript for E!, October 30, 1992.

Ozersky, Josh. *Archie Bunker's America: TV in an Era of Change, 1968–1978.* Carbondale, IL: Southern Illinois University Press, 2003.

Paley, William S. *As It Happened: A Memoir.* New York: Doubleday & Co., 1979.

Papazian, Ed. *Medium Rare: The Evolution, Workings and Impact of Commercial Television.* New York: Media Dynamics, 1989.

Pasetta, Marty. Interview transcript for E!, November 13, 1992.

Paulsen, Pat. Interview transcript for E!, October 26, 1992.

———. Interview with author, August 2, 1996.

Randall, Tony. Interview transcript for E!, December 8, 1992.

———. Interview with author, February 15, 1999.

Ray, Robert Alan. *Stand-Up Comedy in the 1960s: An Analysis of the Smothers Brothers.* Memphis, TN: Memphis State University, PhD thesis, 1980.

Reiner, Carl. Interview transcript for E!, November 27, 1992.

———. Television Critics Association press conference, Pasadena, CA, July 16, 2003.

———. Interview with author, August 14, 2003.

Reunion: The Smothers Brothers Comedy Hour. US Comedy Arts Festival. Participants: Dick Smothers, Tom Smothers, Steve Martin, Mason Williams, Bob Einstein, Bill Maher. Aspen, CO, February 11, 2000.

Rickles, Don. Interview transcript for E!, September 5, 1992.

Rogers, Kenny. Interview transcript for E!, December 7, 1992.

Satire or Sacrilege? Social and Political Commentary on Television. Museum of Television & Radio Satellite Seminar Series, February 25, 2003.

Schlatter, George. Interview with author, June 6, 2001.

Schlesinger, Arthur M. Jr., ed. *The Almanac of American History.* Greenwich, CT: Brompton Books, 1993.

Schneider, Alfred R., with Kaye Pullen. *The Gatekeeper: My 30 Years as a TV Censor.* Syracuse, NY: Syracuse University Press, 2001.

Seeger, Pete. Interview transcript for E!, October 27, 1992.

———. Interview with author, May 18, 1994.

Silverman, David. *You Can't Air That.* Syracuse, NY: Syracuse University Press, 2007.

Silverman, Fred. Interview with author, August 5, 2002.

60 Minutes. "The Smothers Brothers." CBS, January 1969 (vol. I, no. 8).

Skornia, Harry J., and Jack Wilson Kitson, eds. *Problems and Controversies in Television and Radio.* Palo Alto, CA: Pacific Books, 1968.

Slater, Robert. *This . . . Is CBS: A Chronicle of 60 Years.* Englewood Cliffs, NJ: Prentice Hall, 1988.

Slick, Grace. Interview transcript for E!, November 10, 1992.

"Smothers Brothers Comedy Hour 20th Reunion," CBS transcript, TCA Press Tour, Hollywood, CA, January 13, 1988.

Smothers, Dick. Interview with author, July 1, 1999.

———. Interview with author, May 21, 2001.

———. Interview with author, June 5, 2001.

———. Interview with author, September 8, 2003.

———. Interview with author, September 10, 2003.

———. Interview with author, October 6, 2008.

———. Interview with author, October 21, 2008.

Smothers, Sherry. Interview with author, November 9, 2008.

———. Interview with author, November 11, 2008.

Smothers, Tom. *Fresh Air,* National Public Radio, interview with author, August 11, 1997, plus recorded interview outtakes.

———. Interview with author, May 12, 1998.

———. Interview with author, Aug. 27, 1998.

———. Interview with author, July 1, 1999.

———. Interview with author, May 23, 2001.

———. Interview with author, June 5, 2001.

———. Interview with author, September 9, 2003.

———. Interview with author, October 5, 2008.

———. Interview with author, October 24, 2008.

Smothers, Tom and Dick. Joint interview with author, July 22, 1997.

———. Joint interview with author, Feb. 12, 2000.

Spigel, Lynn, and Michael Curtin. *The Revolution Wasn't Televised: Sixties Television and Social Conflict.* NY: Routledge, 1997.

Steinberg, David. Interview transcript for E!, November 18, 1992.

———. Interview with author, September 4, 1998.

———. Interview with author, May 30, 2009.

———. Interview with author, June 6, 2009.

Tankersley, William. Interview with author, September 13, 2008.

———. Interview with author, September 15, 2008.

Terrace, Vincent. *Encyclopedia of Television: Series, Pilots and Specials, 1937–1973.* New York: New York Zoetrope, 1986.

Toll, Robert C. *The Entertainment Machine: American Show Business in the Twentieth Century.* Oxford: Oxford University Press, 1982.

Trudeau, Garry. Interview with author, July 21, 2004.

———. Interview with author, September 22, 2004.

Urdang, Laurence, ed. *The Timetables of American History.* NY: Touchstone, 1996.

Wallechinsky, David, and Irving Wallace. *The People's Almanac.* Garden City, NY: Doubleday & Co., 1975.

Warnes, Jennifer. Interview transcript for E!, November 19, 1992.

Wetterau, Bruce. *The New York Public Library Book of Chronologies.* New York: Prentice Hall, 1990.

Williams, Mason. Personal journals, 1966–67.

———. *The Mason Williams FCC Rapport.* New York: Liveright Publishing Corporation, 1969.

———. *The Mason Williams Reading Matter.* Garden City, NY: Doubleday & Co., 1969.

———. *Flavors.* Garden City, NY: Doubleday & Co., 1970.

———. Interview transcript for E!, November 4, 1992.

———. Interview with author, February 24, 1997.

———. Interview with author, March 14–18, 2000.

———. *Classical Gas: The Music of Mason Williams.* Miami, FL: Warner Bros. Publications, 2003.

Wilson, Nancy. Interview transcript for E!, November 1, 1992.

Witcover, Jules. *The Year the Dream Died: Revisiting 1968 in America.* New York: Warner Books, 1997.

Wober, J. Mallory. *The Use and Abuse of Television: A Social Psychological Analysis of the Changing Screen.* Hillsdale, NJ: Lawrence Erlbaum Associates, 1988.

Index

program practices, CBS. *See* censors; *specific person*

Purple Onion (San Francisco club), Smothers Brothers at, 16–20, 21, 29, 30, 31, 35

race: and Belafonte as *Comedy Hour* guest, 194; and Belafonte-Clark touching, 180, 200; and black entertainers on television, 111; and censorship, 88, 180, 200; and *Comedy Hour* skits, 165, 200, 209, 252–53, 270–72, 288, 291; and interracial touching, 180, 200
Reagan, Ronald, 162, 190, 191, 216, 218
Reasoner, Harry, 241, 243–45
"red frog/green frog" sketch, 165, 288
The Red Skelton Show (TV show), 56, 70–71, 147, 209, 318
Redding, Otis, 141, 179
Reiner, Carl, 38, 66, 85, 150, 181, 182, 223
Reiner, Rob, 181, 182, 186, 188–89, 244
religion, 244, 247, 273, 293. *See also* Steinberg, David: sermonettes of
Remick, Bertha (grandmother), 7, 10, 75
Remick, Dick (uncle), 6–7, 8, 14
Remick, Ed (grandfather), 7, 9, 286, 327
Remick, Ruth. *See* Smothers, Ruth Remick (mother)
Remick, Winifred (aunt), 6–7, 8
The Return of the Smothers Brothers (TV special), 324
Riddle, Nelson, 67–68, 71, 77, 90, 180, 240, 249
Roman, Murray, 208, 210, 227, 244, 250, 252
Rose, Biff, 283, 301
Rowan & Martin's Laugh-In (TV show): *Comedy Hour* comments about, 169; *Comedy Hour* compared with, 209–10, 334–37, 346; Emmy Award for, 179, 223, 270, 321; format of, 236–37; Groening's comment about, 353; influence of *Comedy Hour* on, 165; NBC relationship with, 313; Nixon appearance on, 235–36; Pastore's comments about, 280; pilot special for, 111; popularity of, 288; premiere of, 147–48, 165, 259; ratings for, 172, 177, 234–35; and *Summer Show,* 186; *TV Guide* comments about, 272; as unbilled *Comedy Hour* guests, 235
Rowan, Dan, 169, 235, 236, 288, 290, 291, 294–95, 302, 303, 310, 311, 312, 318, 323
"rowing to Galveston" comment, 260

Sahl, Mort, 69, 274–75
San Jose State University, Smothers Brothers at, 14, 16
Satire, the (Denver club), 28–29
Saturday Night Live (TV show), 66, 97, 118, 238, 336, 347, 348, 356, 358
Schlatter, George, 236, 279
Seeger, Pete: and "Big Muddy" controversy, 135–39, 166–72, 174, 190, 195, 220, 258; as blacklisted, 97, 130–32, 137, 191, 193; as

Columbia recording artist, 78, 137; as *Comedy Hour* guest, 97, 129–39, 146, 147, 153, 164, 166–72, 184, 220, 235, 311, 345; as hero to Smothers Brothers, 133; hits of, 15; and *Hootenanny,* 40; influence on Smothers Brothers of, 129; *Waist Deep in the Big Muddy* album of, 137; with the Weavers, 15, 129–30, 131, 133
Serling, Rod, 53, 265–66
"Sex and the Single Student" skit, 86
Shakespeare, William, skits about works of, 76, 256
Shankar, Ravi, 140, 159
shoe box suggestions, 69–70
Shore, Dinah, 302, 323
"Siblings" (song), 44
Silverman, Fred, 54–55, 58, 92, 93, 304, 305, 313, 318, 357
Simon and Garfunkel, 60, 78, 112, 113, 115, 116, 140, 159, 179, 313–14, 323, 353
Simon, David, 350–51
Sinatra, Frank, 61, 67, 184
Sinatra, Nancy, 61, 159, 187, 188, 203, 209
60 Minutes (CBS TV show), 241, 243–45, 247, 251, 253
Skelton, Red, 57, 70–71, 75, 259, 265, 266, 267
Slaff, George, 330–31
Slaughterhouse Five (film), 332–33
Smith and Dale, 339, 359
Smith, Kate, 160, 308, 358
Smothers, Bo (Tom's son), 339
Smothers, Denby Franklin (Dick's wife), 339
Smothers, Dick Jr. (Dick's son), 42
Smothers, Dick (Richard Remick): birth of, 3; car racing and motorcycling interests of, 151, 152, 286, 287–88, 341; career aspirations of, 14, 21; in *Casino,* 333; casual style of, 104; CBS firing of, 319; childhood and youth of, 1–9, 10–14, 74–75; deafness of, 5, 26; education of, 6, 7, 14; "faking it" by, 13; "firing" of, 288; first performances of, 11–12; harassment of, 327; and IRS, 325; lifestyle of, 286–88; marriages of, 21, 339, 359; as performer, 286–87; reaction to cancellation of *Comedy Hour* by, 309, 314, 359; reaction to CBS court case by, 331; role in *Comedy Hour* of, 150–53; Rowan as "replacing," 288; separations/divorces of, 70, 287, 319, 339; as straight man, 26, 27, 36. *See also* Smothers Brothers; *specific topic*
Smothers, Linda Miller (Dick's first wife), 21, 28, 42, 319, 339
Smothers, Lorraine Martin (Dick's wife), 339
Smothers, Marcy Carriker (Tom's wife), 339, 345
Smothers, Riley Rose (Tom's son), 339
Smothers, Rochelle Robley (Tom's wife), 339
Smothers, Ruth Remick (mother), 1–2, 3, 4–6, 9, 10, 75, 79, 113, 126, 242–43, 336–37

Vietnam War (*cont.*)
for, 319; and elections of 1968, 192; LBJ troop commitment to, 135, 136; and legacy of Smothers Brothers, 349, 350, 354; Paris peace talks about, 179; and Paulsen for president campaign, 219; and Pentagon Papers, 328; public opinion about, 146, 174; and Seeger as *Comedy Hour* guest, 136, 168, 172; Tet Offensive in, 166; and "We're Still Here" number, 197

Wagon Wheel (Lake Tahoe club), Smothers Brothers at, 20
"Waltzing Matilda" musical spot, 156–57
Warnes, Jennifer (Warren), 187, 240, 247, 274, 275, 286, 301, 337, 338
Washington, D. C.: Paulsen trip to, 220–21; Tom Smothers trip to, 295–97
Washington Post, 92–93, 289, 325, 335, 337
"water closet" joke, 24–25, 36, 114
Weavers, 15, 16, 129–30, 131, 132, 133, 135
"We're Still Here" number, 196–98
Who, the, 118, 141–45, 146, 147, 156, 161, 319, 353
Williams, Mason: albums of, 44, 127; and "rowing to Galveston" comment, 260; in Aspen, 27; and backlog of Smothers Brothers comedy routines, 149; and Belafonte, 194, 204; books by, 284; and Campbell, 184, 190–91; censoring of, 312; and censorship of *Comedy Hour,* 86, 98, 102, 103, 106, 124, 158, 260, 283–84; and changes in Comedy Hour, 214; on *Comedy Hour,* 117, 127, 252; comments about Tom of, 322; and disagreements among *Comedy Hour* personnel, 148; and drugs, 183, 186; on early albums of Smothers Brothers, 44; Emmy Award for, 321; FCC testimony of, 322; and final first season *Comedy Hour* show, 127; and French-Tom skit, 124, 125; and frigget skit, 94, 95; Grammy Award for, 283; and guests on *Comedy Hour* shows, 84, 97; and Hartford hiring, 160, 183; and "Honey house" skit, 210; journals of, 68; and legacy of Smothers Brothers, 353, 358; marriage and divorce of, 349; and Martin hiring, 184; and McKay visuals, 112; at Monterey Festival, 126, 135; musical compositions by, 63, 99, 114–15, 117, 122, 127, 137, 153, 175–76, 177, 188, 197, 209, 241, 337, 353; and Nixon *Comedy Hour* campaign spot, 204–5; and "One Man's Country" sketch, 120; and Paulsen as

presidential candidate, 213, 215, 216, 217, 218; as Paulsen fan, 113; and Paulsen's editorials, 85; personal and professional background of, 62; and *Petula,* 179–80, 194; and planning for *Comedy Hour,* 44, 63–64, 65–66, 67–70, 71–72; as poet, 252, 284, 301, 312; and political comments on *Comedy Hour,* 111, 163–64; and premier of *Comedy Hour,* 73, 75–76; and production schedule for *Comedy Hour,* 128; and question-and-answer pieces, 104; recording career of, 127; and relationship between Smothers Brothers, 288; second show comments of, 78; and Seeger as *Comedy Hour* guest, 133, 138, 139; Smothers Brothers' early appearances with, 62–63; Smothers Brothers' relationship with, 61–62; and Smothers Brothers reunion show, 337; and Steinberg sermonettes, 233; and *Summer Show,* 181, 187, 188, 190–91; and talent development on *Comedy Hour,* 77; and television-press relationship, 105; and tensions between CBS–Smothers Brothers, 211; and theme song for *Comedy Hour,* 67–68; and third season of *Comedy Hour,* 241; and Tom and drugs, 286; Tom's relationship with, 27, 63, 175, 186; and "We're Still Here," 197
Wilson, Nancy, 111, 160, 165, 288, 290–91, 295, 303
Winters, Jonathan, 150, 273, 286–87
Wood, Robert: and Baez comments, 276; and cancellation of *Comedy Hour,* 307–8, 311, 312–13; cancellation of popular programs by, 318; as Dawson replacement, 261; and escalation in CBS–Smothers Brothers tensions, 261–62, 263, 277–79, 298–99, 304, 305; and Free Speech Movement, 42, 69; professional background of, 289; and replacement show for *Comedy Hour,* 312–13; shelving of *Comedy Hour* show by, 301; and Stanton's stand on CBS broadcast standards, 297; and Steinberg sermonette controversy, 304; and summer replacement series for *Comedy Hour,* 301; Tom's meeting with, 285, 288, 289–90, 292, 298; Tom's relationship with, 302
Woodstock Music and Arts Fair, 322
Writers Guild of America, 181, 337–38

X rating, 316

Your Show of Shows (TV show), 66, 85, 148, 150, 181, 182

Permissions

About the Author

DAVID BIANCULLI has been a TV critic since 1975. On daily newspapers, he began at Florida's *Gainesville Sun* and ended in 2007 after fourteen years at the New York *Daily News*. Since 1987, he has been heard as TV critic for National Public Radio's *Fresh Air with Terry Gross*, where he also serves as substitute host. He now is an associate professor, teaching TV and film, at Rowan University in New Jersey.

Bianculli has written two other books, *Teleliteracy: Taking Television Seriously* (1992) and *Dictionary of Teleliteracy: Television's 500 Biggest Hits, Misses, and Events* (1996), both published by Continuum. He much prefers the title, and the cover, of the book you're now holding.